SwiftUI Essentials

iOS 16 Edition

SwiftUI Essentials – iOS 16 Edition

ISBN-13: 978-1-951442-51-4

Rev: 1.0

Contents

Table of Contents

Chapter 1

1. Start Here

This book aims to teach the skills necessary to build iOS 16 applications using SwiftUI, Xcode 14, and the Swift 5.7 programming language.

Beginning with the basics, this book outlines the steps to set up an iOS development environment, together with an introduction to using Swift Playgrounds to learn and experiment with Swift.

The book also includes in-depth chapters introducing the Swift 5.7 programming language, including data types, control flow, functions, object oriented programming, property wrappers, structured concurrency, and error handling.

A guided tour of Xcode in SwiftUI development mode follows an introduction to the key concepts of SwiftUI and project architecture. The book also covers creating custom SwiftUI views and explains how these views are combined to create user interface layouts, including stacks, frames, and forms.

Other topics covered include data handling using state properties and observable, state, and environment objects, as are key user interface design concepts such as modifiers, lists, tabbed views, context menus, user interface navigation, and outline groups.

The book also includes chapters covering graphics and chart drawing, user interface animation, view transitions and gesture handling, WidgetKit, document-based apps, Core Data, CloudKit, and SiriKit integration.

Chapters also explain how to integrate SwiftUI views into existing UIKit-based projects and integrate UIKit code into SwiftUI.

Finally, the book explains how to package up a completed app and upload it to the App Store for publication.

Along the way, the topics covered in the book are put into practice through detailed tutorials, the source code for which is also available for download.

The aim of this book, therefore, is to teach you the skills to build your own apps for iOS 16 using SwiftUI. Assuming you are ready to download the iOS 16 SDK and Xcode 14 and have an Apple Mac system, you are ready to get started.

1.1 For Swift Programmers

This book has been designed to address the needs of both existing Swift programmers and those new to Swift and iOS app development. If you are familiar with the Swift programming language, you can probably skip the Swift-specific chapters. If you are not yet familiar with the SwiftUI-specific language features of Swift, however, we recommend that you at least read the sections covering implicit returns from single expressions, opaque return types, and property wrappers. These features are central to the implementation and understanding of SwiftUI.

1.2 For Non-Swift Programmers

If you are new to programming in Swift, then the entire book is appropriate for you. Just start at the beginning and keep going.

1.3 Source Code Download

The source code and Xcode project files for the examples contained in this book are available for download at:

https://www.ebookfrenzy.com/retail/swiftui-ios16/

1.4 Download the Color eBook

Thank you for purchasing the print edition of this book. Your purchase includes a color copy of the book in PDF format.

If you would like to download the PDF version of this book, please email proof of purchase (for example, a receipt, delivery notice, or photo of the physical book) to *feedback@ebookfrenzy.com*, and we will provide you with a download link.

1.5 Feedback

We want you to be satisfied with your purchase of this book. Therefore, if you find any errors in the book or have any comments, questions, or concerns, please contact us at *feedback@ebookfrenzy.com*.

1.6 Errata

While we make every effort to ensure the accuracy of the content of this book, inevitably, a book covering a subject area of this size and complexity may include some errors and oversights. Any known issues with the book will be outlined, together with solutions, at the following URL:

https://www.ebookfrenzy.com/errata/swiftui-ios16.html

In the event that you find an error not listed in the errata, please let us know by emailing our technical support team at *feedback@ebookfrenzy.com*.

Chapter 2

2. Joining the Apple Developer Program

The first step in the process of learning to develop iOS 16 based applications involves gaining an understanding of the advantages of enrolling in the Apple Developer Program and deciding the point at which it makes sense to pay to join. With these goals in mind, this chapter will outline the costs and benefits of joining the developer program and, finally, walk through the steps involved in enrolling.

2.1 Downloading Xcode 14 and the iOS 16 SDK

The latest versions of both the iOS SDK and Xcode can be downloaded free of charge from the macOS App Store. Since the tools are free, this raises the question of whether to enroll in the Apple Developer Program, or to wait until it becomes necessary later in your app development learning curve.

2.2 Apple Developer Program

Membership in the Apple Developer Program currently costs $99 per year to enroll as an individual developer. Organization level membership is also available.

Prior to the introduction of iOS 9 and Xcode 7, one of the key advantages of the developer program was that it permitted the creation of certificates and provisioning profiles to test your applications on physical iOS devices. Fortunately, this is no longer the case and all that is now required to test apps on physical iOS devices is an Apple ID.

Clearly much can be achieved without the need to pay to join the Apple Developer program. There are, however, areas of app development which cannot be fully tested without program membership. Of particular significance is the fact that Siri integration, iCloud access, Apple Pay, Game Center and In-App Purchasing can only be enabled and tested with Apple Developer Program membership.

Of further significance is the fact that Apple Developer Program members have access to technical support from Apple's iOS support engineers (though the annual fee initially covers the submission of only two support incident reports, more can be purchased). Membership also includes access to the Apple Developer forums; an invaluable resource both for obtaining assistance and guidance from other iOS developers, and for finding solutions to problems that others have encountered and subsequently resolved.

Program membership also provides early access to the pre-release Beta versions of Xcode, macOS and iOS.

By far the most important aspect of the Apple Developer Program is that membership is a mandatory requirement in order to publish an application for sale or download in the App Store.

Clearly, program membership is going to be required at some point before your application reaches the App Store. The only question remaining is when exactly to sign up.

2.3 When to Enroll in the Apple Developer Program?

Clearly, there are many benefits to Apple Developer Program membership and, eventually, membership will be necessary to begin selling your apps. As to whether to pay the enrollment fee now or later will depend on individual circumstances. If you are still in the early stages of learning to develop iOS apps or have yet to come up with a compelling idea for an app to develop then much of what you need is provided without program membership. As your skill level increases and your ideas for apps to develop take shape you can, after all, always enroll in the developer program later.

If, on the other hand, you are confident that you will reach the stage of having an application ready to publish, or know that you will need access to more advanced features such as Siri support, iCloud storage, In-App Purchasing and Apple Pay then it is worth joining the developer program sooner rather than later.

2.4 Enrolling in the Apple Developer Program

If your goal is to develop iOS apps for your employer, then it is first worth checking whether the company already has membership. That being the case, contact the program administrator in your company and ask them to send you an invitation from within the Apple Developer Program Member Center to join the team. Once they have done so, Apple will send you an email entitled *You Have Been Invited to Join an Apple Developer Program* containing a link to activate your membership. If you or your company is not already a program member, you can enroll online at:

https://developer.apple.com/programs/enroll/

Apple provides enrollment options for businesses and individuals. To enroll as an individual, you will need to provide credit card information in order to verify your identity. To enroll as a company, you must have legal signature authority (or access to someone who does) and be able to provide documentation such as a Dun & Bradstreet D-U-N-S number and documentation confirming legal entity status.

Acceptance into the developer program as an individual member typically takes less than 24 hours with notification arriving in the form of an activation email from Apple. Enrollment as a company can take considerably longer (sometimes weeks or even months) due to the burden of the additional verification requirements.

While awaiting activation you may log in to the Member Center with restricted access using your Apple ID and password at the following URL:

https://developer.apple.com/membercenter

Once logged in, clicking on the *Your Account* tab at the top of the page will display the prevailing status of your application to join the developer program as *Enrollment Pending*. Once the activation email has arrived, log in to the Member Center again and note that access is now available to a wide range of options and resources as illustrated in Figure 2-1:

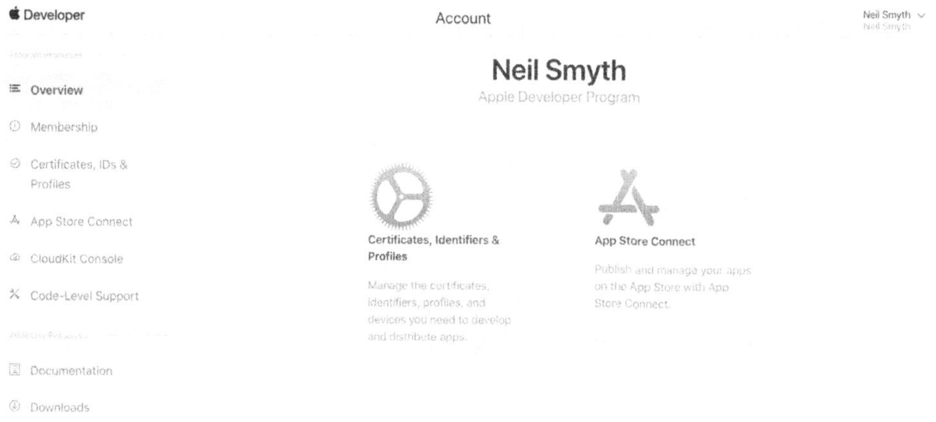

Figure 2-1

2.5 Summary

An important early step in the iOS 16 application development process involves identifying the best time to enroll in the Apple Developer Program. This chapter has outlined the benefits of joining the program, provided some guidance to keep in mind when considering developer program membership and walked briefly through the enrollment process. The next step is to download and install the iOS 16 SDK and Xcode 14 development environment.

Chapter 3

3. Installing Xcode 14 and the iOS 16 SDK

iOS apps are developed using the iOS SDK in conjunction with Apple's Xcode development environment. Xcode is an integrated development environment (IDE) within which you will code, compile, test and debug your iOS applications.

All of the examples in this book are based on Xcode version 14 and make use of features unavailable in earlier Xcode versions. In this chapter we will cover the steps involved in installing both Xcode 14 and the iOS 16 SDK on macOS.

3.1 Identifying Your macOS Version

When developing with SwiftUI, the Xcode 14 environment requires a system running macOS Monterey 12.4 or later. If you are unsure of the version of macOS on your Mac, you can find this information by clicking on the Apple menu in the top left-hand corner of the screen and selecting the *About This Mac* option from the menu. In the resulting dialog check the *Version* line.

If the "About This Mac" dialog does not indicate that macOS 11.0 or later is running, click on the *Software Update...* button to download and install the appropriate operating system upgrades.

Figure 3-1

3.2 Installing Xcode 14 and the iOS 16 SDK

The best way to obtain the latest versions of Xcode and the iOS SDK is to download them from the Apple Mac App Store. Launch the App Store on your macOS system, enter Xcode into the search box and click on the *Get* button to initiate the installation. This will install both Xcode and the iOS SDK.

3.3 Starting Xcode

Having successfully installed the SDK and Xcode, the next step is to launch it so that we are ready to start development work. To start up Xcode, open the macOS Finder and search for *Xcode*. Since you will be making frequent use of this tool take this opportunity to drag and drop it onto your dock for easier access in the future. Click on the Xcode icon in the dock to launch the tool. The first time Xcode runs you may be prompted to install additional components. Follow these steps, entering your username and password when prompted to do so.

Once Xcode has loaded, and assuming this is the first time you have used Xcode on this system, you will be presented with the *Welcome* screen from which you are ready to proceed:

Figure 3-2

3.4 Adding Your Apple ID to the Xcode Preferences

Regardless of whether or not you choose to enroll in the Apple Developer Program it is worth adding your Apple ID to Xcode now that it is installed and running. Select the *Xcode -> Preferences...* menu option followed by the *Accounts* tab. On the Accounts screen, click on the + button highlighted in Figure 3-3, select *Apple ID* from the resulting panel and click on the *Continue* button. When prompted, enter your Apple ID and password before clicking on the *Sign In* button to add the account to the preferences.

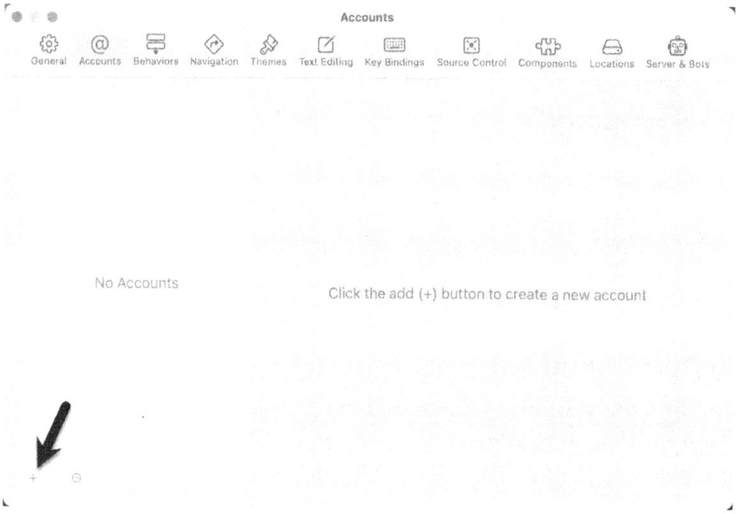

Figure 3-3

3.5 Developer and Distribution Signing Identities

Once the Apple ID has been entered the next step is to generate signing identities. To view the current signing identities, select the newly added Apple ID in the Accounts panel and click on the *Manage Certificates...* button to display a list of available signing identity types. To create a signing identity, simply click on the + button highlighted in Figure 3-4 and make the appropriate selection from the menu:

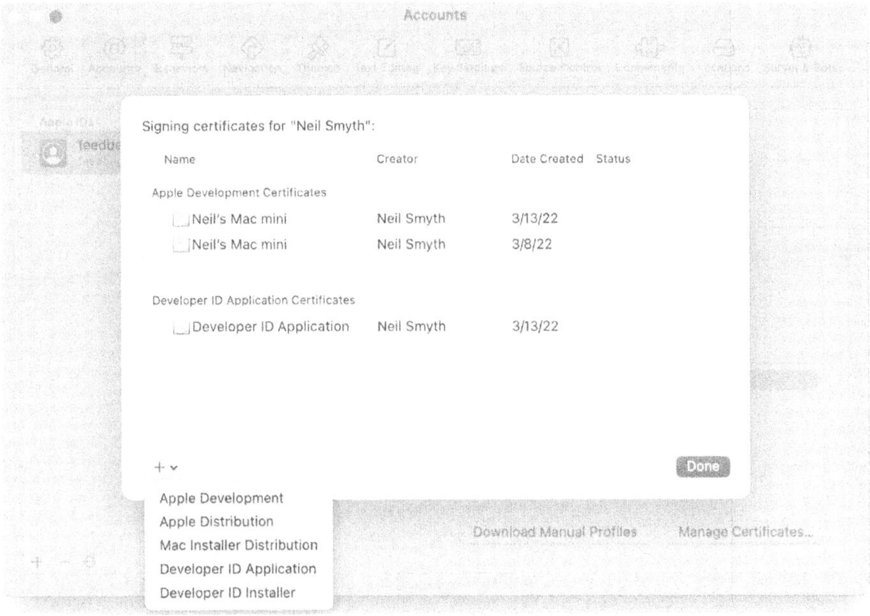

Figure 3-4

If the Apple ID has been used to enroll in the Apple Developer program, the option to create an *Apple Distribution* certificate will appear in the menu which will, when clicked, generate the signing identity required to submit the app to the Apple App Store. You will also need to create a *Developer ID Application* certificate if you plan to integrate features such as iCloud and Siri into your app projects. If you have not yet signed up for the Apple Developer program, select the *Apple Development* option to allow apps to be tested during development.

3.6 Summary

This book was written using Xcode version 14 and the iOS 16 SDK running on macOS 12.5 (Monterey). Before beginning SwiftUI development, the first step is to install Xcode and configure it with your Apple ID via the accounts section of the Preferences screen. Once these steps have been performed, a development certificate must be generated which will be used to sign apps developed within Xcode. This will allow you to build and test your apps on physical iOS-based devices.

When you are ready to upload your finished app to the App Store, you will also need to generate a distribution certificate, a process requiring membership in the Apple Developer Program as outlined in the previous chapter.

Having installed the iOS SDK and successfully launched Xcode 14 we can now look at Xcode in more detail, starting with Playgrounds.

Chapter 4

4. An Introduction to Xcode 14 Playgrounds

Before introducing the Swift programming language in the chapters that follow, it is first worth learning about a feature of Xcode known as *Playgrounds*. This is a feature of Xcode designed to make learning Swift and experimenting with the iOS SDK much easier. The concepts covered in this chapter can be put to use when experimenting with many of the introductory Swift code examples contained in the chapters that follow.

4.1 What is a Playground?

A playground is an interactive environment where Swift code can be entered and executed with the results appearing in real-time. This makes an ideal environment in which to learn the syntax of Swift and the visual aspects of iOS app development without the need to work continuously through the edit/compile/run/debug cycle that would ordinarily accompany a standard Xcode iOS project. With support for rich text comments, playgrounds are also a good way to document code for future reference or as a training tool.

4.2 Creating a New Playground

To create a new Playground, start Xcode and select the *File -> New -> Playground...* menu option. Choose the iOS option on the resulting panel and select the Blank template.

The Blank template is useful for trying out Swift coding. The Single View template, on the other hand, provides a view controller environment for trying out code that requires a user interface layout. The game and map templates provide preconfigured playgrounds that allow you to experiment with the iOS MapKit and SpriteKit frameworks respectively.

On the next screen, name the playground *LearnSwift* and choose a suitable file system location into which the playground should be saved before clicking on the *Create* button.

Once the playground has been created, the following screen will appear ready for Swift code to be entered:

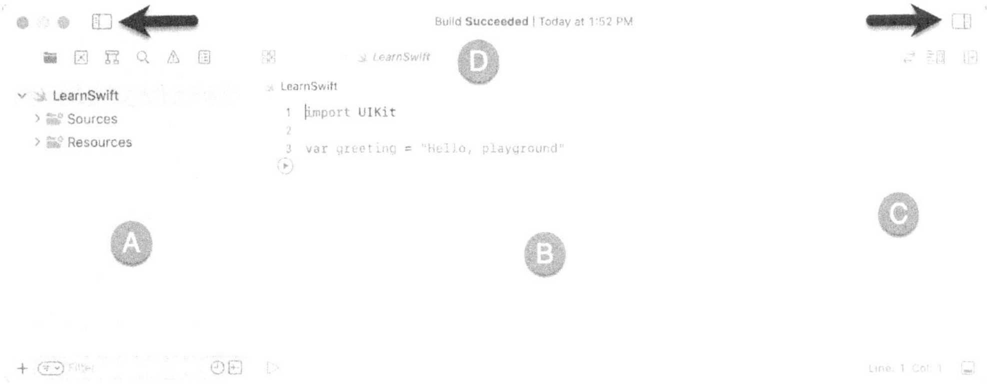

Figure 4-1

The panel on the left-hand side of the window (marked A in Figure 4-1) is the Navigator panel which provides access to the folders and files that make up the playground. To hide and show this panel, click on the button indicated by the left-most arrow. The center panel (B) is the *playground editor* where the lines of Swift code are entered. The right-hand panel (C) is referred to as the *results panel* and is where the results of each Swift expression entered into the playground editor panel are displayed. The tab bar (D) will contain a tab for each file currently open within the playground editor. To switch to a different file, simply select the corresponding tab. To close an open file, hover the mouse pointer over the tab and click on the "X" button when it appears to the left of the file name.

The button marked by the right-most arrow in the above figure is used to hide and show the Inspectors panel (marked A in Figure 4-2 below) where a variety of properties relating to the playground may be configured. Clicking and dragging the bar (B) upward will display the Debug Area (C) where diagnostic output relating to the playground will appear when code is executed:

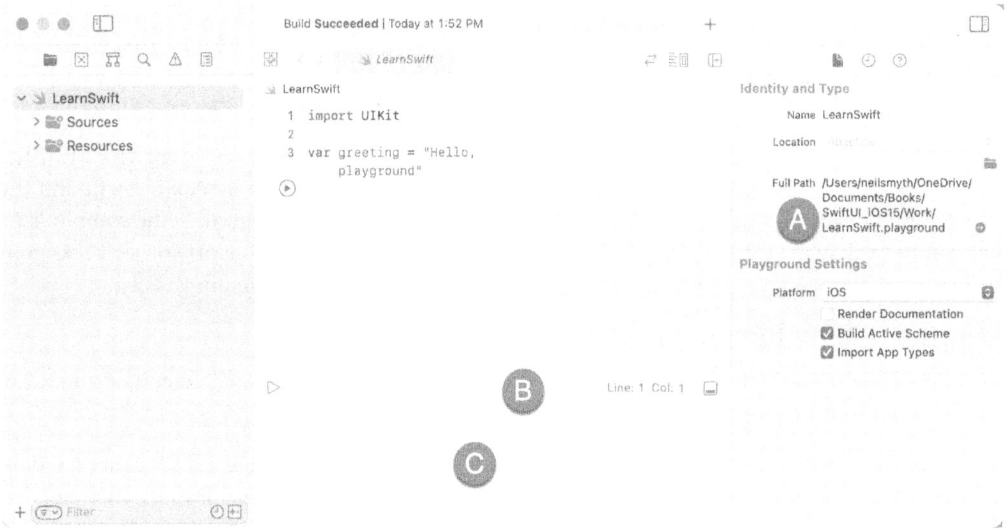

Figure 4-2

By far the quickest way to gain familiarity with the playground environment is to work through some simple examples.

4.3 A Swift Playground Example

Perhaps the simplest of examples in any programming language (that at least does something tangible) is to write some code to output a single line of text. Swift is no exception to this rule so, within the playground window, begin adding another line of Swift code so that it reads as follows:

```
import UIKit

var greeting = "Hello, playground"

print("Welcome to Swift")
```

All that the additional line of code does is make a call to the built-in Swift *print* function which takes as a parameter a string of characters to be displayed on the console. Those familiar with other programming languages will note the absence of a semi-colon at the end of the line of code. In Swift, semi-colons are optional and generally only used as a separator when multiple statements occupy the same line of code.

Note that although some extra code has been entered, nothing yet appears in the results panel. This is because the code has yet to be executed. One option to run the code is to click on the Execute Playground button located in the bottom left-hand corner of the main panel as indicated by the arrow in Figure 4-3:

Figure 4-3

When clicked, this button will execute all the code in the current playground page from the first line of code to the last. Another option is to execute the code in stages using the run button located in the margin of the code editor as shown in Figure 4-4:

Figure 4-4

This button executes the line numbers with the shaded blue background including the line on which the button is currently positioned. In the above figure, for example, the button will execute lines 1 through 3 and then stop.

The position of the run button can be moved by hovering the mouse pointer over the line numbers in the editor. In Figure 4-5, for example, the run button is now positioned on line 5 and will execute lines 4 and 5 when clicked. Note that lines 1 to 3 are no longer highlighted in blue indicating that these have already been executed and are not eligible to be run this time:

Figure 4-5

This technique provides an easy way to execute the code in stages making it easier to understand how the code functions and to identify problems in code execution.

To reset the playground so that execution can be performed from the start of the code, simply click on the stop button as indicated in Figure 4-6:

Figure 4-6

Using this incremental execution technique, execute lines 1 through 3 and note that output now appears in the results panel indicating that the variable has been initialized:

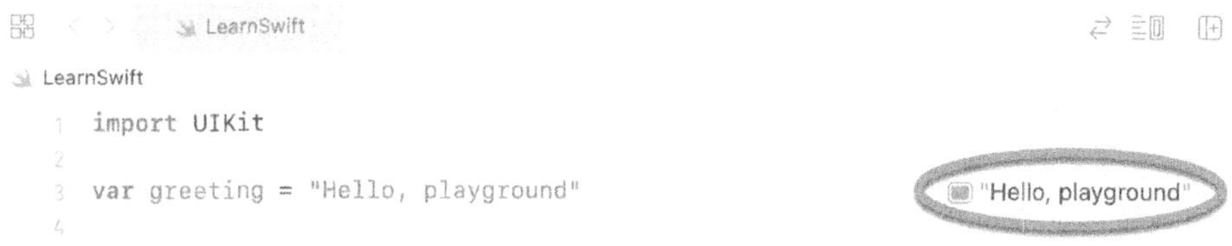

Figure 4-7

Next, execute the remaining lines up to and including line 5 at which point the "Welcome to Swift" output should appear both in the results panel and debug area:

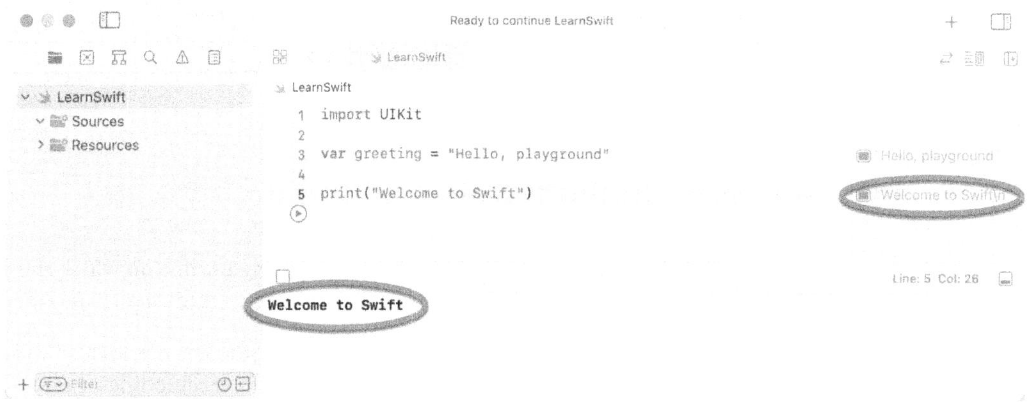

Figure 4-8

4.4 Viewing Results

Playgrounds are particularly useful when working and experimenting with Swift algorithms. This can be useful when combined with the Quick Look feature. Remaining within the playground editor, enter the following lines of code beneath the existing print statement:

```
var x = 10

for index in 1...20 {
    let y = index * x
    x -= 1
    print(y)
}
```

This expression repeats a loop 20 times, performing arithmetic expressions on each iteration of the loop. Once the code has been entered into the editor, click on the run button positioned at line 13 to execute these new lines of code. The playground will execute the loop and display in the results panel the number of times the loop was performed. More interesting information, however, may be obtained by hovering the mouse pointer over the results line so that two additional buttons appear as shown in Figure 4-9:

Figure 4-9

Hovering over the output will display the *Quick Look* button on the far right which, when selected, will show a popup panel displaying the results as shown in Figure 4-10:

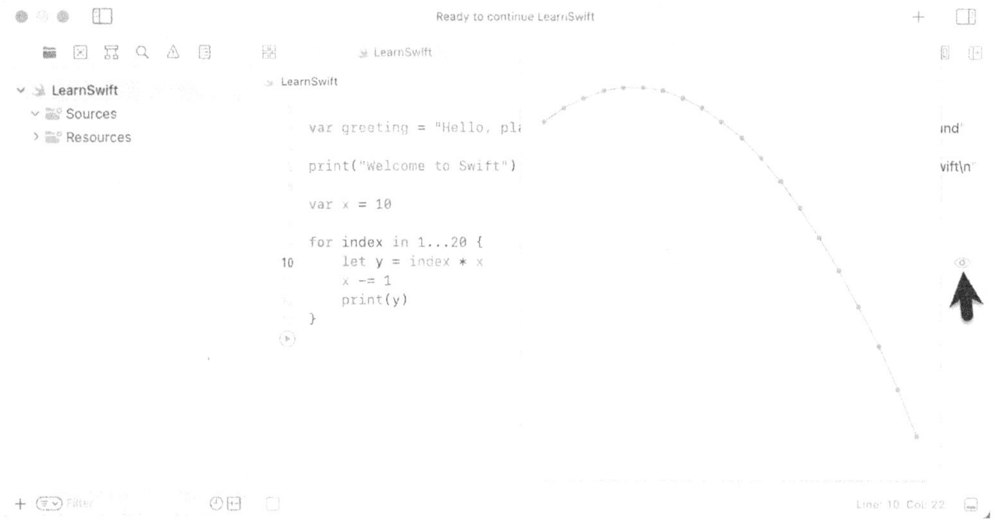

Figure 4-10

The left-most button is the *Show Result* button which, when selected, displays the results in-line with the code:

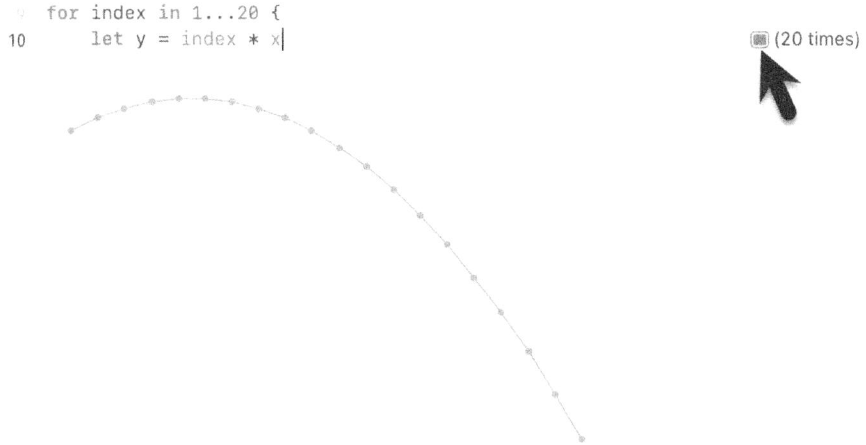

Figure 4-11

4.5 Adding Rich Text Comments

Rich text comments allow the code within a playground to be documented in a way that is easy to format and read. A single line of text can be marked as being rich text by preceding it with a //: marker. For example:

```
//: This is a single line of documentation text
```

Blocks of text can be added by wrapping the text in /*: and */ comment markers:

```
/*:
This is a block of documentation text that is intended
to span multiple lines
*/
```

The rich text uses the Markup language and allows text to be formatted using a lightweight and easy-to-use syntax. A heading, for example, can be declared by prefixing the line with a '#' character while text is displayed in italics when wrapped in '*' characters. Bold text, on the other hand, involves wrapping the text in '**' character sequences. It is also possible to configure bullet points by prefixing each line with a single '*'. Among the many other features of Markup is the ability to embed images and hyperlinks into the content of a rich text comment.

To see rich text comments in action, enter the following markup content into the playground editor immediately after the *print("Welcome to Swift")* line of code:

```
/*:
# Welcome to Playgrounds
This is your *first* playground which is intended to demonstrate:
* The use of **Quick Look**
* Placing results **in-line** with the code
*/
```

As the comment content is added it is said to be displayed in *raw markup* format. To display in *rendered markup* format, either select the *Editor -> Show Rendered Markup* menu option, or enable the *Render Documentation* option located under *Playground Settings* in the Inspector panel (marked A in Figure 4-2). If the Inspector panel is not currently visible, click on the button indicated by the right-most arrow in Figure 4-1 to display it. Once rendered, the above rich text should appear as illustrated in Figure 4-12:

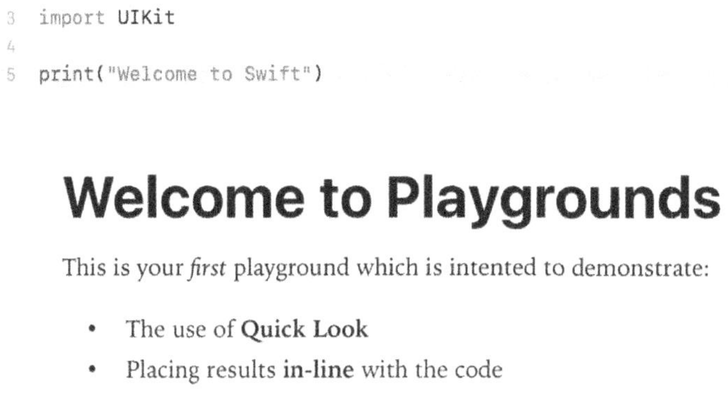

Figure 4-12

Detailed information about the Markup syntax can be found online at the following URL:

https://developer.apple.com/library/content/documentation/Xcode/Reference/xcode_markup_formatting_ref/index.html

4.6 Working with Playground Pages

A playground can consist of multiple pages, with each page containing its own code, resources and, rich text comments. So far, the playground used in this chapter contains a single page. Add a page to the playground now by selecting the LearnSwift entry at the top of the Navigator panel, right-clicking, and selecting the *New Playground Page* menu option. If the Navigator panel is not currently visible, click the button indicated by the left-most arrow in Figure 4-1 above to display it. Note that two pages are now listed in the Navigator named "Untitled Page" and "Untitled Page 2". Select and then click a second time on the "Untitled Page 2" entry so that the name becomes editable and change the name to *SwiftUI Example* as outlined in Figure 4-13:

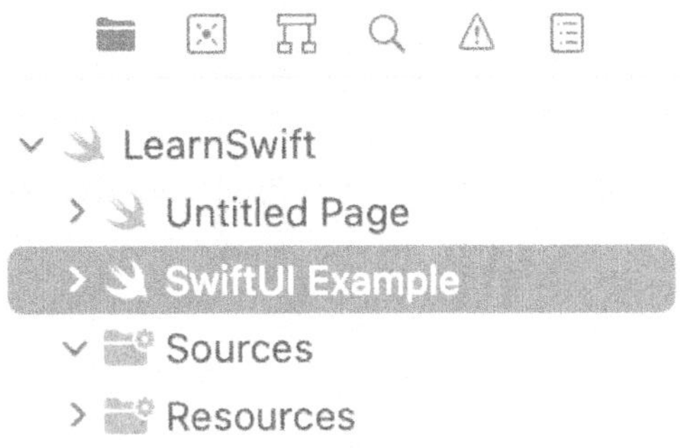

Figure 4-13

Note that the newly added page has Markup links which, when clicked, navigate to the previous or next page in the playground.

4.7 Working with SwiftUI and Live View in Playgrounds

In addition to allowing you to experiment with the Swift programming language, playgrounds may also be used to work with SwiftUI. Not only does this allow SwiftUI views to be prototyped, but when combined with the playground live view feature, it is also possible to run and interact with those views.

To try out SwiftUI and live view, begin by selecting the newly added SwiftUI Example page, deleting the current code lines, and modifying it to import both the SwiftUI and PlaygroundSupport frameworks:

```
import SwiftUI
import PlaygroundSupport
```

The PlaygroundSupport module provides several useful features for playgrounds including the ability to present a live view within the playground timeline.

Beneath the import statements, add the following code (rest assured, all of the techniques used in this example will be thoroughly explained in later chapters):

```
struct ExampleView: View {

    var body: some View {

        VStack {
            Rectangle()
                .fill(Color.blue)
                .frame(width: 200, height: 200)
            Button(action: {
                    }) {
```

```
                        Text("Rotate")
            }
        }
        .padding(10)
    }
}
```

This declaration creates a custom SwiftUI view named *ExampleView* consisting of a blue Rectangle view and a Button, both contained within a vertical stack (VStack).

The PlaygroundSupport module includes a class named PlaygroundPage which allows playground code to interact with the pages that make up a playground. This is achieved through a range of methods and properties of the class, one of which is the *current* property. This property, in turn, provides access to the current playground page. To execute the code within the playground, the *liveView* property of the current page needs to be set to our new container. To display the Live View panel, enable the Xcode *Editor -> Live View* menu option as shown in Figure 4-14:

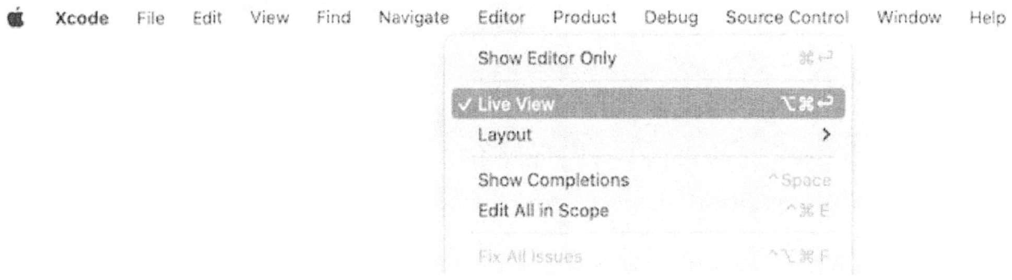

Figure 4-14

Once the live view panel is visible, add the code to assign the container to the live view of the current page as follows:

```
.
.
        VStack {
            Rectangle()
                .fill(Color.blue)
                .frame(width: 200, height: 200)
            Button(action: {
                        }) {
                        Text("Rotate")
            }
        }
        .padding(10)
    }
}

PlaygroundPage.current.setLiveView(ExampleView()
    .padding(100))
```

With the changes made, click on the run button to start the live view. After a short delay, the view should appear as shown in Figure 4-15 below:

Figure 4-15

Since the button is not yet configured to do anything when clicked, it is difficult to see that the view is live. To see the live view in action, click on the stop button and modify the view declaration to rotate the blue square by 60° each time the button is clicked:

```
import SwiftUI
import PlaygroundSupport

struct ExampleView: View {

    @State private var rotation: Double = 0

    var body: some View {

        VStack {
            Rectangle()
                .fill(Color.blue)
                .frame(width: 200, height: 200)
                .rotationEffect(.degrees(rotation))
                .animation(.linear(duration: 2), value: rotation)
            Button(action: {
                 rotation = (rotation < 360 ? rotation + 60 : 0)
                    }) {
                    Text("Rotate")
                }
        }
        .padding(10)
    }
}

PlaygroundPage.current.setLiveView(ExampleView()
    .padding(100))
```

Click the run button to launch the view in the live view and note that the square rotates each time the button is clicked.

Figure 4-16

4.8 Summary

This chapter has introduced the concept of playgrounds. Playgrounds provide an environment in which Swift code can be entered and the results of that code viewed dynamically. This provides an excellent environment both for learning the Swift programming language and for experimenting with many of the classes and APIs included in the iOS SDK without the need to create Xcode projects and repeatedly edit, compile and run code.

Chapter 5

5. Swift Data Types, Constants and Variables

If you are new to the Swift programming language then the next few chapters are recommended reading. Although SwiftUI makes the development of apps easier, it will still be necessary to learn Swift programming both to understand SwiftUI and develop fully functional apps.

If, on the other hand, you are familiar with the Swift programming language you can skip the Swift specific chapters that follow (though if you are not familiar with *implicit returns from single expressions*, *opaque return types* and *property wrappers* you should at least read the sections and chapters relating to these features before moving on to the SwiftUI chapters).

Prior to the introduction of iOS 8, the stipulated programming language for the development of iOS applications was Objective-C. When Apple announced iOS 8, however, the company also introduced an alternative to Objective-C in the form of the Swift programming language.

Due entirely to the popularity of iOS, Objective-C had become one of the more widely used programming languages. With origins firmly rooted in the 40-year-old C Programming Language, however, and despite recent efforts to modernize some aspects of the language syntax, Objective-C was beginning to show its age.

Swift, on the other hand, is a relatively new programming language designed specifically to make programming easier, faster and less prone to programmer error. Starting with a clean slate and no burden of legacy, Swift is a new and innovative language with which to develop applications for iOS, iPadOS, macOS, watchOS and tvOS with the advantage that much of the syntax will be familiar to those with experience of other programming languages.

The next several chapters will provide an overview and introduction to Swift programming. The intention of these chapters is to provide enough information so that you can begin to confidently program using Swift. For an exhaustive and in-depth guide to all the features, intricacies and capabilities of Swift, some time spent reading Apple's excellent book entitled "The Swift Programming Language" (available free of charge from within the Apple Books app) is strongly recommended.

5.1 Using a Swift Playground

Both this and the following few chapters are intended to introduce the basics of the Swift programming language. As outlined in the previous chapter, entitled *"An Introduction to Xcode 14 Playgrounds"* the best way to learn Swift is to experiment within a Swift playground environment. Before starting this chapter, therefore, create a new playground and use it to try out the code in both this and the other Swift introduction chapters that follow.

5.2 Swift Data Types

When we look at the different types of software that run on computer systems and mobile devices, from financial applications to graphics intensive games, it is easy to forget that computers are really just binary machines. Binary systems work in terms of 0 and 1, true or false, set and unset. All the data sitting in RAM, stored on disk drives and flowing through circuit boards and buses are nothing more than sequences of 1s and 0s. Each 1 or 0 is referred to as a *bit* and bits are grouped together in blocks of 8, each group being referred to as a *byte*. When people talk about 32-bit and 64-bit computer systems they are talking about the number of bits that can be handled simultaneously by the CPU bus. A 64-bit CPU, for example, is able to handle data in 64-bit blocks, resulting in faster performance than a 32-bit based system.

Humans, of course, don't think in binary. We work with decimal numbers, letters and words. In order for a human to easily (easily being a subjective term in this context) program a computer, some middle ground between human and computer thinking is needed. This is where programming languages such as Swift come into play. Programming languages allow humans to express instructions to a computer in terms and structures we understand, and then compile that down to a format that can be executed by a CPU.

One of the fundamentals of any program involves data, and programming languages such as Swift define a set of *data types* that allow us to work with data in a format we understand when programming. For example, if we want to store a number in a Swift program, we could do so with syntax similar to the following:

```
var mynumber = 10
```

In the above example, we have created a variable named *mynumber* and then assigned to it the value of 10. When we compile the source code down to the machine code used by the CPU, the number 10 is seen by the computer in binary as:

```
1010
```

Now that we have a basic understanding of the concept of data types and why they are necessary we can take a closer look at some of the more commonly used data types supported by Swift.

5.2.1 Integer Data Types

Swift integer data types are used to store whole numbers (in other words a number with no decimal places). Integers can be *signed* (capable of storing positive, negative and zero values) or *unsigned* (positive and zero values only).

Swift provides support for 8, 16, 32 and 64-bit integers (represented by the Int8, Int16, Int32 and Int64 types respectively). The same variants are also available for unsigned integers (UInt8, UInt16, UInt32 and UInt64).

In general, Apple recommends using the *Int* data type rather than one of the above specifically sized data types. The Int data type will use the appropriate integer size for the platform on which the code is running.

All integer data types contain bounds properties which can be accessed to identify the minimum and maximum supported values of that particular type. The following code, for example, outputs the minimum and maximum bounds for the 32-bit signed integer data type:

```
print("Int32 Min = \(Int32.min) Int32 Max = \(Int32.max)")
```

When executed, the above code will generate the following output:

```
Int32 Min = -2147483648 Int32 Max = 2147483647
```

5.2.2 Floating Point Data Types

The Swift floating point data types are able to store values containing decimal places. For example, 4353.1223 would be stored in a floating-point data type. Swift provides two floating point data types in the form of *Float* and *Double*. Which type to use depends on the size of value to be stored and the level of precision required. The Double type can be used to store up to 64-bit floating point numbers with a level of precision of 15 decimal places or greater. The Float data type, on the other hand, is limited to 32-bit floating point numbers and offers a level of precision as low as 6 decimal places depending on the native platform on which the code is running. Alternatively, the Float16 type may be used to store 16-bit floating point values. Float16 provides greater performance at the expense of lower precision.

5.2.3 Bool Data Type

Swift, like other languages, includes a data type for the purpose of handling true or false (1 or 0) conditions. Two Boolean constant values (*true* and *false*) are provided by Swift specifically for working with Boolean data types.

5.2.4 Character Data Type

The Swift Character data type is used to store a single character of rendered text such as a letter, numerical digit, punctuation mark or symbol. Internally characters in Swift are stored in the form of *grapheme clusters*. A grapheme cluster is made of two or more Unicode scalars that are combined to represent a single visible character.

The following lines assign a variety of different characters to Character type variables:

```
var myChar1 = "f"
var myChar2 = ":"
var myChar3 = "X"
```

Characters may also be referenced using Unicode code points. The following example assigns the 'X' character to a variable using Unicode:

```
var myChar4 = "\u{0058}"
```

5.2.5 String Data Type

The String data type is a sequence of characters that typically make up a word or sentence. In addition to providing a storage mechanism, the String data type also includes a range of string manipulation features allowing strings to be searched, matched, concatenated and modified. Strings in Swift are represented internally as collections of characters (where a character is, as previously discussed, comprised of one or more Unicode scalar values).

Strings can also be constructed using combinations of strings, variables, constants, expressions, and function calls using a concept referred to as *string interpolation*. For example, the following code creates a new string from a variety of different sources using string interpolation before outputting it to the console:

```
var userName = "John"
var inboxCount = 25
let maxCount = 100

var message = "\(userName) has \(inboxCount) messages. Message capacity remaining
is \(maxCount - inboxCount) messages."

print(message)
```

When executed, the code will output the following message:

```
John has 25 messages. Message capacity remaining is 75 messages.
```

A multiline string literal may be declared by encapsulating the string within triple quotes as follows:

```
var multiline = """

    The console glowed with flashing warnings.
    Clearly time was running out.

    "I thought you said you knew how to fly this!" yelled Mary.

    "It was much easier on the simulator" replied her brother,
```

```
     trying to keep the panic out of his voice.

"""

print(multiline)
```

The above code will generate the following output when run:

```
The console glowed with flashing warnings.
Clearly time was running out.

"I thought you said you knew how to fly this!" yelled Mary.

"It was much easier on the simulator" replied her brother,
trying to keep the panic out of his voice.
```

The amount by which each line is indented within a multiline literal is calculated as the number of characters by which the line is indented minus the number of characters by which the closing triple quote line is indented. If, for example, the fourth line in the above example had a 10-character indentation and the closing triple quote was indented by 5 characters, the actual indentation of the fourth line within the string would be 5 characters. This allows multiline literals to be formatted tidily within Swift code while still allowing control over indentation of individual lines.

5.2.6 Special Characters/Escape Sequences

In addition to the standard set of characters outlined above, there is also a range of *special characters* (also referred to as *escape sequences*) available for specifying items such as a new line, tab or a specific Unicode value within a string. These special characters are identified by prefixing the character with a backslash (a concept referred to as *escaping*). For example, the following assigns a new line to the variable named newline:

```
var newline = "\n"
```

In essence, any character that is preceded by a backslash is considered to be a special character and is treated accordingly. This raises the question as to what to do if you actually want a backslash character. This is achieved by *escaping* the backslash itself:

```
var backslash = "\\"
```

Commonly used special characters supported by Swift are as follows:

- **\n** - New line
- **\r** - Carriage return
- **\t** - Horizontal tab
- **** - Backslash
- **\"** - Double quote (used when placing a double quote into a string declaration)
- **\'** - Single quote (used when placing a single quote into a string declaration)
- **\u{*nn*}** – Single byte Unicode scalar where *nn* is replaced by two hexadecimal digits representing the Unicode character.
- **\u{*nnnn*}** – Double byte Unicode scalar where *nnnn* is replaced by four hexadecimal digits representing the Unicode character.

- **\u{*nnnnnnnn*}** – Four-byte Unicode scalar where *nnnnnnnn* is replaced by eight hexadecimal digits representing the Unicode character.

5.3 Swift Variables

Variables are essentially locations in computer memory reserved for storing the data used by an application. Each variable is given a name by the programmer and assigned a value. The name assigned to the variable may then be used in the Swift code to access the value assigned to that variable. This access can involve either reading the value of the variable or changing the value. It is, of course, the ability to change the value of variables which gives them the name *variable*.

5.4 Swift Constants

A constant is like a variable in that it provides a named location in memory to store a data value. Constants differ in one significant way in that once a value has been assigned to a constant it cannot subsequently be changed.

Constants are particularly useful if there is a value which is used repeatedly throughout the application code. Rather than use the value each time, it makes the code easier to read if the value is first assigned to a constant which is then referenced in the code. For example, it might not be clear to someone reading your Swift code why you used the value 5 in an expression. If, instead of the value 5, you use a constant named interestRate the purpose of the value becomes much clearer. Constants also have the advantage that if the programmer needs to change a widely used value, it only needs to be changed once in the constant declaration and not each time it is referenced.

As with variables, constants have a type, a name and a value. Unlike variables, however, once a value has been assigned to a constant, that value cannot subsequently be changed.

5.5 Declaring Constants and Variables

Variables are declared using the *var* keyword and may be initialized with a value at creation time. If the variable is declared without an initial value, it must be declared as being *optional* (a topic which will be covered later in this chapter). The following, for example, is a typical variable declaration:

```
var userCount = 10
```

Constants are declared using the *let* keyword.

```
let maxUserCount = 20
```

For greater code efficiency and execution performance, Apple recommends the use of constants rather than variables whenever possible.

5.6 Type Annotations and Type Inference

Swift is categorized as a *type safe* programming language. This essentially means that once the data type of a variable has been identified, that variable cannot subsequently be used to store data of any other type without inducing a compilation error. This contrasts to *loosely typed* programming languages where a variable, once declared, can subsequently be used to store other data types.

There are two ways in which the type of a constant or variable will be identified. One approach is to use a *type annotation* at the point the variable or constant is declared in the code. This is achieved by placing a colon after the constant or variable name followed by the type declaration. The following line of code, for example, declares a variable named userCount as being of type Int:

```
var userCount: Int = 10
```

In the absence of a type annotation in a declaration, the Swift compiler uses a technique referred to as *type inference* to identify the type of the constant or variable. When relying on type inference, the compiler looks to see what type of value is being assigned to the constant or variable at the point that it is initialized and uses that as the type. Consider, for example, the following variable and constant declarations:

```
var signalStrength = 2.231
let companyName = "My Company"
```

During compilation of the above lines of code, Swift will infer that the signalStrength variable is of type Double (type inference in Swift defaults to Double for all floating-point numbers) and that the companyName constant is of type String.

When a constant is declared without a type annotation it must be assigned a value at the point of declaration:

```
let bookTitle = "SwiftUI Essentials"
```

If a type annotation is used when the constant is declared, however, the value can be assigned later in the code. For example:

```
let bookTitle: String
.
.
if iosBookType {
    bookTitle = "SwiftUI Essentials"
} else {
    bookTitle = "Android Studio Development Essentials"
}
```

It is important to note that a value may only be assigned to a constant once. A second attempt to assign a value to a constant will result in a syntax error.

5.7 The Swift Tuple

Before proceeding, now is a good time to introduce the Swift tuple. The tuple is perhaps one of the simplest, yet most powerful features of the Swift programming language. A tuple is, quite simply, a way to temporarily group together multiple values into a single entity. The items stored in a tuple can be of any type and there are no restrictions requiring that those values all be of the same type. A tuple could, for example, be constructed to contain an Int value, a Double value and a String as follows:

```
let myTuple = (10, 432.433, "This is a String")
```

The elements of a tuple can be accessed using a number of different techniques. A specific tuple value can be accessed simply by referencing the index position (with the first value being at index position 0). The code below, for example, extracts the string resource (at index position 2 in the tuple) and assigns it to a new string variable:

```
let myTuple = (10, 432.433, "This is a String")
let myString = myTuple.2
print(myString)
```

Alternatively, all the values in a tuple may be extracted and assigned to variables or constants in a single statement:

```
let (myInt, myFloat, myString) = myTuple
```

This same technique can be used to extract selected values from a tuple while ignoring others by replacing the values to be ignored with an underscore character. The following code fragment extracts the integer and string values from the tuple and assigns them to variables, but ignores the floating-point value:

```
var (myInt, _, myString) = myTuple
```

When creating a tuple, it is also possible to assign a name to each value:

```
let myTuple = (count: 10, length: 432.433, message: "This is a String")
```

The names assigned to the values stored in a tuple may then be used to reference those values in code. For example, to output the *message* string value from the *myTuple* instance, the following line of code could be used:

```
print(myTuple.message)
```

Perhaps the most powerful use of tuples is, as will be seen in later chapters, the ability to return multiple values from a function.

5.8 The Swift Optional Type

The Swift optional data type is a new concept that does not exist in most other programming languages. The purpose of the optional type is to provide a safe and consistent approach to handling situations where a variable or constant may not have any value assigned to it.

Variables are declared as being optional by placing a ? character after the type declaration. The following code declares an optional Int variable named index:

```
var index: Int?
```

The variable *index* can now either have an integer value assigned to it or have nothing assigned to it. Behind the scenes, and as far as the compiler and runtime are concerned, an optional with no value assigned to it actually has a value of nil.

An optional can easily be tested (typically using an if statement) to identify whether it has a value assigned to it as follows:

```
var index: Int?

if index != nil {
    // index variable has a value assigned to it
} else {
    // index variable has no value assigned to it
}
```

If an optional has a value assigned to it, that value is said to be "wrapped" within the optional. The value wrapped in an optional may be accessed using a concept referred to as *forced unwrapping*. This simply means that the underlying value is extracted from the optional data type, a procedure that is performed by placing an exclamation mark (!) after the optional name.

To explore this concept of unwrapping optional types in more detail, consider the following code:

```
var index: Int?

index = 3

var treeArray = ["Oak", "Pine", "Yew", "Birch"]

if index != nil {
    print(treeArray[index!])
} else {
    print("index does not contain a value")
}
```

The code simply uses an optional variable to hold the index into an array of strings representing the names of tree species (Swift arrays will be covered in more detail in the chapter entitled *"Working with Array and Dictionary Collections in Swift"*). If the index optional variable has a value assigned to it, the tree name at that location in the array is printed to the console. Since the index is an optional type, the value has been unwrapped by placing an exclamation mark after the variable name:

```
print(treeArray[index!])
```

Had the index not been unwrapped (in other words the exclamation mark omitted from the above line), the compiler would have issued an error similar to the following:

```
Value of optional type 'Int?' must be unwrapped to a value of type 'Int'
```

As an alternative to forced unwrapping, the value assigned to an optional may be allocated to a temporary variable or constant using *optional binding*, the syntax for which is as follows:

```
if let constantname = optionalName {

}

if var variablename = optionalName {

}
```

The above constructs perform two tasks. In the first instance, the statement ascertains whether the designated optional contains a value. Second, in the event that the optional has a value, that value is assigned to the declared constant or variable and the code within the body of the statement is executed. The previous forced unwrapping example could, therefore, be modified as follows to use optional binding instead:

```
var index: Int?

index = 3

var treeArray = ["Oak", "Pine", "Yew", "Birch"]

if let myvalue = index {
    print(treeArray[myvalue])
} else {
    print("index does not contain a value")
}
```

In this case the value assigned to the index variable is unwrapped and assigned to a temporary (also referred to as *shadow*) constant named *myvalue* which is then used as the index reference into the array. Note that the *myvalue* constant is described as temporary since it is only available within the scope of the if statement. Once the if statement completes execution, the constant will no longer exist. For this reason, there is no conflict in using the same temporary name as that assigned to the optional. The following is, for example, valid code:

```
.
.
if let index = index {
    print(treeArray[index])
} else {
.
.
```

When considering the above example, the use of the temporary value begins to seem redundant. Fortunately, the Swift development team arrived at the same conclusion and introduced the following shorthand if-let syntax in Swift 5.7:

```
var index: Int?

index = 3

var treeArray = ["Oak", "Pine", "Yew", "Birch"]

if let index {
    print(treeArray[index])
} else {
    print("index does not contain a value")
}
```

Using this approach it is no longer necessary to assign the optional to a temporary value.

Optional binding may also be used to unwrap multiple optionals and include a Boolean test condition, the syntax for which is as follows:

```
if let constname1 = optName1, let constname2 = optName2,
     let optName3 = …, <boolean statement> {

}
```

The shorthand if-let syntax is also available when working with multiple optionals and test conditions avoiding the need to use temporary values:

```
if let constname1, let constname2,
     let optName3, ... <boolean statement> {

}
```

The following code, for example, uses shorthand optional binding to unwrap two optionals within a single statement:

```
var pet1: String?
var pet2: String?

pet1 = "cat"
pet2 = "dog"

if let pet1, let pet2 {
    print(pet1)
    print(pet2)
} else {
    print("insufficient pets")
}
```

The code fragment below, on the other hand, also makes use of the Boolean test clause condition:

```
if let pet1, let pet2, petCount > 1 {
```

```
    print(pet1)
    print(pet2)
} else {
    print("insufficient pets")
}
```

In the above example, the optional binding will not be attempted unless the value assigned to *petCount* is greater than 1.

It is also possible to declare an optional as being *implicitly unwrapped*. When an optional is declared in this way, the underlying value can be accessed without having to perform forced unwrapping or optional binding. An optional is declared as being implicitly unwrapped by replacing the question mark (?) with an exclamation mark (!) in the declaration. For example:

```
var index: Int! // Optional is now implicitly unwrapped

index = 3

var treeArray = ["Oak", "Pine", "Yew", "Birch"]

if index != nil {
    print(treeArray[index])
} else {
    print("index does not contain a value")
}
```

With the index optional variable now declared as being implicitly unwrapped, it is no longer necessary to unwrap the value when it is used as an index into the array in the above print call.

One final observation with regard to optionals in Swift is that only optional types are able to have no value or a value of nil assigned to them. In Swift it is not, therefore, possible to assign a nil value to a non-optional variable or constant. The following declarations, for instance, will all result in errors from the compiler since none of the variables are declared as optional:

```
var myInt = nil // Invalid code
var myString: String = nil // Invalid Code
let myConstant = nil // Invalid code
```

5.9 Type Casting and Type Checking

When writing Swift code, situations will occur where the compiler is unable to identify the specific type of a value. This is often the case when a value of ambiguous or unexpected type is returned from a method or function call. In this situation it may be necessary to let the compiler know the type of value that your code is expecting or requires using the *as* keyword (a concept referred to as *type casting*).

The following code, for example, lets the compiler know that the value returned from the *object(forKey:)* method needs to be treated as a String type:

```
let myValue = record.object(forKey: "comment") as! String
```

In fact, there are two types of casting which are referred to as *upcasting* and *downcasting*. Upcasting occurs when an object of a particular class is cast to one of its superclasses. Upcasting is performed using the *as* keyword and is also referred to as *guaranteed conversion* since the compiler can tell from the code that the cast will be successful. The UIButton class, for example, is a subclass of the UIControl class as shown in the fragment of the

UIKit class hierarchy shown in Figure 5-1:

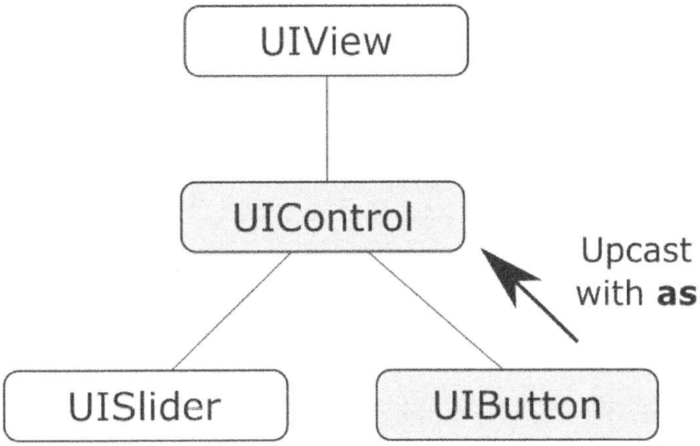

Figure 5-1

Since UIButton is a subclass of UIControl, the object can be safely upcast as follows:

```
let myButton: UIButton = UIButton()

let myControl = myButton as UIControl
```

Downcasting, on the other hand, occurs when a conversion is made from one class to another where there is no guarantee that the cast can be made safely or that an invalid casting attempt will be caught by the compiler. When an invalid cast is made in downcasting and not identified by the compiler it will most likely lead to an error at runtime.

Downcasting usually involves converting from a class to one of its subclasses. Downcasting is performed using the *as!* keyword syntax and is also referred to as *forced conversion*. Consider, for example, the UIKit UIScrollView class which has as subclasses both the UITableView and UITextView classes as shown in Figure 5-2:

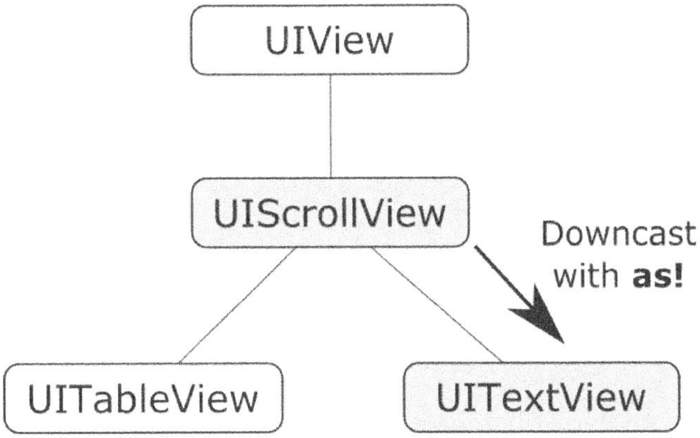

Figure 5-2

In order to convert a UIScrollView object to a UITextView class a downcast operation needs to be performed. The following code attempts to downcast a UIScrollView object to UITextView using the *guaranteed conversion* or *upcast* approach:

```
let myScrollView: UIScrollView = UIScrollView()
```

```
let myTextView = myScrollView as UITextView
```

The above code will result in the following error:

```
'UIScrollView' is not convertible to 'UITextView'
```

The compiler is indicating that a UIScrollView instance cannot be safely converted to a UITextView class instance. This does not necessarily mean that it is incorrect to do so, the compiler is simply stating that it cannot guarantee the safety of the conversion for you. The downcast conversion could instead be forced using the *as!* annotation:

```
let myTextView = myScrollView as! UITextView
```

Now the code will compile without an error. As an example of the dangers of downcasting, however, the above code will crash on execution stating that UIScrollView cannot be cast to UITextView. Forced downcasting should, therefore, be used with caution.

A safer approach to downcasting is to perform an optional binding using *as?*. If the conversion is performed successfully, an optional value of the specified type is returned, otherwise the optional value will be nil:

```
if let myTextView = myScrollView as? UITextView {
    print("Type cast to UITextView succeeded")
} else {
    print("Type cast to UITextView failed")
}
```

It is also possible to *type check* a value using the *is* keyword. The following code, for example, checks that a specific object is an instance of a class named MyClass:

```
if myobject is MyClass {
    // myobject is an instance of MyClass
}
```

5.10 Summary

This chapter has begun the introduction to Swift by exploring data types together with an overview of how to declare constants and variables. The chapter has also introduced concepts such as type safety, type inference and optionals, each of which is an integral part of Swift programming and designed specifically to make code writing less prone to error.

Chapter 6

6. Swift Operators and Expressions

So far we have looked at using variables and constants in Swift and also described the different data types. Being able to create variables, however, is only part of the story. The next step is to learn how to use these variables and constants in Swift code. The primary method for working with data is in the form of *expressions*.

6.1 Expression Syntax in Swift

The most basic Swift expression consists of an *operator*, two *operands* and an *assignment*. The following is an example of an expression:

```
var myresult = 1 + 2
```

In the above example, the (+) operator is used to add two operands (1 and 2) together. The *assignment operator* (=) subsequently assigns the result of the addition to a variable named *myresult*. The operands could just have easily been variables (or a mixture of constants and variables) instead of the actual numerical values used in the example.

In the remainder of this chapter we will look at the basic types of operators available in Swift.

6.2 The Basic Assignment Operator

We have already looked at the most basic of assignment operators, the = operator. This assignment operator simply assigns the result of an expression to a variable. In essence, the = assignment operator takes two operands. The left-hand operand is the variable or constant to which a value is to be assigned and the right-hand operand is the value to be assigned. The right-hand operand is, more often than not, an expression which performs some type of arithmetic or logical evaluation, the result of which will be assigned to the variable or constant. The following examples are all valid uses of the assignment operator:

```
var x: Int? // Declare an optional Int variable
var y = 10 // Declare and initialize a second Int variable

x = 10 // Assign a value to x
x = x! + y // Assign the result of x + y to x
x = y // Assign the value of y to x
```

6.3 Swift Arithmetic Operators

Swift provides a range of operators for the purpose of creating mathematical expressions. These operators primarily fall into the category of *binary* operators in that they take two operands. The exception is the *unary negative operator* (-) which serves to indicate that a value is negative rather than positive. This contrasts with the *subtraction operator* (-) which takes two operands (i.e. one value to be subtracted from another). For example:

```
var x = -10 // Unary - operator used to assign -10 to variable x
x = x - 5 // Subtraction operator. Subtracts 5 from x
```

The following table lists the primary Swift arithmetic operators:

Operator	Description
-(unary)	Negates the value of a variable or expression

*	Multiplication
/	Division
+	Addition
-	Subtraction
%	Remainder/Modulo

Table 6-1

Note that multiple operators may be used in a single expression.

For example:

```
x = y * 10 + z - 5 / 4
```

6.4 Compound Assignment Operators

In an earlier section we looked at the basic assignment operator (=). Swift provides a number of operators designed to combine an assignment with a mathematical or logical operation. These are primarily of use when performing an evaluation where the result is to be stored in one of the operands. For example, one might write an expression as follows:

```
x = x + y
```

The above expression adds the value contained in variable x to the value contained in variable y and stores the result in variable x. This can be simplified using the addition compound assignment operator:

```
x += y
```

The above expression performs exactly the same task as *x = x + y* but saves the programmer some typing.

Numerous compound assignment operators are available in Swift, the most frequently used of which are outlined in the following table:

Operator	Description
x += y	Add x to y and place result in x
x -= y	Subtract y from x and place result in x
x *= y	Multiply x by y and place result in x
x /= y	Divide x by y and place result in x
x %= y	Perform Modulo on x and y and place result in x

Table 6-2

6.5 Comparison Operators

Swift also includes a set of logical operators useful for performing comparisons. These operators all return a Boolean result depending on the result of the comparison. These operators are *binary operators* in that they work with two operands.

Comparison operators are most frequently used in constructing program flow control logic. For example, an *if* statement may be constructed based on whether one value matches another:

```
if x == y {
      // Perform task
}
```

The result of a comparison may also be stored in a *Bool* variable. For example, the following code will result in a *true* value being stored in the variable result:

```
var result: Bool?
var x = 10
var y = 20

result = x < y
```

Clearly 10 is less than 20, resulting in a *true* evaluation of the *x* < *y* expression. The following table lists the full set of Swift comparison operators:

Operator	Description
x == y	Returns true if x is equal to y
x > y	Returns true if x is greater than y
x >= y	Returns true if x is greater than or equal to y
x < y	Returns true if x is less than y
x <= y	Returns true if x is less than or equal to y
x != y	Returns true if x is not equal to y

Table 6-3

6.6 Boolean Logical Operators

Swift also provides a set of so-called logical operators designed to return Boolean *true* or *false* values. These operators both return Boolean results and take Boolean values as operands. The key operators are NOT (!), AND (&&) and OR (||).

The NOT (!) operator simply inverts the current value of a Boolean variable, or the result of an expression. For example, if a variable named *flag* is currently true, prefixing the variable with a '!' character will invert the value to false:

```
var flag = true // variable is true
var secondFlag = !flag // secondFlag set to false
```

The OR (||) operator returns true if one of its two operands evaluates to true, otherwise it returns false. For example, the following code evaluates to true because at least one of the expressions either side of the OR operator is true:

```
if (10 < 20) || (20 < 10) {
        print("Expression is true")
}
```

The AND (&&) operator returns true only if both operands evaluate to be true. The following example will return false because only one of the two operand expressions evaluates to true:

```
if (10 < 20) && (20 < 10) {
      print("Expression is true")
}
```

6.7 Range Operators

Swift includes several useful operators that allow ranges of values to be declared. As will be seen in later chapters, these operators are invaluable when working with looping in program logic.

The syntax for the *closed range operator* is as follows:

```
x...y
```

This operator represents the range of numbers starting at x and ending at y where both x and y are included within the range. The range operator 5...8, for example, specifies the numbers 5, 6, 7 and 8.

The *half-open range operator,* on the other hand uses the following syntax:

```
x..<y
```

In this instance, the operator encompasses all the numbers from x up to, but not including, y. A half-closed range operator 5..<8, therefore, specifies the numbers 5, 6 and 7.

Finally, the *one-sided range* operator specifies a range that can extend as far as possible in a specified range direction until the natural beginning or end of the range is reached (or until some other condition is met). A one-sided range is declared by omitting the number from one side of the range declaration, for example:

```
x...
```

or

```
...y
```

The previous chapter, for example, explained that a String in Swift is actually a collection of individual characters. A range to specify the characters in a string starting with the character at position 2 through to the last character in the string (regardless of string length) would be declared as follows:

```
2...
```

Similarly, to specify a range that begins with the first character and ends with the character at position 6, the range would be specified as follows:

```
...6
```

6.8 The Ternary Operator

Swift supports the *ternary operator* to provide a shortcut way of making decisions within code. The syntax of the ternary operator (also known as the conditional operator) is as follows:

```
condition ? true expression : false expression
```

The way the ternary operator works is that *condition* is replaced with an expression that will return either *true* or *false.* If the result is true then the expression that replaces the *true expression* is evaluated. Conversely, if the result was *false* then the *false expression* is evaluated. Let's see this in action:

```
let x = 10
let y = 20

print("Largest number is \(x > y ? x : y)")
```

The above code example will evaluate whether x is greater than y. Clearly this will evaluate to false resulting in y being returned to the print call for display to the user:

```
Largest number is 20
```

6.9 Nil Coalescing Operator

The *nil coalescing operator* (??) allows a default value to be used in the event that an optional has a nil value. The following example will output text which reads "Welcome back, customer" because the *customerName* optional is set to nil:

```
let customerName: String? = nil
print("Welcome back, \(customerName ?? "customer")")
```

If, on the other hand, *customerName* is not nil, the optional will be unwrapped and the assigned value displayed:

```
let customerName: String? = "John"
print("Welcome back, \(customerName ?? "customer")")
```

On execution, the print statement output will now read "Welcome back, John".

6.10 Bitwise Operators

As previously discussed, computer processors work in binary. These are essentially streams of ones and zeros, each one referred to as a bit. Bits are formed into groups of 8 to form bytes. As such, it is not surprising that we, as programmers, will occasionally end up working at this level in our code. To facilitate this requirement, Swift provides a range of *bit operators*.

Those familiar with bitwise operators in other languages such as C, C++, C#, Objective-C and Java will find nothing new in this area of the Swift language syntax. For those unfamiliar with binary numbers, now may be a good time to seek out reference materials on the subject in order to understand how ones and zeros are formed into bytes to form numbers. Other authors have done a much better job of describing the subject than we can do within the scope of this book.

For the purposes of this exercise we will be working with the binary representation of two numbers (for the sake of brevity we will be using 8-bit values in the following examples). First, the decimal number 171 is represented in binary as:

```
10101011
```

Second, the number 3 is represented by the following binary sequence:

```
00000011
```

Now that we have two binary numbers with which to work, we can begin to look at the Swift bitwise operators:

6.10.1 Bitwise NOT

The Bitwise NOT is represented by the tilde (~) character and has the effect of inverting all of the bits in a number. In other words, all the zeros become ones and all the ones become zeros. Taking our example 3 number, a Bitwise NOT operation has the following result:

```
00000011 NOT
========
11111100
```

The following Swift code, therefore, results in a value of -4:

```
let y = 3
let z = ~y

print("Result is \(z)")
```

6.10.2 Bitwise AND

The Bitwise AND is represented by a single ampersand (&). It makes a bit by bit comparison of two numbers. Any corresponding position in the binary sequence of each number where both bits are 1 results in a 1 appearing in the same position of the resulting number. If either bit position contains a 0 then a zero appears in the result. Taking our two example numbers, this would appear as follows:

```
10101011 AND
```

```
00000011
========
00000011
```

As we can see, the only locations where both numbers have 1s are the last two positions. If we perform this in Swift code, therefore, we should find that the result is 3 (00000011):

```
let x = 171
let y = 3
let z = x & y

print("Result is \(z)")
```

6.10.3 Bitwise OR

The bitwise OR also performs a bit by bit comparison of two binary sequences. Unlike the AND operation, the OR places a 1 in the result if there is a 1 in the first or second operand. The operator is represented by a single vertical bar character (|). Using our example numbers, the result will be as follows:

```
10101011 OR
00000011
========
10101011
```

If we perform this operation in a Swift example the result will be 171:

```
let x = 171
let y = 3
let z = x | y

print("Result is \(z)")
```

6.10.4 Bitwise XOR

The bitwise XOR (commonly referred to as *exclusive OR* and represented by the caret '^' character) performs a similar task to the OR operation except that a 1 is placed in the result if one or other corresponding bit positions in the two numbers is 1. If both positions are a 1 or a 0 then the corresponding bit in the result is set to a 0. For example:

```
10101011 XOR
00000011
========
10101000
```

The result in this case is 10101000 which converts to 168 in decimal. To verify this we can, once again, try some Swift code:

```
let x = 171
let y = 3
let z = x ^ y

print("Result is \(z)")
```

6.10.5 Bitwise Left Shift

The bitwise left shift moves each bit in a binary number a specified number of positions to the left. Shifting an integer one position to the left has the effect of doubling the value.

As the bits are shifted to the left, zeros are placed in the vacated right most (low order) positions. Note also that once the left most (high order) bits are shifted beyond the size of the variable containing the value, those high order bits are discarded:

```
10101011 Left Shift one bit
========
101010110
```

In Swift the bitwise left shift operator is represented by the '<<' sequence, followed by the number of bit positions to be shifted. For example, to shift left by 1 bit:

```
let x = 171
let z = x << 1

print("Result is \(z)")
```

When compiled and executed, the above code will display a message stating that the result is 342 which, when converted to binary, equates to 101010110.

6.10.6 Bitwise Right Shift

A bitwise right shift is, as you might expect, the same as a left except that the shift takes place in the opposite direction. Shifting an integer one position to the right has the effect of halving the value.

Note that since we are shifting to the right there is no opportunity to retain the lower most bits regardless of the data type used to contain the result. As a result, the low order bits are discarded. Whether or not the vacated high order bit positions are replaced with zeros or ones depends on whether the *sign bit* used to indicate positive and negative numbers is set or not.

```
10101011 Right Shift one bit
========
01010101
```

The bitwise right shift is represented by the '>>' character sequence followed by the shift count:

```
let x = 171
let z = x >> 1

print("Result is \(z)")
```

When executed, the above code will report the result of the shift as being 85, which equates to binary 01010101.

6.11 Compound Bitwise Operators

As with the arithmetic operators, each bitwise operator has a corresponding compound operator that allows the operation and assignment to be performed using a single operator:

Operator	Description
x &= y	Perform a bitwise AND of x and y and assign result to x
x |= y	Perform a bitwise OR of x and y and assign result to x
x ^= y	Perform a bitwise XOR of x and y and assign result to x
x <<= n	Shift x left by n places and assign result to x
x >>= n	Shift x right by n places and assign result to x

Table 6-4

6.12 Summary

Operators and expressions provide the underlying mechanism by which variables and constants are manipulated and evaluated within Swift code. This can take the simplest of forms whereby two numbers are added using the addition operator in an expression and the result stored in a variable using the assignment operator. Operators fall into a range of categories, details of which have been covered in this chapter.

Chapter 7

7. Swift Control Flow

Regardless of the programming language used, application development is largely an exercise in applying logic, and much of the art of programming involves writing code that makes decisions based on one or more criteria. Such decisions define which code gets executed, how many times it is executed and, conversely, which code gets by-passed when the program is executing. This is often referred to as *control flow* since it controls the *flow* of program execution. Control flow typically falls into the categories of *looping control* (how often code is executed) and *conditional control flow* (whether code is executed). This chapter is intended to provide an introductory overview of both types of control flow in Swift.

7.1 Looping Control Flow

This chapter will begin by looking at control flow in the form of loops. Loops are essentially sequences of Swift statements which are to be executed repeatedly until a specified condition is met. The first looping statement we will explore is the *for-in* loop.

7.2 The Swift for-in Statement

The *for-in* loop is used to iterate over a sequence of items contained in a collection or number range and provides a simple to use looping option.

The syntax of the for-in loop is as follows:

```
for constant name in collection or range {
    // code to be executed
}
```

In this syntax, *constant name* is the name to be used for a constant that will contain the current item from the collection or range through which the loop is iterating. The code in the body of the loop will typically use this constant name as a reference to the current item in the loop cycle. The *collection* or *range* references the item through which the loop is iterating. This could, for example, be an array of string values, a range operator or even a string of characters (the topic of collections will be covered in greater detail within the chapter entitled *"Working with Array and Dictionary Collections in Swift"*).

Consider, for example, the following for-in loop construct:

```
for index in 1...5 {
      print("Value of index is \(index)")
}
```

The loop begins by stating that the current item is to be assigned to a constant named *index*. The statement then declares a closed range operator to indicate that the for loop is to iterate through a range of numbers, starting at 1 and ending at 5. The body of the loop simply prints out a message to the console panel indicating the current value assigned to the *index* constant, resulting in the following output:

```
Value of index is 1
Value of index is 2
Value of index is 3
Value of index is 4
Value of index is 5
```

As will be demonstrated in the *"Working with Array and Dictionary Collections in Swift"* chapter of this book, the *for-in* loop is of particular benefit when working with collections such as arrays and dictionaries.

The declaration of a constant name in which to store a reference to the current item is not mandatory. In the event that a reference to the current item is not required in the body of the *for* loop, the constant name in the *for* loop declaration can be replaced by an underscore character. For example:

```
var count = 0

for _ in 1...5 {
    // No reference to the current value is required.
    count += 1
}
```

7.2.1 The while Loop

The Swift *for* loop described previously works well when it is known in advance how many times a particular task needs to be repeated in a program. There will, however, be instances where code needs to be repeated until a certain condition is met, with no way of knowing in advance how many repetitions are going to be needed to meet that criteria. To address this need, Swift provides the *while* loop.

Essentially, the *while* loop repeats a set of tasks while a specified condition is met. The *while* loop syntax is defined as follows:

```
while condition {
      // Swift statements go here
}
```

In the above syntax, *condition* is an expression that will return either *true* or *false* and the *// Swift statements go here* comment represents the code to be executed while the *condition* expression is *true*. For example:

```
var myCount = 0

while  myCount < 100 {
      myCount += 1
}
```

In the above example, the *while* expression will evaluate whether the *myCount* variable is less than 100. If it is already greater than 100, the code in the braces is skipped and the loop exits without performing any tasks.

If, on the other hand, *myCount* is not greater than 100 the code in the braces is executed and the loop returns to the *while* statement and repeats the evaluation of *myCount*. This process repeats until the value of *myCount* is greater than 100, at which point the loop exits.

7.3 The repeat ... while loop

The *repeat ... while* loop replaces the Swift 1.x *do .. while* loop. It is often helpful to think of the *repeat ... while* loop as an inverted *while* loop. The *while* loop evaluates an expression before executing the code contained in the body of the loop. If the expression evaluates to *false* on the first check then the code is not executed. The *repeat ... while* loop, on the other hand, is provided for situations where you know that the code contained in the body of the loop will *always* need to be executed at least once. For example, you may want to keep stepping through the items in an array until a specific item is found. You know that you have to at least check the first item in the array to have any hope of finding the entry you need. The syntax for the *repeat ... while* loop is as follows:

```
repeat {
       // Swift statements here
```

```
} while conditional expression
```

In the *repeat ... while* example below the loop will continue until the value of a variable named *i* equals 0:

```
var i = 10

repeat {
        i -= 1
} while (i > 0)
```

7.4 Breaking from Loops

Having created a loop, it is possible that under certain conditions you might want to break out of the loop before the completion criteria have been met (particularly if you have created an infinite loop). One such example might involve continually checking for activity on a network socket. Once activity has been detected it will most likely be necessary to break out of the monitoring loop and perform some other task.

For the purpose of breaking out of a loop, Swift provides the *break* statement which breaks out of the current loop and resumes execution at the code directly after the loop. For example:

```
var j = 10

for _ in 0 ..< 100
{
    j += j

    if j > 100 {
        break
    }

    print("j = \(j)")
}
```

In the above example the loop will continue to execute until the value of j exceeds 100 at which point the loop will exit and execution will continue with the next line of code after the loop.

7.5 The continue Statement

The *continue* statement causes all remaining code statements in a loop to be skipped, and execution to be returned to the top of the loop. In the following example, the print function is only called when the value of variable *i* is an even number:

```
var i = 1

while i < 20
{
        i += 1

        if (i % 2) != 0 {
            continue
        }

        print("i = \(i)")
```

```
}
```

The *continue* statement in the above example will cause the print call to be skipped unless the value of *i* can be divided by 2 with no remainder. If the *continue* statement is triggered, execution will skip to the top of the while loop and the statements in the body of the loop will be repeated (until the value of *i* exceeds 19).

7.6 Conditional Control Flow

In the previous chapter we looked at how to use logical expressions in Swift to determine whether something is *true* or *false*. Since programming is largely an exercise in applying logic, much of the art of programming involves writing code that makes decisions based on one or more criteria. Such decisions define which code gets executed and, conversely, which code gets by-passed when the program is executing.

7.7 Using the if Statement

The *if* statement is perhaps the most basic of control flow options available to the Swift programmer. Programmers who are familiar with C, Objective-C, C++ or Java will immediately be comfortable using Swift *if* statements.

The basic syntax of the Swift *if* statement is as follows:

```
if boolean expression {
    // Swift code to be performed when expression evaluates to true
}
```

Unlike some other programming languages, it is important to note that the braces ({}) are mandatory in Swift, even if only one line of code is executed after the *if* expression.

Essentially if the *Boolean expression* evaluates to *true* then the code in the body of the statement is executed. The body of the statement is enclosed in braces ({}). If, on the other hand, the expression evaluates to *false* the code in the body of the statement is skipped.

For example, if a decision needs to be made depending on whether one value is greater than another, we would write code similar to the following:

```
let x = 10


if x > 9 {
      print("x is greater than 9!")
}
```

Clearly, x is indeed greater than 9 causing the message to appear in the console panel.

7.8 Using if ... else ... Statements

The next variation of the *if* statement allows us to also specify some code to perform if the expression in the *if* statement evaluates to *false*. The syntax for this construct is as follows:

```
if boolean expression {
    // Code to be executed if expression is true
} else {
    // Code to be executed if expression is false
}
```

Using the above syntax, we can now extend our previous example to display a different message if the comparison expression evaluates to be *false*:

```
let x = 10
```

```
if x > 9 {
        print("x is greater than 9!")
} else {
        print("x is less than 10!")
}
```

In this case, the second print statement would execute if the value of x was less than or equal to 9.

7.9 Using if ... else if ... Statements

So far we have looked at *if* statements which make decisions based on the result of a single logical expression. Sometimes it becomes necessary to make decisions based on a number of different criteria. For this purpose, we can use the *if ... else if ...* construct, an example of which is as follows:

```
let x = 9

if x == 10 {
        print("x is 10")
} else if x == 9 {
        print("x is 9")
} else if x == 8 {
        print("x is 8")
}
```

This approach works well for a moderate number of comparisons but can become cumbersome for a larger volume of expression evaluations. For such situations, the Swift *switch* statement provides a more flexible and efficient solution. For more details on using the *switch* statement refer to the next chapter entitled*"The Swift Switch Statement"*.

7.10 The guard Statement

The *guard* statement is a Swift language feature introduced as part of Swift 2. A guard statement contains a Boolean expression which must evaluate to true in order for the code located *after* the guard statement to be executed. The guard statement must include an *else* clause to be executed in the event that the expression evaluates to false. The code in the else clause must contain a statement to exit the current code flow (i.e. a *return*, *break*, *continue* or *throw* statement). Alternatively, the *else* block may call any other function or method that does not itself return.

The syntax for the guard statement is as follows:

```
guard <boolean expressions> else {
   // code to be executed if expression is false
   <exit statement here>
}

// code here is executed if expression is true
```

The guard statement essentially provides an "early exit" strategy from the current function or loop in the event that a specified requirement is not met.

The following code example implements a guard statement within a function:

```
func multiplyByTen(value: Int?) {
```

```
    guard let number = value, number < 10 else {
        print("Number is too high")
        return
    }

    let result = number * 10
    print(result)
}

multiplyByTen(value: 5)
multiplyByTen(value: 10)
```

The function takes as a parameter an integer value in the form of an optional. The guard statement uses optional binding to unwrap the value and verify that it is less than 10. In the event that the variable could not be unwrapped, or that its value is greater than 9, the else clause is triggered, the error message printed, and the return statement executed to exit the function.

If the optional contains a value less than 10, the code after the guard statement executes to multiply the value by 10 and print the result. A particularly important point to note about the above example is that the unwrapped *number* variable is available to the code outside of the guard statement. This would not have been the case had the variable been unwrapped using an *if* statement.

7.11 Summary

The term *control flow* is used to describe the logic that dictates the execution path that is taken through the source code of an application as it runs. This chapter has looked at the two types of control flow provided by Swift (looping and conditional) and explored the various Swift constructs that are available to implement both forms of control flow logic.

Chapter 8

8. The Swift Switch Statement

In *"Swift Control Flow"* we looked at how to control program execution flow using the *if* and *else* statements. While these statement constructs work well for testing a limited number of conditions, they quickly become unwieldy when dealing with larger numbers of possible conditions. To simplify such situations, Swift has inherited the *switch* statement from the C programming language. Those familiar with the switch statement from other programming languages should be aware, however, that the Swift switch statement has some key differences from other implementations. In this chapter we will explore the Swift implementation of the *switch* statement in detail.

8.1 Why Use a switch Statement?

For a small number of logical evaluations of a value the *if... else if...* construct is perfectly adequate. Unfortunately, any more than two or three possible scenarios can quickly make such a construct both time consuming to write and difficult to read. For such situations, the *switch* statement provides an excellent alternative.

8.2 Using the switch Statement Syntax

The syntax for a basic Swift *switch* statement implementation can be outlined as follows:

```
switch expression
{
     case match1:
          statements

     case match2:
          statements

     case match3, match4:
          statements

     default:
          statements
}
```

In the above syntax outline, *expression* represents either a value, or an expression which returns a value. This is the value against which the *switch* operates.

For each possible match a *case* statement is provided, followed by a *match* value. Each potential match must be of the same type as the governing expression. Following on from the *case* line are the Swift statements that are to be executed in the event of the value matching the case condition.

Finally, the *default* section of the construct defines what should happen if none of the case statements present a match to the *expression.*

8.3 A Swift switch Statement Example

With the above information in mind we may now construct a simple *switch* statement:

```
let value = 4

switch (value)
{
      case 0:
        print("zero")

      case 1:
        print("one")

      case 2:
        print("two")

      case 3:
        print("three")

      case 4:
        print("four")

      case 5:
        print("five")

      default:
        print("Integer out of range")
}
```

8.4 Combining case Statements

In the above example, each case had its own set of statements to execute. Sometimes a number of different matches may require the same code to be executed. In this case, it is possible to group case matches together with a common set of statements to be executed when a match for any of the cases is found. For example, we can modify the switch construct in our example so that the same code is executed regardless of whether the value is 0, 1 or 2:

```
let value = 1

switch (value)
{
      case 0, 1, 2:
        print("zero, one or two")

      case 3:
        print("three")

      case 4:
        print("four")

      case 5:
```

```
        print("five")

      default:
        print("Integer out of range")
}
```

8.5 Range Matching in a switch Statement

The case statements within a switch construct may also be used to implement range matching. The following switch statement, for example, checks a temperature value for matches within three number ranges:

```
let temperature = 83

switch (temperature)
{
      case 0...49:
        print("Cold")

      case 50...79:
        print("Warm")

      case 80...110:
        print("Hot")

      default:
        print("Temperature out of range")
}
```

8.6 Using the where statement

The *where* statement may be used within a switch case match to add additional criteria required for a positive match. The following switch statement, for example, checks not only for the range in which a value falls, but also whether the number is odd or even:

```
let temperature = 54

switch (temperature)
{
      case 0...49 where temperature % 2 == 0:
        print("Cold and even")

      case 50...79 where temperature % 2 == 0:
        print("Warm and even")

      case 80...110 where temperature % 2 == 0:
        print("Hot and even")

      default:
        print("Temperature out of range or odd")
}
```

8.7 Fallthrough

Those familiar with switch statements in other languages such as C and Objective-C will notice that it is no longer necessary to include a *break* statement after each case declaration. Unlike other languages, Swift automatically breaks out of the statement when a matching case condition is met. The fallthrough effect of other switch implementations (whereby the execution path continues through the remaining case statements) can be emulated using the *fallthrough* statement:

```
let temperature = 10

switch (temperature)
{
      case 0...49 where temperature % 2 == 0:
        print("Cold and even")
        fallthrough

      case 50...79 where temperature % 2 == 0:
        print("Warm and even")
        fallthrough

      case 80...110 where temperature % 2 == 0:
        print("Hot and even")
        fallthrough

      default:
        print("Temperature out of range or odd")
}
```

Although *break* is less commonly used in Swift switch statements, it is useful when no action needs to be taken for the default case. For example:

```
.
.
.
default:
     break
}
```

8.8 Summary

While the *if.. else..* construct serves as a good decision-making option for small numbers of possible outcomes, this approach can become unwieldy in more complex situations. As an alternative method for implementing flow control logic in Swift when many possible outcomes exist as the result of an evaluation, the *switch* statement invariably makes a more suitable option. As outlined in this chapter, however, developers familiar with switch implementations from other programming languages should be aware of some subtle differences in the way that the Swift switch statement works.

Chapter 9

9. Swift Functions, Methods and Closures

Swift functions, methods and closures are a vital part of writing well-structured and efficient code and provide a way to organize programs while avoiding code repetition. In this chapter we will look at how functions, methods and closures are declared and used within Swift.

9.1 What is a Function?

A function is a named block of code that can be called upon to perform a specific task. It can be provided data on which to perform the task and is capable of returning results to the code that called it. For example, if a particular arithmetic calculation needs to be performed in a Swift program, the code to perform the arithmetic can be placed in a function. The function can be programmed to accept the values on which the arithmetic is to be performed (referred to as *parameters*) and to return the result of the calculation. At any point in the program code where the calculation is required the function is simply called, parameter values passed through as *arguments* and the result returned.

The terms *parameter* and *argument* are often used interchangeably when discussing functions. There is, however, a subtle difference. The values that a function is able to accept when it is called are referred to as *parameters*. At the point that the function is actually called and passed those values, however, they are referred to as *arguments*.

9.2 What is a Method?

A method is essentially a function that is associated with a particular class, structure or enumeration. If, for example, you declare a function within a Swift class (a topic covered in detail in the chapter entitled *"The Basics of Swift Object-Oriented Programming"*), it is considered to be a method. Although the remainder of this chapter refers to functions, the same rules and behavior apply equally to methods unless otherwise stated.

9.3 How to Declare a Swift Function

A Swift function is declared using the following syntax:

```
func <function name> (<para name>: <para type>,
                      <para name>: <para type>, ... ) -> <return type> {
    // Function code
}
```

This combination of function name, parameters and return type are referred to as the *function signature*. Explanations of the various fields of the function declaration are as follows:

- **func** – The prefix keyword used to notify the Swift compiler that this is a function.
- **<function name>** - The name assigned to the function. This is the name by which the function will be referenced when it is called from within the application code.
- **<para name>** - The name by which the parameter is to be referenced in the function code.
- **<para type>** - The type of the corresponding parameter.

- **<return type>** - The data type of the result returned by the function. If the function does not return a result then no return type is specified.

- **Function code** - The code of the function that does the work.

As an example, the following function takes no parameters, returns no result and simply displays a message:

```
func sayHello() {
    print("Hello")
}
```

The following sample function, on the other hand, takes an integer and a string as parameters and returns a string result:

```
func buildMessageFor(name: String, count: Int) -> String {
        return("\(name), you are customer number \(count)")
}
```

9.4 Implicit Returns from Single Expressions

In the previous example, the *return* statement was used to return the string value from within the *buildMessageFor()* function. It is worth noting that if a function contains a single expression (as was the case in this example), the return statement may be omitted. The *buildMessageFor()* method could, therefore, be rewritten as follows:

```
func buildMessageFor(name: String, count: Int) -> String {
        "\(name), you are customer number \(count)"
}
```

The return statement can only be omitted if the function contains a single expression. The following code, for example, will fail to compile since the function contains two expressions requiring the use of the return statement:

```
func buildMessageFor(name: String, count: Int) -> String {
        let uppername = name.uppercased()
        "\(uppername), you are customer number \(count)" // Invalid expression
}
```

9.5 Calling a Swift Function

Once declared, functions are called using the following syntax:

```
<function name> (<arg1>, <arg2>, ... )
```

Each argument passed through to a function must match the parameters the function is configured to accept. For example, to call a function named *sayHello* that takes no parameters and returns no value, we would write the following code:

```
sayHello()
```

9.6 Handling Return Values

To call a function named *buildMessageFor* that takes two parameters and returns a result, on the other hand, we might write the following code:

```
let message = buildMessageFor(name: "John", count: 100)
```

In the above example, we have created a new variable called *message* and then used the assignment operator (=) to store the result returned by the function.

When developing in Swift, situations may arise where the result returned by a method or function call is not used. When this is the case, the return value may be discarded by assigning it to '_'. For example:

```
_ = buildMessageFor(name: "John", count: 100)
```

9.7 Local and External Parameter Names

When the preceding example functions were declared, they were configured with parameters that were assigned names which, in turn, could be referenced within the body of the function code. When declared in this way, these names are referred to as *local parameter names*.

In addition to local names, function parameters may also have *external parameter names*. These are the names by which the parameter is referenced when the function is called. By default, function parameters are assigned the same local and external parameter names. Consider, for example, the previous call to the *buildMessageFor* method:

```
let message = buildMessageFor(name: "John", count: 100)
```

As declared, the function uses "name" and "count" as both the local and external parameter names.

The default external parameter names assigned to parameters may be removed by preceding the local parameter names with an underscore (_) character as follows:

```
func buildMessageFor(_ name: String, _ count: Int) -> String {
        return("\(name), you are customer number \(count)")
}
```

With this change implemented, the function may now be called as follows:

```
let message = buildMessageFor("John", 100)
```

Alternatively, external parameter names can be added simply by declaring the external parameter name before the local parameter name within the function declaration. In the following code, for example, the external names of the first and second parameters have been set to "username" and "usercount" respectively:

```
func buildMessageFor(username name: String, usercount count: Int)
                                                    -> String {
        return("\(name), you are customer number \(count)")
}
```

When declared in this way, the external parameter name must be referenced when calling the function:

```
let message = buildMessageFor(username: "John", usercount: 100)
```

Regardless of the fact that the external names are used to pass the arguments through when calling the function, the local names are still used to reference the parameters within the body of the function. It is important to also note that when calling a function using external parameter names for the arguments, those arguments must still be placed in the same order as that used when the function was declared.

9.8 Declaring Default Function Parameters

Swift provides the ability to designate a default parameter value to be used in the event that the value is not provided as an argument when the function is called. This simply involves assigning the default value to the parameter when the function is declared. Swift also provides a default external name based on the local parameter name for defaulted parameters (unless one is already provided) which must then be used when calling the function.

To see default parameters in action the *buildMessageFor* function will be modified so that the string "Customer" is used as a default in the event that a customer name is not passed through as an argument:

```
func buildMessageFor(_ name: String = "Customer", count: Int ) -> String
```

```
{
    return ("\(name), you are customer number \(count)")
}
```

The function can now be called without passing through a name argument:

```
let message = buildMessageFor(count: 100)
print(message)
```

When executed, the above function call will generate output to the console panel which reads:

```
Customer, you are customer 100
```

9.9 Returning Multiple Results from a Function

A function can return multiple result values by wrapping those results in a tuple. The following function takes as a parameter a measurement value in inches. The function converts this value into yards, centimeters and meters, returning all three results within a single tuple instance:

```
func sizeConverter(_ length: Float) -> (yards: Float, centimeters: Float,
                                          meters: Float) {

    let yards = length * 0.0277778
    let centimeters = length * 2.54
    let meters = length * 0.0254

    return (yards, centimeters, meters)
}
```

The return type for the function indicates that the function returns a tuple containing three values named yards, centimeters and meters respectively, all of which are of type Float:

```
-> (yards: Float, centimeters: Float, meters: Float)
```

Having performed the conversion, the function simply constructs the tuple instance and returns it.

Usage of this function might read as follows:

```
let lengthTuple = sizeConverter(20)

print(lengthTuple.yards)
print(lengthTuple.centimeters)
print(lengthTuple.meters)
```

9.10 Variable Numbers of Function Parameters

It is not always possible to know in advance the number of parameters a function will need to accept when it is called within application code. Swift handles this possibility through the use of *variadic parameters*. Variadic parameters are declared using three periods (…) to indicate that the function accepts zero or more parameters of a specified data type. Within the body of the function, the parameters are made available in the form of an array object. The following function, for example, takes as parameters a variable number of String values and then outputs them to the console panel:

```
func displayStrings(_ strings: String...)
{
    for string in strings {
        print(string)
```

```
    }
}

displayStrings("one", "two", "three", "four")
```

9.11 Parameters as Variables

All parameters accepted by a function are treated as constants by default. This prevents changes being made to those parameter values within the function code. If changes to parameters need to be made within the function body, therefore, *shadow copies* of those parameters must be created. The following function, for example, is passed length and width parameters in inches, creates shadow variables of the two values and converts those parameters to centimeters before calculating and returning the area value:

```
func calcuateArea(length: Float, width: Float) -> Float {

    var length = length
    var width = width

    length = length * 2.54
    width = width * 2.54
    return length * width
}

print(calcuateArea(length: 10, width: 20))
```

9.12 Working with In-Out Parameters

When a variable is passed through as a parameter to a function, we now know that the parameter is treated as a constant within the body of that function. We also know that if we want to make changes to a parameter value we have to create a shadow copy as outlined in the above section. Since this is a copy, any changes made to the variable are not, by default, reflected in the original variable. Consider, for example, the following code:

```
var myValue = 10

func doubleValue (_ value: Int) -> Int {
    var value = value
    value += value
    return(value)
}

print("Before function call myValue = \(myValue)")

print("doubleValue call returns \(doubleValue(myValue))")

print("After function call myValue = \(myValue)")
```

The code begins by declaring a variable named *myValue* initialized with a value of 10. A new function is then declared which accepts a single integer parameter. Within the body of the function, a shadow copy of the value is created, doubled and returned.

The remaining lines of code display the value of the *myValue* variable before and after the function call is made. When executed, the following output will appear in the console:

```
Before function call myValue = 10
doubleValue call returns 20
After function call myValue = 10
```

Clearly, the function has made no change to the original myValue variable. This is to be expected since the mathematical operation was performed on a copy of the variable, not the *myValue* variable itself.

In order to make any changes made to a parameter persist after the function has returned, the parameter must be declared as an *in-out parameter* within the function declaration. To see this in action, modify the *doubleValue* function to include the *inout* keyword, and remove the creation of the shadow copy as follows:

```
func doubleValue (_ value: inout Int) -> Int {
    var value = value
    value += value
    return(value)
}
```

Finally, when calling the function, the inout parameter must now be prefixed with an & modifier:

```
print("doubleValue call returned \(doubleValue(&myValue))")
```

Having made these changes, a test run of the code should now generate output clearly indicating that the function modified the value assigned to the original *myValue* variable:

```
Before function call myValue = 10
doubleValue call returns 20
After function call myValue = 20
```

9.13 Functions as Parameters

An interesting feature of functions within Swift is that they can be treated as data types. It is perfectly valid, for example, to assign a function to a constant or variable as illustrated in the declaration below:

```
func inchesToFeet (_ inches: Float) -> Float {
    return inches * 0.0833333
}

let toFeet = inchesToFeet
```

The above code declares a new function named *inchesToFeet* and subsequently assigns that function to a constant named *toFeet*. Having made this assignment, a call to the function may be made using the constant name instead of the original function name:

```
let result = toFeet(10)
```

On the surface this does not seem to be a particularly compelling feature. Since we could already call the function without assigning it to a constant or variable data type it does not seem that much has been gained.

The possibilities that this feature offers become more apparent when we consider that a function assigned to a constant or variable now has the capabilities of many other data types. In particular, a function can now be passed through as an argument to another function, or even returned as a result from a function.

Before we look at what is, essentially, the ability to plug one function into another, it is first necessary to explore the concept of function data types. The data type of a function is dictated by a combination of the parameters it accepts and the type of result it returns. In the above example, since the function accepts a floating-point parameter and returns a floating-point result, the function's data type conforms to the following:

```
(Float) -> Float
```

A function which accepts an Int and a Double as parameters and returns a String result, on the other hand, would have the following data type:

```
(Int, Double) -> String
```

In order to accept a function as a parameter, the receiving function simply declares the data type of the function it is able to accept.

For the purposes of an example, we will begin by declaring two unit conversion functions and assigning them to constants:

```
func inchesToFeet (_ inches: Float) -> Float {

    return inches * 0.0833333
}

func inchesToYards (_ inches: Float) -> Float {

    return inches * 0.0277778
}

let toFeet = inchesToFeet
let toYards = inchesToYards
```

The example now needs an additional function, the purpose of which is to perform a unit conversion and print the result in the console panel. This function needs to be as general purpose as possible, capable of performing a variety of different measurement unit conversions. In order to demonstrate functions as parameters, this new function will take as a parameter a function type that matches both the inchesToFeet and inchesToYards function data type together with a value to be converted. Since the data type of these functions is equivalent to (Float) -> Float, our general-purpose function can be written as follows:

```
func outputConversion(_ converterFunc: (Float) -> Float, value: Float) {

    let result = converterFunc(value)

    print("Result of conversion is \(result)")
}
```

When the outputConversion function is called, it will need to be passed a function matching the declared data type. That function will be called to perform the conversion and the result displayed in the console panel. This means that the same function can be called to convert inches to both feet and yards, simply by "plugging in" the appropriate converter function as a parameter. For example:

```
outputConversion(toYards, value: 10) // Convert to Yards
outputConversion(toFeet, value: 10) // Convert to Inches
```

Functions can also be returned as a data type simply by declaring the type of the function as the return type. The following function is configured to return either our toFeet or toYards function type (in other words a function which accepts and returns a Float value) based on the value of a Boolean parameter:

```
func decideFunction(_ feet: Bool) -> (Float) -> Float
{
    if feet {
        return toFeet
```

```
    } else {
        return toYards
    }
}
```

9.14 Closure Expressions

Having covered the basics of functions in Swift it is now time to look at the concept of *closures* and *closure expressions*. Although these terms are often used interchangeably there are some key differences.

Closure expressions are self-contained blocks of code. The following code, for example, declares a closure expression and assigns it to a constant named sayHello and then calls the function via the constant reference:

```
let sayHello = { print("Hello") }
sayHello()
```

Closure expressions may also be configured to accept parameters and return results. The syntax for this is as follows:

```
{(<para name>: <para type>, <para name> <para type>, ... ) ->
                                                <return type> in
        // Closure expression code here
}
```

The following closure expression, for example, accepts two integer parameters and returns an integer result:

```
let multiply = {(_ val1: Int, _ val2: Int) -> Int in
    return val1 * val2
}
let result = multiply(10, 20)
```

Note that the syntax is similar to that used for declaring Swift functions with the exception that the closure expression does not have a name, the parameters and return type are included in the braces and the *in* keyword is used to indicate the start of the closure expression code. Functions are, in fact, just named closure expressions.

Before the introduction of structured concurrency in Swift 5.5 (a topic covered in detail in the chapter entitled *"An Overview of Swift Structured Concurrency"*), closure expressions were often (and still are) used when declaring completion handlers for asynchronous method calls. In other words, when developing iOS applications, it will often be necessary to make calls to the operating system where the requested task is performed in the background allowing the application to continue with other tasks. Typically, in such a scenario, the system will notify the application of the completion of the task and return any results by calling the completion handler that was declared when the method was called. Frequently the code for the completion handler will be implemented in the form of a closure expression. Consider the following code example:

```
eventstore.requestAccess(to: .reminder, completion: {(granted: Bool,
                          error: Error?) -> Void in
    if !granted {
            print(error!.localizedDescription)
    }
})
```

When the tasks performed by the *requestAccess(to:)* method call are complete it will execute the closure expression declared as the *completion:* parameter. The completion handler is required by the method to accept a Boolean value and an Error object as parameters and return no results, hence the following declaration:

```
{(granted: Bool, error: Error?) -> Void in
```

In actual fact, the Swift compiler already knows about the parameter and return value requirements for the completion handler for this method call and is able to infer this information without it being declared in the closure expression. This allows a simpler version of the closure expression declaration to be written:

```
eventstore.requestAccess(to: .reminder, completion: {(granted, error) in
    if !granted {
            print(error!.localizedDescription)
    }
})
```

9.15 Shorthand Argument Names

A useful technique for simplifying closures involves using *shorthand argument names*. This allows the parameter names and "in" keyword to be omitted from the declaration and the arguments to be referenced as $0, $1, $2 etc.

Consider, for example, a closure expression designed to concatenate two strings:

```
let join = { (string1: String, string2: String) -> String in
    string1 + string2
}
```

Using shorthand argument names, this declaration can be simplified as follows:

```
let join: (String, String) -> String = {
    $0 + $1
}
```

Note that the type declaration (*(String, String) -> String*) has been moved to the left of the assignment operator since the closure expression no longer defines the argument or return types.

9.16 Closures in Swift

A *closure* in computer science terminology generally refers to the combination of a self-contained block of code (for example a function or closure expression) and one or more variables that exist in the context surrounding that code block. Consider, for example the following Swift function:

```
func functionA() -> () -> Int {

    var counter = 0

    func functionB() -> Int {
        return counter + 10
    }
    return functionB
}

let myClosure = functionA()
let result = myClosure()
```

In the above code, *functionA* returns a function named *functionB*. In actual fact functionA is returning a closure since functionB relies on the *counter* variable which is declared outside the functionB's local scope. In other words, functionB is said to have *captured* or *closed over* (hence the term closure) the counter variable and, as such, is considered a closure in the traditional computer science definition of the word.

To a large extent, and particularly as it relates to Swift, the terms *closure* and *closure expression* have started to be used interchangeably. The key point to remember, however, is that both are supported in Swift.

9.17 Summary

Functions, closures and closure expressions are self-contained blocks of code that can be called upon to perform a specific task and provide a mechanism for structuring code and promoting reuse. This chapter has introduced the concepts of functions and closures in terms of declaration and implementation.

Chapter 10

10. The Basics of Swift Object-Oriented Programming

Swift provides extensive support for developing object-oriented applications. The subject area of object-oriented programming is, however, large. It is not an exaggeration to state that entire books have been dedicated to the subject. As such, a detailed overview of object-oriented software development is beyond the scope of this book. Instead, we will introduce the basic concepts involved in object-oriented programming and then move on to explaining the concept as it relates to Swift application development. Once again, while we strive to provide the basic information you need in this chapter, we recommend reading a copy of Apple's *The Swift Programming Language* book for more extensive coverage of this subject area.

10.1 What is an Instance?

Objects (also referred to as class *instances*) are self-contained modules of functionality that can be easily used and re-used as the building blocks for a software application.

Instances consist of data variables (called *properties*) and functions (called *methods*) that can be accessed and called on the instance to perform tasks and are collectively referred to as *class members*.

10.2 What is a Class?

Much as a blueprint or architect's drawing defines what an item or a building will look like once it has been constructed, a class defines what an instance will look like when it is created. It defines, for example, what the methods will do and what the properties will be.

10.3 Declaring a Swift Class

Before an instance can be created, we first need to define the class 'blueprint' for the instance. In this chapter we will create a bank account class to demonstrate the basic concepts of Swift object-oriented programming.

In declaring a new Swift class we specify an optional *parent class* from which the new class is derived and also define the properties and methods that the class will contain. The basic syntax for a new class is as follows:

```
class NewClassName: ParentClass {
   // Properties
   // Instance Methods
   // Type methods
}
```

The *Properties* section of the declaration defines the variables and constants that are to be contained within the class. These are declared in the same way that any other variable or constant would be declared in Swift.

The *Instance methods* and *Type methods* sections define the methods that are available to be called on the class and instances of the class. These are essentially functions specific to the class that perform a particular operation when called upon and will be described in greater detail later in this chapter.

To create an example outline for our BankAccount class, we would use the following:

```
class BankAccount {
```

```
}
```

Now that we have the outline syntax for our class, the next step is to add some instance properties to it.

When naming classes, note that the convention is for the first character of each word to be declared in uppercase (a concept referred to as UpperCamelCase). This contrasts with property and function names where lower case is used for the first character (referred to as lowerCamelCase).

10.4 Adding Instance Properties to a Class

A key goal of object-oriented programming is a concept referred to as *data encapsulation*. The idea behind data encapsulation is that data should be stored within classes and accessed only through methods defined in that class. Data encapsulated in a class are referred to as *properties* or *instance variables.*

Instances of our BankAccount class will be required to store some data, specifically a bank account number and the balance currently held within the account. Properties are declared in the same way any other variables and constants are declared in Swift. We can, therefore, add these variables as follows:

```
class BankAccount {
    var accountBalance: Float = 0
    var accountNumber: Int = 0
}
```

Having defined our properties, we can now move on to defining the methods of the class that will allow us to work with our properties while staying true to the data encapsulation model.

10.5 Defining Methods

The methods of a class are essentially code routines that can be called upon to perform specific tasks within the context of that class.

Methods come in two different forms, *type methods* and *instance methods*. Type methods operate at the level of the class, such as creating a new instance of a class. Instance methods, on the other hand, operate only on the instances of a class (for example performing an arithmetic operation on two property variables and returning the result).

Instance methods are declared within the opening and closing braces of the class to which they belong and are declared using the standard Swift function declaration syntax.

Type methods are declared in the same way as instance methods with the exception that the declaration is preceded by the *class* keyword.

For example, the declaration of a method to display the account balance in our example might read as follows:

```
class BankAccount {

    var accountBalance: Float = 0
    var accountNumber: Int = 0

    func displayBalance()
    {
       print("Number \(accountNumber)")
       print("Current balance is \(accountBalance)")
    }
```

```
}
```

The method is an *instance method* so it is not preceded by the *class* keyword.

When designing the BankAccount class it might be useful to be able to call a type method on the class itself to identify the maximum allowable balance that can be stored by the class. This would enable an application to identify whether the BankAccount class is suitable for storing details of a new customer without having to go through the process of first creating a class instance. This method will be named *getMaxBalance* and is implemented as follows:

```
class BankAccount {

    var accountBalance: Float = 0
    var accountNumber: Int = 0

    func displayBalance()
    {
       print("Number \(accountNumber)")
       print("Current balance is \(accountBalance)")
    }

    class func getMaxBalance() -> Float {
        return 100000.00
    }
}
```

10.6 Declaring and Initializing a Class Instance

So far all we have done is define the blueprint for our class. In order to do anything with this class, we need to create instances of it. The first step in this process is to declare a variable to store a reference to the instance when it is created. We do this as follows:

```
var account1: BankAccount = BankAccount()
```

When executed, an instance of our BankAccount class will have been created and will be accessible via the *account1* variable.

10.7 Initializing and De-initializing a Class Instance

A class will often need to perform some initialization tasks at the point of creation. These tasks can be implemented by placing an *init* method within the class. In the case of the BankAccount class, it would be useful to be able to initialize the account number and balance properties with values when a new class instance is created. To achieve this, the *init* method could be written in the class as follows:

```
class BankAccount {

    var accountBalance: Float = 0
    var accountNumber: Int = 0

    init(number: Int, balance: Float)
    {
        accountNumber = number
        accountBalance = balance
```

```
    }

    func displayBalance()
    {
       print("Number \(accountNumber)")
       print("Current balance is \(accountBalance)")
    }
}
```

When creating an instance of the class, it will now be necessary to provide initialization values for the account number and balance properties as follows:

```
var account1 = BankAccount(number: 12312312, balance: 400.54)
```

Conversely, any cleanup tasks that need to be performed before a class instance is destroyed by the Swift runtime system can be performed by implementing the de-initializer within the class definition:

```
class BankAccount {

    var accountBalance: Float = 0
    var accountNumber: Int = 0

    init(number: Int, balance: Float)
    {
        accountNumber = number
        accountBalance = balance
    }

    deinit {
        // Perform any necessary clean up here
    }

    func displayBalance()
    {
       print("Number \(accountNumber)")
       print("Current balance is \(accountBalance)")
    }
}
```

10.8 Calling Methods and Accessing Properties

Now is probably a good time to recap what we have done so far in this chapter. We have now created a new Swift class named *BankAccount*. Within this new class we declared some properties to contain the bank account number and current balance together with an initializer and a method to display the current balance information. In the preceding section we covered the steps necessary to create and initialize an instance of our new class. The next step is to learn how to call the instance methods and access the properties we built into our class. This is most easily achieved using *dot notation*.

Dot notation involves accessing an instance variable, or calling an instance method by specifying a class instance followed by a dot followed in turn by the name of the property or method:

```
classInstance.propertyName
```

```
classInstance.instanceMethod()
```

For example, to get the current value of our *accountBalance* instance variable:

```
var balance1 = account1.accountBalance
```

Dot notation can also be used to set values of instance properties:

```
account1.accountBalance = 6789.98
```

The same technique is used to call methods on a class instance. For example, to call the *displayBalance* method on an instance of the BankAccount class:

```
account1.displayBalance()
```

Type methods are also called using dot notation, though they must be called on the class type instead of a class instance:

```
ClassName.typeMethod()
```

For example, to call the previously declared *getMaxBalance* type method, the BankAccount class is referenced:

```
var maxAllowed = BankAccount.getMaxBalance()
```

10.9 Stored and Computed Properties

Class properties in Swift fall into two categories referred to as *stored properties* and *computed properties.* Stored properties are those values that are contained within a constant or variable. Both the account name and number properties in the BankAccount example are stored properties.

A computed property, on the other hand, is a value that is derived based on some form of calculation or logic at the point at which the property is set or retrieved. Computed properties are implemented by creating *getter* and optional corresponding *setter* methods containing the code to perform the computation. Consider, for example, that the BankAccount class might need an additional property to contain the current balance less any recent banking fees. Rather than use a stored property, it makes more sense to use a computed property which calculates this value on request. The modified BankAccount class might now read as follows:

```
class BankAccount {

    var accountBalance: Float = 0
    var accountNumber: Int = 0;
    let fees: Float = 25.00

    var balanceLessFees: Float {
        get {
            return accountBalance - fees
        }
    }

    init(number: Int, balance: Float)
    {
        accountNumber = number
        accountBalance = balance
    }
.
.
```

```
.
}
```

The above code adds a getter that returns a computed property based on the current balance minus a fee amount. An optional setter could also be declared in much the same way to set the balance value less fees:

```
var balanceLessFees: Float {
    get {
        return accountBalance - fees
    }

    set(newBalance)
    {
        accountBalance = newBalance - fees
    }
}
```

The new setter takes as a parameter a floating-point value from which it deducts the fee value before assigning the result to the current balance property. Although these are computed properties, they are accessed in the same way as stored properties using dot-notation. The following code gets the current balance less the fees value before setting the property to a new value:

```
var balance1 = account1.balanceLessFees
account1.balanceLessFees = 12123.12
```

10.10 Lazy Stored Properties

There are several different ways in which a property can be initialized, the most basic being direct assignment as follows:

```
var myProperty = 10
```

Alternatively, a property may be assigned a value within the initializer:

```
class MyClass {
  let title: String

  init(title: String) {
    self.title = title
  }
}
```

For more complex requirements, a property may be initialized using a closure:

```
class MyClass {

    var myProperty: String = {
        var result = resourceIntensiveTask()
        result = processData(data: result)
        return result
    }()
.
.
}
```

Particularly in the case of a complex closure, there is the potential for the initialization to be resource intensive and time consuming. When declared in this way, the initialization will be performed every time an instance of the class is created, regardless of when (or even if) the property is actually used within the code of the app. Also, situations may arise where the value assigned to the property may not be known until a later stage in the execution process, for example after data has been retrieved from a database or user input has been obtained from the user. A far more efficient solution in such situations would be for the initialization to take place only when the property is first accessed. Fortunately, this can be achieved by declaring the property as *lazy* as follows:

```
class MyClass {

    lazy var myProperty: String = {
        var result = resourceIntensiveTask()
        result = processData(data: result)
        return result
    }()
.
.
}
```

When a property is declared as being lazy, it is only initialized when it is first accessed, allowing any resource intensive activities to be deferred until the property is needed and any initialization on which the property is dependent to be completed.

Note that lazy properties must be declared as variables (*var*).

10.11 Using self in Swift

Programmers familiar with other object-oriented programming languages may be in the habit of prefixing references to properties and methods with *self* to indicate that the method or property belongs to the current class instance. The Swift programming language also provides the *self* property type for this purpose and it is, therefore, perfectly valid to write code which reads as follows:

```
class MyClass {
    var myNumber = 1

    func addTen() {
        self.myNumber += 10
    }
}
```

In this context, the *self* prefix indicates to the compiler that the code is referring to a property named *myNumber* which belongs to the MyClass class instance. When programming in Swift, however, it is no longer necessary to use self in most situations since this is now assumed to be the default for references to properties and methods. To quote The Swift Programming Language guide published by Apple, "in practice you don't need to write *self* in your code very often". The function from the above example, therefore, can also be written as follows with the *self* reference omitted:

```
func addTen() {
    myNumber += 10
}
```

In most cases, use of self is optional in Swift. That being said, one situation where it is still necessary to use *self* is when referencing a property or method from within a closure expression. The use of self, for example, is mandatory in the following closure expression:

```
document?.openWithCompletionHandler({(success: Bool) -> Void in
    if success {
        self.ubiquityURL = resultURL
    }
})
```

It is also necessary to use self to resolve ambiguity such as when a function parameter has the same name as a class property. In the following code, for example, the first print statement will output the value passed through to the function via the myNumber parameter while the second print statement outputs the number assigned to the myNumber class property (in this case 10):

```
class MyClass {

    var myNumber = 10 // class property

    func addTen(myNumber: Int) {
        print(myNumber) // Output the function parameter value
        print(self.myNumber) // Output the class property value
    }
}
```

Whether or not to use self in most other situations is largely a matter of programmer preference. Those who prefer to use self when referencing properties and methods can continue to do so in Swift. Code that is written without use of the *self* property type (where doing so is not mandatory) is, however, just as valid when programming in Swift.

10.12 Understanding Swift Protocols

By default, there are no specific rules to which a Swift class must conform as long as the class is syntactically correct. In some situations, however, a class will need to meet certain criteria in order to work with other classes. This is particularly common when writing classes that need to work with the various frameworks that comprise the iOS SDK. A set of rules that define the minimum requirements which a class must meet is referred to as a *Protocol*. A protocol is declared using the *protocol* keyword and simply defines the methods and properties that a class must contain in order to be in conformance. When a class *adopts* a protocol, but does not meet all of the protocol requirements, errors will be reported stating that the class fails to conform to the protocol.

Consider the following protocol declaration. Any classes that adopt this protocol must include both a readable String value called *name* and a method named *buildMessage()* which accepts no parameters and returns a String value:

```
protocol MessageBuilder {

    var name: String { get }
    func buildMessage() -> String
}
```

Below, a class has been declared which adopts the MessageBuilder protocol:

```
class MyClass: MessageBuilder {

}
```

Unfortunately, as currently implemented, MyClass will generate a compilation error because it contains neither the *name* variable nor the *buildMessage()* method as required by the protocol it has adopted. To conform to the protocol, the class would need to meet both requirements, for example:

```
class MyClass: MessageBuilder {

    var name: String

    init(name: String) {
      self.name = name
    }

    func buildMessage() -> String {
        "Hello " + name
    }
}
```

10.13 Opaque Return Types

Now that protocols have been explained it is a good time to introduce the concept of opaque return types. As we have seen in previous chapters, if a function returns a result, the type of that result must be included in the function declaration. The following function, for example, is configured to return an Int result:

```
func doubleFunc1 (value: Int) -> Int {
    return value * 2
}
```

Instead of specifying a specific return type (also referred to as a *concrete type*), opaque return types allow a function to return any type as long as it conforms to a specified protocol. Opaque return types are declared by preceding the protocol name with the *some* keyword. The following changes to the *doubleFunc1()* function, for example, declare that a result will be returned of any type that conforms to the Equatable protocol:

```
func doubleFunc1(value: Int) -> some Equatable {
    value * 2
}
```

To conform to the Equatable protocol, which is a standard protocol provided with Swift, a type must allow the underlying values to be compared for equality. Opaque return types can, however, be used for any protocol, including those you create yourself.

Given that both the Int and String concrete types are in conformance with the Equatable protocol, it is possible to also create a function that returns a String result:

```
func doubleFunc2(value: String) -> some Equatable {
    value + value
}
```

Although these two methods return entirely different concrete types, the only thing known about these types is that they conform to the Equatable protocol. We therefore know the capabilities of the type, but not the actual type.

In fact, we only know the concrete type returned in these examples because we have access to the source code of the functions. If these functions resided in a library or API framework for which the source is not available to us, we would not know the exact type being returned. This is intentional and designed to hide the underlying return type used within public APIs. By masking the concrete return type, programmers will not come to rely on a function returning a specific concrete type or risk accessing internal objects which were not intended to be accessed. This also has the benefit that the developer of the API can make changes to the underlying implementation (including returning a different protocol compliant type) without having to worry about breaking dependencies in any code that uses the API.

This raises the question of what happens when an incorrect assumption is made when working with the opaque return type. Consider, for example, that the assumption could be made that the results from the *doubleFunc1()* and *doubleFunc2()* functions can be compared for equality:

```
let intOne = doubleFunc1(value: 10)
let stringOne = doubleFunc2(value: "Hello")


if (intOne == stringOne) {
    print("They match")
}
```

Working on the premise that we do not have access to the source code for these two functions there is no way to know whether the above code is valid. Fortunately, although we, as programmers, have no way of knowing the concrete type returned by the functions, the Swift compiler has access to this hidden information. The above code will, therefore, generate the following syntax error long before we get to the point of trying to execute invalid code:

```
Binary operator '==' cannot be applied to operands of type 'some
 Equatable' (result of 'doubleFunc1(value:)') and 'some Equatable'
(result of 'doubleFunc2(value:)')
```

Opaque return types are a fundamental foundation of the implementation of the SwiftUI APIs and are used widely when developing apps in SwiftUI (the *some* keyword will appear frequently in SwiftUI View declarations). SwiftUI advocates the creation of apps by composing together small, reusable building blocks and refactoring large view declarations into collections of small, lightweight subviews. Each of these building blocks will typically conform to the View protocol. By declaring these building blocks as returning opaque types that conform to the View protocol, these building blocks become remarkably flexible and interchangeable, resulting in code that is cleaner and easier to reuse and maintain.

10.14 Summary

Object-oriented programming languages such as Swift encourage the creation of classes to promote code reuse and the encapsulation of data within class instances. This chapter has covered the basic concepts of classes and instances within Swift together with an overview of stored and computed properties and both instance and type methods. The chapter also introduced the concept of protocols which serve as templates to which classes must conform and explained how they form the basis of opaque return types.

Chapter 11

11. An Introduction to Swift Subclassing and Extensions

In *"The Basics of Swift Object-Oriented Programming"* we covered the basic concepts of object-oriented programming and worked through an example of creating and working with a new class using Swift. In that example, our new class was not derived from any base class and, as such, did not inherit any traits from a parent or super class. In this chapter we will introduce the concepts of subclassing, inheritance and extensions in Swift.

11.1 Inheritance, Classes and Subclasses

The concept of inheritance brings something of a real-world view to programming. It allows a class to be defined that has a certain set of characteristics (such as methods and properties) and then other classes to be created which are derived from that class. The derived class inherits all of the features of the parent class and typically then adds some features of its own.

By deriving classes we create what is often referred to as a *class hierarchy*. The class at the top of the hierarchy is known as the *base class* or *root class* and the derived classes as *subclasses* or *child classes*. Any number of subclasses may be derived from a class. The class from which a subclass is derived is called the *parent class* or *super class*.

Classes need not only be derived from a root class. For example, a subclass can also inherit from another subclass with the potential to create large and complex class hierarchies.

In Swift a subclass can only be derived from a single direct parent class. This is a concept referred to as *single inheritance*.

11.2 A Swift Inheritance Example

As with most programming concepts, the subject of inheritance in Swift is perhaps best illustrated with an example in *"The Basics of Swift Object-Oriented Programming"* we created a class named *BankAccount* designed to hold a bank account number and corresponding current balance. The BankAccount class contained both properties and instance methods. A simplified declaration for this class is reproduced below:

```
class BankAccount {

    var accountBalance: Float
    var accountNumber: Int

    init(number: Int, balance: Float)
    {
        accountNumber = number
        accountBalance = balance
    }

    func displayBalance()
    {
       print("Number \(accountNumber)")
```

```
        print("Current balance is \(accountBalance)")
    }
}
```

Though this is a somewhat rudimentary class, it does everything necessary if all you need it to do is store an account number and account balance. Suppose, however, that in addition to the BankAccount class you also needed a class to be used for savings accounts. A savings account will still need to hold an account number and a current balance and methods will still be needed to access that data. One option would be to create an entirely new class, one that duplicates all of the functionality of the BankAccount class together with the new features required by a savings account. A more efficient approach, however, would be to create a new class that is a *subclass* of the BankAccount class. The new class will then inherit all the features of the BankAccount class but can then be extended to add the additional functionality required by a savings account.

To create a subclass of BankAccount that we will call SavingsAccount, we simply declare the new class, this time specifying BankAccount as the parent class:

```
class SavingsAccount: BankAccount {


}
```

Note that although we have yet to add any instance variables or methods, the class has actually inherited all the methods and properties of the parent BankAccount class. We could, therefore, create an instance of the SavingsAccount class and set variables and call methods in exactly the same way we did with the BankAccount class in previous examples. That said, we haven't really achieved anything unless we take steps to extend the class.

11.3 Extending the Functionality of a Subclass

So far we have been able to create a subclass that contains all the functionality of the parent class. For this exercise to make sense, however, we now need to extend the subclass so that it has the features we need to make it useful for storing savings account information. To do this, we simply add the properties and methods that provide the new functionality, just as we would for any other class we might wish to create:

```
class SavingsAccount: BankAccount {

    var interestRate: Float = 0.0

    func calculateInterest() -> Float
    {
        return interestRate * accountBalance
    }
}
```

11.4 Overriding Inherited Methods

When using inheritance, it is not unusual to find a method in the parent class that almost does what you need, but requires modification to provide the precise functionality you require. That being said, it is also possible you'll inherit a method with a name that describes exactly what you want to do, but it actually does not come close to doing what you need. One option in this scenario would be to ignore the inherited method and write a new method with an entirely new name. A better option is to *override* the inherited method and write a new version of it in the subclass.

Before proceeding with an example, there are two rules that must be obeyed when overriding a method. First, the overriding method in the subclass must take exactly the same number and type of parameters as the overridden method in the parent class. Second, the new method must have the same return type as the parent method.

In our BankAccount class we have a method named *displayBalance* that displays the bank account number and current balance held by an instance of the class. In our SavingsAccount subclass we might also want to output the current interest rate assigned to the account. To achieve this, we simply declare a new version of the *displayBalance* method in our SavingsAccount subclass, prefixed with the *override* keyword:

```
class SavingsAccount: BankAccount {

    var interestRate: Float

    func calculateInterest() -> Float
    {
        return interestRate * accountBalance
    }

    override func displayBalance()
    {
       print("Number \(accountNumber)")
       print("Current balance is \(accountBalance)")
       print("Prevailing interest rate is \(interestRate)")
    }
}
```

It is also possible to make a call to the overridden method in the super class from within a subclass. The *displayBalance* method of the super class could, for example, be called to display the account number and balance, before the interest rate is displayed, thereby eliminating further code duplication:

```
override func displayBalance()
{
        super.displayBalance()
        print("Prevailing interest rate is \(interestRate)")
}
```

11.5 Initializing the Subclass

As the SavingsAccount class currently stands, it inherits the init initializer method from the parent BankAccount class which was implemented as follows:

```
init(number: Int, balance: Float)
{
        accountNumber = number
        accountBalance = balance
}
```

Clearly this method takes the necessary steps to initialize both the account number and balance properties of the class. The SavingsAccount class, however, contains an additional property in the form of the interest rate variable. The SavingsAccount class, therefore, needs its own initializer to ensure that the interestRate property is initialized when instances of the class are created. This method can perform this task and then make a call to the *init* method of the parent class to complete the initialization of the remaining variables:

```
class SavingsAccount: BankAccount {

    var interestRate: Float
```

```
    init(number: Int, balance: Float, rate: Float)
    {
        interestRate = rate
        super.init(number: number, balance: balance)
    }
.
.
.
}
```

Note that to avoid potential initialization problems, the *init* method of the superclass must always be called *after* the initialization tasks for the subclass have been completed.

11.6 Using the SavingsAccount Class

Now that we have completed work on our SavingsAccount class, the class can be used in some example code in much the same way as the parent BankAccount class:

```
let savings1 = SavingsAccount(number: 12311, balance: 600.00,
                                                 rate: 0.07)


print(savings1.calculateInterest())
savings1.displayBalance()
```

11.7 Swift Class Extensions

Another way to add new functionality to a Swift class is to use an extension. Extensions can be used to add features such as methods, initializers, computed properties and subscripts to an existing class without the need to create and reference a subclass. This is particularly powerful when using extensions to add functionality to the built-in classes of the Swift language and iOS SDK frameworks.

A class is extended using the following syntax:

```
extension ClassName {
  // new features here
}
```

For the purposes of an example, assume that we need to add some additional properties to the standard Double class that will return the value raised to the power 2 and 3. This functionality can be added using the following extension declaration:

```
extension Double {

    var squared: Double {
        return self * self
    }

    var cubed: Double {
        return self * self * self
    }
}
```

Having extended the Double class with two new computed properties we can now make use of the properties as we would any other properties of the Double class:

```
let myValue: Double = 3.0
print(myValue.squared)
```

When executed, the print statement will output the value of 9.0. Note that when declaring the myValue constant we were able to declare it as being of type Double and access the extension properties without the need to use a subclass. In fact, because these properties were added as an extension, rather than using a subclass, we can now access these properties directly on Double values:

```
print(3.0.squared)
print(6.0.cubed)
```

Extensions provide a quick and convenient way to extend the functionality of a class without the need to use subclasses. Subclasses, however, still have some advantages over extensions. It is not possible, for example, to override the existing functionality of a class using an extension and extensions cannot contain stored properties.

11.8 Summary

Inheritance extends the concept of object re-use in object-oriented programming by allowing new classes to be derived from existing classes, with those new classes subsequently extended to add new functionality. When an existing class provides some, but not all, of the functionality required by the programmer, inheritance allows that class to be used as the basis for a new subclass. The new subclass will inherit all the capabilities of the parent class, but may then be extended to add the missing functionality.

Swift extensions provide a useful alternative option to adding functionality to existing classes without the need to create a subclass.

Chapter 12

12. An Introduction to Swift Structures and Enumerations

Having covered Swift classes in the preceding chapters, this chapter will introduce the use of structures in Swift. Although at first glance structures and classes look similar, there are some important differences that need to be understood when deciding which to use. This chapter will outline how to declare and use structures, explore the differences between structures and classes and introduce the concepts of value and reference types.

12.1 An Overview of Swift Structures

As with classes, structures form the basis of object-oriented programming and provide a way to encapsulate data and functionality into re-usable instances. Structure declarations resemble classes with the exception that the *struct* keyword is used in place of the *class* keyword. The following code, for example, declares a simple structure consisting of a String variable, initializer and method:

```
struct SampleStruct {

    var name: String

    init(name: String) {
        self.name = name
    }

    func buildHelloMsg() {
        "Hello " + name
    }
}
```

Consider the above structure declaration in comparison to the equivalent class declaration:

```
class SampleClass {

    var name: String

    init(name: String) {
        self.name = name
    }

    func buildHelloMsg() {
        "Hello " + name
    }
}
```

Other than the use of the *struct* keyword instead of *class*, the two declarations are identical. Instances of each type are also created using the same syntax:

```
let myStruct = SampleStruct(name: "Mark")
let myClass = SampleClass(name: "Mark")
```

In common with classes, structures may be extended and are also able to adopt protocols and contain initializers.

Given the commonality between classes and structures, it is important to gain an understanding of how the two differ. Before exploring the most significant difference it is first necessary to understand the concepts of *value types* and *reference types*.

12.2 Value Types vs. Reference Types

While on the surface structures and classes look alike, major differences in behavior occur when structure and class instances are copied or passed as arguments to methods or functions. This occurs because structure instances are value type while class instances are reference type.

When a structure instance is copied or passed to a method, an actual copy of the instance is created, together with any data contained within the instance. This means that the copy has its own version of the data which is unconnected with the original structure instance. In effect, this means that there can be multiple copies of a structure instance within a running app, each with its own local copy of the associated data. A change to one instance has no impact on any other instances.

In contrast, when a class instance is copied or passed as an argument, the only thing duplicated or passed is a reference to the location in memory where that class instance resides. Any changes made to the instance using those references will be performed on the same instance. In other words, there is only one class instance but multiple references pointing to it. A change to the instance data using any one of those references changes the data for all other references.

To demonstrate reference and value types in action, consider the following code:

```
struct SampleStruct {

    var name: String

    init(name: String) {
        self.name = name
    }

    func buildHelloMsg() {
        "Hello " + name
    }
}

let myStruct1 = SampleStruct(name: "Mark")
print(myStruct1.name)
```

When the code executes, the name "Mark" will be displayed. Now change the code so that a copy of the myStruct1 instance is made, the name property changed and the names from each instance displayed:

```
let myStruct1 = SampleStruct(name: "Mark")
var myStruct2 = myStruct1
myStruct2.name = "David"
```

```
print(myStruct1.name)
print(myStruct2.name)
```

When executed, the output will read as follows:

```
Mark
David
```

Clearly, the change of name only applied to myStruct2 since this is an actual copy of myStruct1 containing its own copy of the data as shown in Figure 12-1:

Figure 12-1

Contrast this with the following class example:

```
class SampleClass {

    var name: String

    init(name: String) {
        self.name = name
    }

    func buildHelloMsg() {
        "Hello " + name
    }
}

let myClass1 = SampleClass(name: "Mark")
var myClass2 = myClass1
myClass2.name = "David"

print(myClass1.name)
print(myClass2.name)
```

When this code executes, the following output will be generated:

```
David
David
```

In this case, the name property change is reflected for both myClass1 and myClass2 because both are references pointing to the same class instance as illustrated in Figure 12-2 below:

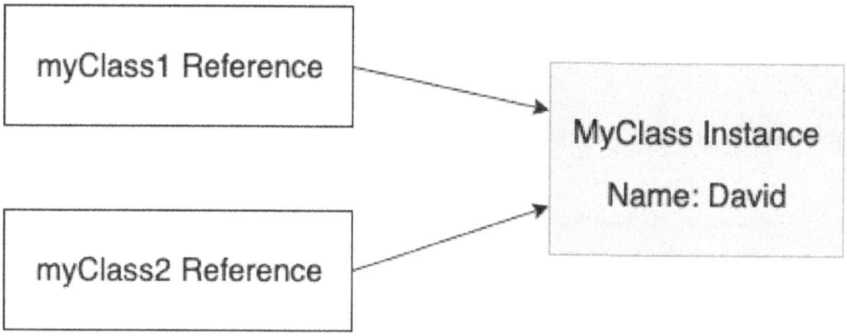

Figure 12-2

In addition to these value and reference type differences, structures do not support inheritance and sub-classing in the way that classes do. In other words, it is not possible for one structure to inherit from another structure. Unlike classes, structures also cannot contain a de-initializer (deinit) method. Finally, while it is possible to identify the type of a class instance at runtime, the same is not true of a struct.

12.3 When to Use Structures or Classes

In general, structures are recommended whenever possible because they are both more efficient than classes and safer to use in multi-threaded code. Classes should be used when inheritance is needed, only one instance of the encapsulated data is required, or extra steps need to be taken to free up resources when an instance is de-initialized.

12.4 An Overview of Enumerations

Enumerations (typically referred to as enums) are used to create custom data types consisting of pre-defined sets of values. Enums are typically used for making decisions within code such as when using switch statements. An enum might, for example be declared as follows:

```
enum Temperature {
    case hot
    case warm
    case cold
}
```

Note that in this example, none of the cases are assigned a value. An enum of this type is essentially used to reference one of a pre-defined set of states (in this case the current temperature being hot, warm or cold). Once declared, the enum may, for example, be used within a switch statement as follows:

```
func displayTempInfo(temp: Temperature) {
    switch temp {
        case .hot:
            print("It is hot.")
        case .warm:
            print("It is warm.")
        case .cold:
            print("It is cold.")
    }
}
```

It is also worth noting that because an enum has a definitive set of valid member values, the switch statement does not need to include a default case. An attempt to pass an invalid enum case through the switch will be caught by the compiler long before it has a chance to cause a runtime error.

To test out the enum, the *displayTempInfo()* function must be passed an instance of the Temperature enum with one of the following three possible states selected:

```
Temperature.hot
Temperature.warm
Temperature.cold
```

For example:

```
displayTempInfo(temp: Temperature.warm)
```

When executed, the above function call will output the following information:

```
It is warm.
```

Individual cases within an enum may also have *associated values*. Assume, for example, that the "cold" enum case needs to have associated with it a temperature value so that the app can differentiate between cold and freezing conditions. This can be defined within the enum declaration as follows:

```
enum Temperature {
    case hot
    case warm
    case cold(centigrade: Int)
}
```

This allows the switch statement to also check for the temperature for the cold case as follows:

```
func displayTempInfo(temp: Temperature) {
    switch temp {
        case .hot:
            print("It is hot")
        case .warm:
            print("It is warm")
        case.cold(let centigrade) where centigrade <= 0:
            print("Ice warning: \(centigrade) degrees.")
        case .cold:
            print("It is cold but not freezing.")
    }
}
```

When the cold enum value is passed to the function, it now does so with a temperature value included:

```
displayTempInfo(temp: Temperature.cold(centigrade: -10))
```

The output from the above function will read as follows:

```
Ice warning: -10 degrees
```

12.5 Summary

Swift structures and classes both provide a mechanism for creating instances that define properties, store values and define methods. Although the two mechanisms appear to be similar, there are significant behavioral differences when structure and class instances are either copied or passed to a method. Classes are categorized as being reference type instances while structures are value type. When a structure instance is copied or passed, an entirely new copy of the instance is created containing its own data. Class instances, on the other hand, are passed and copied by reference, with each reference pointing to the same class instance. Other features unique to classes include support for inheritance and deinitialization and the ability to identify the class type at runtime. Structures should typically be used in place of classes unless specific class features are required.

Enumerations are used to create custom types consisting of a pre-defined set of state values and are of particular use in identifying state within switch statements.

Chapter 13

13. An Introduction to Swift Property Wrappers

Now that the topics of Swift classes and structures have been covered, this chapter will introduce a related topic in the form of property wrappers. Introduced in Swift 5.1, property wrappers provide a way to reduce the amount of duplicated code involved in writing getters, setters and computed properties in class and structure implementations.

13.1 Understanding Property Wrappers

When values are assigned or accessed via a property within a class or structure instance it is sometimes necessary to perform some form of transformation or validation on that value before it is stored or read. As outlined in the chapter entitled *"The Basics of Swift Object-Oriented Programming"*, this type of behavior can be implemented through the creation of computed properties. Frequently, patterns emerge where a computed property is common to multiple classes or structures. Prior to the introduction of Swift 5.1, the only way to share the logic of a computed property was to duplicate the code and embed it into each class or structure implementation. Not only is this inefficient, but a change in the behavior of the computation must be manually propagated across all the entities that use it.

To address this shortcoming, Swift 5.1 introduced a feature known as *property wrappers*. Property wrappers essentially allow the capabilities of computed properties to be separated from individual classes and structures and reused throughout the app code base.

13.2 A Simple Property Wrapper Example

Perhaps the best way to understand property wrappers is to study a very simple example. Imagine a structure with a String property intended to contain a city name. Such a structure might read as follows:

```
struct Address {
    var city: String
}
```

If the class was required to store the city name in uppercase, regardless of how it was entered by the user, a computed property such as the following might be added to the structure:

```
struct Address {

    private var cityname: String = ""

    var city: String {
        get { cityname }
        set { cityname = newValue.uppercased() }
    }
}
```

When a city name is assigned to the property, the setter within the computed property converts it to uppercase before storing it in the private *cityname* variable. This structure can be tested using the following code:

```
var address = Address()

address.city = "London"
print(address.city)
```

When executed, the output from the above code would read as follows:

```
LONDON
```

Clearly the computed property performs the task of converting the city name string to uppercase, but if the same behavior is needed in other structures or classes the code would need to be duplicated in those declarations. In this example this is only a small amount of code, but that won't necessarily be the case for more complex computations.

Instead of using a computed property, this logic can instead be implemented as a property wrapper. The following declaration, for example, implements a property wrapper named FixCase designed to convert a string to uppercase:

```
@propertyWrapper
struct FixCase {
    private(set) var value: String = ""

    var wrappedValue: String {
        get { value }
        set { value = newValue.uppercased() }
    }

    init(wrappedValue initialValue: String) {
        self.wrappedValue = initialValue
    }
}
```

Property wrappers are declared using the @propertyWrapper directive and are implemented in a class or structure (with structures being the preferred choice). All property wrappers must include a wrappedValue property containing the getter and setter code that changes or validates the value. An optional initializer may also be included which is passed the value being assigned. In this case, the initial value is simply assigned to the wrappedValue property where it is converted to uppercase and stored in the private variable.

Now that this property wrapper has been defined, it can be reused by applying it to other property variables wherever the same behavior is needed. To use this property wrapper, simply prefix property declarations with the @FixCase directive in any class or structure declarations where the behavior is needed, for example:

```
struct Contact {
    @FixCase var name: String
    @FixCase var city: String
    @FixCase var country: String
}

var contact = Contact(name: "John Smith", city: "London", country: "United Kingdom")
print("\(contact.name), \(contact.city), \(contact.country)")
```

When executed, the following output will appear:

```
JOHN SMITH, LONDON, UNITED KINGDOM
```

13.3 Supporting Multiple Variables and Types

In the above example, the property wrapper accepted a single value in the form of the value to be assigned to the property being wrapped. More complex property wrappers may also be implemented that accept other values that can be used when performing the computation. These additional values are placed within parentheses after the property wrapper name. A property wrapper designed to restrict a value within a specified range might read as follows:

```
struct Demo {
    @MinMaxVal(min: 10, max: 150) var value: Int = 100
}
```

The code to implement the above MinMaxVal property wrapper could be written as follows:

```
@propertyWrapper
struct MinMaxVal {
  var value: Int
  let max: Int
  let min: Int

    init(wrappedValue: Int, min: Int, max: Int) {
    value = wrappedValue
    self.min = min
    self.max = max
  }

  var wrappedValue: Int {
    get { return value }
    set {
       if newValue > max {
        value = max
       } else if newValue < min {
        value = min
       } else {
        value = newValue
      }
    }
  }
}
```

Note that the *init()* method has been implemented to accept the min and max values in addition to the wrapped value. The wrappedValue setter checks the value and modifies it to the min or max number if it falls above or below the specified range.

The above property wrapper can be tested using the following code:

```
struct Demo {
    @MinMaxVal(min: 100, max: 200) var value: Int = 100
}
```

```
var demo = Demo()
demo.value = 150
print(demo.value)

demo.value = 250
print(demo.value)
```

When executed, the first print statement will output 150 because it falls within the acceptable range, while the second print statement will show that the wrapper restricted the value to the maximum permitted value (in this case 200).

As currently implemented, the property wrapper will only work with integer (Int) values. The wrapper would be more useful if it could be used with any variable type which can be compared with another value of the same type. Fortunately, protocol wrappers can be implemented to work with any types that conform to a specific protocol. Since the purpose of this wrapper is to perform comparisons, it makes sense to modify it to support any data types that conform to the Comparable protocol which is included with the Foundation framework. Types that conform to the Comparable protocol are able to be used in equality, greater-than and less-than comparisons. A wide range of types such as String, Int, Date, Date Interval and Character conform to this protocol.

To implement the wrapper so that it can be used with any types that conform to the Comparable protocol, the declaration needs to be modified as follows:

```
@propertyWrapper
struct MinMaxVal<V: Comparable> {
  var value: V
  let max: V
  let min: V

    init(wrappedValue: V, min: V, max: V) {
    value = wrappedValue
    self.min = min
    self.max = max
  }

  var wrappedValue: V {
    get { return value }
    set {
       if newValue > max {
        value = max
       } else if newValue < min {
        value = min
       } else {
        value = newValue
      }
    }
  }
}
```

The modified wrapper will still work with Int values as before but can now also be used with any of the other types that conform to the Comparable protocol. In the following example, a string value is evaluated to ensure that it fits alphabetically within the min and max string values:

```
struct Demo {
    @MinMaxVal(min: "Apple", max: "Orange") var value: String = ""
}

var demo = Demo()
demo.value = "Banana"
print(demo.value)
// Banana <--- Value fits within alphabetical range and is stored.

demo.value = "Pear"
print(demo.value)
// Orange <--- Value is outside of the alphabetical range so is changed to the
max value.
```

Similarly, this same wrapper will also work with Date instances, as in the following example where the value is limited to a date between the current date and one month in the future:

```
struct DateDemo {
     @MinMaxVal(min: Date(), max: Calendar.current.date(byAdding: .month,
            value: 1, to: Date())! ) var value: Date = Date()
}
```

The following code and output demonstrate the wrapper in action using Date values:

```
var dateDemo = DateDemo()

print(dateDemo.value)
// 2019-08-23 20:05:13 +0000. <--- Property set to today by default.

dateDemo.value = Calendar.current.date(byAdding: .day, value: 10, to: Date())! //
<--- Property is set to 10 days into the future.
print(dateDemo.value)
// 2019-09-02 20:05:13 +0000 <--- Property is within acceptable range and is
stored.
dateDemo.value = Calendar.current.date(byAdding: .month, value: 2, to: Date())!
// <--- Property is set to 2 months into the future.

print(dateDemo.value)
// 2019-09-23 20:08:54 +0000 <--- Property is outside range and set to max date
(i.e. 1 month into the future).
```

13.4 Summary

Introduced with Swift 5.1, property wrappers allow the behavior that would normally be placed in the getters and setters of a property implementation to be extracted and reused through the codebase of an app project avoiding the duplication of code within the class and structure declarations. Property wrappers are declared in the form of structures using the @propertyWrapper directive.

Property wrappers are a powerful Swift feature and allow you to add your own custom behavior to the Swift language. In addition to creating your own property wrappers, you will also encounter them when working with the iOS SDK. In fact, pre-defined property wrappers are used extensively when working with SwiftUI as will be covered in later chapters.

Chapter 14

14. Working with Array and Dictionary Collections in Swift

Arrays and dictionaries in Swift are objects that contain collections of other objects. In this chapter, we will cover some of the basics of working with arrays and dictionaries in Swift.

14.1 Mutable and Immutable Collections

Collections in Swift come in mutable and immutable forms. The contents of immutable collection instances cannot be changed after the object has been initialized. To make a collection immutable, assign it to a *constant* when it is created. Collections are mutable, on the other hand, if assigned to a *variable*.

14.2 Swift Array Initialization

An array is a data type designed specifically to hold multiple values in a single ordered collection. An array, for example, could be created to store a list of String values. Strictly speaking, a single Swift based array is only able to store values that are of the same type. An array declared as containing String values, therefore, could not also contain an Int value. As will be demonstrated later in this chapter, however, it is also possible to create mixed type arrays. The type of an array can be specified specifically using type annotation or left to the compiler to identify using type inference.

An array may be initialized with a collection of values (referred to as an *array literal*) at creation time using the following syntax:

var variableName: [type] = [value 1, value2, value3, …….]

The following code creates a new array assigned to a variable (thereby making it mutable) that is initialized with three string values:

```
var treeArray = ["Pine", "Oak", "Yew"]
```

Alternatively, the same array could have been created immutably by assigning it to a constant:

```
let treeArray = ["Pine", "Oak", "Yew"]
```

In the above instance, the Swift compiler will use type inference to decide that the array contains values of String type and prevent values of other types being inserted into the array elsewhere within the application code.

Alternatively, the same array could have been declared using type annotation:

```
var treeArray: [String] = ["Pine", "Oak", "Yew"]
```

Arrays do not have to have values assigned at creation time. The following syntax can be used to create an empty array:

```
var variableName = [type]()
```

Consider, for example, the following code which creates an empty array designated to store floating point values and assigns it to a variable named priceArray:

```
var priceArray = [Float]()
```

Another useful initialization technique allows an array to be initialized to a certain size with each array element pre-set with a specified default value:

```
var nameArray = [String](repeating: "My String", count: 10)
```

When compiled and executed, the above code will create a new 10 element array with each element initialized with a string that reads "My String".

Finally, a new array may be created by adding together two existing arrays (assuming both arrays contain values of the same type). For example:

```
let firstArray = ["Red", "Green", "Blue"]
let secondArray = ["Indigo", "Violet"]

let thirdArray = firstArray + secondArray
```

14.3 Working with Arrays in Swift

Once an array exists, a wide range of methods and properties are provided for working with and manipulating the array content from within Swift code, a subset of which is as follows:

14.3.1 Array Item Count

A count of the items in an array can be obtained by accessing the array's count property:

```
var treeArray = ["Pine", "Oak", "Yew"]
var itemCount = treeArray.count

print(itemCount)
```

Whether or not an array is empty can be identified using the array's Boolean *isEmpty* property as follows:

```
var treeArray = ["Pine", "Oak", "Yew"]

if treeArray.isEmpty {
    // Array is empty
}
```

14.3.2 Accessing Array Items

A specific item in an array may be accessed or modified by referencing the item's position in the array index (where the first item in the array has index position 0) using a technique referred to as *index subscripting*. In the following code fragment, the string value contained at index position 2 in the array (in this case the string value "Yew") is output by the print call:

```
var treeArray = ["Pine", "Oak", "Yew"]

print(treeArray[2])
```

This approach can also be used to replace the value at an index location:

```
treeArray[1] = "Redwood"
```

The above code replaces the current value at index position 1 with a new String value that reads "Redwood".

14.3.3 Random Items and Shuffling

A call to the *shuffled()* method of an array object will return a new version of the array with the item ordering randomly shuffled, for example:

```
let shuffledTrees = treeArray.shuffled()
```

To access an array item at random, simply make a call to the *randomElement()* method:

```
let randomTree = treeArray.randomElement()
```

14.3.4 Appending Items to an Array

Items may be added to an array using either the *append* method or + and += operators. The following, for example, are all valid techniques for appending items to an array:

```
treeArray.append("Redwood")
treeArray += ["Redwood"]
treeArray += ["Redwood", "Maple", "Birch"]
```

14.3.5 Inserting and Deleting Array Items

New items may be inserted into an array by specifying the index location of the new item in a call to the array's *insert(at:)* method. An insertion preserves all existing elements in the array, essentially moving them to the right to accommodate the newly inserted item:

```
treeArray.insert("Maple", at: 0)
```

Similarly, an item at a specific array index position may be removed using the *remove(at:)* method call:

```
treeArray.remove(at: 2)
```

To remove the last item in an array, simply make a call to the array's *removeLast* method as follows:

```
treeArray.removeLast()
```

14.3.6 Array Iteration

The easiest way to iterate through the items in an array is to make use of the for-in looping syntax. The following code, for example, iterates through all of the items in a String array and outputs each item to the console panel:

```
let treeArray = ["Pine", "Oak", "Yew", "Maple", "Birch", "Myrtle"]

for tree in treeArray {
    print(tree)
}
```

Upon execution, the following output would appear in the console:

```
Pine
Oak
Yew
Maple
Birch
Myrtle
```

The same result can be achieved by calling the *forEach()* array method. When this method is called on an array, it will iterate through each element and execute specified code. For example:

```
treeArray.forEach { tree in
    print(tree)
}
```

Note that since the task to be performed for each array element is declared in a closure expression, the above example may be modified as follows to take advantage of shorthand argument names:

```
treeArray.forEach {
    print($0)
```

```
}
```

14.4 Creating Mixed Type Arrays

A mixed type array is an array that can contain elements of different class types. Clearly an array that is either declared or inferred as being of type String cannot subsequently be used to contain non-String class object instances. Interesting possibilities arise, however, when taking into consideration that Swift includes the *Any* type. Any is a special type in Swift that can be used to reference an object of a non-specific class type. It follows, therefore, that an array declared as containing Any object types can be used to store elements of mixed types. The following code, for example, declares and initializes an array containing a mixture of String, Int and Double elements:

```
let mixedArray: [Any] = ["A String", 432, 34.989]
```

The use of the Any type should be used with care since the use of Any masks from Swift the true type of the elements in such an array thereby leaving code prone to potential programmer error. It will often be necessary, for example, to manually cast the elements in an Any array to the correct type before working with them in code. Performing the incorrect cast for a specific element in the array will most likely cause the code to compile without error but crash at runtime. Consider, for the sake of an example, the following mixed type array:

```
let mixedArray: [Any] = [1, 2, 45, "Hello"]
```

Assume that, having initialized the array, we now need to iterate through the integer elements in the array and multiply them by 10. The code to achieve this might read as follows:

```
for object in mixedArray {
    print(object * 10)
}
```

When entered into Xcode, however, the above code will trigger a syntax error indicating that it is not possible to multiply operands of type Any and Int. In order to remove this error it will be necessary to downcast the array element to be of type Int:

```
for object in mixedArray {
    print(object as! Int * 10)
}
```

The above code will compile without error and work as expected until the final String element in the array is reached at which point the code will crash with the following error:

```
Could not cast value of type 'Swift.String' to 'Swift.Int'
```

The code will, therefore, need to be modified to be aware of the specific type of each element in the array. Clearly, there are both benefits and risks to using Any arrays in Swift.

14.5 Swift Dictionary Collections

String dictionaries allow data to be stored and managed in the form of key-value pairs. Dictionaries fulfill a similar purpose to arrays, except each item stored in the dictionary has associated with it a unique key (to be precise, the key is unique to the particular dictionary object) which can be used to reference and access the corresponding value. Currently only String, Int, Double and Bool data types are suitable for use as keys within a Swift dictionary.

14.6 Swift Dictionary Initialization

A dictionary is a data type designed specifically to hold multiple values in a single unordered collection. Each item in a dictionary consists of a key and an associated value. The data types of the key and value elements type may be specified specifically using type annotation, or left to the compiler to identify using type inference.

A new dictionary may be initialized with a collection of values (referred to as a *dictionary literal*) at creation time using the following syntax:

var *variableName*: [*key type*: *value type*] = [*key 1*: *value 1*, *key 2*: *value2* ....]

The following code creates a new dictionary assigned to a variable (thereby making it mutable) that is initialized with four key-value pairs in the form of ISBN numbers acting as keys for corresponding book titles:

```
var bookDict = ["100-432112" : "Wind in the Willows",
                "200-532874" : "Tale of Two Cities",
                "202-546549" : "Sense and Sensibility",
                "104-109834" : "Shutter Island"]
```

In the above instance, the Swift compiler will use type inference to decide that both the key and value elements of the dictionary are of String type and prevent values or keys of other types being inserted into the dictionary.

Alternatively, the same dictionary could have been declared using type annotation:

```
var bookDict: [String: String] =
               ["100-432112" : "Wind in the Willows",
                "200-532874" : "Tale of Two Cities",
                "202-546549" : "Sense and Sensibility",
                "104-109834" : "Shutter Island"]
```

As with arrays, it is also possible to create an empty dictionary, the syntax for which reads as follows:

var *variableName* = [*key type*: *value type*]()

The following code creates an empty dictionary designated to store integer keys and string values:

```
var myDictionary = [Int: String]()
```

14.7 Sequence-based Dictionary Initialization

Dictionaries may also be initialized using sequences to represent the keys and values. This is achieved using the Swift *zip()* function, passing through the keys and corresponding values. In the following example, a dictionary is created using two arrays:

```
let keys = ["100-432112", "200-532874", "202-546549", "104-109834"]
let values = ["Wind in the Willows", "Tale of Two Cities",
                "Sense and Sensibility", "Shutter Island"]

let bookDict = Dictionary(uniqueKeysWithValues: zip(keys, values))
```

This approach allows keys and values to be generated programmatically. In the following example, a number range starting at 1 is being specified for the keys instead of using an array of predefined keys:

```
let values = ["Wind in the Willows", "Tale of Two Cities",
               "Sense and Sensibility", "Shutter Island"]

var bookDict = Dictionary(uniqueKeysWithValues: zip(1..., values))
```

The above code is a much cleaner equivalent to the following dictionary declaration:

```
var bookDict = [1 : "Wind in the Willows",
                2 : "Tale of Two Cities",
                3 : "Sense and Sensibility",
```

```
                4 : "Shutter Island"]
```

14.8 Dictionary Item Count

A count of the items in a dictionary can be obtained by accessing the dictionary's count property:

```
print(bookDict.count)
```

14.9 Accessing and Updating Dictionary Items

A specific value may be accessed or modified using key subscript syntax to reference the corresponding value. The following code references a key known to be in the bookDict dictionary and outputs the associated value (in this case the book entitled "A Tale of Two Cities"):

```
print(bookDict["200-532874"])
```

When accessing dictionary entries in this way, it is also possible to declare a default value to be used in the event that the specified key does not return a value:

```
print(bookDict["999-546547", default: "Book not found"])
```

Since the dictionary does not contain an entry for the specified key, the above code will output text which reads "Book not found".

Indexing by key may also be used when updating the value associated with a specified key, for example, to change the title of the same book from "A Tale of Two Cities" to "Sense and Sensibility"):

```
bookDict["200-532874"] = "Sense and Sensibility"
```

The same result is also possible by making a call to the *updateValue(forKey:)* method, passing through the key corresponding to the value to be changed:

```
bookDict.updateValue("The Ruins", forKey: "200-532874")
```

14.10 Adding and Removing Dictionary Entries

Items may be added to a dictionary using the following key subscripting syntax:

dictionaryVariable[*key*] = *value*

For example, to add a new key-value pair entry to the books dictionary:

```
bookDict["300-898871"] = "The Overlook"
```

Removal of a key-value pair from a dictionary may be achieved either by assigning a *nil* value to the entry, or via a call to the *removeValueForKey* method of the dictionary instance. Both code lines below achieve the same result of removing the specified entry from the books dictionary:

```
bookDict["300-898871"] = nil
bookDict.removeValue(forKey: "300-898871")
```

14.11 Dictionary Iteration

As with arrays, it is possible to iterate through dictionary entries by making use of the for-in looping syntax. The following code, for example, iterates through all of the entries in the books dictionary, outputting both the key and value for each entry:

```
for (bookid, title) in bookDict {
  print("Book ID: \(bookid) Title: \(title)")
}
```

Upon execution, the following output would appear in the console:

```
Book ID: 100-432112 Title: Wind in the Willows
```

```
Book ID: 200-532874 Title: The Ruins
Book ID: 104-109834 Title: Shutter Island
Book ID: 202-546549 Title: Sense and Sensibility
```

14.12 Summary

Collections in Swift take the form of either dictionaries or arrays. Both provide a way to collect together multiple items within a single object. Arrays provide a way to store an ordered collection of items where those items are accessed by an index value corresponding to the item position in the array. Dictionaries provide a platform for storing key-value pairs, where the key is used to gain access to the stored value. Iteration through the elements of Swift collections can be achieved using the for-in loop construct.

Chapter 15

15. Understanding Error Handling in Swift 5

In a perfect world, a running iOS app would never encounter an error. The reality, however, is that it is impossible to guarantee that an error of some form or another will not occur at some point during the execution of the app. It is essential, therefore, to ensure that the code of an app is implemented such that it gracefully handles any errors that may occur. Since the introduction of Swift 2, the task of handling errors has become much easier for the iOS app developer.

This chapter will cover the handling of errors using Swift and introduce topics such as *error types*, *throwing methods and functions*, the *guard* and *defer* statements and *do-catch* statements.

15.1 Understanding Error Handling

No matter how carefully Swift code is designed and implemented, there will invariably be situations that are beyond the control of the app. An app that relies on an active internet connection cannot, for example, control the loss of signal on an iPhone device, or prevent the user from enabling "airplane mode". What the app can do, however, is to implement robust handling of the error (for example displaying a message indicating to the user that the app requires an active internet connection to proceed).

There are two sides to handling errors within Swift. The first involves triggering (or *throwing*) an error when the desired results are not achieved within the method of an iOS app. The second involves catching and handling the error after it is thrown by a method.

When an error is thrown, the error will be of a particular error type which can be used to identify the specific nature of the error and to decide on the most appropriate course of action to be taken. The error type value can be any value that conforms to the Error protocol.

In addition to implementing methods in an app to throw errors when necessary, it is important to be aware that a number of API methods in the iOS SDK (particularly those relating to file handling) will throw errors which will need to be handled within the code of the app.

15.2 Declaring Error Types

As an example, consider a method that is required to transfer a file to a remote server. Such a method might fail to transfer the file for a variety of reasons such as there being no network connection, the connection being too slow or the failure to find the file to be transferred. All these possible errors could be represented within an enumeration that conforms to the Error protocol as follows:

```
enum FileTransferError: Error {
    case noConnection
    case lowBandwidth
    case fileNotFound
}
```

Once an error type has been declared, it can be used within a method when throwing errors.

15.3 Throwing an Error

A method or function declares that it can throw an error using the *throws* keyword. For example:

```
func transferFile() throws {
}
```

In the event that the function or method returns a result, the *throws* keyword is placed before the return type as follows:

```
func transferFile() throws -> Bool {
}
```

Once a method has been declared as being able to throw errors, code can then be added to throw the errors when they are encountered. This is achieved using the *throw* statement in conjunction with the *guard* statement. The following code declares some constants to serve as status values and then implements the guard and throw behavior for the method:

```
let connectionOK = true
let connectionSpeed = 30.00
let fileFound = false

enum FileTransferError: Error {
    case noConnection
    case lowBandwidth
    case fileNotFound
}

func fileTransfer() throws {

    guard connectionOK else {
        throw FileTransferError.noConnection
    }

    guard connectionSpeed > 30 else {
        throw FileTransferError.lowBandwidth
    }

    guard fileFound else {
        throw FileTransferError.fileNotFound
    }
}
```

Within the body of the method, each guard statement checks a condition for a true or false result. In the event of a false result, the code contained within the *else* body is executed. In the case of a false result, the throw statement is used to throw one of the error values contained in the FileTransferError enumeration.

15.4 Calling Throwing Methods and Functions

Once a method or function is declared as throwing errors, it can no longer be called in the usual manner. Calls to such methods must now be prefixed by the *try* statement as follows:

```
try fileTransfer()
```

In addition to using the try statement, the call must also be made from within a *do-catch* statement to catch and handle any errors that may be thrown. Consider, for example, that the *fileTransfer* method needs to be called from within a method named *sendFile*. The code within this method might be implemented as follows:

```
func sendFile() -> String {

    do {
        try fileTransfer()
    } catch FileTransferError.noConnection {
        return("No Network Connection")
    } catch FileTransferError.lowBandwidth {
        return("File Transfer Speed too Low")
    } catch FileTransferError.fileNotFound {
        return("File not Found")
    } catch {
        return("Unknown error")
    }

    return("Successful transfer")
}
```

The method calls the *fileTransfer* method from within a *do-catch* statement which, in turn, includes catch conditions for each of the three possible error conditions. In each case, the method simply returns a string value containing a description of the error. In the event that no error was thrown, a string value is returned indicating a successful file transfer. Note that a fourth catch condition is included with no pattern matching. This is a "catch all" statement that ensures that any errors not matched by the preceding catch statements are also handled. This is required because do-catch statements must be exhaustive (in other words constructed so as to catch all possible error conditions).

Swift also allows multiple matches to be declared within a single catch statement, with the list of matches separated by commas. For example, a single catch declaration could be used to handle both the noConnection and lowBandwidth errors as follows:

```
func sendFile() -> String {

    do {
        try fileTransfer()
    } catch FileTransferError.noConnection, FileTransferError.lowBandwidth {
        return("Connection problem")
    } catch FileTransferError.fileNotFound {
        return("File not Found")
    } catch {
        return("Unknown error")
    }

    return("Successful transfer")
}
```

15.5 Accessing the Error Object

When a method call fails, it will invariably return an Error object identifying the nature of the failure. A common requirement within the catch statement is to gain access to this object so that appropriate corrective action can be taken within the app code. The following code demonstrates how such an error object is accessed from within a catch statement when attempting to create a new file system directory:

```
do {
    try filemgr.createDirectory(atPath: newDir,
                    withIntermediateDirectories: true,
                    attributes: nil)
    } catch let error {
            print("Error: \(error.localizedDescription)")
}
```

15.6 Disabling Error Catching

A throwing method may be forced to run without the need to enclose the call within a do-catch statement by using the *try!* statement as follows:

```
try! fileTransfer
```

In using this approach we are informing the compiler that we know with absolute certainty that the method call will not result in an error being thrown. In the event that an error is thrown when using this technique, the code will fail with a runtime error. As such, this approach should be used sparingly.

15.7 Using the defer Statement

The previously implemented *sendFile* method demonstrated a common scenario when handling errors. Each of the catch clauses in the do-catch statement contained a return statement that returned control to the calling method. In such a situation, however, it might be useful to be able to perform some other task before control is returned and regardless of the type of error that was encountered. The *sendFile* method might, for example, need to remove temporary files before returning. This behavior can be achieved using the *defer* statement.

The defer statement allows a sequence of code statements to be declared as needing to be run as soon as the method returns. In the following code, the *sendFile* method has been modified to include a defer statement:

```
func sendFile() -> String {

    defer {
        removeTmpFiles()
        closeConnection()
    }

    do {
        try fileTransfer()
    } catch FileTransferError.noConnection {
        return("No Network Connection")
    } catch FileTransferError.lowBandwidth {
        return("File Transfer Speed too Low")
    } catch FileTransferError.fileNotFound {
        return("File not Found")
    } catch {
```

```
        return("Unknown error")
    }

    return("Successful transfer")
}
```

With the defer statement now added, the calls to the *removeTmpFiles* and *closeConnection* methods will always be made before the method returns, regardless of which return call gets triggered.

15.8 Summary

Error handling is an essential part of creating robust and reliable iOS apps. Since the introduction of Swift 2 it is now much easier to both trigger and handle errors. Error types are created using values that conform to the Error protocol and are most commonly implemented as enumerations. Methods and functions that throw errors are declared as such using the *throws* keyword. The *guard* and *throw* statements are used within the body of these methods or functions to throw errors based on the error type.

A throwable method or function is called using the *try* statement which must be encapsulated within a do-catch statement. A do-catch statement consists of an exhaustive list of catch pattern constructs, each of which contains the code to be executed in the event of a particular error being thrown. Cleanup tasks can be defined to be executed when a method returns through the use of the *defer* statement.

Chapter 16

16. An Overview of SwiftUI

Now that Xcode has been installed and the basics of the Swift programing language covered, it is time to start introducing SwiftUI.

First announced at Apple's Worldwide Developer Conference in 2019, SwiftUI is an entirely new approach to developing apps for all Apple operating system platforms. The basic goals of SwiftUI are to make app development easier, faster and less prone to the types of bugs that typically appear when developing software projects. These elements have been combined with SwiftUI specific additions to Xcode that allow SwiftUI projects to be tested in near real-time using a live preview of the app during the development process.

Many of the advantages of SwiftUI originate from the fact that it is both *declarative* and *data driven*, topics which will be explained in this chapter.

The discussion in this chapter is intended as a high-level overview of SwiftUI and does not cover the practical aspects of implementation within a project. Implementation and practical examples will be covered in detail in the remainder of the book.

16.1 UIKit and Interface Builder

To understand the meaning and advantages of SwiftUI's declarative syntax, it helps to understand how user interface layouts were designed before the introduction of SwiftUI. Up until the introduction of SwiftUI, iOS apps were built entirely using UIKit together with a collection of associated frameworks that make up the iOS Software Development Kit (SDK).

To aid in the design of the user interface layouts that make up the screens of an app, Xcode includes a tool called Interface Builder. Interface Builder is a powerful tool that allows storyboards to be created which contain the individual scenes that make up an app (with a scene typically representing a single app screen).

The user interface layout of a scene is designed within Interface Builder by dragging components (such as buttons, labels, text fields and sliders) from a library panel to the desired location on the scene canvas. Selecting a component in a scene provides access to a range of inspector panels where the attributes of the components can be changed.

The layout behavior of the scene (in other words how it reacts to different device screen sizes and changes to device orientation between portrait and landscape) is defined by configuring a range of constraints that dictate how each component is positioned and sized in relation to both the containing window and the other components in the layout.

Finally, any components that need to respond to user events (such as a button tap or slider motion) are connected to methods in the app source code where the event is handled.

At various points during this development process, it is necessary to compile and run the app on a simulator or device to test that everything is working as expected.

16.2 SwiftUI Declarative Syntax

SwiftUI introduces a declarative syntax that provides an entirely different way of implementing user interface layouts and behavior from the UIKit and Interface Builder approach. Instead of manually designing the intricate details of the layout and appearance of components that make up a scene, SwiftUI allows the scenes to be described using a simple and intuitive syntax. In other words, SwiftUI allows layouts to be created by declaring how the user interface should appear without having to worry about the complexity of how the layout is actually built.

This essentially involves declaring the components to be included in the layout, stating the kind of layout manager in which they are to be contained (vertical stack, horizontal stack, form, list etc.) and using modifiers to set attributes such as the text on a button, the foreground color of a label, or the method to be called in the event of a tap gesture. Having made these declarations, all the intricate and complicated details of how to position, constrain and render the layout are handled automatically by SwiftUI.

SwiftUI declarations are structured hierarchically, which also makes it easy to create complex views by composing together small, re-usable custom subviews.

While the view layout is being declared and tested, Xcode provides a preview canvas which changes in real-time to reflect the appearance of the layout. Xcode also includes a *live preview* mode which allows the app to be launched within the preview canvas and fully tested without the need to build and run on a simulator or device.

Coverage of the SwiftUI declaration syntax begins with the chapter entitled *"Creating Custom Views with SwiftUI"*.

16.3 SwiftUI is Data Driven

When we say that SwiftUI is data driven, this is not to say that it is no longer necessary to handle events generated by the user (in other words the interaction between the user and the app user interface). It is still necessary, for example, to know when the user taps a button and to react in some app specific way. Being data driven relates more to the relationship between the underlying app data and the user interface and logic of the app.

Prior to the introduction of SwiftUI, an iOS app would contain code responsible for checking the current values of data within the app. If data is likely to change over time, code has to be written to ensure that the user interface always reflects the latest state of the data (perhaps by writing code to frequently check for changes to the data, or by providing a refresh option for the user to request a data update). Similar problems arise when keeping the user interface state consistent and making sure issues like toggle button settings are stored appropriately. Requirements such as these can become increasingly complex when multiple areas of an app depend on the same data sources.

SwiftUI addresses this complexity by providing several ways to *bind* the data model of an app to the user interface components and logic that provide the app functionality.

When implemented, the data model *publishes* data variables to which other parts of the app can then *subscribe*. Using this approach, changes to the published data are automatically reported to all subscribers. If the binding is made from a user interface component, any data changes will automatically be reflected within the user interface by SwiftUI without the need to write any additional code.

16.4 SwiftUI vs. UIKit

With the choice of using UIKit and SwiftUI now available, the obvious question arises as to which is the best option. When making this decision it is important to understand that SwiftUI and UIKit are not mutually exclusive. In fact, several integration solutions are available (a topic area covered starting with the chapter entitled *"Integrating UIViews with SwiftUI"*).

If supporting devices running older versions of iOS is not of concern and you are starting a new project, it makes sense to use SwiftUI wherever possible. Not only does SwiftUI provide a faster, more efficient app development environment, it also makes it easier to make the same app available on multiple Apple platforms (iOS, iPadOS, macOS, watchOS and tvOS) without making significant code changes.

If you have an existing app developed using UIKit there is no easy migration path to convert that code to SwiftUI, so it probably makes sense to keep using UIKit for that part of the project. UIKit will continue to be a valuable part of the app development toolset and will be extended, supported and enhanced by Apple for the foreseeable future. When adding new features to an existing project, however, consider doing so using SwiftUI and integrating it into the existing UIKit codebase.

When adopting SwiftUI for new projects, it will probably not be possible to avoid using UIKit entirely. Although SwiftUI comes with a wide array of user interface components, it will still be necessary to use UIKit for certain functionality not yet available in SwiftUI.

In addition, for extremely complex user interface layout designs, it may also be necessary to use Interface Builder in situations where layout needs cannot be satisfied using the SwiftUI layout container views.

16.5 Summary

SwiftUI introduces a different approach to app development than that offered by UIKit and Interface Builder. Rather than directly implement the way in which a user interface is to be rendered, SwiftUI allows the user interface to be declared in descriptive terms and then does all the work of deciding the best way to perform the rendering when the app runs.

SwiftUI is also data driven in that data changes drive the behavior and appearance of the app. This is achieved through a publisher and subscriber model.

This chapter has provided a very high-level view of SwiftUI. The remainder of this book will explore SwiftUI in greater depth.

17. Using Xcode in SwiftUI Mode

When creating a new project, Xcode now provides a choice of creating either a Storyboard or SwiftUI-based user interface for the project. When creating a SwiftUI project, Xcode appears and behaves significantly differently when designing the user interface for an app project compared to the UIKit Storyboard mode.

When working in SwiftUI mode, most of your time as an app developer will be spent in the code editor and preview canvas, both of which will be explored in detail in this chapter.

17.1 Starting Xcode 14

As with all the examples in this book, the development of our example will take place within the Xcode 14 development environment. If you have not already installed this tool together with the latest iOS SDK refer first to the *"Installing Xcode 14 and the iOS 16 SDK"* chapter of this book. Assuming the installation is complete, launch Xcode either by clicking on the icon on the dock (assuming you created one) or using the macOS Finder to locate Xcode in the Applications folder of your system.

When launched for the first time, and until you turn off the *Show this window when Xcode launches* toggle, the screen illustrated in Figure 17-1 will appear by default:

Figure 17-1

If you do not see this window, simply select the *Window -> Welcome to Xcode* menu option to display it. From within this window, click on the option to *Create a new Xcode project*.

17.2 Creating a SwiftUI Project

When creating a new project, the project template screen includes options to select how the app project is to be implemented. Options are available to design an app for a specific Apple platform (such as iOS, watchOS, macOS, DriveKit, or tvOS), or to create a *multiplatform* project. Selecting a platform-specific option will also provide the choice of creating either a Storyboard (UIKit) or SwiftUI-based project.

A multiplatform project allows an app to be designed for multiple Apple platforms with a minimum of platform-specific code. Even if you plan to initially only target iOS the multiplatform option is still recommended since it provides the flexibility to make the app available on other platforms in the future without having to restructure the project.

Templates are also available for creating a basic app, a document-based app, or a game project. For this chapter, use the multiplatform app option:

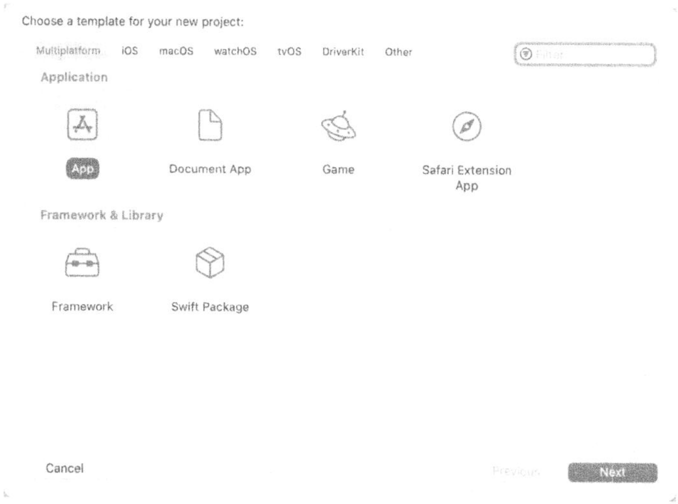

Figure 17-2

Clicking *Next* will display the project options screen where the project name needs to be entered (in this case, name the project *DemoProject*).

The Organization Identifier is typically the reversed URL of your company's website, for example, "com. mycompany". This will be used when creating provisioning profiles and certificates to enable the testing of advanced features of iOS on physical devices. It also serves to uniquely identify the app within the Apple App Store when the app is published:

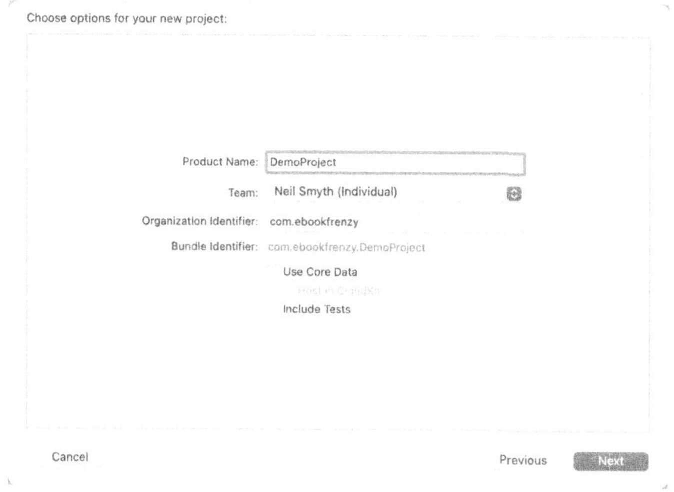

Figure 17-3

Click *Next* once again and choose a location on your filesystem in which to place the project before clicking on the *Create* button.

Once a new project has been created, the main Xcode panel will appear with the default layout for SwiftUI development displayed.

17.3 Xcode in SwiftUI Mode

Before beginning work on a SwiftUI user interface, it is worth taking some time to gain familiarity with how Xcode works in SwiftUI mode. A newly created multiplatform "app" project includes two SwiftUI View files named *<app name>App.swift* (in this case *DemoProjectApp.swift*) and *ContentView.swift* which, when selected from the project navigation panel, will appear within Xcode as shown in Figure 17-4 below:

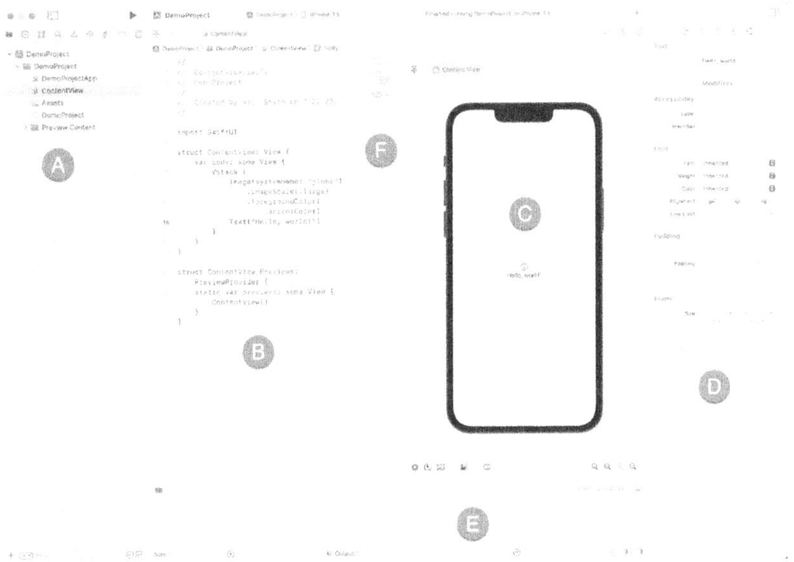

Figure 17-4

When the project loads for the first time, Xcode may default to macOS as the destination platform for building and testing your app. Before continuing, use the run destination chooser to select an iPhone device as illustrated in Figure 17-5 below:

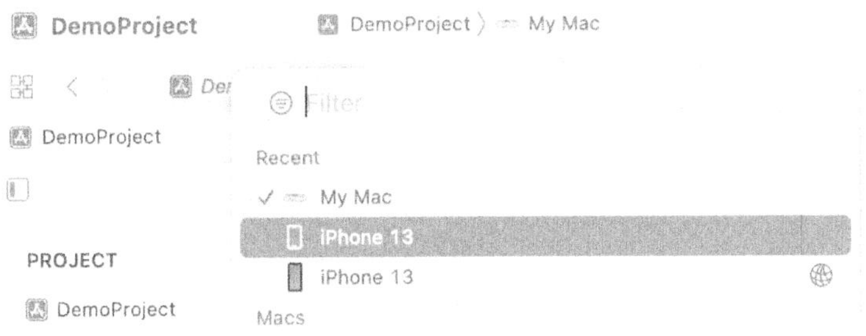

Figure 17-5

Located to the right of the project navigator (A) is the code editor (B). To the right of this is the preview canvas (C) where any changes made to the SwiftUI layout declaration will appear in real-time.

Selecting a view in the canvas will automatically select and highlight the corresponding entry in the code editor, and vice versa. Attributes for the currently selected item will appear in the attributes inspector panel (D).

During debugging, the debug panel (E) will appear containing debug output from both the iOS frameworks and any diagnostic print statements you have included in your code. If the console is not currently visible, display it by clicking on the button indicated by the arrow in Figure 17-6:

Figure 17-6

The debug panel can be configured to show a variable view, a console view, or both views in a split panel arrangement. The variable view displays variables within the app at the point that the app crashes or reaches a debugging breakpoint. The console view, on the other hand, displays print output and messages from the running app. Figure 17-7 shows both views displayed together with an arrow indicating the buttons used to hide and show the different views:

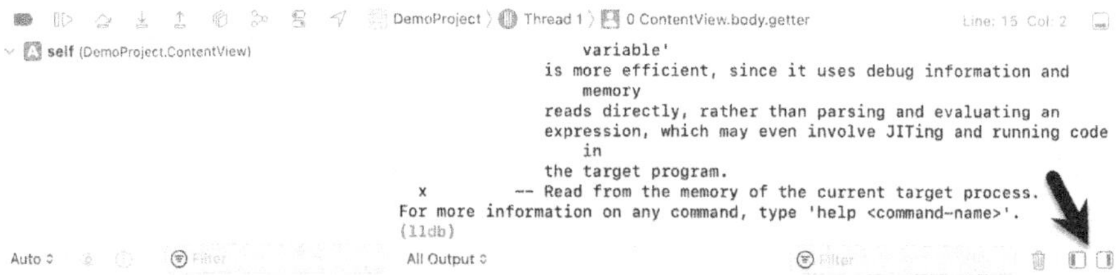

Figure 17-7

The button indicated in Figure 17-6 above may be used to hide the debug panel (E), while the two buttons highlighted in Figure 17-8 below hide and show the project navigator and inspector panels:

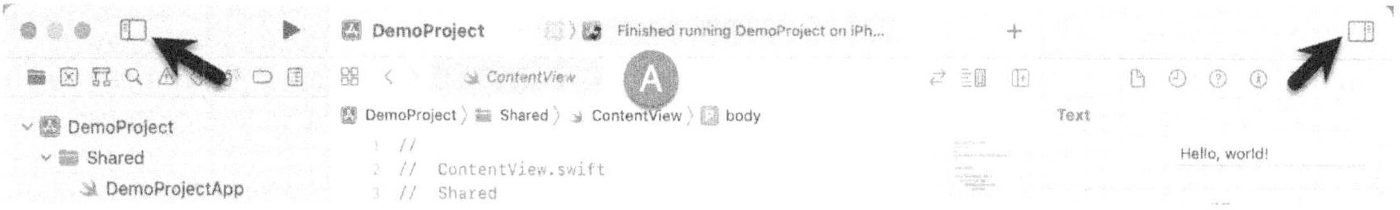

Figure 17-8

The tab bar (marked A above) displays a tab for each currently open file. When a tab is clicked, the corresponding file is loaded into the editor. Hovering the mouse pointer over a tab will display an "X" button within the tab which will close the file when clicked.

The area marked F in Figure 17-4 is called the *minimap*. This map provides a miniaturized outline of the source code in the editor. Particularly useful when working with large source files, the minimap panel provides a quick way to move to different areas of the code. Hovering the mouse pointer of a line in the minimap will display a label indicating the class, property, or function at that location as illustrated in Figure 17-9:

Figure 17-9

Clicking either on the label or within the map will take you to that line in the code editor. Holding down the

Command key while hovering will display all of the elements contained within the source file as shown in Figure 17-10:

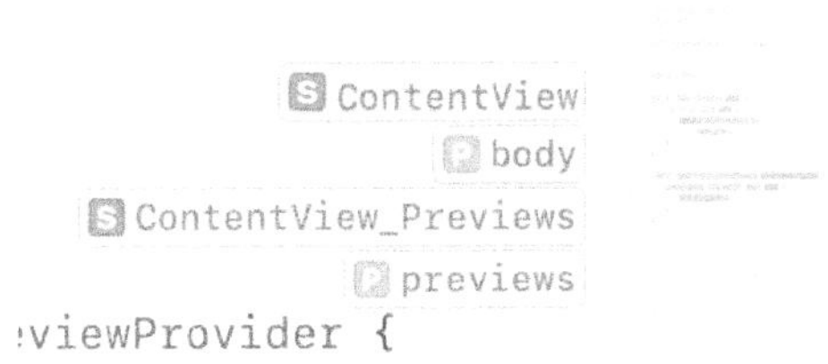

Figure 17-10

The minimap can be displayed and hidden by toggling the *Editor -> Minimap* menu option.

17.4 The Preview Canvas

The preview canvas provides both a visual representation of the user interface design and a tool for adding and modifying views within the layout design. The canvas may also be used to perform live testing of the running app without the need to launch an iOS simulator. Figure 17-11 illustrates a typical preview canvas for a newly created project:

Figure 17-11

If the canvas is not visible it can be displayed using the Xcode *Editor -> Canvas* menu option.

The main canvas area (A) represents the current view as it will appear when running on a physical device (also referred to as the *canvas device*). When changes are made to the code in the editor, those changes are reflected within the preview canvas. To avoid continually updating the canvas, and depending on the nature of the changes being made, the preview will occasionally pause live updates. When this happens, the Resume button will appear which, when clicked, will once again begin updating the preview:

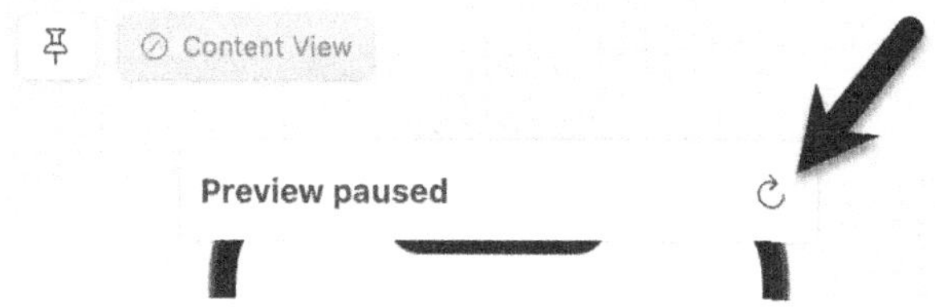

Figure 17-12

The size buttons (B) will zoom in and out of the canvas, zoom to 100%, and fit the available space.

17.5 Preview Pinning

When building an app in Xcode it will likely consist of several SwiftUI View files in addition to the default *ContentView.swift* file. When a SwiftUI View file is selected from the project navigator, both the code editor and preview canvas will change to reflect the currently selected file. Sometimes you may want the user interface layout for one SwiftUI file to appear in the preview canvas while editing the code in a different file. This can be particularly useful if the layout from one file is dependent on or embedded in another view. The pin button (labeled C in Figure 17-11 above) pins the current preview to the canvas so that it remains accessible on the canvas after navigating to a different view. Switch between pinned views by clicking on the view buttons along the top of the preview panel. In Figure 17-13, for example, buttons are provided to switch between views named ContentView and SalesView:

Figure 17-13

17.6 The Preview Toolbar

The preview toolbar (marked D in Figure 17-11 above and shown below) provides a range of options for changing the preview panel:

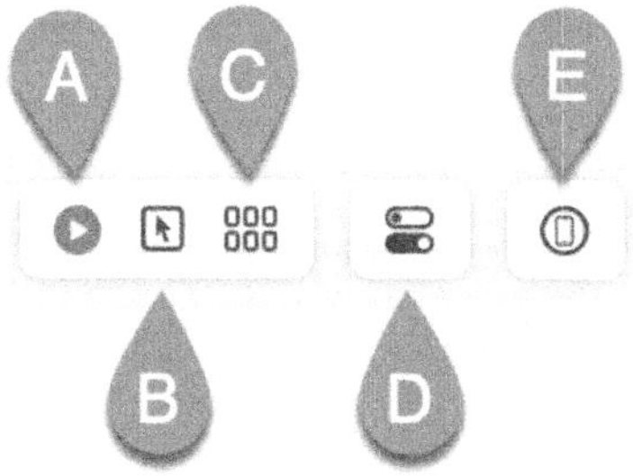

Figure 17-14

The preview panel can display the current view in either *live* or *selectable* mode. In live mode, the app runs interactively within the canvas and allows you to interact with it as if it is running on a device or simulator. Selectable mode allows you to select items in the canvas view to edit attributes and also to add and remove components. To switch between modes, use the buttons marked A (for live mode) and B (for selectable mode) as marked in the above figure.

The current version of the app may also be previewed on an attached physical device by clicking on the Preview on Device button (E). As with the preview canvas, the running app on the device will update dynamically as changes are made to the code in the editor.

The Variants button (C) allows the view to be previewed in a variety of dynamic text sizes, color schemes, and device orientations:

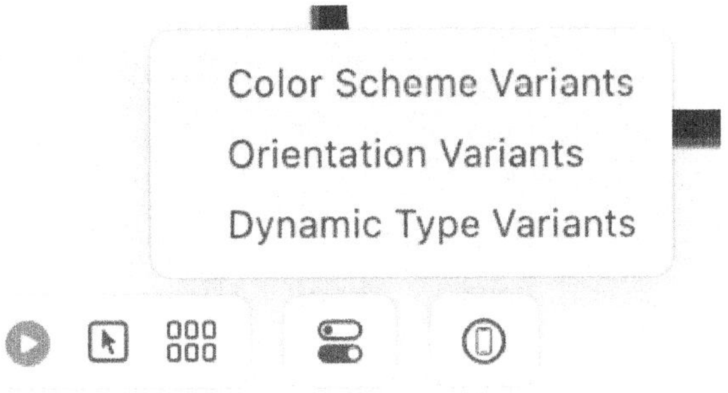

Figure 17-15

Figure 17-16, for example, shows the result of selecting the orientation variations option:

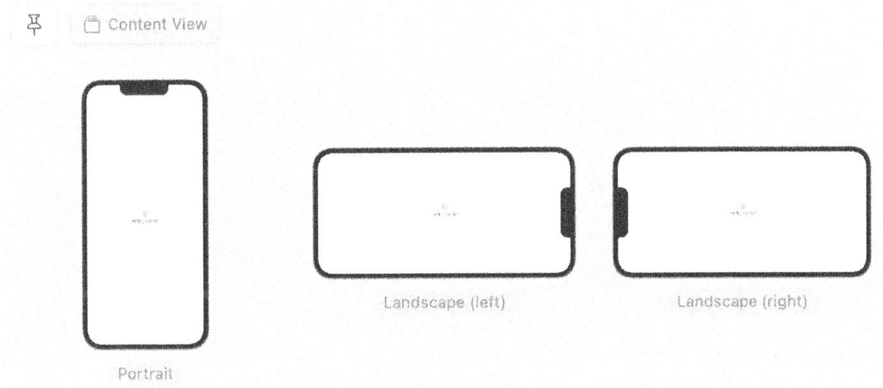

Figure 17-16

The Device Settings button (D) controls the color scheme (light or dark), orientation (portrait or landscape), and dynamic font size of the canvas device:

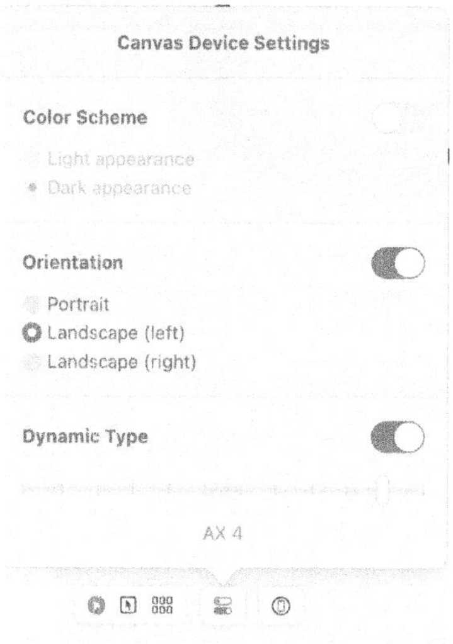

Figure 17-17

17.7 Modifying the Design

Working with SwiftUI primarily involves adding additional views, customizing those views using modifiers, adding logic, and interacting with state and other data instance bindings. All of these tasks can be performed exclusively by modifying the structure in the code editor. The font used to display the "Hello, world!" Text view, for example, can be changed by adding the appropriate modifier in the editor:

```
Text("Hello, world!")
    .font(.largeTitle)
```

An alternative to this is to make changes to the SwiftUI views by dragging and dropping items from the Library panel. The Library panel is displayed by clicking on the toolbar button highlighted in Figure 17-18:

Figure 17-18

When displayed, the Library panel will appear as shown in Figure 17-19:

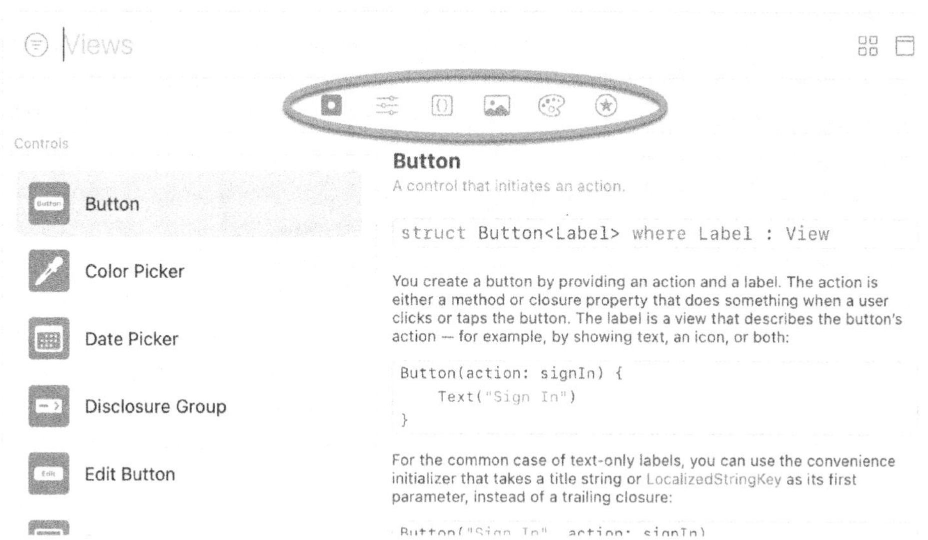

Figure 17-19

When launched in this way, the Library panel is transient and will disappear either after a selection has been made, or a click is performed outside of the panel. To keep the panel displayed, hold down the Option key when clicking on the Library button.

When first opened, the panel displays a list of views available for inclusion in the user interface design. The list can be browsed, or the search bar used to narrow the list to specific views. The toolbar (highlighted in the above figure) can be used to switch to other categories such as modifiers, commonly used code snippets, images, color resources, and symbols.

An item within the library can be applied to the user interface design in several ways. To apply a font modifier to the "Hello, world!" Text view, one option is to place the cursor in the code editor at the location where the code is to be added, locate the font modifier in the Library panel, and double-click on it. Xcode will then automatically insert the font modifier at the cursor position.

Another option is to locate the Library item and then drag and drop it onto the desired location either in the code editor or the preview canvas. In Figure 17-20 below, for example, the font modifier is being dragged to the Text view within the canvas (note that the canvas must be in selectable mode):

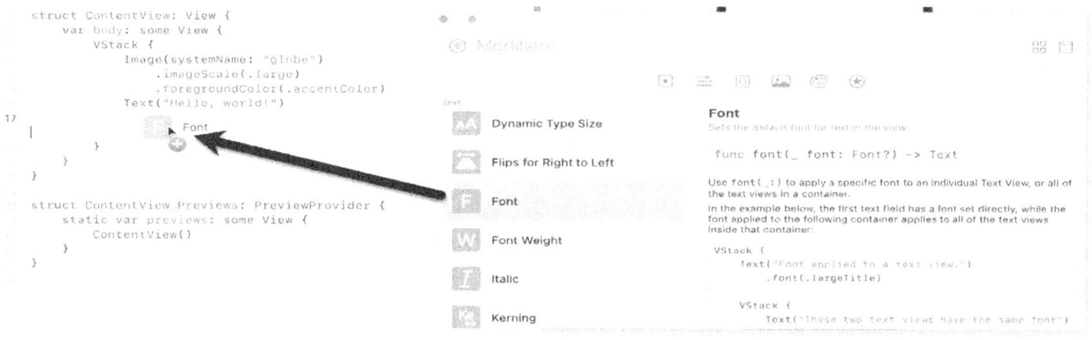

Figure 17-20

The same result can be achieved by dragging an item from the library onto the preview canvas. In the case of Figure 17-21, a Button view is being added to the layout beneath the existing Text view:

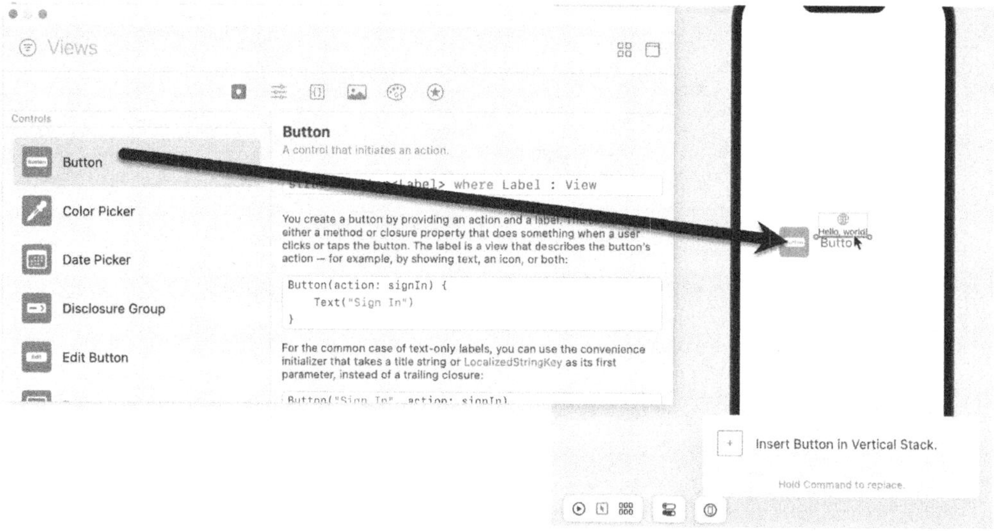

Figure 17-21

In this example, the side along which the view will be placed if released highlights and the preview canvas displays a notification that the Button and existing Text view will automatically be placed in a Vertical Stack container view (stacks will be covered later in the chapter entitled *"SwiftUI Stacks and Frames"*).

Once a view or modifier has been added to the SwiftUI view file it is highly likely that some customization will be necessary, such as specifying the color for a foreground modifier. One option is, of course, to simply make the changes within the editor, for example:

```
Text("Hello, world!")
    .font(.largeTitle)
    .foregroundColor(.red)
```

Another option is to select the view in either the editor or preview panel and then make the necessary changes within the Attributes Inspector panel:

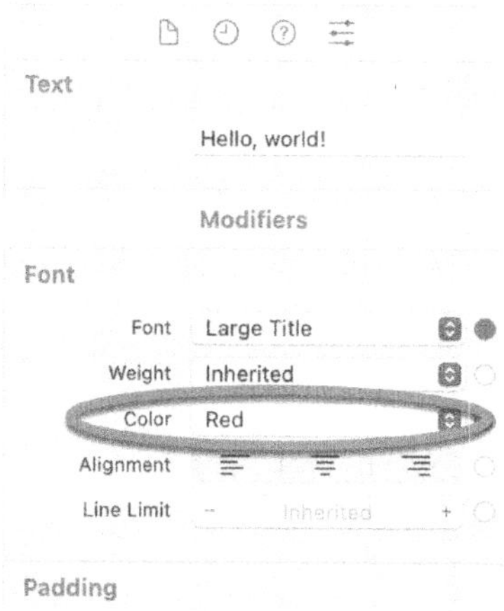

Figure 17-22

The Attributes inspector will provide the option to make changes to any modifiers already applied to the selected view.

Before moving on to the next topic, it is also worth noting that the Attributes inspector provides yet another way to add modifiers to a view via the Add Modifier menu located at the bottom of the panel. When clicked, this menu will display a long list of modifiers available for the current view type. To apply a modifier, simply select it from the menu. An entry for the new modifier will subsequently appear in the inspector where it can be configured with the required properties.

17.8 Editor Context Menu

Holding down the Command key while clicking on an item in the code editor will display the menu shown in Figure 17-23:

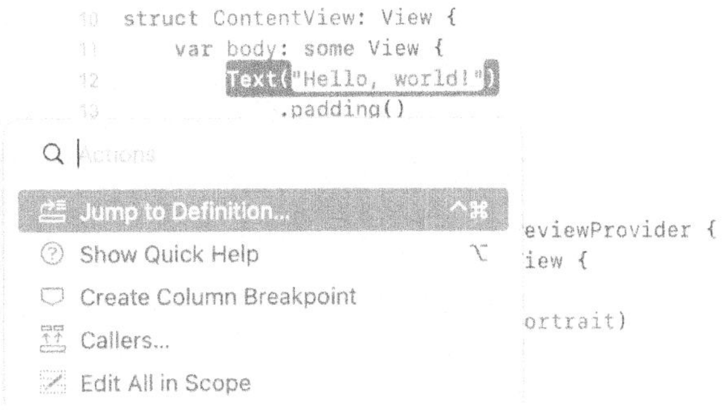

Figure 17-23

This menu provides a list of options that will vary depending on the type of item selected. Options typically include a shortcut to a popup version of the Attributes inspector for the current view, together with options to embed the current view in a stack or list container. This menu is also useful for extracting part of a view into its own self-contained subview. Creating subviews is strongly encouraged to promote reuse, improve performance and unclutter complex design structures.

17.9 Previewing on Multiple Device Configurations

Every newly created SwiftUI View file includes an additional declaration at the bottom of the file that resembles the following:

```
struct ContentView_Previews: PreviewProvider {
    static var previews: some View {
        ContentView()
    }
}
```

This structure, which conforms to the PreviewProvider protocol, returns an instance of the primary view within the file. This instructs Xcode to display the preview for that view within the preview canvas (without this declaration, nothing will appear in the canvas).

By default, the preview canvas shows the user interface on a single device based on the current selection in the run target menu to the right of the run and stop buttons in the Xcode toolbar (as highlighted in Figure 17-25 below). To preview on other device models, one option is to simply change the run target and wait for the preview canvas to change.

A better option, however, is to modify the previews structure to specify a different device. In the following example, the canvas previews the user interface on an iPhone SE:

```
struct ContentView_Previews: PreviewProvider {
    static var previews: some View {
```

```
        ContentView()
            .previewDevice("iPhone SE (2nd generation)")
            .previewDisplayName("iPhone SE")
    }
}
```

It is possible using this technique to preview multiple device types simultaneously by placing them into a Group view as follows:

```
struct ContentView_Previews: PreviewProvider {
    static var previews: some View {

        Group {
            ContentView()
                .previewDevice("iPhone 13")
                .previewDisplayName("iPhone 13")
            ContentView()
                .previewDevice("iPhone SE (2nd generation)")
                .previewDisplayName("iPhone SE")
        }
    }
}
```

When multiple devices are previewed, you can switch between each preview using the buttons located at the top of the preview panel as shown in Figure 17-24:

Figure 17-24

The environment modifier may also be used to preview the layout in other configurations, for example, to preview in dark mode:

```
ContentView()
    .preferredColorScheme(.dark)
    .previewDevice("iPhone SE (2nd generation)")
```

This preview structure is also useful for passing sample data into the enclosing view for testing purposes within the preview canvas, a technique that will be used in later chapters. For example:

```
struct ContentView_Previews: PreviewProvider {
    static var previews: some View {
        ContentView(sampleData: mySampleData)
    }
}
```

17.10 Running the App on a Simulator

Although much can be achieved using the preview canvas, there is no substitute for running the app on physical devices and simulators during testing.

Within the main Xcode project window, the menu marked C in Figure 17-25 is used to choose a target simulator. This menu will include simulators that have been configured and any physical devices connected to the development system:

Figure 17-25

Clicking on the *Run* toolbar button (marked B in Figure 17-25 above) will compile the code and run the app on the selected target. The small panel in the center of the Xcode toolbar (D) will report the progress of the build process together with any problems or errors that cause the build process to fail. Once the app is built, the simulator will start and the app will run. Clicking on the stop button (A) will terminate the running app.

The simulator includes several options not available in the Live Preview for testing different aspects of the app. The Hardware and Debug menus, for example, include options for testing Face ID authentication and simulating geographical location changes for navigation and map-based apps.

17.11 Running the App on a Physical iOS Device

Although the Simulator environment provides a useful way to test an app on a variety of different iOS device models, it is important to also test on a physical iOS device.

If you have entered your Apple ID in the Xcode preferences screen as outlined in the *"Joining the Apple Developer Program"* chapter and selected a development team for the project, it is possible to run the app on a physical device simply by connecting it to the development Mac system with a USB cable and selecting it as the run target within Xcode.

With a device connected to the development system, and an application ready for testing, refer to the device menu located in the Xcode toolbar. There is a reasonable chance that this will have defaulted to one of the iOS Simulator configurations. Switch to the physical device by selecting this menu and changing it to the device name listed under the iOS Devices section as shown in Figure 17-26:

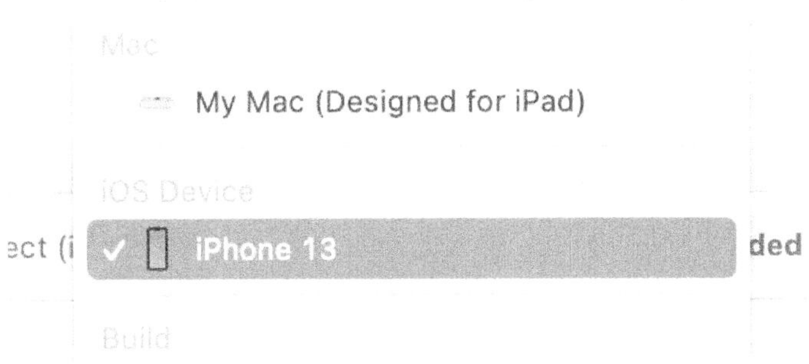

Figure 17-26

With the target device selected, make sure the device is unlocked and click on the run button at which point Xcode will install and launch the app on the device.

As will be discussed later in this chapter, a physical device may also be configured for network testing, whereby apps are installed and tested on the device via a network connection without the need to have the device connected by a USB cable.

17.12 Managing Devices and Simulators

Currently connected iOS devices and the simulators configured for use with Xcode can be viewed and managed using the Xcode Devices window which is accessed via the *Window -> Devices and Simulators* menu option. Figure 17-27, for example, shows a typical Device screen on a system where an iPhone has been detected:

Figure 17-27

A wide range of simulator configurations are set up within Xcode by default and can be viewed by selecting the *Simulators* button at the top of the left-hand panel. Other simulator configurations can be added by clicking on the + button located in the bottom left-hand corner of the window. Once selected, a dialog will appear allowing the simulator to be configured in terms of the device model, iOS version, and name.

17.13 Enabling Network Testing

In addition to testing an app on a physical device connected to the development system via a USB cable, Xcode also supports testing via a network connection. This option is enabled on a per device basis within the Devices and Simulators dialog introduced in the previous section. With the device connected via the USB cable, display this dialog, select the device from the list and enable the *Connect via network* option as highlighted in Figure 17-28:

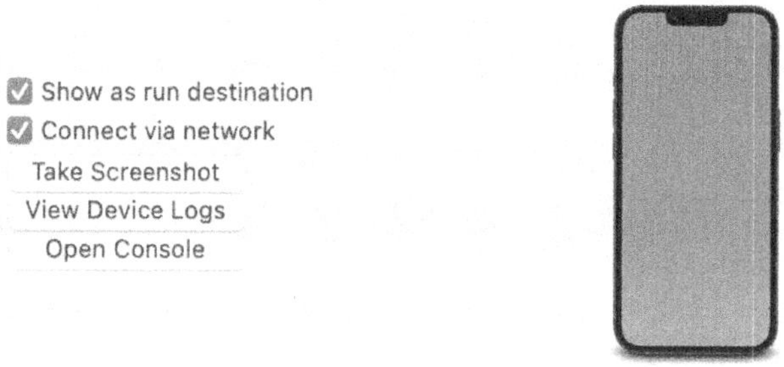

Figure 17-28

Once the setting has been enabled, the device may continue to be used as the run target for the app even when the USB cable is disconnected. The only requirement is that both the device and development computer be connected to the same WiFi network. Assuming this requirement has been met, clicking on the run button with the device selected in the run menu will install and launch the app over the network connection.

17.14 Dealing with Build Errors

If for any reason a build fails, the status window in the Xcode toolbar will report that an error has been detected by displaying "Build" together with the number of errors detected and any warnings. In addition, the left-hand panel of the Xcode window will update with a list of the errors. Selecting an error from this list will take you to the location in the code where corrective action needs to be taken.

17.15 Monitoring Application Performance

Another useful feature of Xcode is the ability to monitor the performance of an application while it is running, either on a device or simulator or within the Live Preview canvas. This information is accessed by displaying the *Debug Navigator*.

When Xcode is launched, the project navigator is displayed in the left-hand panel by default. Along the top of this panel is a bar with a range of other options. The seventh option from the left displays the debug navigator when selected as illustrated in Figure 17-29. When displayed, this panel shows real-time statistics relating to the performance of the currently running application such as memory, CPU usage, disk access, energy efficiency, network activity, and iCloud storage access.

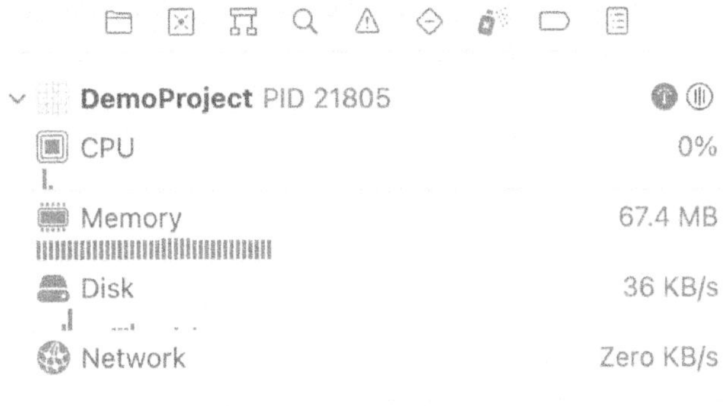

Figure 17-29

When one of these categories is selected, the main panel (Figure 17-30) updates to provide additional information about that particular aspect of the application's performance:

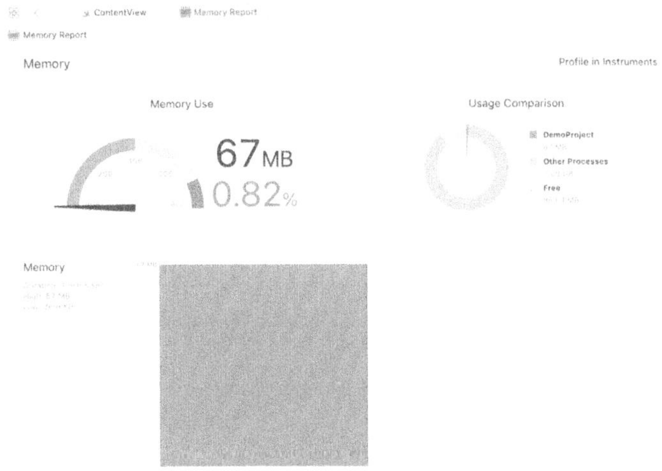

Figure 17-30

Yet more information can be obtained by clicking on the *Profile in Instruments* button in the top right-hand corner of the panel.

17.16 Exploring the User Interface Layout Hierarchy

Xcode also provides an option to break the user interface layout out into a rotatable 3D view that shows how the view hierarchy for a user interface is constructed. This can be particularly useful for identifying situations where one view instance is obscured by another appearing on top of it or a layout is not appearing as intended. This is also useful for learning how SwiftUI works behind the scenes to construct a SwiftUI layout if only to appreciate how much work SwiftUI is saving us from having to do.

To access the view hierarchy in this mode, the app needs to be running on a device or simulator. Once the app is running, click on the *Debug View Hierarchy* button indicated in Figure 17-31:

Figure 17-31

Once activated, a 3D "exploded" view of the layout will appear. Clicking and dragging within the view will rotate the hierarchy allowing the layers of views that make up the user interface to be inspected:

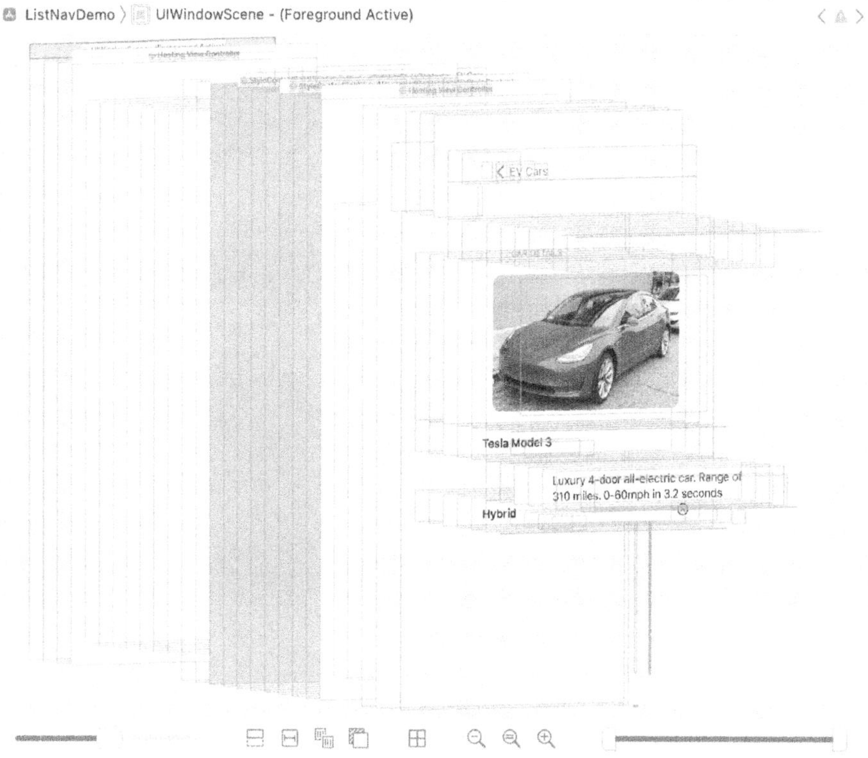

Figure 17-32

Moving the slider in the bottom left-hand corner of the panel will adjust the spacing between the different views in the hierarchy. The two markers in the right-hand slider (Figure 17-33) may also be used to narrow the range of views visible in the rendering. This can be useful, for example, to focus on a subset of views located in the middle of the hierarchy tree:

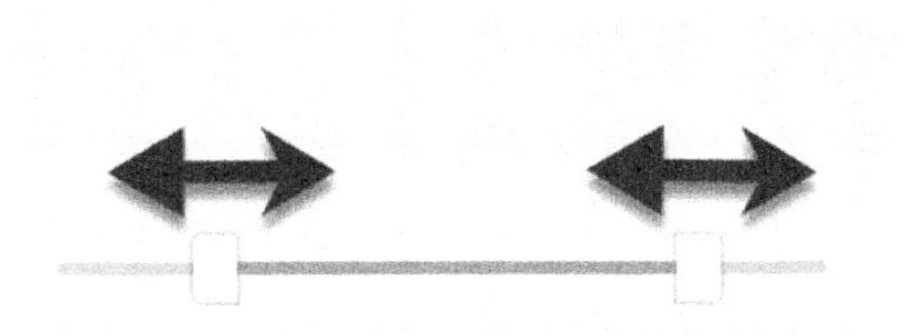

Figure 17-33

While the hierarchy is being debugged, the left-hand panel will display the entire view hierarchy tree for the layout as shown in Figure 17-34 below:

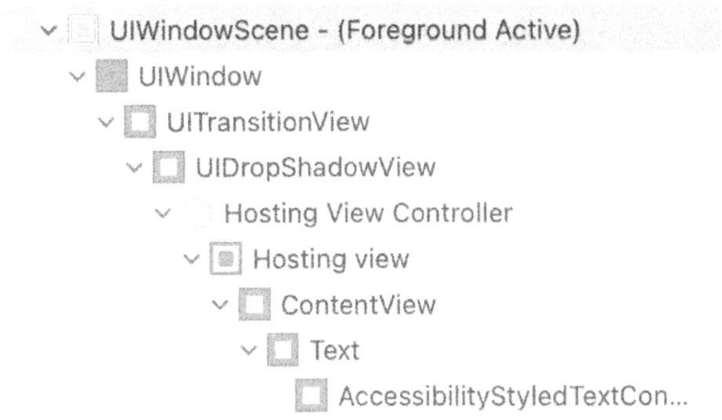

Figure 17-34

Selecting an object in the hierarchy tree will highlight the corresponding item in the 3D rendering and vice versa. The far right-hand panel will also display the attributes of the selected object. Figure 17-35, for example, shows the inspector panel while a Text view is selected within the view hierarchy.

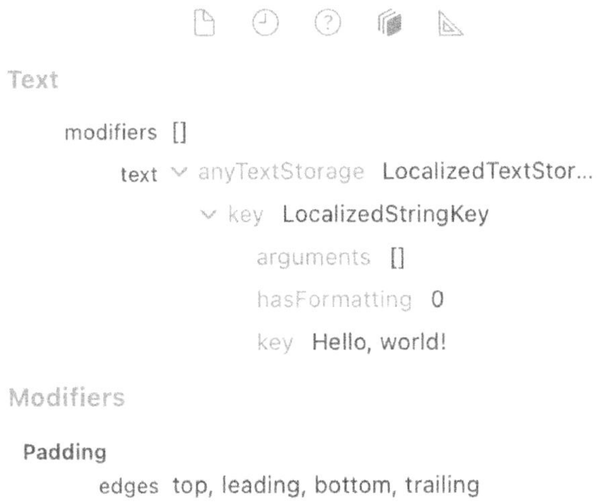

Figure 17-35

17.17 Summary

When creating a new project, Xcode provides the option to use either UIKit Storyboards or SwiftUI as the basis of the user interface of the app. When in SwiftUI mode, most of the work involved in developing an app takes place in the code editor and the preview canvas. New views can be added to the user interface layout and configured either by typing into the code editor or dragging and dropping components from the Library either onto the editor or the preview canvas.

The preview canvas will usually update in real-time to reflect code changes as they are typed into the code editor, though will occasionally pause updates in response to larger changes. When in the paused state, clicking the Resume button will restart updates. The Attribute inspector allows the properties of a selected view to be changed and new modifiers added. Holding down the Command key while clicking on a view in the editor or canvas displays the context menu containing a range of options such as embedding the view in a container or extracting the selection to a subview.

The preview structure at the end of the SwiftUI View file allows previewing on multiple device models simultaneously and with different environment settings.

Chapter 18

18. SwiftUI Architecture

A completed SwiftUI app is constructed from multiple components which are assembled in a hierarchical manner. Before embarking on the creation of even the most basic of SwiftUI projects, it is useful to first gain an understanding of how SwiftUI apps are structured. With this goal in mind, this chapter will introduce the key elements of SwiftUI app architecture, with an emphasis on App, Scene and View elements.

18.1 SwiftUI App Hierarchy

When considering the structure of a SwiftUI application, it helps to view a typical hierarchy visually. Figure 18-1, for example, illustrates the hierarchy of a simple SwiftUI app:

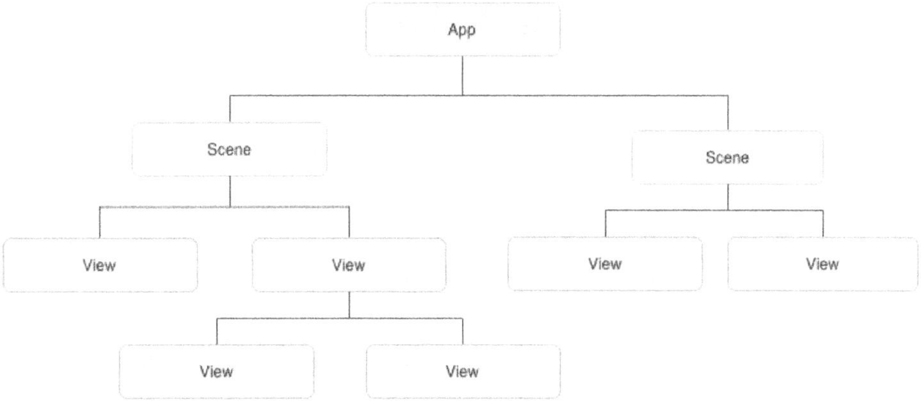

Figure 18-1

Before continuing, it is important to distinguish the difference between the term "app" and the "App" element outlined in the above figure. The software applications that we install and run on our mobile devices have come to be referred to as "apps". In this chapter reference will be made both to these apps and the App element in the above figure. To avoid confusion, we will use the term "application" to refer to the completed, installed and running app, while referring to the App element as "App". The remainder of the book will revert to using the more common "app" when talking about applications.

18.2 App

The App object is the top-level element within the structure of a SwiftUI application and is responsible for handling the launching and lifecycle of each running instance of the application.

The App element is also responsible for managing the various Scenes that make up the user interface of the application. An application will include only one App instance.

18.3 Scenes

Each SwiftUI application will contain one or more scenes. A scene represents a section or region of the application's user interface. On iOS and watchOS a scene will typically take the form of a window which takes up the entire device screen. SwiftUI applications running on macOS and iPadOS, on the other hand, will likely be comprised of multiple scenes. Different scenes might, for example, contain context specific layouts to be displayed when tabs are selected by the user within a dialog, or to design applications that consist of multiple windows.

SwiftUI includes some pre-built primitive scene types that can be used when designing applications, the most common of which being WindowGroup and DocumentGroup. It is also possible to group scenes together to create your own custom scenes.

18.4 Views

Views are the basic building blocks that make up the visual elements of the user interface such as buttons, labels and text fields. Each scene will contain a hierarchy of the views that make up a section of the application's user interface. Views can either be individual visual elements such as text views or buttons, or take the form of containers that manage other views. The Vertical Stack view, for example, is designed to display child views in a vertical layout. In addition to the Views provided with SwiftUI, you will also create custom views when developing SwiftUI applications. These custom views will comprise groups of other views together with customizations to the appearance and behavior of those views to meet the requirements of the application's user interface.

Figure 18-2, for example, illustrates a scene containing a simple view hierarchy consisting of a Vertical Stack containing a Button and TextView combination:

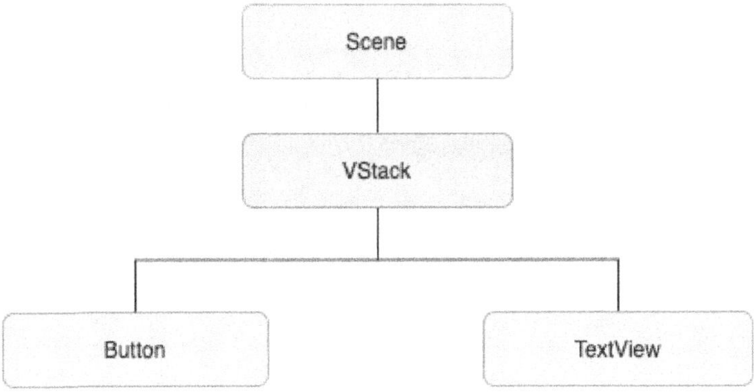

Figure 18-2

18.5 Summary

SwiftUI applications are constructed hierarchically. At the top of the hierarchy is the App instance which is responsible for the launching and lifecycle of the application. One or more child Scene instances contain hierarchies of the View instances that make up the user interface of the application. These scenes can either be derived from one of the SwiftUI primitive Scene types such as WindowGroup, or custom built.

On iOS or watchOS, an application will typically contain a single scene which takes the form of a window occupying the entire display. On a macOS or iPadOS system, however, an application may comprise multiple scene instances, often represented by separate windows which can be displayed simultaneously or grouped together in a tabbed interface.

19. The Anatomy of a Basic SwiftUI Project

When a new SwiftUI project is created in Xcode using the Multiplatform App template, Xcode generates a collection of files and folders which form the basis of the project, and on which the finished app will eventually be built.

Although it is not necessary to know in detail about the purpose of each of these files when beginning with SwiftUI development, each of them will become useful as you progress to developing more complex applications.

This chapter will provide a brief overview of each element of a basic Xcode project structure.

19.1 Creating an Example Project

If you have not already done so, it may be useful to create a sample project to review while working through this chapter. To do so, launch Xcode and, on the welcome screen, select the option to create a new project. On the resulting template selection panel, select the Multiplatform tab followed by the App option before proceeding to the next screen:

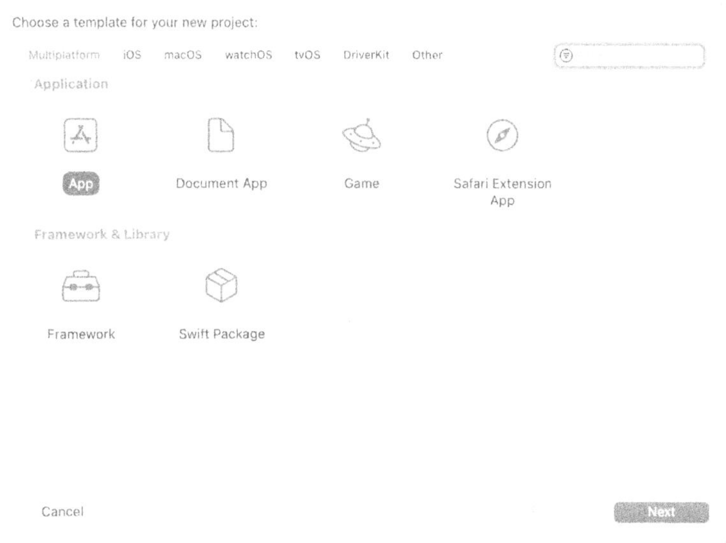

Figure 19-1

On the project options screen, name the project *DemoProject*. Click Next to proceed to the final screen, choose a suitable filesystem location for the project and click on the Create button.

19.2 The DemoProjectApp.swift File

The *DemoProjectApp.swift* file contains the declaration for the App object as described in the chapter entitled *"SwiftUI Architecture"* and will read as follows:

```
import SwiftUI
```

```
@main
struct DemoProjectApp: App {
    var body: some Scene {
        WindowGroup {
            ContentView()
        }
    }
}
```

As implemented, the declaration returns a Scene consisting of a WindowGroup containing the View defined in the *ContentView.swift* file. Note that the declaration is prefixed with *@main*. This indicates to SwiftUI that this is the entry point for the app when it is launched on a device.

19.3 The ContentView.swift File

This is a SwiftUI View file that, by default, contains the content of the first screen to appear when the app starts. This file and others like it are where most of the work is performed when developing apps in SwiftUI. By default, it contains an Image view and a Text view displaying the words "Hello, world!" arranged within a vertical stack container:

```
import SwiftUI

struct ContentView: View {
    var body: some View {
        VStack {
            Image(systemName: "globe")
                .imageScale(.large)
                .foregroundColor(.accentColor)
            Text("Hello, world!")
        }
    }
}

struct ContentView_Previews: PreviewProvider {
    static var previews: some View {
        ContentView()
    }
}
```

19.4 Assets.xcassets

The *Assets.xcassets* folder contains the asset catalog that is used to store resources used by the app such as images, icons, and colors.

19.5 DemoProject.entitlements

The entitlements file is used to enable support for specific iOS features within the app. For example, if your app needs access to iCloud storage or the device microphone, or if you plan to integrate voice control via Siri, these entitlements will first need to be enabled within this file.

19.6 Preview Content

The preview assets folder contains any assets and data that are needed when previewing the app during development, but that are not required in the completed app. When you are ready to package your app for submission to the app store, Xcode will remove these assets from the delivery archive so that they do not take up unnecessary space.

19.7 Summary

When a new SwiftUI project is created in Xcode using the Multiplatform App template, Xcode automatically generates the minimal set of files required for the app to function. All of these files and folders can be modified to add functionality to the app, both in terms of adding resource assets, performing initialization and de-initialization tasks, and building the user interface and logic of the app.

Chapter 20

20. Creating Custom Views with SwiftUI

A key step in learning to develop apps using SwiftUI is learning how to declare user interface layouts both by making use of the built-in SwiftUI views as well as building your own custom views. This chapter will introduce the basic concepts of SwiftUI views and outline the syntax used to declare user interface layouts and modify view appearance and behavior.

20.1 SwiftUI Views

User interface layouts are composed in SwiftUI by using, creating, and combining views. An important first step is to understand what is meant by the term "view". Views in SwiftUI are declared as structures that conform to the View protocol. To conform with the View protocol, a structure is required to contain a body property and it is within this body property that the view is declared.

SwiftUI includes a wide range of built-in views that can be used when constructing a user interface including text label, button, text field, menu, toggle, and layout manager views. Each of these is a self-contained instance that complies with the View protocol. When building an app with SwiftUI you will use these views to create custom views of your own which, when combined, constitute the appearance and behavior of your user interface.

These custom views will range from subviews that encapsulate a reusable subset of view components (perhaps a secure text field and a button for logging in to screens within your app) to views that encapsulate the user interface for an entire screen. Regardless of the size and complexity of a custom view or the number of child views encapsulated within, a view is still just an instance that defines some user interface appearance and behavior.

20.2 Creating a Basic View

In Xcode, custom views are contained within SwiftUI View files. When a new SwiftUI project is created, Xcode will create a single SwiftUI View file containing a single custom view consisting of a single Text view component. Additional view files can be added to the project by selecting the *File -> New -> File...* menu option and choosing the SwiftUI View file entry from the template screen.

The default SwiftUI View file is named *ContentView.swift* and reads as follows:

```
import SwiftUI

struct ContentView: View {
    var body: some View {
        VStack {
            Image(systemName: "globe")
                .imageScale(.large)
                .foregroundColor(.accentColor)
            Text("Hello, world!")
        }
    }
}
```

```
struct ContentView_Previews: PreviewProvider {
    static var previews: some View {
        ContentView()
    }
}
```

The view is named ContentView and is declared as conforming to the View protocol. It also includes the mandatory body property which, in turn, contains a vertical stack layout container containing an Image component configured to display a globe graphic and an instance of the built-in Text view component displaying text that reads "Hello, World!".

The second structure in the file is needed to create an instance of ContentView so that it appears in the preview canvas, a topic that will be covered in detail in later chapters.

20.3 Adding Views

Additional views can be added to a parent view by placing them in the body. The body property, however, is designed to return a single view. In this example, the body element is returning the VStack instance containing the child Image and Text views. Adding a view outside the scope of the VStack container will cause Xcode to create a second preview containing just the "Goodbye, world!" text view:

```
struct ContentView: View {
    var body: some View {
        VStack {
            Image(systemName: "globe")
                .imageScale(.large)
                .foregroundColor(.accentColor)
            Text("Hello, world!")
        }
        Text("Goodbye, world!")
    }
}
```

After this change, Xcode will add another preview button that can be clicked to display the "Goodbye, world!" preview as shown below:

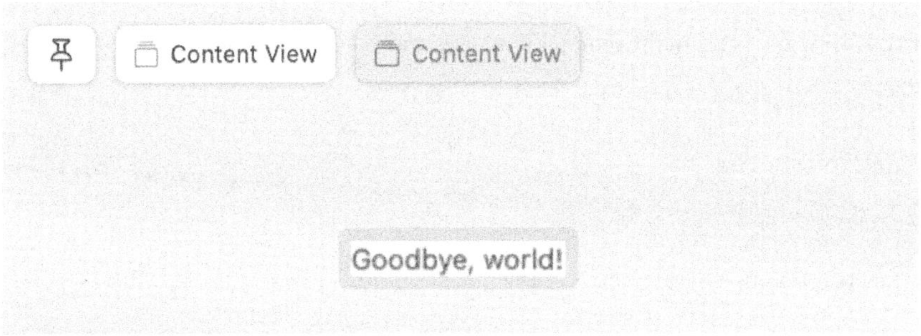

Figure 20-1

To correctly add additional views, those views must be placed in a container view such as a stack or form. The above example should, therefore, be modified to place the additional Text view within the VStack view which, as the name suggests, positions views vertically within the containing view:

```
struct ContentView: View {
    var body: some View {
        VStack {
            Image(systemName: "globe")
                .imageScale(.large)
                .foregroundColor(.accentColor)
            Text("Hello, world!")
            Text("Goodbye, world!")
        }
    }
}
```

SwiftUI views are hierarchical by nature, starting with parent and child views. This allows views to be nested to multiple levels to create user interfaces of any level of complexity. Consider, for example, the following view hierarchy diagram:

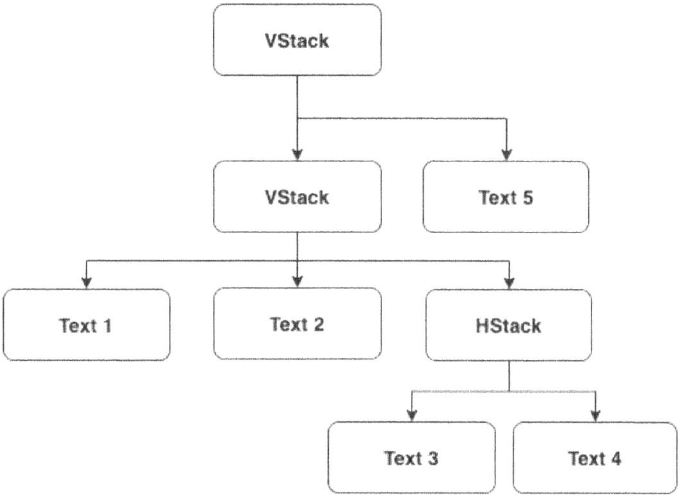

Figure 20-2

The equivalent view declaration for the above view would read as follows:

```
struct ContentView: View {
    var body: some View {
        VStack {
            VStack {
                Text("Text 1")
                Text("Text 2")
                HStack {
                    Text("Text 3")
                    Text("Text 4")
                }
            }
            Text("Text 5")
        }
    }
```

```
}
```

A notable exception to the requirement that multiple views be embedded in a container is that multiple Text views count as a single view when concatenated. The following, therefore, is a valid view declaration:

```
struct ContentView: View {
    var body: some View {
        Text("Hello, ") + Text("how ") + Text("are you?")
    }
}
```

Note that in the above examples the closure for the body property does not have a return statement. This is because the closure essentially contains a single expression (implicit returns from single expressions were covered in the chapter entitled *"Swift Functions, Methods and Closures"*). As soon as extra expressions are added to the closure, however, it will be necessary to add a return statement, for example:

```
struct ContentView: View {

    @State var fileopen: Bool = true

    var body: some View {

        var myString: String = "File closed"

        if (fileopen) {
            myString = "File open"
        }

        return VStack {
            HStack {
                Text(myString)
                    .padding()
                Text("Goodbye, world")
                }
            }
    }
}
```

When the following syntax error appears within the code editor it usually means a return statement is needed.

```
Type '()' cannot conform to 'View'
```

20.4 Working with Subviews

Apple recommends that views be kept as small and lightweight as possible. This promotes the creation of reusable components, makes view declarations easier to maintain, and results in more efficient layout rendering.

If you find that a custom view declaration has become large and complex, identify areas of the view that can be extracted into a subview. As a very simplistic example, the HStack view in the above example could be extracted as a subview named "MyHStackView" as follows:

```
struct ContentView: View {
    var body: some View {
```

```
        VStack {
            VStack {
                Text("Text 1")
                Text("Text 2")
                MyHStackView()
            }
            Text("Text 5")
        }
    }
}

struct MyHStackView: View {
    var body: some View {
        HStack {
            Text("Text 3")
            Text("Text 4")
        }
    }
}
```

20.5 Views as Properties

In addition to creating subviews, views may also be assigned to properties as a way to organize complex view hierarchies. Consider the following example view declaration:

```
struct ContentView: View {

    var body: some View {

        VStack {
            Text("Main Title")
                .font(.largeTitle)
            HStack {
                Text("Car Image")
                Image(systemName: "car.fill")
            }
        }
    }
}
```

Any part of the above declaration can be moved to a property value, and then referenced by name. In the following declaration, the HStack has been assigned to a property named carStack which is then referenced within the VStack layout:

```
struct ContentView: View {

    let carStack = HStack {
        Text("Car Image")
        Image(systemName: "car.fill")
```

```
    }

    var body: some View {
        VStack {
            Text("Main Title")
                .font(.largeTitle)
            carStack
        }
    }
}
```

20.6 Modifying Views

It is unlikely that any of the views provided with SwiftUI will appear and behave exactly as required without some form of customization. These changes are made by applying *modifiers* to the views.

All SwiftUI views have sets of modifiers that can be applied to make appearance and behavior changes. These modifiers take the form of methods that are called on the instance of the view and essentially wrap the original view inside another view which applies the necessary changes. This means that modifiers can be chained together to apply multiple modifications to the same view. The following, for example, changes the font and foreground color of a Text view:

```
Text("Text 1")
    .font(.headline)
    .foregroundColor(.red)
```

Similarly, the following example uses modifiers to configure an Image view to be resizable with the aspect ratio set to fit proportionally within the available space:

```
Image(systemName: "car.fill")
    .resizable()
    .aspectRatio(contentMode: .fit)
```

Modifiers may also be applied to custom subviews. In the following example, the font for both Text views in the previously declared MyHStackView custom view will be changed to use the large title font style:

```
MyHStackView()
    .font(.largeTitle)
```

20.7 Working with Text Styles

In the above example, the font used to display text on a view was declared using a built-in text style (in this case the large title style).

iOS provides a way for the user to select a preferred text size that applications are expected to adopt when displaying text. The current text size can be configured on a device via the *Settings -> Display & Brightness -> Text Size* screen which provides a slider to adjust the font size as shown below:

Figure 20-3

If a font has been declared on a view using a text style, the text size will dynamically adapt to the user's preferred font size. Almost without exception, the built-in iOS apps adopt the preferred size setting selected by the user when displaying text and Apple recommends that third-party apps also conform to the user's chosen text size. The following text style options are currently available:

- Large Title
- Title, Title2, Title 3
- Headline
- Subheadline
- Body
- Callout
- Footnote
- Caption1, Caption2

If none of the text styles meet your requirements, it is also possible to apply custom fonts by declaring the font family and size. Although the font size is specified in the custom font, the text will still automatically resize based on the user's preferred dynamic type text size selection:

```
Text("Sample Text")
    .font(.custom("Copperplate", size: 70))
```

The above custom font selection will render the Text view as follows:

Figure 20-4

20.8 Modifier Ordering

When chaining modifiers, it is important to be aware that the order in which they are applied can be significant. Both border and padding modifiers have been applied to the following Text view.

```
Text("Sample Text")
    .border(Color.black)
    .padding()
```

The border modifier draws a black border around the view and the padding modifier adds space around the view. When the above view is rendered it will appear as shown in Figure 20-5:

Figure 20-5

Given that padding has been applied to the text, it might be reasonable to expect there to be a gap between the text and the border. In fact, the border was only applied to the original Text view. Padding was then applied to the modified view returned by the border modifier. The padding is still applied to the view, but outside of the border. For the border to encompass the padding, the order of the modifiers needs to be changed so that the border is drawn on the view returned by the padding modifier:

```
Text("Sample Text")
    .padding()
    .border(Color.black)
```

With the modifier order switched, the view will now be rendered as follows:

Figure 20-6

If you don't see the expected effects when working with chained modifiers, keep in mind this may be because of the order in which they are being applied to the view.

20.9 Custom Modifiers

SwiftUI also allows you to create your own custom modifiers. This can be particularly useful if you have a standard set of modifiers that are frequently applied to views. Suppose that the following modifiers are a common requirement within your view declarations:

```
Text("Text 1")
    .font(.largeTitle)
    .background(Color.white)
    .border(Color.gray, width: 0.2)
    .shadow(color: Color.black, radius: 5, x: 0, y: 5)
```

Instead of applying these four modifiers each time text with this appearance is required, a better solution is to group them into a custom modifier and then reference that modifier each time the modification is needed. Custom modifiers are declared as structs that conform to the ViewModifier protocol and, in this instance, might be implemented as follows:

```
struct StandardTitle: ViewModifier {
   func body(content: Content) -> some View {
        content
            .font(.largeTitle)
            .background(Color.white)
            .border(Color.gray, width: 0.2)
            .shadow(color: Color.black, radius: 5, x: 0, y: 5)
    }
}
```

The custom modifier is then applied when needed by passing it through to the *modifier()* method:

```
Text("Text 1")
    .modifier(StandardTitle())
Text("Text 2")
    .modifier(StandardTitle())
```

With the custom modifier implemented, changes can be made to the StandardTitle implementation and those changes will automatically propagate through to all views that use the modifier. This avoids the need to manually change the modifiers on multiple views.

20.10 Basic Event Handling

Although SwiftUI is described as being data-driven, it is still necessary to handle the events that are generated when a user interacts with the views in the user interface. Some views, such as the Button view, are provided solely to solicit user interaction. In fact, the Button view can be used to turn a variety of different views into a "clickable" button. A Button view needs to be declared with the action method to be called when a click is detected together with the view to act as the button content. It is possible, for example, to designate an entire stack of views as a single button. In most cases, however, a Text view will typically be used as the Button content. In the following implementation, a Button view is used to wrap a Text view which, when clicked, will call a method named *buttonPressed()*:

```
struct ContentView: View {
    var body: some View {
        Button(action: buttonPressed) {
            Text("Click Me")
        }
```

```
    }

    func buttonPressed() {
        // Code to perform action here
    }
}
```

Instead of specifying an action function, the code to be executed when the button is clicked may also be specified as a closure in-line with the declaration:

```
Button(action: {
    // Code to perform action here
}) {
    Text("Click Me")
}
```

Another common requirement is to turn an Image view into a button, for example:

```
Button(action: {
    print("Button clicked")
}) {
    Image(systemName: "square.and.arrow.down")
}
```

20.11 Building Custom Container Views

As outlined earlier in this chapter, subviews provide a useful way to divide a view declaration into small, lightweight, and reusable blocks. One limitation of subviews, however, is that the content of the container view is static. In other words, it is not possible to dynamically specify the views that are to be included at the point that a subview is included in a layout. The only children included in the subview are those that are specified in the original declaration.

Consider the following subview which consists of three TextViews contained within a VStack and modified with custom spacing and font settings.

```
struct MyVStack: View {
    var body: some View {
        VStack(spacing: 10) {
            Text("Text Item 1")
            Text("Text Item 2")
            Text("Text Item 3")
        }
        .font(.largeTitle)
    }
}
```

To include an instance of MyVStack in a declaration, it would be referenced as follows:

```
MyVStack()
```

Suppose, however, that a VStack with a spacing of 10 and a large font modifier is something that is needed frequently within a project, but in each case, different child views are required to be contained within the stack. While this flexibility isn't possible using subviews, it can be achieved using the SwiftUI ViewBuilder closure attribute when constructing custom container views.

A ViewBuilder takes the form of a Swift closure which can be used to create a custom view comprised of multiple child views, the content of which does not need to be declared until the view is used within a layout declaration. The ViewBuilder closure takes the content views and returns them as a single view which is, in effect, a dynamically built subview.

The following is an example of using the ViewBuilder attribute to implement our custom MyVStack view:

```
struct MyVStack<Content: View>: View {
  let content: () -> Content
  init(@ViewBuilder content: @escaping () -> Content) {
    self.content = content
  }

  var body: some View {
    VStack(spacing: 10) {
      content()
    }
    .font(.largeTitle)
  }
}
```

Note that this declaration still returns an instance that complies with the View protocol and that the body contains the VStack declaration from the previous subview. Instead of including static views to be included in the stack, however, the child views of the stack will be passed to the initializer, handled by ViewBuilder, and embedded into the VStack as child views. The custom MyVStack view can now be initialized with different child views wherever it is used in a layout, for example:

```
MyVStack {
    Text("Text 1")
    Text("Text 2")
    HStack {
        Image(systemName: "star.fill")
        Image(systemName: "star.fill")
        Image(systemName: "star")
    }
}
```

20.12 Working with the Label View

The Label view is different from most other SwiftUI views in that it comprises two elements in the form of an icon and text positioned side-by-side. The image can take the form of any image asset, a SwiftUI Shape rendering, or an SF Symbol.

SF Symbols is a collection of thousands of scalable vector drawings available for use when developing apps for Apple platforms and designed to complement Apple's San Francisco system font.

The full set of symbols can be browsed and selected via the Symbols screen of the Library panel as illustrated in Figure 20-7:

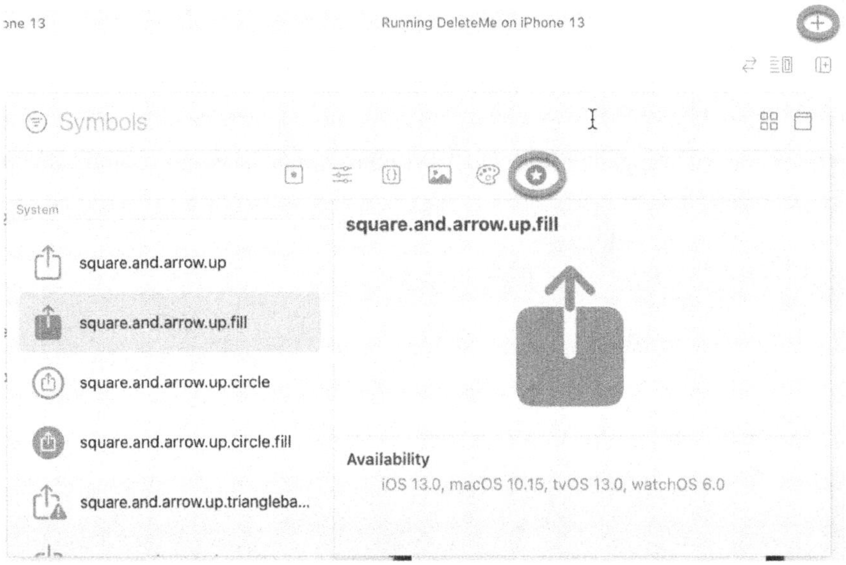

Figure 20-7

The following is an example of the Label view using an SF Symbol together with a *font()* modifier to increase the size of the icon and text:

```
Label("Welcome to SwiftUI", systemImage: "person.circle.fill")
    .font(.largeTitle)
```

The above view will be rendered as shown in Figure 20-8 below:

Figure 20-8

By referencing *systemImage:* in the Label view declaration, we are indicating that the icon is to be taken from the built-in SF Symbol collection. To display an image from the app's asset catalog, the following syntax would be used instead:

```
Label("Welcome to SwiftUI", image: "myimage")
```

Instead of specifying a text string and an image, the Label may also be declared using separate views for the title and icon. The following Label view declaration, for example, uses a Text view for the title and a Circle drawing for the icon:

```
Label(
    title: {
        Text("Welcome to SwiftUI")
        .font(.largeTitle)
    },
    icon: { Circle()
        .fill(Color.blue)
```

```
            .frame(width: 25, height: 25)
        }
)
```

When rendered, the above Label view will appear as shown in Figure 20-9:

Figure 20-9

20.13 Summary

SwiftUI user interfaces are declared in SwiftUI View files and are composed of components that conform to the View protocol. To conform with the View protocol a structure must contain a property named body which is itself a View.

SwiftUI provides a library of built-in components for use when designing user interface layouts. The appearance and behavior of a view can be configured by applying modifiers, and views can be modified and grouped to create custom views and subviews. Similarly, custom container views can be created using the ViewBuilder closure property.

When a modifier is applied to a view, a new modified view is returned and subsequent modifiers are then applied to this modified view. This can have significant implications for the order in which modifiers are applied to a view.

Chapter 21

21. SwiftUI Stacks and Frames

User interface design is largely a matter of selecting the appropriate interface components, deciding how those views will be positioned on the screen, and then implementing navigation between the different screens and views of the app.

As is to be expected, SwiftUI includes a wide range of user interface components to be used when developing an app such as button, label, slider and toggle views. SwiftUI also provides a set of layout views for the purpose of defining both how the user interface is organized and the way in which the layout responds to changes in screen orientation and size.

This chapter will introduce the Stack container views included with SwiftUI and explain how they can be used to create user interface designs with relative ease.

Once stack views have been explained, this chapter will cover the concept of flexible frames and explain how they can be used to control the sizing behavior of views in a layout.

21.1 SwiftUI Stacks

SwiftUI includes three stack layout views in the form of VStack (vertical), HStack (horizontal) and ZStack (views are layered on top of each other).

A stack is declared by embedding child views into a stack view within the SwiftUI View file. In the following view, for example, three Image views have been embedded within an HStack:

```
struct ContentView: View {
    var body: some View {
        HStack {
            Image(systemName: "goforward.10")
            Image(systemName: "goforward.15")
            Image(systemName: "goforward.30")
        }
    }
}
```

Within the preview canvas, the above layout will appear as illustrated in Figure 21-1:

Figure 21-1

A similarly configured example using a VStack would accomplish the same results with the images stacked vertically:

```
VStack {
    Image(systemName: "goforward.10")
```

```
    Image(systemName: "goforward.15")
    Image(systemName: "goforward.30")
}
```

To embed an existing component into a stack, either wrap it manually within a stack declaration, or hover the mouse pointer over the component in the editor so that it highlights, hold down the Command key on the keyboard and left-click on the component. From the resulting menu (Figure 21-2) select the appropriate option :

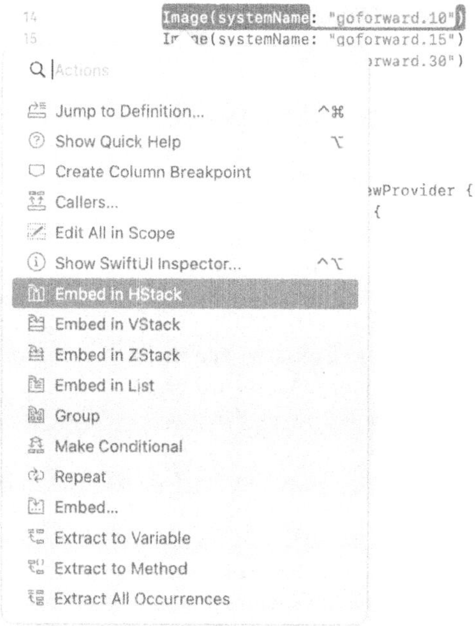

Figure 21-2

Layouts of considerable complexity can be designed simply by embedding stacks within other stacks, for example:

```
VStack {
    Text("Financial Results")
        .font(.title)

    HStack {
        Text("Q1 Sales")
            .font(.headline)

        VStack {
            Text("January")
            Text("February")
            Text("March")
        }

        VStack {
            Text("$1000")
            Text("$200")
            Text("$3000")
```

```
            }
        }
}
```

The above layout will appear as shown in Figure 21-3:

Figure 21-3

As currently configured the layout clearly needs some additional work, particularly in terms of alignment and spacing. The layout can be improved in this regard using a combination of alignment settings, the Spacer component and the padding modifier.

21.2 Spacers, Alignment and Padding

To add space between views, SwiftUI includes the Spacer component. When used in a stack layout, the spacer will flexibly expand and contract along the axis of the containing stack (in other words either horizontally or vertically) to provide a gap between views positioned on either side, for example:

```
HStack(alignment: .top) {
    Text("Q1 Sales")
        .font(.headline)
    Spacer()
    VStack(alignment: .leading) {
        Text("January")
        Text("February")
        Text("March")
    }
    Spacer()
.
.
```

In terms of aligning the content of a stack, this can be achieved by specifying an alignment value when the stack is declared, for example:

```
VStack(alignment: .center) {
            Text("Financial Results")
                .font(.title)
```

Alignments may also be specified with a corresponding spacing value:

```
VStack(alignment: .center, spacing: 15) {
            Text("Financial Results")
                .font(.title)
```

Spacing around the sides of any view may also be implemented using the *padding()* modifier. When called without a parameter SwiftUI will automatically use the best padding for the layout, content and screen size (referred to as *adaptable padding*). The following example sets adaptable padding on all four sides of a Text view:

```
Text("Hello, world!")
    .padding()
```

Alternatively, a specific amount of padding may be passed as a parameter to the modifier as follows:

```
Text("Hello, world!")
    .padding(15)
```

Padding may also be applied to a specific side of a view with or without a specific value. In the following example a specific padding size is applied to the top edge of a Text view:

```
Text("Hello, world!")
    .padding(.top, 10)
```

Making use of these options, the example layout created earlier in the chapter can be modified as follows:

```
VStack(alignment: .center, spacing: 15) {
        Text("Financial Results")
            .font(.title)

        HStack(alignment: .top) {
            Text("Q1 Sales")
                .font(.headline)
            Spacer()
            VStack(alignment: .leading) {
                Text("January")
                Text("February")
                Text("March")
            }
            Spacer()
            VStack(alignment: .leading) {
                Text("$1000")
                Text("$200")
                Text("$3000")
            }
            .padding(5)
        }
        .padding(5)
    }
    .padding(5)
}
```

With the alignments, spacers and padding modifiers added, the layout should now resemble the following figure:

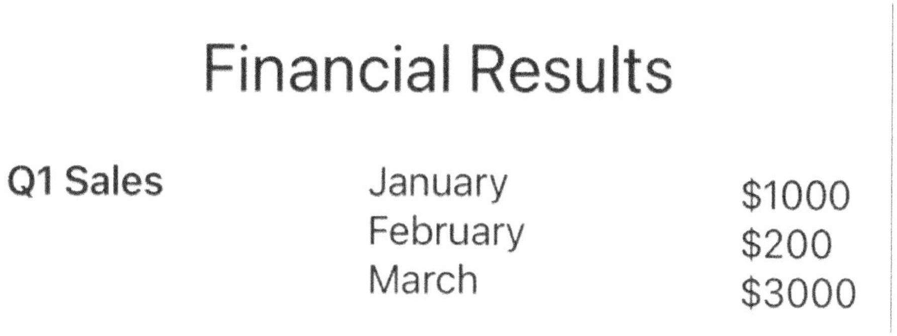

Figure 21-4

More advanced stack alignment topics will be covered in a later chapter entitled *"SwiftUI Stack Alignment and Alignment Guides"*.

21.3 Container Child Limit

Container views are limited to 10 direct descendant views. If a stack contains more than 10 direct children, Xcode will likely display the following syntax error:

```
Extra arguments at positions #11, #12 in call
```

If a stack exceeds the 10 direct children limit, the views will need to be embedded into multiple containers. This can, of course, be achieved by adding stacks as subviews, but another useful container is the Group view. In the following example, a VStack can contain 12 Text views by splitting the views between Group containers giving the VStack only two direct descendants:

```
VStack {

    Group {
        Text("Sample Text")
        Text("Sample Text")
        Text("Sample Text")
        Text("Sample Text")
        Text("Sample Text")
        Text("Sample Text")
    }

    Group {
        Text("Sample Text")
        Text("Sample Text")
        Text("Sample Text")
        Text("Sample Text")
        Text("Sample Text")
        Text("Sample Text")
    }
}
```

In addition to providing a way to avoid the 10-view limit, groups are also useful when performing an operation on multiple views (for example, a set of related views can all be hidden in a single operation by embedding them in a Group and hiding that view).

21.4 Dynamic HStack and VStack Conversion

The choice between an HStack and a VStack during the design phase does need to be final. SwiftUI allows the type of stack used in a layout to be changed dynamically from within the app code. We achieve this by creating an AnyLayout instance and assigning it either an HStackLayout or VStackLayout container. In the example below, we have assigned an AnyLayout instance to a state variable and configured it to stack children using the HStackLayout container. We then use this layout to arrange two Image views. Finally, we add two Button views to switch between horizontal and vertical orientation by changing the container type assigned to myLayout:

```
@State var myLayout: AnyLayout = AnyLayout(VStackLayout())


var body: some View {


    VStack {
        myLayout {
            Image(systemName: "goforward.10")
                .resizable()
                .aspectRatio(contentMode: .fit)
            Image(systemName: "goforward.15")
                .resizable()
                .aspectRatio(contentMode: .fit)
        }


        HStack {
            Button(action: {
                layout = AnyLayout(HStackLayout()) }){
                Text("HStack")
            }
            Button(action: {
                layout = AnyLayout(VStackLayout()) }) {
                Text("VStack")
            }
        }
    }
}
```

21.5 Text Line Limits and Layout Priority

By default, an HStack will attempt to display the text within its Text view children on a single line. Take, for example, the following HStack declaration containing an Image view and two Text views:

```
HStack {
    Image(systemName: "airplane")
    Text("Flight times:")
    Text("London")
}
.font(.largeTitle)
```

If the stack has enough room, the above layout will appear as follows:

Figure 21-5

If a stack has insufficient room (for example if it is constrained by a frame or is competing for space with sibling views) the text will automatically wrap onto multiple lines when necessary:

Figure 21-6

While this may work for some situations, it may become an issue if the user interface is required to display this text in a single line. The number of lines over which text can flow can be restricted using the *lineCount()* modifier. The example HStack could, therefore, be limited to 1 line of text with the following change:

```
HStack {
    Image(systemName: "airplane")
    Text("Flight times:")
    Text("London")
}
.font(.largeTitle)
.lineLimit(1)
```

A line limit restriction can also be specified as a range that provides the maximum and minimum number lines over which text can be displayed:

```
.lineLimit(1...4)
```

When an HStack has insufficient space to display the full text and is not permitted to wrap the text over enough lines, the view will resort to truncating the text, as is the case in Figure 21-7:

Figure 21-7

In the absence of any priority guidance, the stack view will decide how to truncate the Text views based on the available space and the length of the views. Obviously, the stack has no way of knowing whether the text in one view is more important than the text in another unless the text view declarations include some priority information. This is achieved by making use of the *layoutPriority()* modifier. This modifier can be added to the views in the stack and passed values indicating the level of priority for the corresponding view. The higher the number, the greater the layout priority and the less the view will be subjected to truncation.

Assuming the flight destination city name is more important than the "Flight times:" text, the example stack could be modified as follows:

```
HStack {
    Image(systemName: "airplane")
    Text("Flight times:")
    Text("London")
        .layoutPriority(1)
}
.font(.largeTitle)
.lineLimit(1)
```

With a higher priority assigned to the city Text view (in the absence of a layout priority the other text view defaults to a priority of 0) the layout will now appear as illustrated in Figure 21-8:

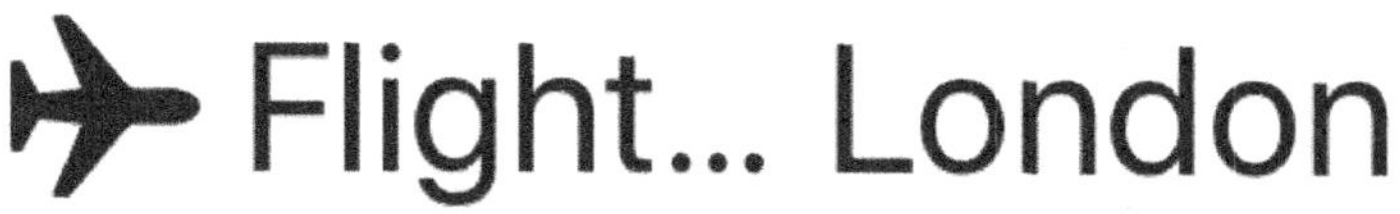

Figure 21-8

21.6 Traditional vs. Lazy Stacks

So far in this chapter we have only covered the HStack, VStack and ZStack views. Although the stack examples shown so far contain relatively few child views, it is possible for a stack to contain large quantities of views. This is particularly common when a stack is embedded in a ScrollView. ScrollView is a view which allows the user to scroll through content that extends beyond the visible area of either the containing view or device the screen.

When using the traditional HStack and VStack views, the system will create all the views child views at initialization, regardless of whether those views are currently visible to the user. While this may not be an issue for most requirements, this can lead to performance degradation in situations where a stack has thousands of child views.

To address this issue, SwiftUI also provides "lazy" vertical and horizontal stack views. These views (named LazyVStack and LazyHStack) use exactly the same declaration syntax as the traditional stack views, but are designed to only create child views as they are needed. For example, as the user scrolls through a stack, views that are currently off screen will only be created once they approach the point of becoming visible to the user. Once those views pass out of the viewing area, SwiftUI releases those views so that they no longer take up system resources.

When deciding whether to use traditional or lazy stacks, it is generally recommended to start out using the traditional stacks and to switch to lazy stacks if you encounter performance issues relating to a high number of child views.

21.7 SwiftUI Frames

By default, a view will be sized automatically based on its content and the requirements of any layout in which it may be embedded. Although much can be achieved using the stack layouts to control the size and positioning of a view, sometimes a view is required to be a specific size or to fit within a range of size dimensions. To address this need, SwiftUI includes the flexible frame modifier.

Consider the following Text view which has been modified to display a border:

```
Text("Hello World")
    .font(.largeTitle)
    .border(Color.black)
```

Within the preview canvas, the above text view will appear as follows:

Figure 21-9

In the absence of a frame, the text view has been sized to accommodate its content. If the Text view was required to have height and width dimensions of 100, however, a frame could be applied as follows:

```
Text("Hello World")
    .font(.largeTitle)
    .border(Color.black)
    .frame(width: 100, height: 100, alignment: .center)
```

Now that the Text view is constrained within a frame, the view will appear as follows:

Figure 21-10

In many cases, fixed dimensions will provide the required behavior. In other cases, such as when the content of a view changes dynamically, this can cause problems. Increasing the length of the text, for example, might cause the content to be truncated:

Figure 21-11

This can be resolved by creating a frame with minimum and maximum dimensions:

```
Text("Hello World, how are you?")
            .font(.largeTitle)
            .border(Color.black)
            .frame(minWidth: 100, maxWidth: 300, minHeight: 100,
                   maxHeight: 100, alignment: .center)
```

Now that the frame has some flexibility, the view will be sized to accommodate the content within the defined minimum and maximum limits. When the text is short enough, the view will appear as shown in Figure 21-10 above. Longer text, however, will be displayed as follows:

Figure 21-12

Frames may also be configured to take up all the available space by setting the minimum and maximum values to 0 and infinity respectively:

```
.frame(minWidth: 0, maxWidth: .infinity, minHeight: 0,
          maxHeight: .infinity)
```

Remember that the order in which modifiers are chained often impacts the appearance of a view. In this case, if the border is to be drawn at the edges of the available space it will need to be applied to the frame:

```
Text("Hello World, how are you?")
    .font(.largeTitle)
    .frame(minWidth: 0, maxWidth: .infinity, minHeight: 0,
          maxHeight: .infinity)
    .border(Color.black, width: 5)
```

By default, the frame will honor the safe areas on the screen when filling the display. Areas considered to be outside the safe area include those occupied by the camera notch on some device models and the bar across the top of the screen displaying the time and WiFi and cellular signal strength icons. To configure the frame to extend beyond the safe area, simply use the *edgesIgnoringSafeArea()* modifier, specifying the safe area edges to ignore:

```
.edgesIgnoringSafeArea(.all)
```

21.8 Frames and the Geometry Reader

Frames can also be implemented so that they are sized relative to the size of the container within which the corresponding view is embedded. This is achieved by wrapping the view in a GeometryReader and using the reader to identify the container dimensions. These dimensions can then be used to calculate the frame size. The following example uses a frame to set the dimensions of two Text views relative to the size of the containing VStack:

```
GeometryReader { geometry in
```

```
    VStack {
        Text("Hello World, how are you?")
            .font(.largeTitle)
            .frame(width: geometry.size.width / 2,
                height: (geometry.size.height / 4) * 3)
        Text("Goodbye World")
            .font(.largeTitle)
            .frame(width: geometry.size.width / 3,
                height: geometry.size.height / 4)
    }
}
```

The topmost Text view is configured to occupy half the width and three quarters of the height of the VStack while the lower Text view occupies one third of the width and one quarter of the height.

21.9 Summary

User interface design mostly involves gathering components and laying them out on the screen in a way that provides a pleasant and intuitive user experience. User interface layouts must also be responsive so that they appear correctly on any device regardless of screen size and, ideally, device orientation. To ease the process of user interface layout design, SwiftUI provides several layout views and components. In this chapter we have looked at layout stack views and the flexible frame.

By default, a view will be sized according to its content and the restrictions imposed on it by any view in which it may be contained. When insufficient space is available, a view may be restricted in size resulting in truncated content. Priority settings can be used to control the amount by which views are reduced in size relative to container sibling views.

For greater control of the space allocated to a view, a flexible frame can be applied to the view. The frame can be fixed in size, constrained within a range of minimum and maximum values or, using a Geometry Reader, sized relative to the containing view.

Chapter 22

22. SwiftUI State Properties, Observable, State, and Environment Objects

Earlier chapters have described how SwiftUI emphasizes a data-driven approach to app development whereby the views in the user interface are updated in response to changes in the underlying data without the need to write handling code. This approach is achieved by establishing a publisher and subscriber binding between the data and the views in the user interface.

SwiftUI offers four options for implementing this behavior in the form of *state properties*, *observable objects*, *state objects*, and *environment objects*, all of which provide the *state* that drives the way the user interface appears and behaves. In SwiftUI, the views that make up a user interface layout are never updated directly within code. Instead, the views are updated automatically based on the state objects to which they have been bound as they change over time.

This chapter will describe these four options and outline when they should be used. Later chapters *"A SwiftUI Example Tutorial"* and *"SwiftUI Observable and Environment Objects – A Tutorial"*) will provide practical examples that demonstrate their use.

22.1 State Properties

The most basic form of state is the state property. State properties are used exclusively to store state that is local to a view layout such as whether a toggle button is enabled, the text being entered into a text field, or the current selection in a Picker view. State properties are used for storing simple data types such as a String or an Int value and are declared using the *@State* property wrapper, for example:

```
struct ContentView: View {

    @State private var wifiEnabled = true
    @State private var userName = ""

    var body: some View {
.
.
```

Note that since state values are local to the enclosing view they should be declared as private properties.

Every change to a state property value is a signal to SwiftUI that the view hierarchy within which the property is declared needs to be re-rendered. This involves rapidly recreating and displaying all of the views in the hierarchy. This, in turn, has the effect of ensuring that any views that rely on the property in some way are updated to reflect the latest value.

Once declared, bindings can be established between state properties and the views contained in the layout. Changes within views that reference the binding are then automatically reflected in the corresponding state property. A binding could, for example, be established between a Toggle view and the Boolean wifiEnabled property declared above. Whenever the user switches the toggle, SwiftUI will automatically update the state property to match the new toggle setting.

A binding to a state property is implemented by prefixing the property name with a '$' sign. In the following example, a TextField view establishes a binding to the userName state property to use as the storage for text entered by the user:

```
struct ContentView: View {

    @State private var wifiEnabled = true
    @State private var userName = ""

    var body: some View {
        VStack {
            TextField("Enter user name", text: $userName)
        }
    }
}
```

With each keystroke performed as the user types into the TextField, the binding will store the current text into the userName property. Each change to the state property will, in turn, cause the view hierarchy to be re-rendered by SwiftUI.

Of course, storing something in a state property is only one side of the process. As previously discussed, a change of state usually results in a change to other views in the layout. In this case, a Text view might need to be updated to reflect the user's name as it is being typed. This can be achieved by declaring the userName state property value as the content for a Text view:

```
var body: some View {
    VStack {
        TextField("Enter user name", text: $userName)
        Text(userName)
    }
}
```

As the user types, the Text view will automatically update to reflect the user's input. Note that in this case the userName property is declared without the '$' prefix. This is because we are now referencing the value assigned to the state property (i.e. the String value being typed by the user) instead of a binding to the property.

Similarly, the hypothetical binding between a Toggle view and the wifiEnabled state property described above could be implemented as follows:

```
var body: some View {

    VStack {
        Toggle(isOn: $wifiEnabled) {
            Text("Enable Wi-Fi")
        }
        TextField("Enter user name", text: $userName)
        Text(userName)
        Image(systemName: wifiEnabled ? "wifi" : "wifi.slash")
```

```
    }
}
```

In the above declaration, a binding is established between the Toggle view and the state property. The value assigned to the property is then used to decide which image is to be displayed on an Image view.

22.2 State Binding

A state property is local to the view in which it is declared and any child views. Situations may occur, however, where a view contains one or more subviews that may also need access to the same state properties. Consider, for example, a situation whereby the WiFi Image view in the above example has been extracted into a subview:

```
.
.
    VStack {
        Toggle(isOn: $wifiEnabled) {
            Text("Enable WiFi")
        }
        TextField("Enter user name", text: $userName)
        WifiImageView()
    }
}
.
.
struct WifiImageView: View {

    var body: some View {
        Image(systemName: wifiEnabled ? "wifi" : "wifi.slash")
    }
}
```

Clearly, the WifiImageView subview still needs access to the wifiEnabled state property. As an element of a separate subview, however, the Image view is now out of the scope of the main view. Within the scope of WifiImageView, the wifiEnabled property is an undefined variable.

This problem can be resolved by declaring the property using the *@Binding* property wrapper as follows:

```
struct WifiImageView: View {

    @Binding var wifiEnabled : Bool

    var body: some View {
        Image(systemName: wifiEnabled ? "wifi" : "wifi.slash")
    }
}
```

Now, when the subview is called, it simply needs to be passed a binding to the state property:

```
WifiImageView(wifiEnabled: $wifiEnabled)
```

22.3 Observable Objects

State properties provide a way to locally store the state of a view, are available only to the local view and, as such, cannot be accessed by other views unless they are subviews and state binding is implemented. State properties are also transient in that when the parent view goes away the state is also lost. Observable objects, on the other hand, are used to represent persistent data that is both external and accessible to multiple views.

An Observable object takes the form of a class or structure that conforms to the ObservableObject protocol. Though the implementation of an observable object will be application-specific depending on the nature and source of the data, it will typically be responsible for gathering and managing one or more data values that are known to change over time. Observable objects can also be used to handle events such as timers and notifications.

The observable object *publishes* the data values for which it is responsible as *published properties*. Observer objects then *subscribe* to the publisher and receive updates whenever changes to the published properties occur. As with the state properties outlined above, by binding to these published properties SwiftUI views will automatically update to reflect changes in the data stored in the observable object.

Observable objects are part of the Combine framework, which was first introduced with iOS 13 to make it easier to establish relationships between publishers and subscribers.

The Combine framework provides a platform for building custom publishers for performing a variety of tasks from the merging of multiple publishers into a single stream to transforming published data to match subscriber requirements. This allows for complex, enterprise-level data processing chains to be implemented between the original publisher and the resulting subscriber. That being said, one of the built-in publisher types will typically be all that is needed for most requirements. In fact, the easiest way to implement a published property within an observable object is to simply use the *@Published* property wrapper when declaring a property. This wrapper simply sends updates to all subscribers each time the wrapped property value changes.

The following structure declaration shows a simple observable object declaration with two published properties:

```
import Foundation
import Combine

class DemoData : ObservableObject {

    @Published var userCount = 0
    @Published var currentUser = ""

    init() {
        // Code here to initialize data
        updateData()
    }

    func updateData() {
        // Code here to keep data up to date
    }
}
```

A subscriber uses either the *@ObservedObject* or *@StateObject* property wrapper to subscribe to the observable object. Once subscribed, that view and any of its child views access the published properties using the same techniques used with state properties earlier in the chapter. A sample SwiftUI view designed to subscribe to an instance of the above DemoData class might read as follows:

```
import SwiftUI

struct ContentView: View {

    @ObservedObject var demoData : DemoData = DemoData()

    var body: some View {
        Text("\(demoData.currentUser), you are user number \(demoData.
userCount)")
    }
}

struct ContentView_Previews: PreviewProvider {
    static var previews: some View {
        ContentView()
    }
}
```

As the published data changes, SwiftUI will automatically re-render the view layout to reflect the new state.

22.4 State Objects

Introduced in iOS 14, the State Object property wrapper (@StateObject) is an alternative to the @ObservedObject wrapper. The key difference between a state object and an observed object is that an observed object reference is not owned by the view in which it is declared and, as such, is at risk of being destroyed or recreated by the SwiftUI system while still in use (for example as the result of the view being re-rendered).

Using @StateObject instead of @ObservedObject ensures that the reference is owned by the view in which it is declared and, therefore, will not be destroyed by SwiftUI while it is still needed, either by the local view in which it is declared or any child views.

As a general rule, unless there is a specific need to use @ObservedObject, the recommendation is to use a State Object to subscribe to observable objects. In terms of syntax, the two are entirely interchangeable:

```
import SwiftUI

struct ContentView: View {

    @StateObject var demoData : DemoData = DemoData()

    var body: some View {
        Text("\(demoData.currentUser), you are user number \(demoData.
userCount)")
    }
}
.
.
```

22.5 Environment Objects

Observed objects are best used when a particular state needs to be used by a few SwiftUI views within an app. When one view navigates to another view that needs access to the same observed or state object, the originating view will need to pass a reference to the observed object to the destination view during the navigation (navigation will be covered in the chapter entitled *"SwiftUI Lists and Navigation"*). Consider, for example, the following code:

```
.
.
@StateObject var demoData : DemoData = DemoData()
.
.
NavigationLink(destination: SecondView(demoData)) {
    Text("Next Screen")
}
```

In the above declaration, a navigation link is used to navigate to another view named SecondView, passing through a reference to the demoData observed object.

While this technique is acceptable for many situations, it can become complex when many views within an app need access to the same observed object. In this situation, it may make more sense to use an environment object.

An environment object is declared in the same way as an observable object (in that it must conform to the ObservableObject protocol and appropriate properties must be published). The key difference, however, is that the object is stored in the environment of the view in which it is declared and, as such, can be accessed by all child views without needing to be passed from view to view.

Consider the following example observable object declaration:

```
class SpeedSetting: ObservableObject {
    @Published var speed = 0.0
}
```

Views needing to subscribe to an environment object simply reference the object using the @EnvironmentObject property wrapper instead of the @StateObject or @ObservedObject wrapper. For example, the following views both need access to the same SpeedSetting data:

```
struct SpeedControlView: View {
    @EnvironmentObject var speedsetting: SpeedSetting

    var body: some View {
        Slider(value: $speedsetting.speed, in: 0...100)
    }
}

struct SpeedDisplayView: View {
    @EnvironmentObject var speedsetting: SpeedSetting

    var body: some View {
        Text("Speed = \(speedsetting.speed)")
    }
}
```

At this point, we have an observable object named SpeedSetting and two views that reference an environment object of that type, but we have not yet initialized an instance of the observable object. The logical place to perform this task is within the parent view of the above sub-views. In the following example, both views are sub-views of the main ContentView:

```
struct ContentView: View {
    let speedsetting = SpeedSetting()

    var body: some View {
        VStack {
            SpeedControlView()
            SpeedDisplayView()
        }
    }
}
```

If the app were to run at this point, however, it would crash shortly after launching with the following diagnostics:

```
Thread 1: Fatal error: No ObservableObject of type SpeedSetting found. A View.
environmentObject(_:) for SpeedSetting may be missing as an ancestor of this
view.
```

The problem here is that while we have created an instance of the observable object within the ContentView declaration, we have not yet inserted it into the view hierarchy. This is achieved using the *environmentObject()* modifier, passing through the observable object instance as follows:

```
struct ContentView: View {
    let speedsetting = SpeedSetting()

    var body: some View {
        VStack {
            SpeedControlView()
            SpeedDisplayView()
        }
        .environmentObject(speedsetting)
    }
}
```

Once these steps have been taken the object will behave in the same way as an observed object, except that it will be accessible to all child views of the content view without having to be passed down through the view hierarchy. When the slider in SpeedControlView is moved, the Text view in SpeedDisplayView will update to reflect the current speed setting, thereby demonstrating that both views are accessing the same environment object:

Figure 22-1

22.6 Summary

SwiftUI provides three ways to bind data to the user interface and logic of an app. State properties are used to store the state of the views in a user interface layout and are local to the current content view. These transient values are lost when the view goes away.

For data that is external to the user interface and is required only by a subset of the SwiftUI view structures in an app, the observable object protocol should be used. Using this approach, the class or structure which represents the data must conform to the ObservableObject protocol, and any properties to which views will bind must be declared using the @Published property wrapper. To bind to an observable object property in a view declaration the property must use the @ObservedObject or @StateObject property wrapper (@StateObject being the preferred option in the majority of cases).

For data that is external to the user interface, but for which access is required for many views, the environment object provides the best solution. Although declared in the same way as observable objects, environment object bindings are declared in SwiftUI View files using the @EnvironmentObject property wrapper. Before becoming accessible to child views, the environment object must also be initialized before being inserted into the view hierarchy using the *environmentObject()* modifier.

23. A SwiftUI Example Tutorial

Now that some of the fundamentals of SwiftUI development have been covered, this chapter will begin to put this theory into practice by building an example SwiftUI-based project.

This chapter's objective is to demonstrate using Xcode to design a simple interactive user interface using views, modifiers, state variables, and some basic animation effects. This tutorial will use various techniques to add and modify views. While this may appear inconsistent, the objective is to gain familiarity with the different options available.

23.1 Creating the Example Project

Start Xcode and select the option to create a new project. Then, on the template selection screen, make sure Multiplatform is selected and choose the App option as shown in Figure 23-1 before proceeding to the next screen:

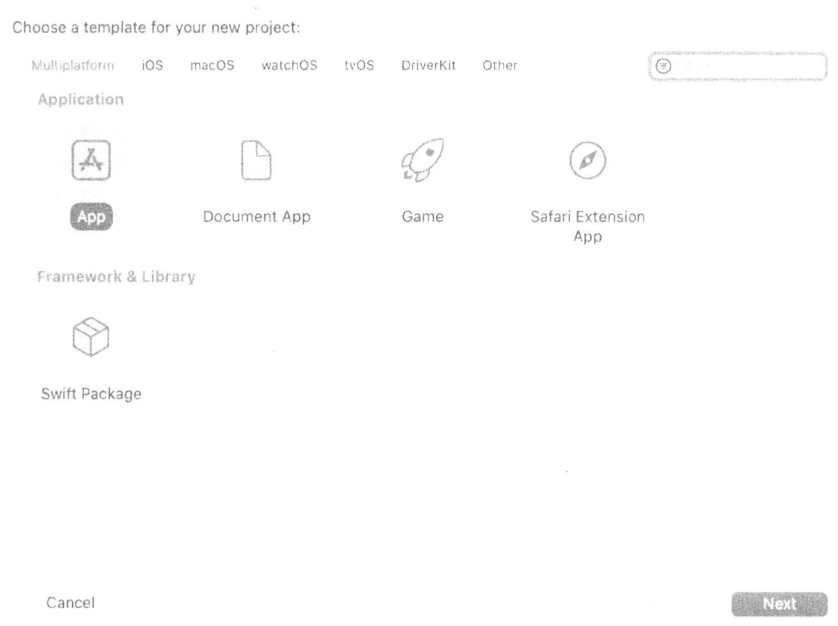

Figure 23-1

On the project options screen, name the project *SwiftUIDemo* before clicking Next to proceed to the final screen. Choose a suitable filesystem location for the project and click on the Create button.

23.2 Reviewing the Project

Once the project has been created, it will contain the *SwiftUIDemoApp.swift* file along with a SwiftUI View file named *ContentView.swift* which should have loaded into the editor and preview canvas ready for modification (if it has not loaded, select it in the project navigator panel). Next, from the target device menu (Figure 23-2) select an iPhone 13 simulator:

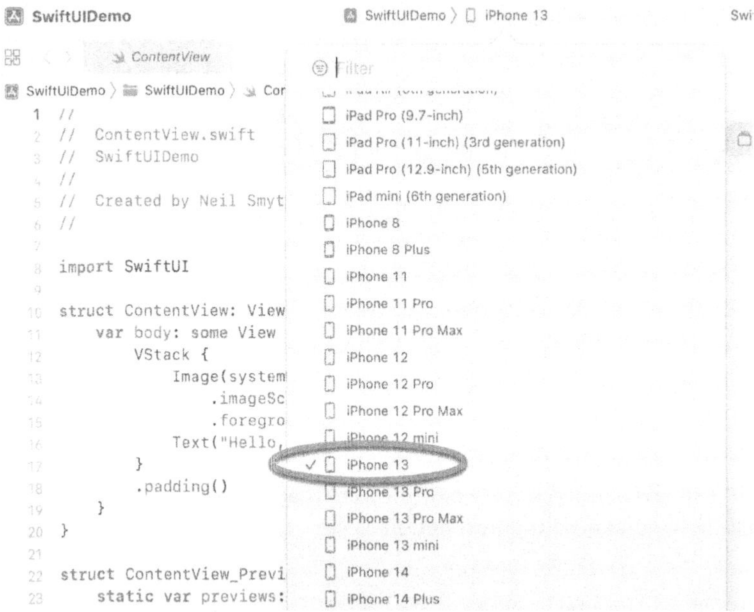

Figure 23-2

If the preview canvas is in the paused state, click on the Resume button to build the project and display the preview:

Figure 23-3

23.3 Modifying the Layout

The view body currently consists of a vertical stack layout (VStack) containing an Image and a Text view. Although we could reuse some of the existing layout for our example, we will learn more by deleting the current views are starting over. Within the Code Editor, delete the existing views from the ContentView body:

```
import SwiftUI

struct ContentView: View {
    var body: some View {
        VStack {
            Image(systemName: "globe")
                .imageScale(.large)
                .foregroundColor(.accentColor)
            Text("Hello, world!")
        }
        .padding()
    }
}
```

Next, add a Text view to the layout as follows:

```
struct ContentView: View {
    var body: some View {
        Text("Hello, world!")
    }
}
```

Within the code editor, select the Text view entry, hold down the Command key on the keyboard and perform a left-click. From the resulting menu, select the *Embed in VStack* option:

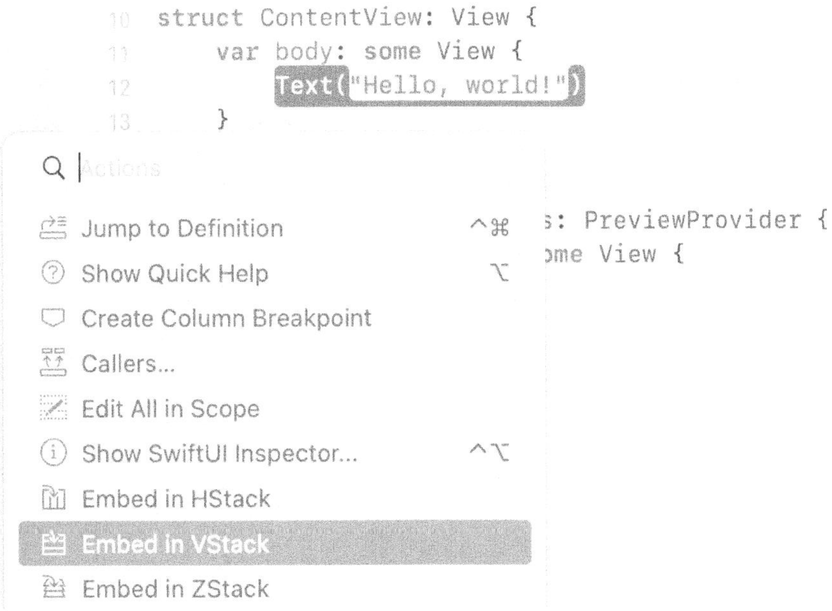

Figure 23-4

Once the Text view has been embedded into the VStack the declaration will read as follows:

```
struct ContentView: View {
    var body: some View {
        VStack {
            Text("Hello, world!")
        }
    }
}
```

23.4 Adding a Slider View to the Stack

The next item to be added to the layout is a Slider view. Before doing that, however, we need to switch the Preview panel from live to selectable mode by clicking the button indicated by the arrow in Figure 23-5:

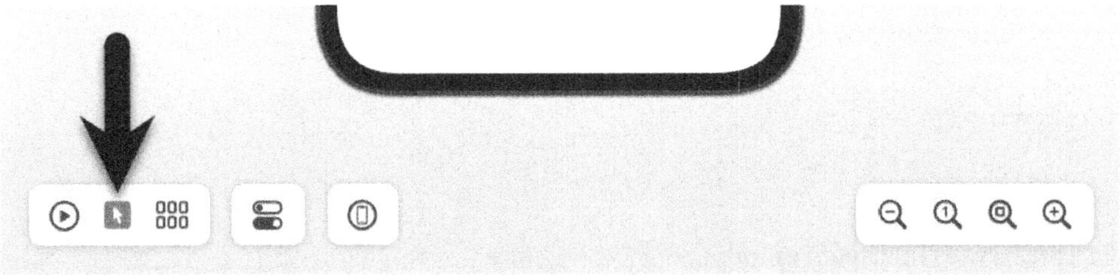

Figure 23-5

Next, display the Library panel by clicking on the '+' button highlighted in Figure 23-6, locate the Slider in the View list and drag it over the top of the existing Text view within the preview canvas. Ensure the notification panel (also highlighted in Figure 23-6) indicates that the view will be inserted into the existing stack (as opposed to being placed in a new vertical stack) before dropping the view into place.

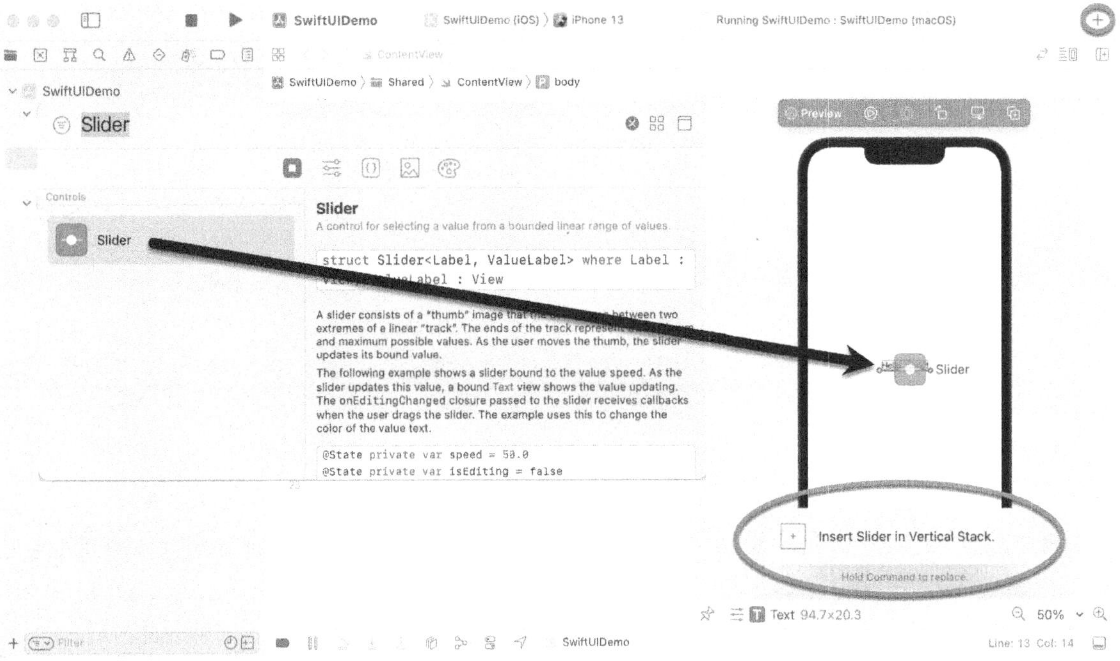

Figure 23-6

Once the slider has been dropped into place, the view implementation should read as follows:

```
struct ContentView: View {
    var body: some View {
        VStack {
            VStack {
                Text("Hello, world!")
                Slider(value: Value)
            }
        }
    }
}
```

23.5 Adding a State Property

The slider will be used to control the degree to which the Text view is to be rotated. As such, a binding must be established between the Slider view and a state property into which the current rotation angle will be stored. Within the code editor, declare this property and configure the Slider to use a range between 0 and 360 in increments of 0.1:

```
struct ContentView: View {

    @State private var rotation: Double = 0

    var body: some View {
        VStack {
            VStack {
                Text("Hello, world!")
                Slider(value: $rotation, in: 0 ... 360, step: 0.1)
            }
        }
    }
}
```

Note that since we are declaring a binding between the Slider view and the rotation state property it is prefixed by a '$' character.

23.6 Adding Modifiers to the Text View

The next step is to add some modifiers to the Text view to change the font and adopt the rotation value stored by the Slider view. Begin by displaying the Library panel, switch to the modifier list, and drag and drop a font modifier onto the Text view entry in the code editor:

Figure 23-7

Select the modifier line in the editor, refer to the Attributes inspector panel and change the font property from Title to Large Title, as shown in Figure 23-8:

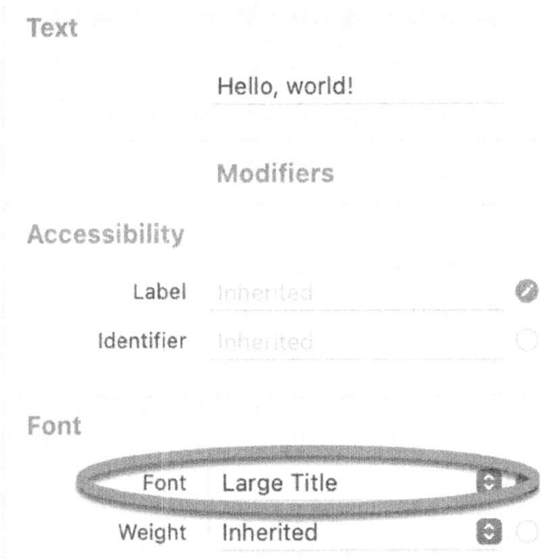

Figure 23-8

Note that the modifier added above does not change the font weight. Since modifiers may also be added to a view from within the Attributes inspector, take this opportunity to change the setting of the Weight menu from Inherited to Heavy.

On completion of these steps, the View body should read as follows:

```
var body: some View {
    VStack {
        VStack {
            Text("Hello, world!")
                .font(.largeTitle)
```

```
                .fontWeight(.heavy)
                Slider(value: $rotation, in: 0 ... 360, step: 0.1)
        }
    }
}
```

23.7 Adding Rotation and Animation

The next step is to add the rotation and animation effects to the Text view using the value stored by the Slider (animation is covered in greater detail in the *"SwiftUI Animation and Transitions"* chapter). This can be implemented using a modifier as follows:

```
Text("Hello, world!")
    .font(.largeTitle)
    .fontWeight(.heavy)
    .rotationEffect(.degrees(rotation))
```

Note that since we are simply reading the value assigned to the rotation state property, as opposed to establishing a binding, the property name is not prefixed with the '$' sign notation.

Click on the Live button (indicated by the arrow in Figure 23-9), wait for the code to compile, then use the slider to rotate the Text view:

Figure 23-9

Next, add an animation modifier to the Text view to animate the rotation over 5 seconds using the Ease In Out effect:

```
Text("Hello, world!")
    .font(.largeTitle)
    .fontWeight(.heavy)
    .rotationEffect(.degrees(rotation))
    .animation(.easeInOut(duration: 5), value: rotation)
```

Use the slider once again to rotate the text, and note that rotation is now smoothly animated.

23.8 Adding a TextField to the Stack

In addition to supporting text rotation, the app will also allow custom text to be entered and displayed on the Text view. This will require the addition of a TextField view to the project. To achieve this, either directly edit the View structure or use the Library panel to add a TextField so that the structure reads as follows (also note the addition of a state property in which to store the custom text string and the change to the Text view to use this property):

```
struct ContentView: View {

    @State private var rotation: Double = 0
    @State private var text: String = "Welcome to SwiftUI"

    var body: some View {
        VStack {
            VStack {
                Text(text)
                    .font(.largeTitle)
                    .fontWeight(.heavy)
                    .rotationEffect(.degrees(rotation))
                    .animation(.easeInOut(duration: 5))

                Slider(value: $rotation, in: 0 ... 360, step: 0.1)

                TextField("Enter text here", text: $text)
                    .textFieldStyle(RoundedBorderTextFieldStyle())
            }
        }
    }
}
```

When the user enters text into the TextField view, that text will be stored in the *text* state property and will automatically appear on the Text view via the binding.

Return to the preview canvas and ensure that the changes work as expected.

23.9 Adding a Color Picker

A Picker view is the final view to be added to the stack before we start to tidy up the layout. The purpose of this view will be to allow the foreground color of the Text view to be chosen by the user from a range of color options. Begin by adding some arrays of color names and Color objects, together with a state property to hold the current array index value as follows:

```
import SwiftUI

struct ContentView: View {

    var colors: [Color] = [.black, .red, .green, .blue]
    var colornames = ["Black", "Red", "Green", "Blue"]

    @State private var colorIndex = 0
    @State private var rotation: Double = 0
    @State private var text: String = "Welcome to SwiftUI"
```

With these variables configured, display the Library panel, locate the Picker in the Views screen and drag and drop it beneath the TextField view in the code editor so that it is embedded in the existing VStack layout. Once added, the view entry will read as follows:

```
Picker(selection: .constant(1), label: Text("Picker")) {
    Text("1").tag(1)
    Text("2").tag(2)
}
```

The Picker view needs to be configured to store the current selection in the *colorIndex* state property and to display an option for each color name in the *colorNames* array. In addition, to make the Picker more visually appealing, we will change the background color for each Text view to the corresponding color in the *colors* array.

To iterate through the colorNames array, the code will make use of the SwiftUI *ForEach* structure. At first glance, ForEach looks like just another Swift programing language control flow statement. In fact, *ForEach* is very different from the Swift *forEach()* array method outlined earlier in the book.

ForEach is itself a SwiftUI view structure designed specifically to generate multiple views by looping through a data set such as an array or range. We may also configure the Picker view to display the color choices in various ways. For this project, we need to select the WheelPickerStyle (*.wheel*) style via the *pickerStyle()* modifier. Within the editor, modify the Picker view declaration so that it reads as follows:

```
Picker(selection: $colorIndex, label: Text("Color")) {
    ForEach (0 ..< colornames.count, id:\.self)  { color in
        Text(colornames[color])
            .foregroundColor(colors[color])
    }
}
.pickerStyle(.wheel)
```

In the above implementation, ForEach is used to loop through the elements of the colornames array, generating a Text view for each color, setting the displayed text and background color on each view accordingly.

The ForEach loop in the above example is contained within a closure expression. As outlined in the chapter entitled *"Swift Functions, Methods and Closures"* this expression can be simplified using *shorthand argument names*. Using this technique, modify the Picker declaration so that it reads as follows:

```
Picker(selection: $colorIndex, label: Text("Color")) {
    ForEach (0 ..< colornames.count, id:\.self) { color in
        Text(colornames[$0])
            .foregroundColor(colors[$0])
```

```
    }
}
.pickerStyle(.wheel)
```

Remaining in the code editor, locate the Text view and add a foreground color modifier to set the foreground color based on the current Picker selection value:

```
Text(text)
    .font(.largeTitle)
    .fontWeight(.heavy)
    .rotationEffect(.degrees(rotation))
    .animation(.easeInOut(duration: 5))
    .foregroundColor(colors[colorIndex])
```

Test the app in the preview canvas and confirm that the Picker view appears with all of the color names using the corresponding foreground color and that color selections are reflected in the Text view.

23.10 Tidying the Layout

Up until this point the focus of this tutorial has been on the appearance and functionality of the individual views. Aside from making sure the views are stacked vertically, however, no attention has been paid to the overall appearance of the layout. At this point the layout should resemble that shown in Figure 23-10:

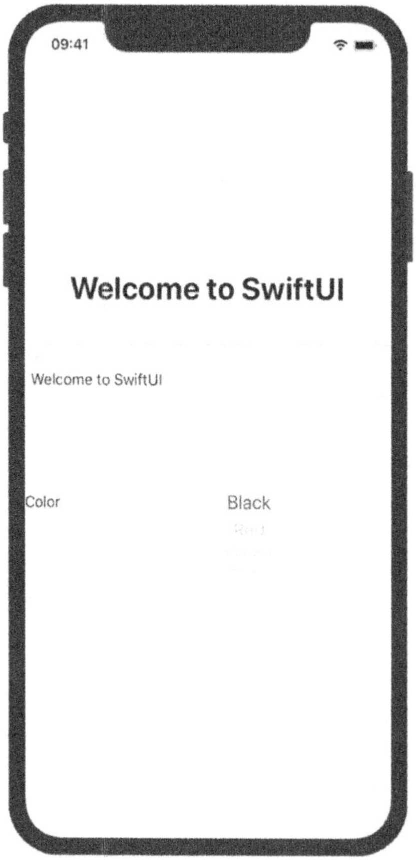

Figure 23-10

The first improvement needed is to add some space around the Slider, TextField, and Picker views so that they are not so close to the edge of the device display. To implement this, we will add some padding modifiers to the views:

```
Slider(value: $rotation, in: 0 ... 360, step: 0.1)
    .padding()

TextField("Enter text here", text: $text)
    .textFieldStyle(RoundedBorderTextFieldStyle())
    .padding()

Picker(selection: $colorIndex, label: Text("Color")) {
    ForEach (0 ..< colornames.count, id:\.self) {
        Text(colornames[$0])
            .foregroundColor(colors[$0])
    }
}
.pickerStyle(.wheel)
.padding()
```

Next, the layout would probably look better if the Views were evenly spaced. One way to implement this is to add some Spacer views before and after the Text view:

```
VStack {
        Spacer()
        Text(text)
            .font(.largeTitle)
            .fontWeight(.heavy)
            .rotationEffect(.degrees(rotation))
            .animation(.easeInOut(duration: 5))
            .foregroundColor(colors[colorIndex])
        Spacer()
        Slider(value: $rotation, in: 0 ... 360, step: 0.1)
            .padding()
.
.
```

The Spacer view provides a flexible space between views that will expand and contract based on the requirements of the layout. If a Spacer is contained in a stack, it will resize along the stack axis. When used outside of a stack container, a Spacer view can resize both horizontally and vertically.

To make the separation between the Text view and the Slider more obvious, also add a Divider view to the layout:

```
.
.
VStack {
    Spacer()
    Text(text)
        .font(.largeTitle)
        .fontWeight(.heavy)
```

```
        .rotationEffect(.degrees(rotation))
        .animation(.easeInOut(duration: 5))
        .foregroundColor(colors[colorIndex])
    Spacer()
    Divider()
.
.
```

The Divider view draws a line to indicate separation between two views in a stack container.

With these changes made, the layout should now appear in the preview canvas, as shown in Figure 23-11:

Figure 23-11

23.11 Summary

The goal of this chapter has been to put into practice some of the theory covered in the previous chapters through the creation of an example app project. In particular, the tutorial used various techniques for adding views to a layout in addition to the use of modifiers and state property bindings. The chapter also introduced the Spacer and Divider views and used the ForEach structure to generate views from a data array dynamically.

Chapter 24

24. An Overview of Swift Structured Concurrency

Concurrency can be defined as the ability of software to perform multiple tasks in parallel. Many app development projects will need to make use of concurrent processing at some point and concurrency is essential for providing a good user experience. Concurrency, for example, is what allows the user interface of an app to remain responsive while performing background tasks such as downloading images or processing data.

In this chapter, we will explore the *structured concurrency* features of the Swift programming language and explain how these can be used to add multi-tasking support to your app projects.

24.1 An Overview of Threads

Threads are a feature of modern CPUs and provide the foundation of concurrency in any multitasking operating system. Although modern CPUs can run large numbers of threads, the actual number of threads that can be run in parallel at any one time is limited by the number of CPU cores (depending on the CPU model, this will typically be between 4 and 16 cores). When more threads are required than there are CPU cores, the operating system performs thread scheduling to decide how the execution of these threads is to be shared between the available cores.

Threads can be thought of as mini-processes running within a main process, the purpose of which is to enable at least the appearance of parallel execution paths within application code. The good news is that although structured concurrency uses threads behind the scenes, it handles all of the complexity for you and you should never need to interact with them directly.

24.2 The Application Main Thread

When an app is first started, the runtime system will typically create a single thread in which the app will run by default. This thread is generally referred to as the *main thread*. The primary role of the main thread is to handle the user interface in terms of UI layout rendering, event handling, and user interaction with views in the user interface.

Any additional code within an app that performs a time-consuming task using the main thread will cause the entire application to appear to lock up until the task is completed. This can be avoided by launching the tasks to be performed in separate threads, allowing the main thread to continue unhindered with other tasks.

24.3 Completion Handlers

As outlined in the chapter entitled *"Swift Functions, Methods and Closures"*, Swift previously used completion handlers to implement asynchronous code execution. In this scenario, an asynchronous task would be started and a completion handler assigned to be called when the task finishes. In the meantime, the main app code would continue to run while the asynchronous task is performed in the background. On completion of the asynchronous task, the completion handler would be called and passed any results. The body of the completion handler would then execute and process those results.

Unfortunately, completion handlers tend to result in complex and error-prone code constructs that are difficult to write and understand. Completion handlers are also unsuited to handling errors thrown by the asynchronous tasks and generally result in large and confusing nested code structures.

24.4 Structured Concurrency

Structured concurrency was introduced into the Swift language with Swift version 5.5 to make it easier for app developers to implement concurrent execution safely, and in a way that is logical and easy to both write and understand. In other words, structured concurrency code can be read from top to bottom without having to jump back to completion handler code to understand the logic flow. Structured concurrency also makes it easier to handle errors thrown by asynchronous functions.

Swift provides several options for implementing structured concurrency, each of which will be introduced in this chapter.

24.5 Preparing the Project

Launch Xcode and select the option to create a new Multiplatform App project named ConcurrencyDemo. Once created, edit the *ContentView.swift* file so that it reads as follows:

```
import SwiftUI

struct ContentView: View {
    var body: some View {
        Button(action: {
            doSomething()
        }) {
            Text("Do Something")
        }
    }

    func doSomething() {
    }

    func takesTooLong() {
    }
}

struct ContentView_Previews: PreviewProvider {
    static var previews: some View {
        ContentView()
    }
}
```

The above changes create a Button view configured to call the *doSomething()* function when clicked. In the remainder of this chapter, we will make changes to this template code to demonstrate structured concurrency in Swift.

24.6 Non-Concurrent Code

Before exploring concurrency, we will first look at an example of non-concurrent code (also referred to as *synchronous code*) execution. Begin by adding the following code to the two stub functions. The changes to the *doSomething()* function print out the current date and time before calling the *takesTooLong()* function. Finally, the date and time are output once again before the *doSomething()* function exits.

The *takesTooLong()* function uses the system *sleep()* method to simulate the effect of performing a time-consuming task that blocks the main thread until it is complete before printing out another timestamp:

```
func doSomething() {
    print("Start \(Date())")
    takesTooLong()
    print("End \(Date())")
}

func takesTooLong() {
    sleep(5)
    print("Async task completed at \(Date())")
}
```

Run the app on a device or simulator and click on the "Do Something" button. Output similar to the following should appear in the Xcode console panel:

```
Start 2022-07-29 17:55:16 +0000
Async task completed at 2022-03-29 17:55:21 +0000
End 2022-07-29 17:55:21 +0000
```

The key point to note in the above timestamps is that the end time is 5 seconds after the start time. This tells us not only that the call to *takesTooLong()* lasted 5 seconds as expected, but that any code after the call was made within the *doSomething()* function was not able to execute until after the call returned. During that 5 seconds, the app would appear to the user to be frozen.

The answer to this problem is to implement a Swift *async/await* concurrency structure.

24.7 Introducing async/await Concurrency

The foundation of structured concurrency is the *async/await* pair. The *async* keyword is used when declaring a function to indicate that it is to be executed asynchronously relative to the thread from which it was called. We need, therefore, to declare both of our example functions as follows (any errors that appear will be addressed later):

```
func doSomething() async {
    print("Start \(Date())")
    takesTooLong()
    print("End \(Date())")
}

func takesTooLong() async {
    sleep(5)
    print("Async task completed at \(Date())")
}
```

Marking a function as async achieves several objectives. First, it indicates that the code in the function needs to be executed on a different thread to the one from which it was called. It also notifies the system that the function itself can be suspended during execution to allow the system to run other tasks. As we will see later, these *suspend points* within an async function are specified using the *await* keyword.

Another point to note about async functions is that they can generally only be called from within the scope of other async functions though, as we will see later in the chapter, the Task object can be used to provide a bridge between synchronous and asynchronous code. Finally, if an async function calls other async functions, the parent function cannot exit until all child tasks have also completed.

Most importantly, once a function has been declared as being asynchronous, it can only be called using the *await* keyword. Before looking at the await keyword, we need to understand how to call async functions from synchronous code.

24.8 Asynchronous Calls from Synchronous Functions

The rules of structured concurrency state that an async function can only be called from within an asynchronous context. If the entry point into your program is a synchronous function, this raises the question of how any async functions can ever get called. The answer is to use the Task object from within the synchronous function to launch the async function. Suppose we have a synchronous function named *main()* from which we need to call one of our async functions and attempt to do so as follows:

```
func main() {
    doSomething()
}
```

The above code will result in the following error notification in the code editor:

```
'async' call in a function that does not support concurrency
```

The only options we have are to make *main()* an async function or to launch the function in an unstructured task. Assuming that declaring *main()* as an async function is not a viable option, in this case, the code will need to be changed as follows:

```
func main() {
    Task {
        await doSomething()
    }
}
```

24.9 The await Keyword

As we have previously discussed, the await keyword is required when making a call to an async function and can only usually be used within the scope of another async function. Attempting to call an async function without the await keyword will result in the following syntax error:

```
Expression is 'async' but is not marked with 'await'
```

To call the *takesTooLong()* function, therefore, we need to make the following change to the *doSomething()* function:

```
func doSomething() async {
    print("Start \(Date())")
    await takesTooLong()
    print("End \(Date())")
}
```

One more change is now required because we are attempting to call the async *doSomething()* function from a synchronous context (in this case the action closure of the Button view). To resolve this, we need to use the Task object to launch the *doSomething()* function:

```
var body: some View {
    Button(action: {
        Task {
```

```
            await doSomething()
        }
    }) {
        Text("Do Something")
    }
}
```

When tested now, the console output should be similar to the following:

```
Start 2022-03-30 13:27:42 +0000
Async task completed at 2022-03-30 13:27:47 +0000
End 2022-03-30 13:27:47 +0000
```

This is where the await keyword can be a little confusing. As you have probably noticed, the *doSomething()* function still had to wait for the *takesTooLong()* function to return before continuing, giving the impression that the task was still blocking the thread from which it was called. In fact, the task was performed on a different thread, but the await keyword told the system to wait until it completed. The reason for this is that, as previously mentioned, a parent async function cannot complete until all of its sub-functions have also completed. This means that the call has no choice but to wait for the async *takesTooLong()* function to return before executing the next line of code. In the next section, we will explain how to defer the wait until later in the parent function using the *async-let* binding expression. Before doing that, however, we need to look at another effect of using the await keyword in this context.

In addition to allowing us to make the async call, the await keyword has also defined a *suspend point* within the *doSomething()* function. When this point is reached during execution, it tells the system that the *doSomething()* function can be temporarily suspended and the thread on which it is running used for other purposes. This allows the system to allocate resources to any higher priority tasks and will eventually return control to the *doSomething()* function so that execution can continue. By marking suspend points, the *doSomething()* function is essentially being forced to be a good citizen by allowing the system to briefly allocate processing resources to other tasks. Given the speed of the system, it is unlikely that a suspension will last more than fractions of a second and will not be noticeable to the user while benefiting the overall performance of the app.

24.10 Using async-let Bindings

In our example code, we have identified that the default behavior of the await keyword is to wait for the called function to return before resuming execution. A more common requirement, however, is to continue executing code within the calling function while the async function is executing in the background. This can be achieved by deferring the wait until later in the code using an async-let binding. To demonstrate this, we first need to modify our *takesTooLong()* function to return a result (in this case our task completion timestamp):

```
func takesTooLong() async -> Date {
    sleep(5)
    return Date()
}
```

Next, we need to change the call within *doSomething()* to assign the returned result to a variable using a *let* expression but also marked with the *async* keyword:

```
func doSomething() async {
    print("Start \(Date())")
    async let result = takesTooLong()
    print("End \(Date())")
}
```

Now, all we need to do is specify where within the *doSomething()* function we want to wait for the result value to be returned. We do this by accessing the result variable using the await keyword. For example:

```
func doSomething() async {
    print("Start \(Date())")
    async let result = takesTooLong()
    print("After async-let \(Date())")
    // Additional code to run concurrently with async function goes here
    print ("result = \(await result)")
    print("End \(Date())")
}
```

When printing the result value, we are using await to let the system know that execution cannot continue until the async *takesTooLong()* function returns with the result value. At this point, execution will stop until the result is available. Any code between the async-let and the await, however, will execute concurrently with the *takesTooLong()* function.

Execution of the above code will generate output similar to the following:

```
Start 2022-07-30 14:18:40 +0000
After async-let 2022-07-30 14:18:40 +0000
result = 2022-07-30 14:18:45 +0000
End 2022-07-30 14:18:45 +0000
```

Note that the "After async-let" message has a timestamp that is 5 seconds earlier than the "result =" call return stamp confirming that the code was executed while *takesTooLong()* was also running.

24.11 Handling Errors

Error handling in structured concurrency makes use of the throw/do/try/catch mechanism previously covered in the chapter entitled *"Understanding Error Handling in Swift 5"*. The following example modifies our original async *takesTooLong()* function to accept a sleep duration parameter and to throw an error if the delay is outside of a specific range:

```
enum DurationError: Error {
    case tooLong
    case tooShort
}
.
.
func takesTooLong(delay: UInt32) async throws {

    if delay < 5 {
        throw DurationError.tooShort
    } else if delay > 20 {
        throw DurationError.tooLong
    }

    sleep(delay)
    print("Async task completed at \(Date())")
}
```

Now when the function is called, we can use a do/try/catch construct to handle any errors that get thrown:

```
func doSomething() async {
    print("Start \(Date())")
    do {
        try await takesTooLong(delay: 25)
    } catch DurationError.tooShort {
        print("Error: Duration too short")
    } catch DurationError.tooLong {
        print("Error: Duration too long")
    } catch {
        print("Unknown error")
    }
    print("End \(Date())")
}
```

When executed, the resulting output will resemble the following:

```
Start 2022-03-30 19:29:43 +0000
Error: Duration too long
End 2022-03-30 19:29:43 +0000
```

24.12 Understanding Tasks

Any work that executes asynchronously is running within an instance of the Swift *Task* class. An app can run multiple tasks simultaneously and structures these tasks hierarchically. When launched, the async version of our *doSomething()* function will run within a Task instance. When the *takesTooLong()* function is called, the system creates a *sub-task* within which the function code will execute. In terms of the task hierarchy tree, this sub-task is a child of the *doSomething()* parent task. Any calls to async functions from within the sub-task will become children of that task, and so on.

This task hierarchy forms the basis on which structured concurrency is built. For example, child tasks inherit attributes such as priority from their parents, and the hierarchy ensures that a parent task does not exit until all descendant tasks have been completed.

As we will see later in the chapter, tasks can be grouped to enable the dynamic launching of multiple asynchronous tasks.

24.13 Unstructured Concurrency

Individual tasks can be created manually using the Task object, a concept referred to as unstructured concurrency. As we have already seen, a common use for unstructured tasks is to call async functions from within synchronous functions.

Unstructured tasks also provide more flexibility because they can be externally canceled at any time during execution. This is particularly useful if you need to provide the user with a way to cancel a background activity, such as tapping on a button to stop a background download task. This flexibility comes with some extra cost in terms of having to do a little more work to create and manage tasks.

Unstructured tasks are created and launched by making a call to the Task initializer and providing a closure containing the code to be performed. For example:

```
Task {
    await doSomething()
```

```
}
```

These tasks also inherit the configuration of the parent from which they are called, such as the actor context (a topic we will explore in the chapter entitled *"An Introduction to Swift Actors"*), priority, and task local variables. Tasks can also be assigned a new priority when they are created, for example:

```
Task(priority: .high) {
    await doSomething()
}
```

This provides a hint to the system about how the task should be scheduled relative to other tasks. Available priorities ranked from highest to lowest are as follows:

- .high / .userInitiated
- .medium
- .low / .utility
- .background

When a task is manually created, it returns a reference to the Task instance. This can be used to cancel the task, or to check whether the task has already been canceled from outside the task scope:

```
let task = Task(priority: .high) {
    await doSomething()
}
.
.
if (!task.isCancelled) {
    task.cancel()
}
```

24.14 Detached Tasks

Detached tasks are another form of unstructured concurrency, but differ in that they do not inherit any properties from the calling parent. Detached tasks are created by calling the *Task.detached()* method as follows:

```
Task.detached {
    await doSomething()
}
```

Detached tasks may also be passed a priority value, and checked for cancellation using the same techniques as outlined above:

```
let detachedTask = Task(priority: .medium) {
    await doSomething()
}
.
.
if (!detachedTask.isCancelled) {
    detachedTask.cancel()
}
```

24.15 Task Management

Regardless of whether you are using structured or unstructured tasks, the Task class provides a set of static methods and properties that can be used to manage the task from within the task scope.

A task may, for example, use the *currentPriority* property to identify the priority assigned when it was created:

```
Task {
    let priority = Task.currentPriority
    await doSomething()
}
```

Unfortunately, this is a read-only property so cannot be used to change the priority of the running task.

It is also possible for a task to check if it has been canceled by accessing the *isCancelled* property:

```
if Task.isCancelled {
    // perform task cleanup
}
```

Another option for detecting cancellation is to call the *checkCancellation()* method which will throw a CancellationError error if the task has been canceled:

```
do {
    try Task.checkCancellation()
} catch {
   // Perform task cleanup
}
```

A task may cancel itself at any time by calling the *cancel()* Task method:

```
Task.cancel()
```

Finally, if there are locations within the task code where execution could safely be suspended, these can be declared to the system via the *yield()* method:

```
Task.yield()
```

24.16 Working with Task Groups

So far in this chapter, all of our examples have involved creating one or two tasks (a parent and a child). In each case, we knew in advance of writing the code how many tasks were required. Situations often arise, however, where several tasks need to be created and run concurrently based on dynamic criteria. We might, for example, need to launch a separate task for each item in an array, or within the body of a *for* loop. Swift addresses this by providing *task groups.*

Task groups allow a dynamic number of tasks to be created and are implemented using either the *withThrowingTaskGroup()* or *withTaskGroup()* functions (depending on whether or not the async functions in the group throw errors). The looping construct to create the tasks is then defined within the corresponding closure, calling the group *addTask()* function to add each new task.

Modify the two functions as follows to create a task group consisting of five tasks, each running an instance of the *takesTooLong()* function.

```
func doSomething() async {
    await withTaskGroup(of: Void.self) { group in
        for i in 1...5 {
            group.addTask {
```

```
                let result = await takesTooLong()
                print("Completed Task \(i) = \(result)")
            }
        }
    }
}

func takesTooLong() async -> Date {
    sleep(5)
    return Date()
}
```

When executed, there will be a 5-second delay while the tasks run before output similar to the following appears:

```
Completed Task 1 = 2022-03-31 17:36:32 +0000
Completed Task 2 = 2022-03-31 17:36:32 +0000
Completed Task 5 = 2022-03-31 17:36:32 +0000
Completed Task 3 = 2022-03-31 17:36:32 +0000
Completed Task 4 = 2022-03-31 17:36:32 +0000
```

Note that the tasks all show the same completion timestamp indicating that they were executed concurrently. It is also interesting to notice that the tasks did not complete in the order in which they were launched. When working with concurrency, it is important to keep in mind that there is no guarantee that tasks will complete in the order that they were created.

In addition to the *addTask()* function, several other methods and properties are accessible from within the task group including the following:

- **cancelAll()** - Method call to cancel all tasks in the group
- **isCancelled** - Boolean property indicating whether the task group has already been canceled.
- **isEmpty** - Boolean property indicating whether any tasks remain within the task group.

24.17 Avoiding Data Races

In the above task group example, the group did not store the results of the tasks. In other words, the results did not leave the scope of the task group and were not retained when the tasks ended. As an example, let's assume that we want to store the task number and result timestamp for each task within a Swift dictionary object (with the task number as the key and the timestamp as the value). When working with synchronous code, we might consider a solution that reads as follows:

```
func doSomething() async {

    var timeStamps: [Int: Date] = [:]

    await withTaskGroup(of: Void.self) { group in
        for i in 1...5 {
            group.addTask {
                timeStamps[i] = await takesTooLong()
            }
        }
```

```
    }
}
```

Unfortunately, the above code will report the following error on the line where the result from the *takesTooLong()* function is added to the dictionary:

```
Mutation of captured var 'timeStamps' in concurrently-executing code
```

The problem here is that we have multiple tasks accessing the data concurrently and risk encountering a data race condition. A data race occurs when multiple tasks attempt to access the same data concurrently, and one or more of these tasks is performing a write operation. This generally results in data corruption problems that can be hard to diagnose.

One option is to create an *actor* in which to store the data. Actors, and how they might be used to solve this particular problem, will be covered in the chapter entitled *"An Introduction to Swift Actors"*.

Another solution is to adapt our task group to return the task results sequentially and add them to the dictionary. We originally declared the task group as returning no results by passing Void.self as the return type to the *withTaskGroup()* function as follows:

```
await withTaskGroup(of: Void.self) { group in
.
.
```

The first step is to design the task group so that each task returns a tuple containing the task number (Int) and timestamp (Date) as follows. We also need a dictionary in which to store the results:

```
func doSomething() async {

    var timeStamps: [Int: Date] = [:]

    await withTaskGroup(of: (Int, Date).self) { group in
        for i in 1...5 {
            group.addTask {
                return(i, await takesTooLong())
            }
        }
    }
}
```

Next, we need to declare a second loop to handle the results as they are returned from the group. Because the results are being returned individually from async functions, we cannot simply write a loop to process them all at once. Instead, we need to wait until each result is returned. For this situation, Swift provides the *for-await* loop.

24.18 The for-await Loop

The *for-await* expression allows us to step through sequences of values that are being returned asynchronously and *await* the receipt of values as they are returned by concurrent tasks. The only requirement for using for-await is that the sequential data conforms to the AsyncSequence protocol (which should always be the case when working with task groups).

In our example, we need to add a for-await loop within the task group scope, but after the addTask loop as follows:

```
func doSomething() async {
```

```
    var timeStamps: [Int: Date] = [:]

    await withTaskGroup(of: (Int, Date).self) { group in

        for i in 1...5 {
            group.addTask {
                return(i, await takesTooLong())
            }
        }

        for await (task, date) in group {
            timeStamps[task] = date
        }
    }
}
```

As each task returns, the for-await loop will receive the resulting tuple and store it in the timeStamps dictionary. To verify this, we can add some code to print the dictionary entries after the task group exits:

```
func doSomething() async {
.
.
        for await (task, date) in group {
            timeStamps[task] = date
        }
    }

    for (task, date) in timeStamps {
        print("Task = \(task), Date = \(date)")
    }
}
```

When executed, the output from the completed example should be similar to the following:

```
Task = 5, Date = 2022-09-12 17:26:43 +0000
Task = 1, Date = 2022-09-12 17:26:23 +0000
Task = 4, Date = 2022-09-12 17:26:38 +0000
Task = 2, Date = 2022-09-12 17:26:28 +0000
Task = 3, Date = 2022-09-12 17:26:33 +0000
```

24.19 Asynchronous Properties

In addition to async functions, Swift also supports async properties within class and struct types. Asynchronous properties are created by explicitly declaring a getter and marking it as async as demonstrated in the following example. Currently, only read-only properties can be asynchronous.

```
struct MyStruct {
    var myResult: Date {
        get async {
            return await self.getTime()
```

```
        }
    }
    func getTime() async -> Date {
        sleep(5)
        return Date()
    }
}
.
.
func doSomething() async {

    let myStruct = MyStruct()

    Task {
        let date = await myStruct.myResult
        print(date)
    }
}
```

24.20 Summary

Modern CPUs and operating systems are designed to execute code concurrently allowing multiple tasks to be performed at the same time. This is achieved by running tasks on different *threads* with the *main thread* being primarily responsible for rendering the user interface and responding to user events. By default, most code in an app is also executed on the main thread unless specifically configured to run on a different thread. If that code performs tasks that occupy the main thread for too long the app will appear to freeze until the task completes. To avoid this, Swift provides the structured concurrency API. When using structured concurrency, code that would block the main thread is instead placed in an asynchronous function (async properties are also supported) so that it is performed on a separate thread. The calling code can be configured to wait for the async code to complete before continuing using the *await* keyword, or to continue executing until the result is needed using *async-let*.

Tasks can be run individually or as groups of multiple tasks. The for-await loop provides a useful way to asynchronously process the results of asynchronous task groups. When working with concurrency, it is important to avoid data races, a problem that can usually be resolved using Swift Actors, a topic we will cover in the next chapter entitled *"An Introduction to Swift Actors"*.

Chapter 25

25. An Introduction to Swift Actors

Structured concurrency in Swift provides a powerful platform for performing multiple tasks at the same time, greatly increasing app performance and responsiveness. One of the downsides of concurrency is that it can lead to problems when multiple tasks access the same data concurrently, and that access includes a mix of reading and writing operations. This type of problem is referred to as a *data race* and can lead to intermittent crashes and unpredictable app behavior.

In the previous chapter, we looked at a solution to this problem that involved sequentially processing the results from multiple concurrent tasks. Unfortunately, that solution only really works when the tasks involved all belong to the same task group. A more flexible solution and one that works regardless of where the concurrent tasks are launched involves the use of Swift actors.

25.1 An Overview of Actors

Actors are a Swift type that controls asynchronous access to internal mutable state so that only one task at a time can access data. Actors are much like classes in that they are a reference type and contain properties, initializers, and methods. Like classes, actors can also conform to protocols and be enhanced using extensions. The primary difference when declaring an actor is that the word "actor" is used in place of "class".

25.2 Declaring an Actor

A simple Swift class that contains a property and a method might be declared as follows:

```
class BuildMessage {

    var message: String = ""
    let greeting = "Hello"

    func setName(name: String) {
        self.message = "\(greeting) \(name)"
    }
}
```

To make the class into an actor we just need to change the type declaration from "class" to "actor":

```
actor BuildMessage {

    var message: String = ""
    let greeting = "Hello"

    func setName(name: String) {
        self.message = "\(greeting) \(name)"
    }
}
```

Once declared, actor instances are created in the same way as classes, for example:

```
let hello = BuildMessage()
```

A key difference between classes and actors, however, is that actors can only be created and accessed from within an asynchronous context, such as within an async function or Task closure. Also, when calling an actor method or accessing a property, the *await* keyword must be used, for example:

```
func someFunction() async {
    let builder = BuildMessage()
    await builder.setName(name: "Jane Smith")
    let message = await builder.message
    print(message)

}
```

25.3 Understanding Data Isolation

The data contained in an actor instance is said to be isolated from the rest of the code in the app. This isolation is imposed in part by ensuring that when a method that changes the instance data (in this case, changing the *name* variable) is called, the method is executed to completion before the method can be called from anywhere else in the code. This prevents multiple tasks from concurrently attempting to change the data. This, of course, means that method calls and property accesses may have to wait until a previous task has been handled, hence the need for the await statement.

Isolation also prevents code from directly changing the mutable internal properties of an actor. Consider, for example, the following code to directly assign a new value to the message property of our BuildMessage instance.

```
builder.message = "hello"
```

Though valid when working with class instances, the above code will generate the following error when attempted on an actor instance:

```
Actor-isolated property 'message' can not be mutated from a non-isolated context
```

By default, all methods and mutable properties within an actor are considered to be isolated and, as such, can only be called using the await keyword. Actor methods that do not access mutable properties may be excluded from isolation using the *nonisolated* keyword. Once declared in this way, the method can be called without the await keyword, and also called from synchronous code. We can, for example, add a nonisolated method to our BuildMessage actor that returns the greeting string:

```
actor BuildMessage {

    var message: String = ""
    let greeting = "Hello"

    func setName(name: String) {
        self.message = "\(greeting) \(name)"
    }

    nonisolated func getGreeting() -> String {
        return greeting
    }
}
```

This new method can be called without the await keyword from both synchronous and asynchronous contexts:

```
var builder = BuildMessage()
```

```
func asyncFunction() async {
    let greeting = builder.getGreeting()
    print(greeting)
}

func syncFunction() {
    let greeting = builder.getGreeting()
    print(greeting)
}
```

It is only possible to declare *getGreeting()* as nonisolated because the method only accesses the immutable greeting property. If the method attempted to access the mutable message property, the following error would be reported:

```
Actor-isolated property 'message' can not be referenced from a non-isolated
context
```

Note that although immutable properties are excluded from isolation by default, the *nonisolated* keyword may still be declared for clarity:

```
nonisolated let greeting = "Hello"
```

25.4 A Swift Actor Example

In the previous chapter, we looked at data races and explored how the compiler will prevent us from writing code that could cause one with the following error message:

```
Mutation of captured var 'timeStamps' in concurrently-executing code
```

We encountered this error when attempting to write entries to a dictionary object using the following asynchronous code:

```
func doSomething() async {

    var timeStamps: [Int: Date] = [:]

    await withTaskGroup(of: Void.self) { group in
        for i in 1...5 {
            group.addTask {
                timeStamps[i] = await takesTooLong()
            }
        }
    }
}
```

One option to avoid this problem, and the one implemented in the previous chapter, was to process the results from the asynchronous tasks sequentially using a for-await loop. As we have seen in this chapter, however, the problem could also be resolved using an actor.

With the ConcurrencyDemo project loaded into Xcode, edit the *ContentView.swift* file to add the following actor declaration to encapsulate the timeStamps dictionary and to provide a method via which data can be added:

```
import SwiftUI

actor TimeStore {
```

```
    var timeStamps: [Int: Date] = [:]

    func addStamp(task: Int, date: Date) {
        timeStamps[task] = date
    }
}
.
.
```

Having declared the actor, we can now modify the *doSomething()* method to add new timestamps via the *addStamp()* method:

```
func doSomething() async {

    let store = TimeStore()

    await withTaskGroup(of: Void.self) { group in
        for i in 1...5 {
            group.addTask {
                await store.addStamp(task: i, date: await takesTooLong())
            }
        }
    }

    for (task, date) in await store.timeStamps {
            print("Task = \(task), Date = \(date)")
    }
}

func takesTooLong() async -> Date {
    sleep(5)
    return Date()
}
```

With these changes made, the code should now compile and run without error.

25.5 Introducing the MainActor

In the chapter entitled *"An Overview of Swift Structured Concurrency,"* we talked about the main thread (or main queue) and explained how it is responsible both for handling the rendering of the UI and also responding to user events. We also demonstrated the risks of performing thread-blocking tasks on the main thread and how doing so can cause the running program to freeze. As we have also seen, Swift provides a simple and powerful mechanism for running tasks on separate threads from the main thread. What we have not mentioned yet is that it is also essential that updates to the UI are *only* performed on the main thread. Performing UI updates on any separate thread other than the main thread is likely to cause instability and unpredictable app behavior that can be difficult to debug.

Within Swift, the main thread is represented by the *main actor*. This is referred to as a *global actor* because it is accessible throughout your program code when you need code to execute on the main thread.

When developing your app, situations may arise where you have code that you want to run on the main actor, particularly if that code updates the UI in some way. In this situation, the code can be marked using the @ MainActor attribute. This attribute may be used on types, methods, instances, functions, and closures to indicate that the associated operation must be performed on the main actor. We could, for example, configure a class so that it operates only on the main thread:

```
@MainActor
class TimeStore {

    var timeStamps: [Int: Date] = [:]

    func addStamp(task: Int, date: Date) {
        timeStamps[task] = date
    }
}
```

Alternatively, a single value or property can be marked as being main thread dependent:

```
class TimeStore {

    @MainActor var timeStamps: [Int: Date] = [:]

    func addStamp(task: Int, date: Date) {
        timeStamps[task] = date
    }
}
```

Of course, now that the timeStamps dictionary is assigned to the main actor, it cannot be accessed on any other thread. The attempt to add a new date to the dictionary in the above *addStamp()* method will generate the following error:

```
Property 'timeStamps' isolated to global actor 'MainActor' can not be mutated
from this context
```

To resolve this issue, the *addStamp()* method must also be marked using the @MainActor attribute:

```
@MainActor func addStamp(task: Int, date: Date) {
    timeStamps[task] = date
}
```

The run method of the MainActor can also be called directly from within asynchronous code to perform tasks on the main thread as follows:

```
func runExample() async {

    await MainActor.run {
        // Perform tasks on the main thread
    }
}
```

25.6 Summary

A key part of writing asynchronous code is avoiding data races. A data race occurs when two or more tasks access the same data and at least one of those tasks performs a write operation. This can cause data inconsistencies where the concurrent tasks see and act on different versions of the same data.

A useful tool for avoiding data races is the Swift Actor type. Actors are syntactically and behaviorally similar to Swift classes but differ in that the data they encapsulate is said to be isolated from the rest of the code in the app. If a method within an actor that changes instance data is called, that method is executed to completion before the method can be called from anywhere else in the code. This prevents multiple tasks from concurrently attempting to change the data. Actor method calls and property accesses must be called using the await keyword.

The main actor is a special actor that provides access to the main thread from within asynchronous code. The @ MainActor attribute can be used to mark types, methods, instances, functions, and closures to indicate that the associated task must be performed on the main thread.

Chapter 26

26. SwiftUI Concurrency and Lifecycle Event Modifiers

One of the key strengths of SwiftUI is that, through the use of features such as views, state properties, and observable objects, much of the work required in making sure an app handles lifecycle changes correctly is performed automatically.

It is still often necessary, however, to perform additional actions when certain lifecycle events occur. An app might, for example, need to perform a sequence of actions at the point that a view appears or disappears within a layout. Similarly, an app may need to execute some code each time a value changes or to detect when a view becomes active or inactive. It will also be a common requirement to launch one or more asynchronous tasks at the beginning of a view lifecycle.

All of these requirements and more can be met by making use of a set of event modifiers provided by SwiftUI.

Since event modifiers are best understood when seen in action, this chapter will create a project which makes use of the four most commonly used modifiers.

26.1 Creating the LifecycleDemo Project

Launch Xcode and select the option to create a new Multiplatform App project named LifecycleDemo.

26.2 Designing the App

Begin by editing the *ContentView.swift* file and modifying the body declaration so that it reads as follows:

```
import SwiftUI

struct ContentView: View {

    var body: some View {
        TabView {
            TabView {
                FirstTabView()
                    .tabItem {
                        Image(systemName: "01.circle")
                        Text("First")
                    }

                SecondTabView()
                    .tabItem {
                        Image(systemName: "02.circle")
                        Text("Second")
                    }
            }
```

```
        }
    }
}
```

Select the Xcode *File -> New -> File...* menu option and in the resulting template panel, select the SwiftUI View option from the User Interface section as shown in Figure 26-1 below:

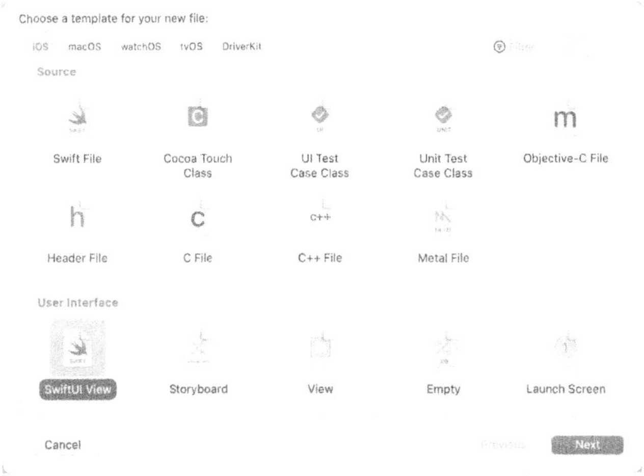

Figure 26-1

Click the Next button and name the file *FirstTabView.swift* before clicking on the Create button. With the new file loaded into the editor, change the Text view to read "View One".

Repeat the above steps to create a second SwiftUI view file named *SecondTabView.swift* with the Text view set to "View Two"

26.3 The onAppear and onDisappear Modifiers

The most basic and frequently used modifiers are *onAppear()* and *onDisappear()*. When applied to a view, these modifiers allow actions to be performed at the point that the view appears or disappears.

Within the *FirstTabView.swift* file, add both modifiers to the Text view as follows:

```
import SwiftUI

struct FirstTabView: View {

    var body: some View {

        Text("View One")
            .onAppear(perform: {
                print("onAppear triggered")
            })
            .onDisappear(perform: {
                print("onDisappeared triggered")
            })
    }
}
```

Run the app on a device or simulator and note that the diagnostic output appears in the console panel when the app first appears. Click on the second tab to display SecondTabView at which point the onDisappear modifier will be triggered. Display the first tab once again and verify that the onAppear diagnostic is output to the console.

26.4 The onChange Modifier

In basic terms, the *onChange()* modifier should be used when an action needs to be performed each time a state changes within an app. This, for example, allows actions to be triggered each time the value of a state property changes. As we will explore later in the chapter, this modifier is also particularly useful when used in conjunction with the ScenePhase environment property.

To experience the *onChange()* modifier in action, begin by editing the *SecondTabView.swift* file so that it reads as follows:

```
import SwiftUI

struct SecondTabView: View {

    @State private var text: String = ""

    var body: some View {
        TextEditor(text: $text)
            .padding()
            .onChange(of: text, perform: { value in
                print("onChange triggered")
            })
    }
}

struct SecondTabView_Previews: PreviewProvider {
    static var previews: some View {
        SecondTabView()
    }
}
```

Run the app again and note that the event is triggered for each keystroke within the TextEditor view.

26.5 ScenePhase and the onChange Modifier

ScenePhase is an @Environment property that is used by SwiftUI to store the state of the current scene. When changes to ScenePhase are monitored by the *onChange()* modifier, an app can take action, for example, when the scene moves between the foreground and background or when it becomes active or inactive. This technique can be used on any view or scene but is also useful when applied to the App declaration. For example, edit the *LifecycleDemoApp.swift* file and modify it so that it reads as follows:

```
import SwiftUI

@main
struct LifecycleDemoApp: App {

    @Environment(\.scenePhase) private var scenePhase
```

```
    var body: some Scene {
        WindowGroup {
            ContentView()
        }
        .onChange(of: scenePhase, perform: { phase in
                switch phase {
                    case .active:
                        print("Active")
                    case .inactive:
                        print("Inactive")
                    case .background:
                        print("Background")
                    default:
                        print("Unknown scenephase")
                }
            })
    }
}
```

When applied to the window group in this way, the scene phase will be based on the state of all scenes within the app. In other words, the phase will be set to active if any scene is currently active and will only be set to inactive when all scenes are inactive.

When applied to an individual view, on the other hand, the phase state will reflect only that of the scene in which the view is located. The modifier could, for example, have been applied to the content view instead of the window group as follows:

```
.
.
var body: some Scene {
    WindowGroup {
        ContentView()
            .onChange(of: scenePhase, perform: { phase in
.
.
    }
.
.
```

Run the app on a device or simulator and place the app in the background. The console should show that the scene phase changed to inactive state followed by the background phase. On returning the app to the foreground the active phase will be entered. The three scene phases can be summarized as follows:

- **active** – The scene is in the foreground, visible, and responsive to user interaction.
- **inactive** –The scene is in the foreground and visible to the user but not interactive.
- **background** – The scene is not visible to the user.

26.6 Launching Concurrent Tasks

The chapter entitled *"An Overview of Swift Structured Concurrency"* covered the topic of structured concurrency in Swift but did not explain how asynchronous tasks can be launched in the context of a SwiftUI view. In practice, all of the techniques described in that earlier chapter still apply when working with SwiftUI. All that is required is a call to the *task()* modifier on a view together with a closure containing the code to be executed. This code will be executed within a new concurrent task at the point that the view is created. We can, for example, modify the FirstTabView to display a different string on the Text view using an asynchronous task:

```
import SwiftUI

struct FirstTabView: View {

    @State var title = "View One"

    var body: some View {
        Text(title)
            .onAppear(perform: {
                print("onAppear triggered")
            })
            .onDisappear(perform: {
                print("onDisappeared triggered")
            })
            .task(priority: .background) {
                title = await changeTitle()
            }

    }

    func changeTitle() async -> String {
        sleep(5)
        return "Async task complete"
    }
}

struct FirstTabView_Previews: PreviewProvider {
    static var previews: some View {
        FirstTabView()
    }
}
```

When the view is created, a task is launched with an optional priority setting. The task calls a function named *changeTitle()* and then waits for the code to execute asynchronously.

The *changeTitle()* function puts the thread to sleep for 5 seconds to simulate a long-running task before returning a new title string. This string is then assigned to the title state variable where it will appear on Text view.

Build and run the app and verify that the tabs remain responsive during the 5-second delay and that the new title appears on the first tab.

26.7 Summary

SwiftUI provides a collection of modifiers designed to allow actions to be taken in the event of lifecycle changes occurring in a running app. The *onAppear()* and *onDisappear()* modifiers can be used to perform actions when a view appears or disappears from view within a user interface layout. The *onChange()* modifier, on the other hand, is useful for performing tasks each time the value assigned to a property changes.

The ScenePhase environment property, when used with the *onChange()* modifier, allows an app to identify when the state of a scene changes. This is of particular use when an app needs to know when it moves between foreground and background modes. Asynchronous tasks can be launched when a view is created using the *task()* modifier.

Chapter 27

27. SwiftUI Observable and Environment Objects – A Tutorial

The chapter entitled *"SwiftUI State Properties, Observable, State, and Environment Objects"* introduced the concept of observable and environment objects and explained how these are used to implement a data driven approach to app development in SwiftUI.

This chapter will build on the knowledge from the earlier chapter by creating a simple example project that makes use of both observable and environment objects.

27.1 About the ObservableDemo Project

Observable objects are particularly powerful when used to wrap dynamic data (in other words, data values that change repeatedly). To simulate data of this type, an observable data object will be created which makes use of the Foundation framework Timer object configured to update a counter once every second. This counter will be published so that it can be observed by views within the app project.

Initially, the data will be treated as an observable object and passed from one view to another. Later in the chapter, the data will be converted to an environment object so that it can be accessed by multiple views without being passed between views.

27.2 Creating the Project

Launch Xcode and select the option to create a new Multiplatform App project named ObservableDemo.

27.3 Adding the Observable Object

The first step after creating the new project is to add a data class implementing the ObservableObject protocol. Within Xcode, select the *File -> New -> File...* menu option and, in the resulting template dialog, select the *Swift File* option. Click the Next button and name the file *TimerData* before clicking the Create button.

With the *TimerData.swift* file loaded into the code editor, implement the TimerData class as follows:

```
import Foundation
import Combine

class TimerData : ObservableObject {

    @Published var timeCount = 0
    var timer : Timer?

    init() {
        timer = Timer.scheduledTimer(timeInterval: 1.0, target: self,
            selector: #selector(timerDidFire), userInfo: nil, repeats: true)
    }
```

```
    @objc func timerDidFire() {
        timeCount += 1
    }

    func resetCount() {
        timeCount = 0
    }
}
```

The class is declared as implementing the ObservableObject protocol and contains an initializer which configures a Timer instance to call a function named *timerDidFire()* once every second. The *timerDidFire()* function, in turn, increments the value assigned to the timeCount variable. The timeCount variable is declared using the @ Published property wrapper so that it can be observed from within views elsewhere in the project. The class also includes a method named *resetCount()* to reset the counter to zero.

27.4 Designing the ContentView Layout

The user interface for the app will consist of two screens, the first of which will be represented by the *ContentView.Swift* file. Select this file to load it into the code editor and modify it so that it reads as follows:

```
import SwiftUI

struct ContentView: View {

    @StateObject var timerData: TimerData = TimerData()

    var body: some View {

        NavigationView {
            VStack {
                Text("Timer count = \(timerData.timeCount)")

                    .font(.largeTitle)
                    .fontWeight(.bold)
                    .padding()

                Button(action: resetCount) {
                    Text("Reset Counter")
                }
            }
        }
    }

    func resetCount() {
        timerData.resetCount()
    }
}
```

```
struct ContentView_Previews: PreviewProvider {
    static var previews: some View {
        ContentView()
    }
}
```

With the changes made, use the Live Preview button to test the view. Once the Live Preview starts, the counter should begin incrementing:

Figure 27-1

Next, click on the Reset Counter button and verify that the counter restarts counting from zero. Now that the initial implementation is working, the next step is to add a second view which will also need access to the same observable object.

27.5 Adding the Second View

Select the *File -> New -> File...* menu option, this time choosing the *SwiftUI View* template option and naming the view SecondView. Edit the *SecondView.swift* file so that it reads as follows:

```
import SwiftUI

struct SecondView: View {

    @StateObject var timerData: TimerData

    var body: some View {
```

```
        VStack {
            Text("Second View")
                .font(.largeTitle)
            Text("Timer Count = \(timerData.timeCount)")
                .font(.headline)
        }
        .padding()
    }
}

struct SecondView_Previews: PreviewProvider {
    static var previews: some View {
        SecondView(timerData: TimerData())
    }
}
```

Use Live Preview to test that the layout matches Figure 27-2 and that the timer begins counting.

In the Live Preview, the view has its own instance of TimerData which was configured in the SecondView_Previews declaration. To make sure that both ContentView and SecondView are using the same TimerData instance, the observed object needs to be passed to the SecondView when the user navigates to the second screen.

Figure 27-2

27.6 Adding Navigation

A navigation link now needs to be added to ContentView and configured to navigate to the second view. Open the *ContentView.swift* file in the code editor and add this link as follows:

```
var body: some View {

    NavigationView {
        VStack {
            Text("Timer count = \(timerData.timeCount)")

                .font(.largeTitle)
                .fontWeight(.bold)
                .padding()

            Button(action: resetCount) {
                Text("Reset Counter")
            }

            NavigationLink(destination:
                        SecondView(timerData: timerData)) {
                Text("Next Screen")
            }
            .padding()
        }
    }
}
```

Once again using Live Preview, test the ContentView and check that the counter increments. Taking note of the current counter value, click on the Next Screen link to display the second view and verify that counting continues from the same number. This confirms that both views are subscribed to the same observable object instance.

27.7 Using an Environment Object

The final step in this tutorial is to convert the observable object to an environment object. This will allow both views to access the same TimerData object without the need for a reference to be passed from one view to the other.

This change does not require any modifications to the *TimerData.swift* class declaration and only minor changes are needed within the two SwiftUI view files. Starting with the *ContentView.swift* file, modify the navigation link destination so that timerData is no longer passed through to SecondView. Also add a call to the *environmentObject()* modifier to insert the timerData instance into the view hierarchy environment:

```
import SwiftUI

struct ContentView: View {

    @StateObject var timerData: TimerData = TimerData()

    var body: some View {
```

```
        NavigationView {
.
.
                NavigationLink(destination: SecondView(timerData: timerData)) {
                    Text("Next Screen")
                }
                .padding()
            }
        }
        .environmentObject(timerData)
    }
.
.
struct ContentView_Previews: PreviewProvider {
    static var previews: some View {
        ContentView()
    }
}
```

Next, modify the *SecondView.swift* file so that it reads as follows:

```
import SwiftUI

struct SecondView: View {

    @EnvironmentObject var timerData: TimerData

    var body: some View {

        VStack {
            Text("Second View")
                .font(.largeTitle)
            Text("Timer Count = \(timerData.timeCount)")
                .font(.headline)
        }.padding()
    }
}

struct SecondView_Previews: PreviewProvider {
    static var previews: some View {
        SecondView().environmentObject(TimerData())
    }
}
```

Test the project one last time, either using Live Preview or by running on a physical device or simulator and check that both screens are accessing the same counter data via the environment.

27.8 Summary

This chapter has worked through a tutorial that demonstrates the use of observed and environment objects to bind dynamic data to the views in a user interface, including implementing an observable object, publishing a property, subscribing to an observable object and the use of environment objects.

Chapter 28

28. SwiftUI Data Persistence using AppStorage and SceneStorage

It is a common requirement for an app to need to store small amounts of data that will persist through app restarts. This is particularly useful for storing user preference settings, or when restoring a scene to the exact state it was in the last time it was accessed by the user. SwiftUI provides two property wrappers (@AppStorage and @SceneStorage) for the specific purpose of persistently storing small amounts of app data, details of which will be covered in this chapter.

28.1 The @SceneStorage Property Wrapper

The @SceneStorage property wrapper is used to store small amounts of data within the scope of individual app scene instances and is ideal for saving and restoring the state of a screen between app launches. Consider a situation where a user, partway through entering information into a form within an app, is interrupted by a phone call or text message and places the app in the background. The user subsequently forgets to return to the app, complete the form and save the entered information. If the background app were to exit (either because of a device restart, the user terminating the app, or the system killing the app to free up resources) the partial information entered into the form would be lost. Situations such as this can be avoided, however, by using scene storage to retain and restore the data.

Scene storage is declared using the @SceneStorage property wrapper together with a key string value which is used internally to store the associated value. The following code, for example, declares a scene storage property designed to store a String value using a key name set to "city" with an initial default value set to an empty string:

```
@SceneStorage("city") var city: String = ""
```

Once declared, the stored property could, for example, be used in conjunction with a TextEditor as follows:

```
var body: some View {
    TextEditor(text: $city)
        .padding()
}
```

When implemented in an app, this will ensure that any text entered into the text field is retained within the scene through app restarts. If multiple instances of the scene are launched by the user on multi-windowing platforms such as iPadOS or macOS, each scene will have its own distinct copy of the saved value.

28.2 The @AppStorage Property Wrapper

The @SceneStorage property wrapper allows each individual scene within an app to have its own copy of stored data. In other words, the data stored by one scene is not accessible to any other scenes in the app (even other instances of the same scene). The @AppStorage property wrapper, on the other hand, is used to store data that is universally available throughout the entire app.

App Storage is built on top of UserDefaults, a feature that has been available in iOS for many years. Primarily provided as a way for apps to access and store default user preferences (such as language preferences or color choices), UserDefaults can also be used to store small amounts of data needed by the app in the form of key-value pairs.

As with scene storage, the @AppStorage property wrapper requires a string value to serve as a key and may be declared as follows:

```
@AppStorage("mystore") var mytext: String = ""
```

By default, data will be stored in the *standard* UserDefaults storage. It is also possible, however, to specify a custom App Group in which to store the data. App Groups allow apps to share data with other apps and targets within the same group. App Groups are assigned a name (typically similar to *group.com.mydomain.myappname*) and are enabled and configured within the Xcode project *Signing & Capabilities* screen. Figure 28-1, for example, shows a project target with App Groups enabled and a name set to *group.com.ebookfrenzy.userdefaults*:

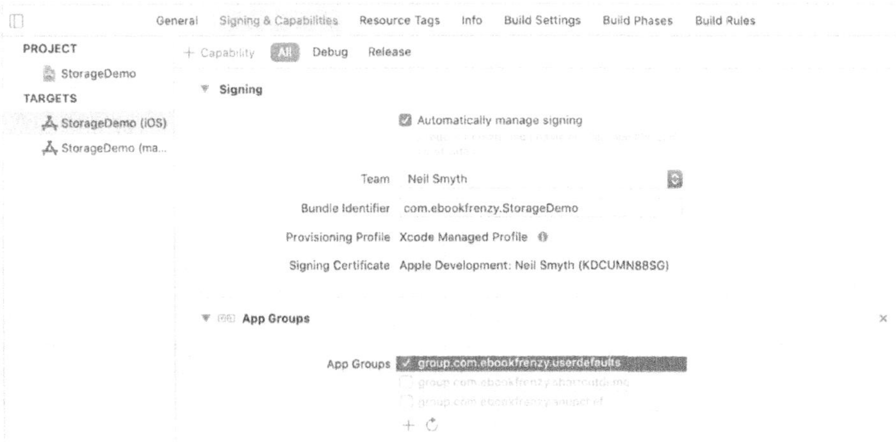

Figure 28-1

The following @AppStorage declaration references an app group to use for storing data:

```
@AppStorage("mystore",
  store: UserDefaults(
        suiteName: "group.com.ebookfrenzy.userdefaults"))
              var mytext: String = ""
```

As with the @State property wrapper, changes to the stored value will cause the user interface to refresh to reflect the new data.

With the basics of app and scene storage covered, the remainder of this chapter will demonstrate these property wrappers in action.

28.3 Creating and Preparing the StorageDemo Project

Begin this tutorial by launching Xcode and selecting the options to create a new Multiplatform App project named *StorageDemo*.

Begin the project design by selecting the *ContentView.swift* file and changing the view body so that it contains a TabView as outlined below:

```
import SwiftUI

struct ContentView: View {

    var body: some View {

        TabView {
```

```
            SceneStorageView()
                .tabItem {
                    Image(systemName: "circle.fill")
                    Text("SceneStorage")
                }

            AppStorageView()
                .tabItem {
                    Image(systemName: "square.fill")
                    Text("AppStorage")
                }
        }
    }
}
.
.
```

Next, use the *File -> New -> File...* menu option to add two new *SwiftUI View* files named SceneStorageView and AppStorageView respectively.

28.4 Using Scene Storage

Edit the *SceneStorageView.swift* file and modify it so that it reads as follows:

```
import SwiftUI

struct SceneStorageView: View {

    @State private var editorText: String = ""

    var body: some View {
        TextEditor(text: $editorText)
            .padding(30)
            .font(.largeTitle)
    }
}
```

This declaration makes use of the TextEditor view. This is a view designed to allow multiline text to be displayed and edited within a SwiftUI app and includes scrolling when the displayed text extends beyond the viewable area. The TextEditor view is passed a binding to a state property into which any typed text will be stored (note that we aren't yet using scene storage).

With the changes made, build and run the app on a device or simulator and, once launched, enter some text into the TextEditor view. Place the app in the background so that the device home screen appears, then terminate the app using the stop button located in the Xcode toolbar.

Run the app a second time and verify that the previously entered text has not been restored into the TextEditor view. Clearly, this app would benefit from the use of scene storage.

Return to the *SceneStorageView.swift* file and convert the @State property to an @SceneStorage property as follows:

```
struct SceneStorageView: View {

        @SceneStorage("mytext") private var editorText = ""
.
.
```

Run the app again, enter some text, place it in the background, and terminate it. This time, when the app is relaunched, the text will be restored into the TextEditor view.

When working with scene storage it is important to keep in mind that each instance of a scene has its own storage which is entirely separate from any other scenes. To experience this in action, run the StorageDemo app on an iPad device or simulator in landscape orientation. Once the app is running, tap the three dots in the top center of the screen and select the Split View menu option:

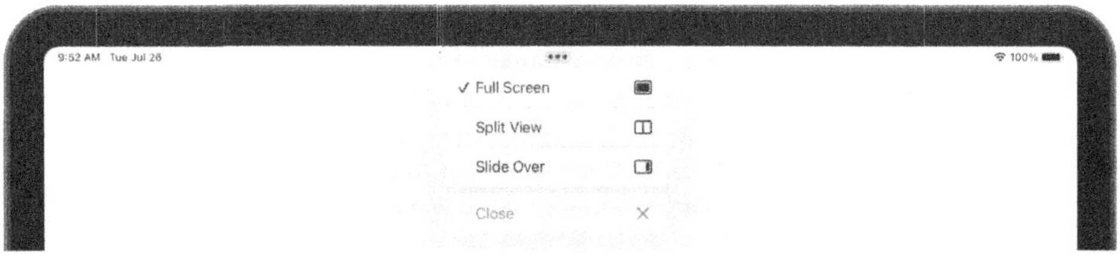

Figure 28-2

When prompted, tap the StorageDemo app icon on the screen to launch a second instance of the app. Once both instances of the app are running, the screen will be equally divided with two scene instances visible. Enter different text into each scene as shown in Figure 28-3 below:

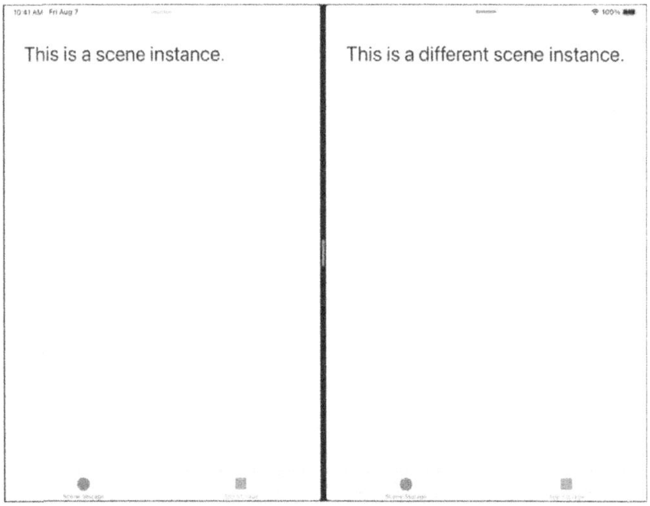

Figure 28-3

Use the home button, or swipe upwards, to place the app into the background, terminate the app, and then re-launch it. On restarting, the two scenes will appear just as they were before the app was placed in the background, thereby demonstrating that each scene has a copy of its own stored data.

28.5 Using App Storage

The final task in this tutorial is to demonstrate the use of app storage. Within Xcode, edit the *AppStorageView.swift* file and modify it so that it reads as follows:

```
import SwiftUI

struct AppStorageView: View {

    @AppStorage("mytext") var editorText: String = "Sample Text"

    var body: some View {
        TextEditor(text: $editorText)
            .padding(30)
            .font(.largeTitle)
    }
}
.
.
```

With the changes made, run the app on the iPad once again and repeat the steps to display two scene instances side-by-side. Select the App Storage tab within both scenes and note that the scene instances are displaying the default sample text. Tap in one of the scenes and add some additional text. As text is added in one scene, the changes are reflected in the second scene as each character is typed:

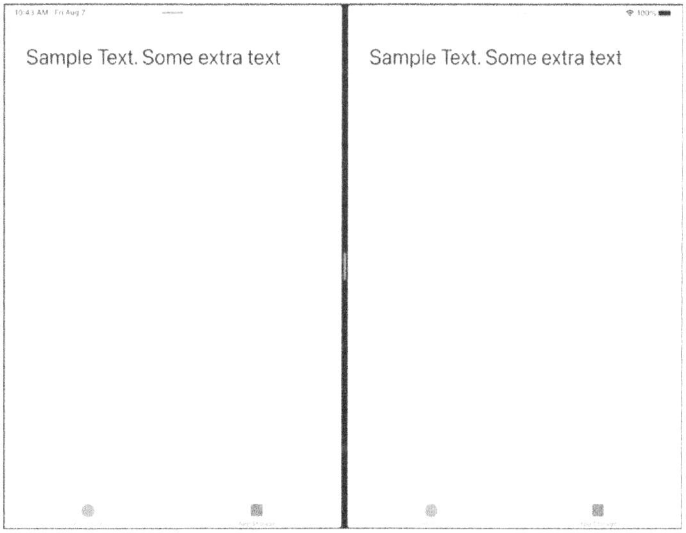

Figure 28-4

Terminate the app while it is in the foreground (unlike scene storage, app storage data is stored in real-time, not just when the app is placed into the background) and relaunch it to confirm that the text changes were saved and restored.

28.6 Storing Custom Types

The @AppStorage and @SceneStorage property wrappers only allow values of certain types to be stored. Specifically Bool, Int, Double, String, URL, and Data types. This means that any other type that needs to be stored must first be encoded as a Swift Data object in order to be stored and subsequently decoded when retrieved.

Consider, for example, the following struct declaration and initialization:

```
struct UserName {
```

```
    var firstName: String
    var secondName: String
}

var username = UserName(firstName: "Mark", secondName: "Wilson")
```

Because UserName is not a supported type, it is not possible to store our username instance directly into app or scene-based storage. Instead, the instance needs to be encoded and encapsulated into a Data instance before it can be saved. The exact steps to perform the encoding and decoding will depend on the type of data being stored. The key requirement, however, is that the type conforms to the Encodable and Decodable protocols. For example:

```
struct UserName: Encodable, Decodable {
    var firstName: String
    var secondName: String
}
```

The following example uses a JSON encoder to encode our username instance and store it using the @AppStorage property wrapper:

```
@AppStorage("username") var namestore: Data = Data()
.
.
let encoder = JSONEncoder()

if let data = try? encoder.encode(username) {
    namestore = data
}
```

When the time comes to retrieve the data from storage, the process is reversed using the JSON decoder:

```
let decoder = JSONDecoder()

if let name = try? decoder.decode(UserName.self, from: namestore) {
    username = name
}
```

Using this technique, it is even possible to store an image using either of the storage property wrappers, for example:

```
@AppStorage("myimage") var imagestore: Data = Data()

var image = UIImage(named: "profilephoto")

// Encode and store image

if let data = image!.pngData() {
    imagestore = data
}

// Retrieve and decode image
```

```
if let decodedImage: UIImage = UIImage(data: imagestore) {
     image = decodedImage
}
```

28.7 Summary

The @SceneStorage and @AppStorage property wrappers provide two ways to persistently store small amounts of data within a SwiftUI app. Scene storage is intended primarily for saving and restoring the state of a scene when an app is terminated while in the background. Each scene within an app has its own local scene storage which is not directly accessible to other areas of the app. App storage uses the UserDefaults system and is used for storing data that is to be accessible from anywhere within an app. Through the use of App Groups, app storage may also be shared between different targets within the same app project, or even entirely different apps. Changes to app storage are immediate regardless of whether the app is currently in the foreground or background.

Both the @AppStorage and @SceneStorage property wrappers support storing Bool, Int, Double, String, URL, and Data types. Other types need to be encoded and encapsulated in Data objects before being placed into storage.

29. SwiftUI Stack Alignment and Alignment Guides

The chapter entitled *"SwiftUI Stacks and Frames"* touched on the basics of alignment in the context of stack container views. Inevitably, when it comes to designing complex user interface layouts, it will be necessary to move beyond the standard alignment options provided with SwiftUI stack views. With this in mind, this chapter will introduce more advanced stack alignment techniques including container alignment, alignment guides, custom alignments, and the implementation of alignments between different stacks.

29.1 Container Alignment

The most basic of alignment options when working with SwiftUI stacks is container alignment. These settings define how the child views contained within a stack are aligned in relation to each other and the containing stack. This alignment value applies to all the contained child views unless different alignment guides have been applied to individual views. Views that do not have their own alignment guide are said to be *implicitly aligned.*

When working with alignments it is important to remember that horizontal stacks (HStack) align child views vertically, while vertical stacks (VStack) align their children horizontally. In the case of the ZStack, both horizontal and vertical alignment values are used.

The following VStack declaration consists of a simple VStack configuration containing three child views:

```
VStack {
    Text("This is some text")
    Text("This is some longer text")
    Text("This is short")
}
```

In the absence of a specific container alignment value, the VStack will default to aligning the centers (.center) of the contained views as shown in Figure 29-1:

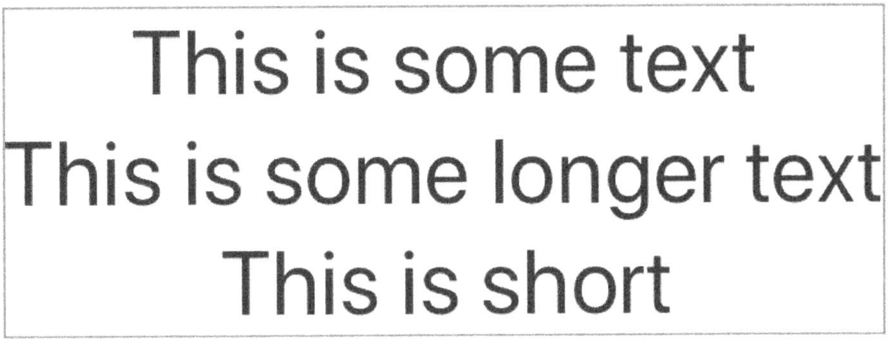

Figure 29-1

In addition to the default center alignment, a VStack can be configured using *.leading* or *.trailing* alignment, for example:

```
VStack(alignment: .trailing) {
    Text("This is some text")
    Text("This is some longer text")
    Text("This is short")
}
```

When rendered, the above VStack layout will appear with the child views aligned along the trailing edges of the views and the container:

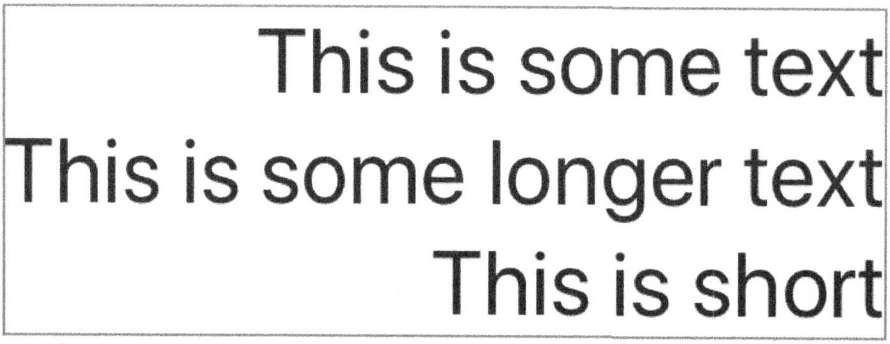

Figure 29-2

Horizontal stacks also default to center alignment in the absence of a specific setting, but also provide top and bottom alignment options in addition to values for aligning text baselines. It is also possible to include spacing values when specifying an alignment. The following HStack uses the default center alignment with spacing and contains three Text view child views, each using a different font size.

```
HStack(spacing: 20) {
    Text("This is some text")
        .font(.largeTitle)
    Text("This is some much longer text")
        .font(.body)
    Text("This is short")
        .font(.headline)
}
```

The above stack will appear as follows when previewed:

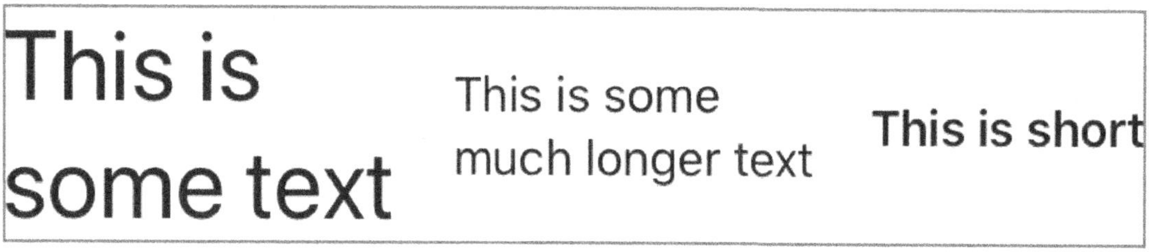

Figure 29-3

Text baseline alignment can be applied based on the baseline of either the first (.firstTextBaseline) or last (.lastTextBaseline) text-based view, for example:

```
HStack(alignment: .lastTextBaseline, spacing: 20) {
    Text("This is some text")
        .font(.largeTitle)
```

```
    Text("This is some much longer text")
        .font(.body)
    Text("This is short")
        .font(.headline)
}
```

Now the three Text views will align with the baseline of the last view:

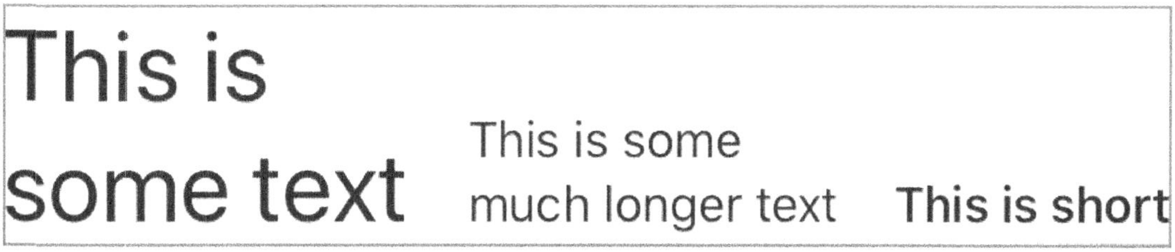

Figure 29-4

29.2 Alignment Guides

An alignment guide is used to define a custom position within a view that is to be used when that view is aligned with other views contained in a stack. This allows more complex alignments to be implemented than those offered by the standard alignment types such as center, leading, and top, though these standard types may still be used when defining an alignment guide. An alignment guide could, for example, be used to align a view based on a position two-thirds along its length or 20 points from the top edge.

Alignment guides are applied to views using the *alignmentGuide()* modifier which takes as arguments a standard alignment type and a closure that must calculate and return a value indicating the point within the view on which the alignment is to be based. To assist in calculating the alignment position within the view, the closure is passed a ViewDimensions object which can be used to obtain the width and height of the view and also the view's standard alignment positions (.top, .bottom, .leading, and so on).

Consider the following VStack containing three rectangles of differing lengths and colors, aligned on their leading edges:

```
VStack(alignment: .leading) {
    Rectangle()
        .foregroundColor(Color.green)
        .frame(width: 120, height: 50)
    Rectangle()
        .foregroundColor(Color.red)
        .frame(width: 200, height: 50)
    Rectangle()
        .foregroundColor(Color.blue)
        .frame(width: 180, height: 50)
}
```

The above layout will be rendered as shown in Figure 29-5:

Figure 29-5

Now, suppose that instead of being aligned on the leading edge, the second view needs to be aligned 120 points inside the leading edge. This can be implemented using an alignment guide as follows:

```
VStack(alignment: .leading) {
    Rectangle()
        .foregroundColor(Color.green)
        .frame(width: 120, height: 50)
    Rectangle()
        .foregroundColor(Color.red)
        .alignmentGuide(.leading, computeValue: { d in 120.0 })
        .frame(width: 200, height: 50)
    Rectangle()
        .foregroundColor(Color.blue)
        .frame(width: 180, height: 50)
}
```

While the first and third rectangles continue to be aligned on their leading edges, the second rectangle is aligned at the specified alignment guide position:

Figure 29-6

When working with alignment guides, the alignment type specified in the *alignmentGuide()* modifier must match the alignment type applied to the parent stack as shown in Figure 29-7. If these do not match, the alignment guide will be ignored by SwiftUI when the layout is rendered.

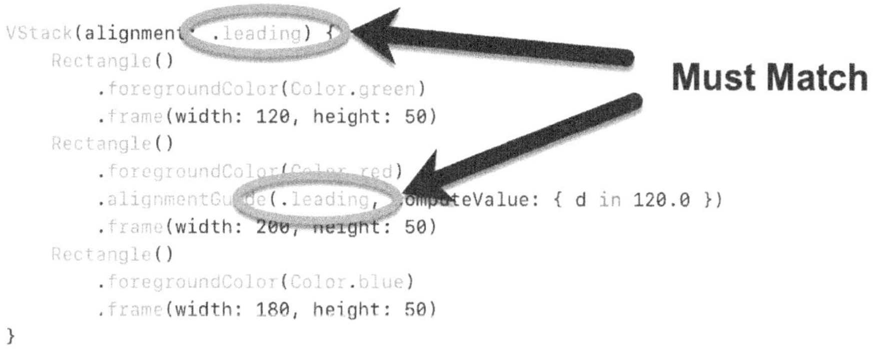

Figure 29-7

Instead of hard-coding an offset, the properties of the ViewDimensions object passed to the closure can be used in calculating the alignment guide position. Using the width property, for example, the alignment guide could be positioned one-third of the way along the view from the leading edge:

```
VStack(alignment: .leading) {
    Rectangle()
        .foregroundColor(Color.green)
        .frame(width: 120, height: 50)
    Rectangle()
        .foregroundColor(Color.red)
        .alignmentGuide(.leading,
                  computeValue: { d in d.width / 3 })
        .frame(width: 200, height: 50)
    Rectangle()
        .foregroundColor(Color.blue)
        .frame(width: 180, height: 50)
}
```

Now when the layout is rendered it will appear as shown in Figure 29-8:

Figure 29-8

The ViewDimensions object also provides access to the HorizontalAlignment and VerticalAlignment properties of the view. In the following example, the trailing edge of the view is identified with an additional 20 points added:

```
.alignmentGuide(.leading, computeValue: {
                    d in d[HorizontalAlignment.trailing] + 20
})
```

This will cause the trailing edge of the view to be aligned 20 points from the leading edges of the other views:

Figure 29-9

29.3 Using the Alignment Guides Tool

The best way to gain familiarity with alignment guides is to experiment with the various settings and options. Fortunately, the SwiftUI Lab has created a useful learning tool for trying out the various alignment settings. To use the tool, begin by creating a new Xcode SwiftUI project named AlignmentTool, open the *ContentView.swift* file, and remove all the existing contents.

Next, open a web browser and navigate to the following URL:

http://bit.ly/2MCioyl

This page contains the source code for a tool in a file named *alignment-guides-tool.swift*. Select and copy the entire source code from the file and paste it into the *ContentView.swift* file in Xcode. Once loaded, compile and run the app on an iPad device or simulator in landscape mode where it will appear as shown in Figure 29-10:

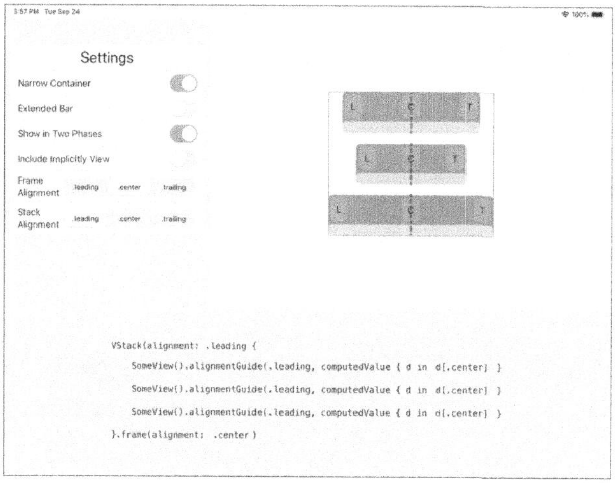

Figure 29-10

Turn on the *Include Implicitly View* option to see what a view will do without any alignment guides and use the yellow bars under each view together with the green L, C, and T buttons and the Stack Alignment options to try different combinations of guide settings. With each selection, the VStack declaration in the bottom section of the screen will change to reflect the current configuration.

29.4 Custom Alignment Types

In the previous examples, changes have been made to view alignments based on the standard alignment types. SwiftUI provides a way for the set of standard types to be extended by declaring custom alignment types. A custom alignment type named *oneThird* could, for example, be created which would make the point of alignment one-third of the distance from a specified edge of a view.

Take, for example, the following HStack configuration consisting of four rectangles centered vertically:

Figure 29-11

The declaration to display the above layout reads as follows:

```
HStack(alignment: .center) {
      Rectangle()
          .foregroundColor(Color.green)
          .frame(width: 50, height: 200)
      Rectangle()
          .foregroundColor(Color.red)
          .frame(width: 50, height: 200)
      Rectangle()
          .foregroundColor(Color.blue)
          .frame(width: 50, height: 200)
      Rectangle()
          .foregroundColor(Color.orange)
          .frame(width: 50, height: 200)
}
```

To change the alignment of one or more of these rectangles, alignment guides could be applied containing the calculations for a computed value. An alternative approach is to create a custom alignment that can be applied to multiple views. This is achieved by extending either VerticalAlignment or HorizontalAlignment to add a new alignment type that returns a calculated value. The following example creates a new vertical alignment type:

```
extension VerticalAlignment {
    private enum OneThird : AlignmentID {
        static func defaultValue(in d: ViewDimensions) -> CGFloat {
            return d.height / 3
        }
    }
    static let oneThird = VerticalAlignment(OneThird.self)
}
```

The extension must contain an enum that conforms to the AlignmentID protocol which, in turn, dictates that a function named *defaultValue()* is implemented. This function must accept a ViewDimensions object for a view and return a CGFloat computed value indicating the alignment guide position. In the above example, a position one-third of the height of the view is returned.

Once implemented, the custom alignment can be used as shown in the following HStack declaration:

```
HStack(alignment: .oneThird) {
    Rectangle()
        .foregroundColor(Color.green)
        .frame(width: 50, height: 200)
    Rectangle()
        .foregroundColor(Color.red)
        .alignmentGuide(.oneThird,
             computeValue: { d in d[VerticalAlignment.top] })
        .frame(width: 50, height: 200)

    Rectangle()
        .foregroundColor(Color.blue)

        .frame(width: 50, height: 200)
    Rectangle()
        .foregroundColor(Color.orange)
        .alignmentGuide(.oneThird,
             computeValue: { d in d[VerticalAlignment.top] })
        .frame(width: 50, height: 200)
}
```

In the above example, the new *oneThird* custom alignment has been applied to two of the rectangle views, resulting in the following layout:

Figure 29-12

In both cases, the alignment was calculated relative to the top of the view with no additional modifications. In fact, the custom alignment can be used in the same way as a standard alignment type. For example, the following changes align the red rectangle relative to the bottom edge of the view:

```
.alignmentGuide(.oneThird,
            computeValue: { d in d[VerticalAlignment.bottom] })
```

Now when the view is rendered, the alignment guide is set to a position one-third of the view height below the bottom edge of the view:

Figure 29-13

29.5 Cross Stack Alignment

A typical user interface layout will be created by nesting stacks to multiple levels. A key shortcoming of the standard alignment types is that they do not provide a way for a view in one stack to be aligned with a view in another stack. Consider the following stack configuration consisting of a VStack embedded inside an HStack. In addition to the embedded VStack, the HStack also contains a single additional view:

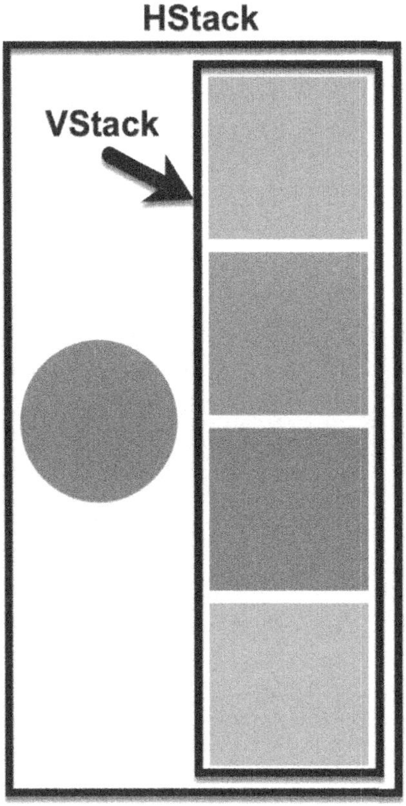

Figure 29-14

The corresponding declaration for the above nested layout reads as follows:

```
HStack(alignment: .center, spacing: 20) {

    Circle()
        .foregroundColor(Color.purple)
        .frame(width: 100, height: 100)

    VStack(alignment: .center) {
        Rectangle()
            .foregroundColor(Color.green)
            .frame(width: 100, height: 100)
        Rectangle()
            .foregroundColor(Color.red)
            .frame(width: 100, height: 100)
```

```
        Rectangle()
            .foregroundColor(Color.blue)
            .frame(width: 100, height: 100)
        Rectangle()
            .foregroundColor(Color.orange)
            .frame(width: 100, height: 100)
    }
}
```

Currently, both the view represented by the circle and the VStack are centered in the vertical plane within the HStack. If we wanted the circle to align with either the top or bottom squares in the VStack we could change the HStack alignment to .top or .bottom and the view would align with the top or bottom squares respectively. If, on the other hand, the purple circle view needed to be aligned with either the second or third square there would be no way of doing so using the standard alignment types. Fortunately, this can be achieved by creating a custom alignment and applying it to both the circle and the square within the VStack with which it is to be aligned.

A simple custom alignment that returns an alignment value relative to the bottom edge of a view can be implemented as follows:

```
extension VerticalAlignment {
    private enum CrossAlignment : AlignmentID {
        static func defaultValue(in d: ViewDimensions) -> CGFloat {
            return d[.bottom]
        }
    }
    static let crossAlignment = VerticalAlignment(CrossAlignment.self)
}
```

This custom alignment can now be used to align views embedded in different stacks. In the following example, the bottom edge of the circle view is aligned with the third square embedded in the VStack:

```
HStack(alignment: .crossAlignment, spacing: 20) {

    Circle()
        .foregroundColor(Color.purple)
        .alignmentGuide(.crossAlignment,
             computeValue: { d in d[VerticalAlignment.center] })
        .frame(width: 100, height: 100)

    VStack(alignment: .center) {
        Rectangle()
            .foregroundColor(Color.green)
            .frame(width: 100, height: 100)
        Rectangle()
            .foregroundColor(Color.red)
            .frame(width: 100, height: 100)
        Rectangle()
            .foregroundColor(Color.blue)
            .alignmentGuide(.crossAlignment, computeValue:
```

```
                                    { d in d[VerticalAlignment.center] })
                    .frame(width: 100, height: 100)
            Rectangle()
                    .foregroundColor(Color.orange)
                    .frame(width: 100, height: 100)
        }

}
```

Note that the alignment of the containing HStack also needs to use the crossAlignment type for the custom alignment to take effect. When rendered, the layout now will appear as illustrated in Figure 29-15 below:

Figure 29-15

29.6 ZStack Custom Alignment

By default, the child views of a ZStack are overlaid on top of each other and center-aligned. The following figure shows three shape views (circle, square, and capsule) stacked on top of each other in a ZStack and center aligned:

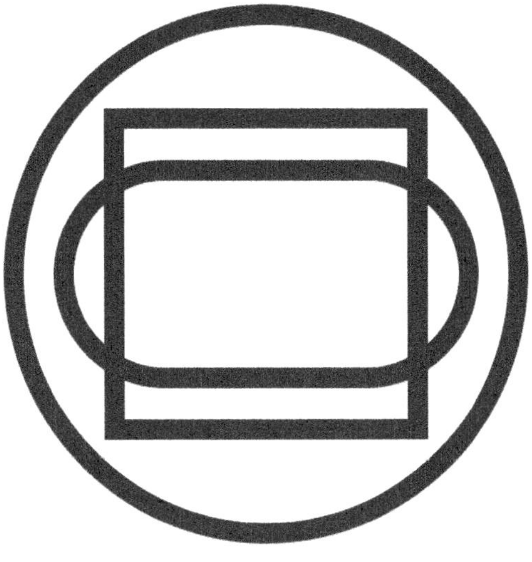

Figure 29-16

Using the standard alignment types, the alignment of all the embedded views can be changed. In Figure 29-17 for example, the ZStack has .leading alignment configured:

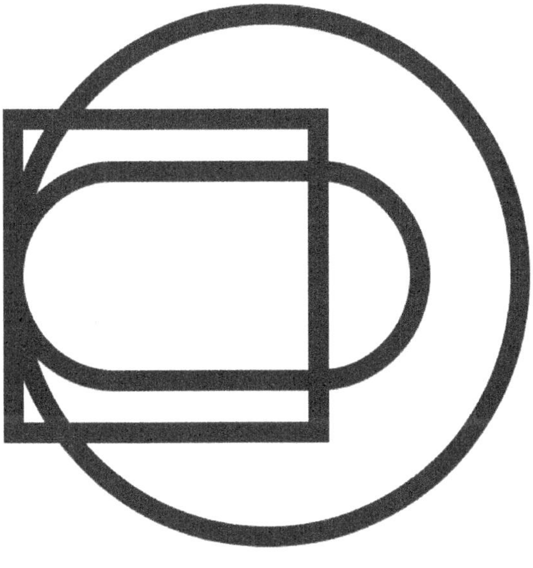

Figure 29-17

To perform more advanced alignment layouts, where each view within the stack has its own alignment, both horizontal and vertical custom alignments must be combined into a single custom alignment, for example:

```
extension HorizontalAlignment {
    enum MyHorizontal: AlignmentID {
        static func defaultValue(in d: ViewDimensions) -> CGFloat
                { d[HorizontalAlignment.center] }
    }
    static let myAlignment =
```

```
                HorizontalAlignment(MyHorizontal.self)
}

extension VerticalAlignment {
    enum MyVertical: AlignmentID {
        static func defaultValue(in d: ViewDimensions) -> CGFloat
                { d[VerticalAlignment.center] }
    }
    static let myAlignment = VerticalAlignment(MyVertical.self)
}

extension Alignment {
    static let myAlignment = Alignment(horizontal: .myAlignment,
                              vertical: .myAlignment)
}
```

Once implemented, the custom alignments can be used to position ZStack child views on both the horizontal and vertical axes:

```
ZStack(alignment: .myAlignment) {
   Rectangle()
        .foregroundColor(Color.green)
        .alignmentGuide(HorizontalAlignment.myAlignment)
                          { d in d[.trailing]}
        .alignmentGuide(VerticalAlignment.myAlignment)
                          { d in d[VerticalAlignment.bottom] }
        .frame(width: 100, height: 100)

   Rectangle()
        .foregroundColor(Color.red)
        .alignmentGuide(VerticalAlignment.myAlignment)
                          { d in d[VerticalAlignment.top] }
        .alignmentGuide(HorizontalAlignment.myAlignment)
                          { d in d[HorizontalAlignment.center] }
        .frame(width: 100, height: 100)

    Circle()
        .foregroundColor(Color.orange)
        .alignmentGuide(HorizontalAlignment.myAlignment)
                          { d in d[.leading] }
        .alignmentGuide(VerticalAlignment.myAlignment)
                          { d in d[.bottom] }
        .frame(width: 100, height: 100)
}
```

The above ZStack will appear as shown in Figure 29-18 when rendered:

Figure 29-18

Take some time to experiment with the alignment settings on each view to gain an understanding of how ZStack custom alignment works. Begin, for example, with the following changes:

```
ZStack(alignment: .myAlignment) {
   Rectangle()
        .foregroundColor(Color.green)
        .alignmentGuide(HorizontalAlignment.myAlignment)
                            { d in d[.leading]}
        .alignmentGuide(VerticalAlignment.myAlignment)
                            { d in d[VerticalAlignment.bottom] }
        .frame(width: 100, height: 100)

   Rectangle()
        .foregroundColor(Color.red)
        .alignmentGuide(VerticalAlignment.myAlignment)
                            { d in d[VerticalAlignment.center] }
        .alignmentGuide(HorizontalAlignment.myAlignment)
                            { d in d[HorizontalAlignment.trailing] }
        .frame(width: 100, height: 100)

    Circle()
        .foregroundColor(Color.orange)
        .alignmentGuide(HorizontalAlignment.myAlignment)
                            { d in d[.leading] }
        .alignmentGuide(VerticalAlignment.myAlignment)
                            { d in d[.top] }
        .frame(width: 100, height: 100)
}
```

With these changes made, check the preview canvas and verify that the layout now matches Figure 29-19:

Figure 29-19

29.7 Summary

The SwiftUI stack container views can be configured using basic alignment settings that control the positioning of all child views relative to the container. The alignment of individual views within a stack may be configured using alignment guides. An alignment guide includes a closure that is passed a ViewDimensions object that can be used to compute the alignment position for the view based on the view's height and width. These alignment guides can be implemented as custom alignments which can be reused in the same way as standard alignments when declaring a stack view layout. Custom alignments are also a useful tool when views contained in different stacks need to be aligned with each other. Custom alignment of ZStack child views requires both horizontal and vertical alignment guides.

Chapter 30

30. SwiftUI Lists and Navigation

The SwiftUI List view provides a way to present information to the user in the form of a vertical list of rows. Often the items within a list will navigate to another area of the app when tapped by the user. Behavior of this type is implemented in SwiftUI using the NavigationStack and NavigationLink components.

The List view can present both static and dynamic data and may also be extended to allow for the addition, removal, and reordering of row entries.

This chapter will provide an overview of the List View used in conjunction with NavigationStack and NavigationLink in preparation for the tutorial in the next chapter entitled *"A SwiftUI List and NavigationStack Tutorial"*.

30.1 SwiftUI Lists

The SwiftUI List control provides similar functionality to the UIKit TableView class in that it presents information in a vertical list of rows with each row containing one or more views contained within a cell. Consider, for example, the following List implementation:

```
struct ContentView: View {
    var body: some View {

        List {
            Text("Wash the car")
            Text("Vacuum house")
            Text("Pick up kids from school bus @ 3pm")
            Text("Auction the kids on eBay")
            Text("Order Pizza for dinner")
        }
    }
}
```

When displayed in the preview, the above list will appear as shown in Figure 30-1:

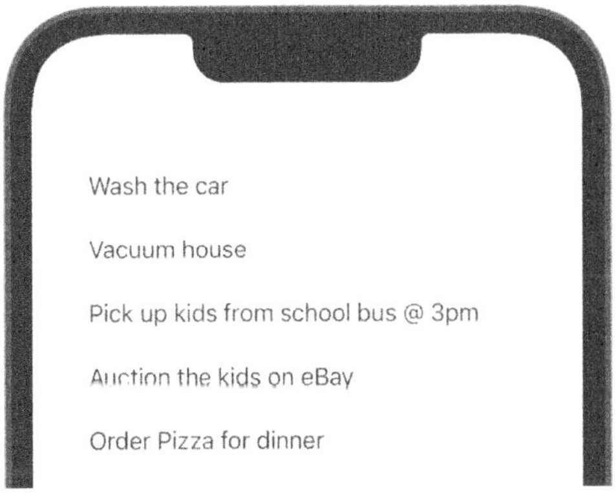

Figure 30-1

A list cell is not restricted to containing a single component. In fact, any combination of components can be displayed in a list cell. Each row of the list in the following example consists of an image and text component within an HStack:

```
List {
    HStack {
        Image(systemName: "trash.circle.fill")
        Text("Take out the trash")
    }
    HStack {
        Image(systemName: "person.2.fill")
        Text("Pick up the kids") }
    HStack {
        Image(systemName: "car.fill")
        Text("Wash the car")
    }
}
```

The preview canvas for the above view structure will appear as shown in Figure 30-2 below:

Figure 30-2

30.2 Modifying List Separators and Rows

The lines used by the List view to separate rows can be hidden by applying the *listRowSeparator()* modifier to the cell content views. The *listRowSeparatorTint()* modifier, on the other hand, can be used to change the color of the lines. It is even possible to assign a view to appear as the background of a row using the *listRowBackground()* modifier. The following code, for example, hides the first separator, changes the tint of the next two separators, and displays a background image on the final row:

```
List {
    Text("Wash the car")
        .listRowSeparator(.hidden)
    Text("Pick up kids from school bus @ 3pm")
        .listRowSeparatorTint(.green)
    Text("Auction the kids on eBay")
        .listRowSeparatorTint(.red)
    Text("Order Pizza for dinner")
        .listRowBackground(Image("MyBackgroundImage"))
}
```

The above examples demonstrate the use of a List to display static information. To display a dynamic list of items a few additional steps are required.

30.3 SwiftUI Dynamic Lists

A list is considered to be dynamic when it contains a set of items that can change over time. In other words, items can be added, edited, and deleted and the list updates dynamically to reflect those changes.

To support a list of this type, each data element to be displayed must be contained within a class or structure that conforms to the Identifiable protocol. The Identifiable protocol requires that the instance contain a property named *id* which can be used to uniquely identify each item in the list. The id property can be any Swift or custom type that conforms to the Hashable protocol which includes the String, Int, and UUID types in addition to several hundred other standard Swift types. If you opt to use UUID as the type for the property, the *UUID()* method can be used to automatically generate a unique ID for each list item.

The following code implements a simple structure for the To Do list example that conforms to the Identifiable protocol. In this case, the id is generated automatically via a call to *UUID()*:

```
struct ToDoItem : Identifiable {
    var id = UUID()
    var task: String
    var imageName: String
}
```

For example, an array of ToDoItem objects can be used to simulate the supply of data to the list which can now be implemented as follows:

```
struct ContentView: View {

    @State var listData: [ToDoItem] = [
       ToDoItem(task: "Take out trash", imageName: "trash.circle.fill"),
       ToDoItem(task: "Pick up the kids", imageName: "person.2.fill"),
       ToDoItem(task: "Wash the car", imageName: "car.fill")
       ]

    var body: some View {

        List(listData) { item in
            HStack {
                Image(systemName: item.imageName)
                Text(item.task)
            }
        }
    }
}
.
.
```

Now the list no longer needs a view for each cell. Instead, the list iterates through the data array and reuses the same HStack declaration, simply plugging in the appropriate data for each array element.

In situations where dynamic and static content needs to be displayed together within a list, the ForEach statement can be used within the body of the list to iterate through the dynamic data while also declaring static entries. The following example includes a static toggle button together with a ForEach loop for the dynamic content:

```
struct ContentView: View {

    @State private var toggleStatus = true
.
.
    var body: some View {

        List {
            Toggle(isOn: $toggleStatus) {
                Text("Allow Notifications")
            }

            ForEach (listData) { item in
                HStack {
                    Image(systemName: item.imageName)
                    Text(item.task)
                }
            }
        }
    }
}
```

Note the appearance of the toggle button and the dynamic list items in Figure 30-3:

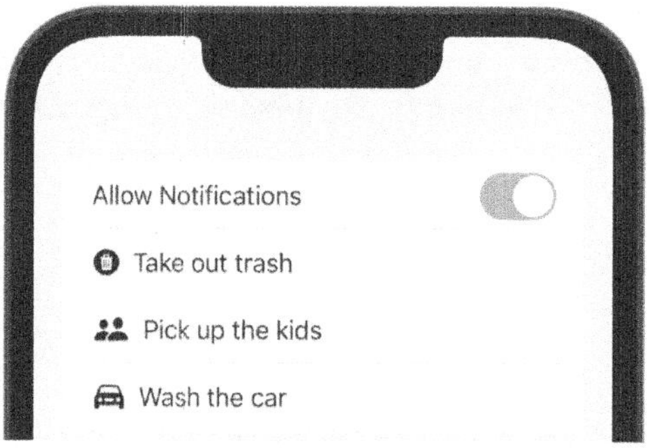

Figure 30-3

A SwiftUI List implementation may also be divided into sections using the Section view, including headers and footers if required. Figure 30-4 shows the list divided into two sections, each with a header:

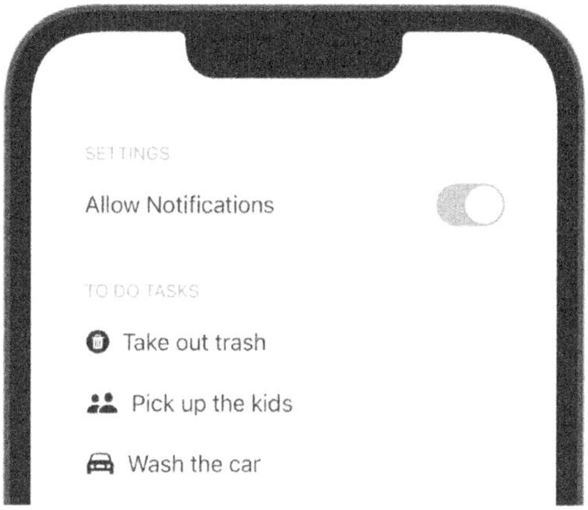

Figure 30-4

The changes to the view declaration to implement these sections are as follows:

```
List {
    Section(header: Text("Settings")) {
        Toggle(isOn: $toggleStatus) {
            Text("Allow Notifications")
        }
    }

    Section(header: Text("To Do Tasks")) {
        ForEach (listData) { item in
            HStack {
                Image(systemName: item.imageName)
                Text(item.task)
            }
        }
    }
}
```

Often the items within a list will navigate to another area of the app when tapped by the user. Behavior of this type is implemented in SwiftUI using the NavigationStack and NavigationLink views.

30.4 Creating a Refreshable List

The data displayed on a screen is often derived from a dynamic source which is subject to change over time. The standard paradigm within iOS apps is for the user to perform a downward swipe to refresh the displayed data. During the refresh process, the app will typically display a spinning progress indicator after which the latest data is displayed. To make it easy to add this type of refresh behavior to your apps, SwiftUI provides the *refreshable()* modifier. When applied to a view, a downward swipe gesture on that view will display the progress indicator and execute the code in the modifier closure. For example, we can add refresh support to our list as follows:

```
List {
    Section(header: Text("Settings")) {
        Toggle(isOn: $toggleStatus) {
            Text("Allow Notifications")
```

```
            }
        }

        Section(header: Text("To Do Tasks")) {
            ForEach (listData) { item in
                HStack {
                    Image(systemName: item.imageName)
                    Text(item.task)
                }
            }
        }
    }
.refreshable {
    listData = [
        ToDoItem(task: "Order dinner", imageName: "dollarsign.circle.fill"),
        ToDoItem(task: "Call financial advisor", imageName: "phone.fill"),
        ToDoItem(task: "Sell the kids", imageName: "person.2.fill")
        ]
}
```

Figure 30-5 demonstrates the effect of performing a downward swipe gesture within the List view after adding the above modifier. Note both the progress indicator at the top of the list and the appearance of the updated to-do list items:

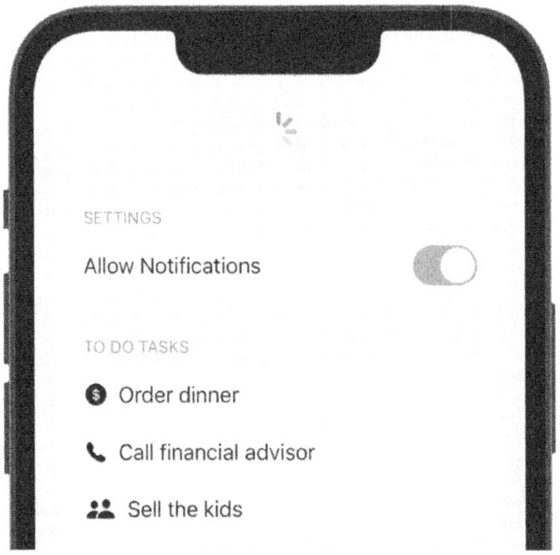

Figure 30-5

When using the *refreshable()* modifier, be sure to perform any time-consuming activities as an asynchronous task using structured concurrency (covered previously in the chapter entitled *"An Overview of Swift Structured Concurrency"*). This will ensure that the app remains responsive during the refresh.

30.5 SwiftUI NavigationStack and NavigationLink

To make items in a list navigable, the first step is to embed the entire list within a NavigationStack. Once the list is embedded, the individual rows must be wrapped in a NavigationLink control which is, in turn, passed a value that uniquely identifies each navigation link within the context of the NavigationStack.

The following changes to our example code embed the List view in a NavigationStack and wrap the row content in a NavigationLink:

```
NavigationStack {
    List {
        Section(header: Text("Settings")) {
            Toggle(isOn: $toggleStatus) {
                Text("Allow Notifications")
            }
        }

        Section(header: Text("To Do Tasks")) {
            ForEach (listData) { item in
                NavigationLink(value: item.task) {
                    HStack {
                        Image(systemName: item.imageName)
                        Text(item.task)
                    }
                }
            }
        }
    }
}
```

Note that we have used the item task string as the NavigationLink value to uniquely identify each row. The next step is to specify the destination view to which the user is to be taken when the row is tapped. We achieve this by applying the *navigationDestination(for:)* modifier to the list. When adding this modifier, we need to pass it the value type for which it is to provide navigation. In our example we are using the task string, so we need to specify *String.self* as the value type. Within the trailing closure of the *navigationDestination(for:)* call we need to call the view that is to be displayed when the row is selected. This closure is passed the value from the NavigationLink, allowing us to display the appropriate view:

```
NavigationStack {
    List {
.
.
        Section(header: Text("To Do Tasks")) {
            ForEach (listData) { item in
                NavigationLink(value: item.task) {
                    HStack {
                        Image(systemName: item.imageName)
                        Text(item.task)
                    }
                }
            }
        }
    }
    .navigationDestination(for: String.self) { task in
```

```
            Text("Selected task = \(task)")
        }
}
```

In this example, the navigation link will simply display a new screen containing the destination Text view displaying the *item.task* string value. The finished list will appear as shown in Figure 30-6 with the title and chevrons on the far right of each row now visible indicating that navigation is available. Tapping the links will navigate to and display the destination Text view.

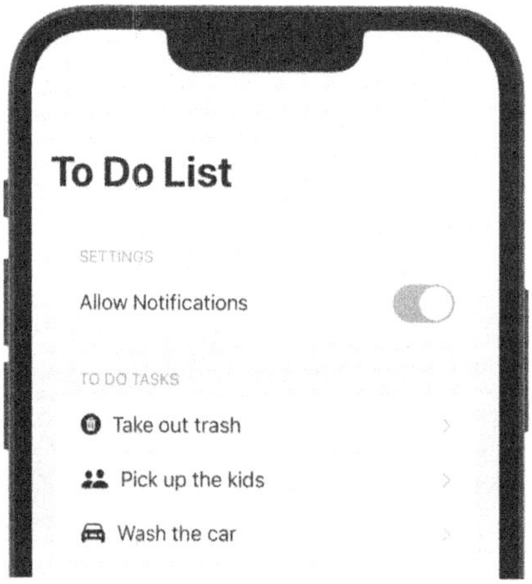

Figure 30-6

30.6 Navigation by Value Type

The *navigationDestination()* modifier is particularly useful for adding navigation support to lists containing values of different types, with each type requiring navigation to a specific view. Suppose, for example, that in addition to the string-based task navigation link, we also have a NavigationLink which is passed an integer value indicating the number of tasks in the list. This could be implemented in our example as follows:

```
NavigationStack {

    List {

        Section(header: Text("Settings")) {
            Toggle(isOn: $toggleStatus) {
                Text("Allow Notifications")
            }

            NavigationLink(value: listData.count) {
                Text("View Task Count")
            }
        }
.
.
```

When this link is selected, we need the app to navigate to a Text view that displays the current task count. All this requires is a second *navigationDestination()* modifier, this time configured to handle Int instead of String values:

.

```
.
}
    .navigationDestination(for: String.self) { task in
        Text("Selected task = \(task)")
    }
    .navigationDestination(for: Int.self) { count in
        Text("Number of tasks = \(count)")
    }
.
.
```

This technique allows us to configure multiple navigation destinations within a single navigation stack based solely on the value type passed to each navigation link.

30.7 Working with Navigation Paths

As the name suggests, NavigationStack provides a stack on which navigation targets are stored as the user navigates through the screens of an app. When a user navigates from one view to another, a reference to the originating view is *pushed* onto the stack. If the user then navigates to another view, the current view will also be placed onto the stack. At any point, the user can tap the back arrow displayed in the navigation bar to move back to the previous view. As the user navigates back through the views, each one is *popped* off the stack until the view from which navigation began is reached.

The views through which a user navigates are called the *navigation path*. SwiftUI allows us to provide our own path by passing an instance of NavigationPath to the NavigationStack instance as follows:

```
struct ContentView: View {

   @State private var stackPath = NavigationPath()

   var body: some View {

        NavigationStack(path: $stackPath) {
.
.
```

With NavigationStack using our path, we can perform tasks such as manually popping targets off the stack to jump back multiple navigation levels instead of making the user navigate through the targets individually. We could, for example, configure a button on a view deep within the stack to take the user directly back to the home screen. We can do this by identifying how many navigation targets are in the stack and then removing them via a call to the *removeLast()* method of the path instance, for example:

```
var stackCount = stackPath.count
stackPath.removeLast(stackCount)
```

We can also programmatically navigate to specific destination views by calling the navigation path's *append()* method and passing through the navigation value associated with the destination:

```
stackPath.append(value)
```

30.8 Navigation Bar Customization

The NavigationStack title bar may also be customized using modifiers on the List component to set the title and to add buttons to perform additional tasks. In the following code fragment the title is set to “To Do List” and a button labeled "Add" is added as a bar item and configured to call a hypothetical method named *addTask()*:

```
NavigationStack {
    List {
.
.
    }
    .navigationBarTitle(Text("To Do List"))
    .navigationBarItems(trailing: Button(action: addTask) {
        Text("Add")
     })
.
.
}
```

30.9 Making the List Editable

It is common for an app to allow the user to delete items from a list and, in some cases, even move an item from one position to another. Deletion can be enabled by adding an *onDelete()* modifier to each list cell, specifying a method to be called which will delete the item from the data source. When this method is called it will be passed an IndexSet object containing the offsets of the rows being deleted and it is the responsibility of this method to remove the selected data from the data source. Once implemented, the user will be able to swipe left on rows in the list to reveal the Delete button as shown in Figure 30-7:

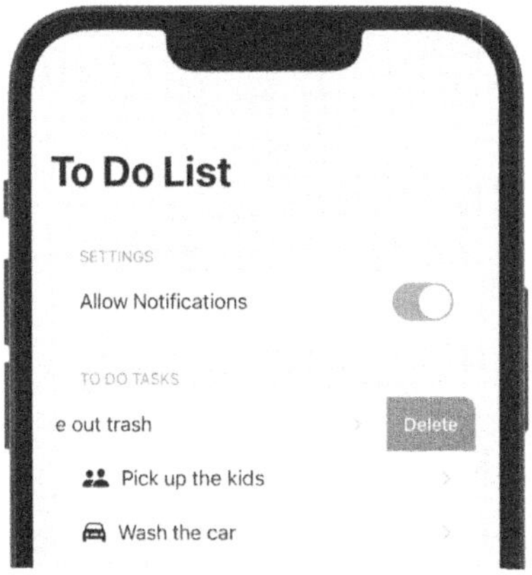

Figure 30-7

The changes to the example List to implement this behavior might read as follows:

```
.
.
List {
    Section(header: Text("Settings")) {
        Toggle(isOn: $toggleStatus) {
            Text("Allow Notifications")
        }
    }

    Section(header: Text("To Do Tasks")) {
```

```
        ForEach (listData) { item in
            NavigationLink(value: item.task) {
                HStack {
                    Image(systemName: item.imageName)
                    Text(item.task)
                }
            }
        }
        .onDelete(perform: deleteItem)
    }
}
.
.
func deleteItem(at offsets: IndexSet) {
    // Delete items from the data source here
}
```

To allow the user to move items up and down in the list the *onMove()* modifier must be applied to the cell, once again specifying a method to be called to modify the ordering of the source data. In this case, the method will be passed an IndexSet object containing the positions of the rows being moved and an integer indicating the destination position.

In addition to adding the *onMove()* modifier, an EditButton instance needs to be added to the List. When tapped, this button automatically switches the list into editable mode and allows items to be moved and deleted by the user. This edit button is added as a navigation bar item which can be attached to a list by applying the *navigationBarItems()* modifier. The List declaration can be modified as follows to add this functionality:

```
List {
    Section(header: Text("Settings")) {
        Toggle(isOn: $toggleStatus) {
            Text("Allow Notifications")
        }
    }

    Section(header: Text("To Do Tasks")) {
        ForEach (listData) { item in
            NavigationLink(value: item.task) {
                HStack {
                    Image(systemName: item.imageName)
                    Text(item.task)
                }
            }
        }
        .onDelete(perform: deleteItem)
        .onMove(perform: moveItem)
    }

}
```

```
.navigationBarTitle(Text("To Do List"))
.navigationBarItems(trailing: EditButton())
.
.
func moveItem(from source: IndexSet, to destination: Int) {
    // Reorder items in source data here
}
```

Viewed within the preview canvas, the list will appear as shown in Figure 30-8 when the Edit button is tapped. Clicking and dragging the three lines on the right side of each row allows the row to be moved to a different list position (in the figure below the "Pick up the kids" entry is in the process of being moved):

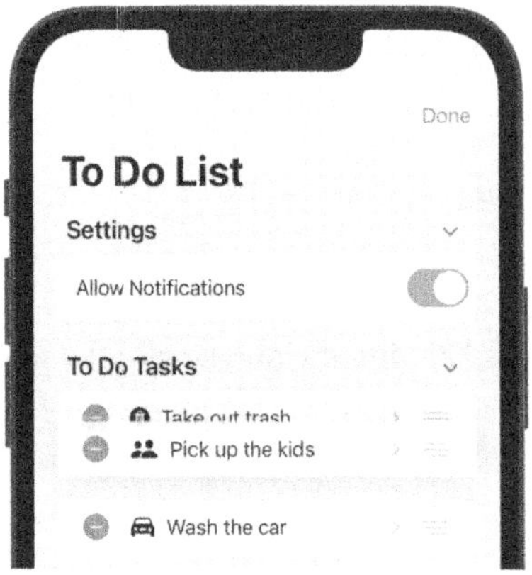

Figure 30-8

30.10 Hierarchical Lists

SwiftUI also includes support for organizing hierarchical data for display in list format as shown in Figure 30-9 below:

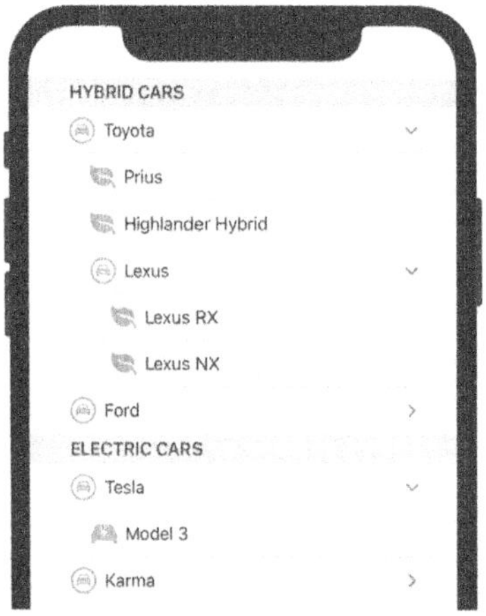

Figure 30-9

This behavior is achieved using features of the List view together with the OutlineGroup and DisclosureGroup views which automatically analyze the parent-child relationships within a data structure to create a browsable list containing controls to expand and collapse branches of data. This topic is covered in detail beginning with the chapter titled *"An Overview of List, OutlineGroup and DisclosureGroup"*.

30.11 Multicolumn Navigation

NavigationStack provides navigation between views where each destination occupies the entire device screen. SwiftUI also supports multicolumn navigation where the destinations appear together on the screen with each appearing in a separate column. Multicolumn navigation is provided by the NavigationSplitView component and will be covered beginning with the chapter titled *"An Overview of Split View Navigation"*.

30.12 Summary

The SwiftUI List view provides a way to order items in a single column of rows, each containing a cell. Each cell, in turn, can contain multiple views when those views are encapsulated in a container view such as a stack layout. The List view provides support for displaying both static and dynamic items or a combination of both. Lists may also be used to group, organize and display hierarchical data.

List views are used to allow the user to navigate to other screens. This navigation is implemented by wrapping the List declaration in a NavigationStack and each row in a NavigationLink, using the *navigationDestination()* modifier to define the navigation target view.

Lists can be divided into titled sections and assigned a navigation bar containing a title and buttons. Lists may also be configured to allow rows to be added, deleted, and moved.

Chapter 31

31. A SwiftUI List and NavigationStack Tutorial

The previous chapter introduced the List, NavigationStack, and NavigationLink views and explained how these can be used to present a navigable and editable list of items to the user. This chapter will create a project that provides a practical example of these concepts.

31.1 About the ListNavDemo Project

When completed, the project will consist of a List view in which each row contains a cell displaying image and text information. Selecting a row within the list will navigate to a details screen containing more information about the selected item. In addition, the List view will include options to add and remove entries and to change the ordering of rows in the list.

The project extensively uses state properties and observable objects to keep the user interface synchronized with the data model.

31.2 Creating the ListNavDemo Project

Launch Xcode and select the option to create a new Multiplatform App named *ListNavDemo*.

31.3 Preparing the Project

Before beginning the development of the app project, some preparatory work needs to be performed involving the addition of image and data assets which will be needed later in the chapter.

The assets to be used in the project are included in the source code sample download provided with the book available from the following URL:

https://www.ebookfrenzy.com/retail/swiftui-ios16/

Once the code samples have been downloaded and unpacked, open a Finder window, and locate the *CarAssets.xcassets* folder and drag and drop it onto the project navigator panel as illustrated in Figure 31-1:

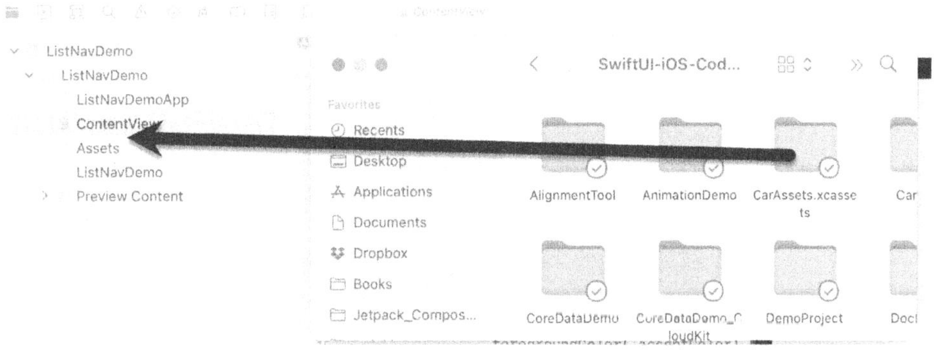

Figure 31-1

When the options dialog appears, enable the *Copy items if needed* option so that the assets are included within the project folder before clicking on the Finish button. With the image assets added, find the *carData.json* file located in the CarData folder and drag and drop it onto the Project navigator panel to also add it to the project.

This JSON file contains entries for different hybrid and electric cars including a unique id, model, description, a Boolean property indicating whether or not it is a hybrid vehicle, and the filename of the corresponding car image in the asset catalog. The following, for example, is the JSON entry for the Tesla Model 3:

```
{
    "id": "aa32jj887hhg55",
    "name": "Tesla Model 3",
    "description": "Luxury 4-door all-electric car. Range of 310 miles. 0-60mph
in 3.2 seconds ",
    "isHybrid": false,
    "imageName": "tesla_model_3"
}
```

31.4 Adding the Car Structure

Now that the JSON file has been added to the project, a structure needs to be declared to represent each car model. Add a new Swift file to the project by selecting the *File -> New -> File...* menu option, selecting Swift File in the template dialog and clicking on the Next button. Name the file *Car.swift* on the subsequent screen before clicking on the Create button.

Once created, the new file will load into the code editor where it needs to be modified so that it reads as follows:

```
import SwiftUI

struct Car : Codable, Identifiable {
    var id: String
    var name: String

    var description: String
    var isHybrid: Bool

    var imageName: String
}
```

As we can see, the structure contains a property for each field in the JSON file and is declared as conforming to the Identifiable protocol so that each instance can be uniquely identified within the List view.

31.5 Loading the JSON Data

The project will also need a way to load the *carData.json* file and translate the car entries into an array of Car objects. For this, we will add another Swift file containing a convenience function that reads the JSON file and initializes an array that can be accessed elsewhere in the project.

Using the steps outlined previously, add another Swift file named *CarData.swift* to the project and modify it as follows:

```
import UIKit
import SwiftUI

var carData: [Car] = loadJson("carData.json")
```

```
func loadJson<T: Decodable>(_ filename: String) -> T {
    let data: Data

    guard let file = Bundle.main.url(forResource: filename,
                                     withExtension: nil)
    else {
        fatalError("\(filename) not found.")
    }

    do {
        data = try Data(contentsOf: file)
    } catch {
        fatalError("Could not load \(filename): \(error)")
    }

    do {
        return try JSONDecoder().decode(T.self, from: data)
    } catch {
        fatalError("Unable to parse \(filename): \(error)")
    }
}
```

The file contains a variable referencing an array of Car objects which is initialized by a call to the *loadJson()* function. The *loadJson()* function is a standard example of how to load a JSON file and can be used in your own projects.

31.6 Adding the Data Store

When the user interface has been designed, the List view will rely on an observable object to ensure that the latest data is always displayed to the user. So far, we have a Car structure and an array of Car objects loaded from the JSON file to act as a data source for the project. The last step in getting the data ready for use in the app is to add a data store structure. This structure will need to contain a published property that can be observed by the user interface to keep the List view up to date. Add another Swift file to the project, this time named *CarStore.swift*, and implement the class as follows:

```
import SwiftUI
import Combine

class CarStore : ObservableObject {

    @Published var cars: [Car]

    init (cars: [Car] = []) {
        self.cars = cars
    }
}
```

This file contains a published property in the form of an array of Car objects and an initializer which is passed the array to be published.

With the data side of the project complete, it is now time to begin designing the user interface.

31.7 Designing the Content View

Select the *ContentView.swift* file and modify it as follows to add a state object binding to an instance of CarStore, passing through to its initializer the carData array created in the *CarData.swift* file:

```
import SwiftUI

struct ContentView: View {

    @StateObject var carStore : CarStore = CarStore(cars: carData)
.
.
```

The content view is going to require a List view to display information about each car. Now that we have access to the array of cars via the carStore property, we can use a ForEach loop to display a row for each car model. The cell for each row will be implemented as an HStack containing an Image and a Text view, the content of which will be extracted from the carData array elements. Remaining in the *ContentView.swift* file, delete the existing views and implement the list as follows:

```
.
.
    var body: some View {

        List {
            ForEach (0..<carStore.cars.count, id: \.self) { i in
                HStack {
                    Image(carStore.cars[i].imageName)
                        .resizable()
                        .aspectRatio(contentMode: .fit)
                        .frame(width: 100, height: 60)
                    Text(carStore.cars[i].name)
                }
            }
        }
    }
}
.
.
```

With the change made to the view, use the preview canvas to verify that the list populates with content as shown in Figure 31-2:

Figure 31-2

Before moving to the next step in the tutorial, the cell declaration will be extracted to a subview to make the declaration tidier. Within the editor, hover the mouse pointer over the HStack declaration and hold down the keyboard Command key so that the declaration highlights. With the Command key still depressed, left-click and select the *Extract Subview* menu option:

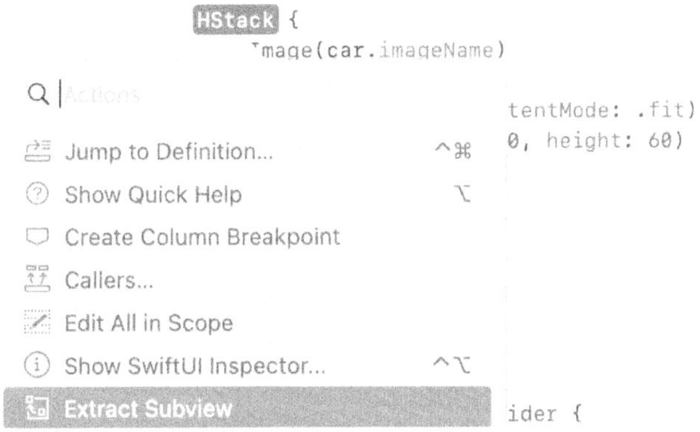

Figure 31-3

Once the view has been extracted, change the name from the default ExtractedView to ListCell. Because the ListCell subview is used within a ForEach statement, the current car will need to be passed through when it is used. Modify both the ListCell declaration and the reference as follows to remove the syntax errors:

```
var body: some View {

        List {
            ForEach (carStore.cars) { car in
                ListCell(car: carStore.cars[i])
        }
    }
}
}
```

```
struct ListCell: View {

    var car: Car

    var body: some View {
        HStack {
            Image(car.imageName)
                .resizable()
                .aspectRatio(contentMode: .fit)
                .frame(width: 100, height: 60)
            Text(car.name)
        }
    }
}
```

Use the preview canvas to confirm that the extraction of the cell as a subview has worked successfully.

31.8 Designing the Detail View

When a user taps a row in the list, a detail screen will appear showing additional information about the selected car. The layout for this screen will be declared in a separate SwiftUI View file which now needs to be added to the project. Use the *File -> New -> File...* menu option once again, this time selecting the SwiftUI View template option and naming the file CarDetail.

When the user navigates to this view from within the List, it will need to be passed the Car instance for the selected car so that the correct details are displayed. Begin by adding a property to the structure and configuring the preview provider to display the details of the first car in the carData array within the preview canvas as follows:

```
import SwiftUI

struct CarDetail: View {

    let selectedCar: Car

    var body: some View {
.
.
    }
}

struct CarDetail_Previews: PreviewProvider {
    static var previews: some View {
        CarDetails(selectedCar: carData[0])
    }
}
```

For this layout, a Form container will be used to organize the views. This is a container view that allows views to be grouped and divided into different sections. The Form also places a line divider between each child view.

Within the body of the *CarDetail.swift* file, implement the layout as follows:

```
var body: some View {
    Form {
        Section(header: Text("Car Details")) {
            Image(selectedCar.imageName)
                .resizable()
                .cornerRadius(12.0)
                .aspectRatio(contentMode: .fit)
                .padding()

                Text(selectedCar.name)
                    .font(.headline)

                Text(selectedCar.description)
                    .font(.body)

                HStack {
                    Text("Hybrid").font(.headline)
                    Spacer()
                    Image(systemName: selectedCar.isHybrid ?
                            "checkmark.circle" : "xmark.circle" )
                }
        }
    }
}
```

Note that the Image view is configured to be resizable and scaled to fit the available space while retaining the aspect ratio. Rounded corners are also applied to make the image more visually appealing and either a circle or checkmark image is displayed in the HStack based on the setting of the isHybrid Boolean setting of the selected car.

When previewed, the screen should match that shown in Figure 31-4:

Figure 31-4

31.9 Adding Navigation to the List

The next step in this tutorial is to return to the List view in the *ContentView.swift* file and implement navigation so that selecting a row displays the detail screen populated with the corresponding car details.

With the *ContentView.swift* file loaded into the code editor, locate the call to the ListCell subview declaration and embed it within a NavigationLink using the current ForEach counter as the link value:

```
var body: some View {
    List {
        ForEach (0..<carStore.cars.count, id: \.self) { i in
            NavigationLink(value: i) {
                ListCell(car: carStore.cars[i])
            }
        }


    }
}
```

For this navigation link to function, the List view must also be embedded in a NavigationStack as follows:

```
var body: some View {
    NavigationStack {
        List {
            ForEach (0..<carStore.cars.count, id: \.self) { i in
                NavigationLink(value: i) {
                    ListCell(car: carStore.cars[i])
                }
            }
        }
    }
}
```

Next, we need to add the navigation destination modifier to the list so that tapping an item navigates to the CarDetail view containing details of the selected car:

```
NavigationStack {
    List {
        ForEach (0..<carStore.cars.count, id: \.self) { i in
            NavigationLink(value: i) {
                ListCell(car: carStore.cars[i])
            }
        }
    }
    .navigationDestination(for: Int.self) { i in
        CarDetail(selectedCar: carStore.cars[i])
    }
}
```

Test that the navigation works using the preview canvas in Live mode and selecting different rows, confirming each time that the detail view appears containing information matching the selected car model.

31.10 Designing the Add Car View

The final view to be added to the project is the screen to be displayed when the user is adding a new car to the list. Add a new SwiftUI View file to the project named *AddNewCar.swift* including some state properties and a declaration for storing a reference to the carStore binding (this reference will be passed to the view from the ContentView when the user taps an Add button). Also, modify the preview provider to pass the carData array into the view for testing purposes:

```
import SwiftUI

struct AddNewCar: View {

    @StateObject var carStore : CarStore
    @State private var isHybrid = false
    @State private var name: String = ""
    @State private var description: String = ""
.
.
struct AddNewCar_Previews: PreviewProvider {
    static var previews: some View {
        AddNewCar(carStore: CarStore(cars: carData))
    }
}
```

Next, add a new subview to the declaration that can be used to display a Text and TextField view pair into which the user will enter details of the new car. This subview will be passed a String value for the text to appear on the Text view and a state property binding into which the user's input is to be stored. As outlined in the chapter entitled *"SwiftUI State Properties, Observable, State, and Environment Objects"*, a property must be declared using the @Binding property wrapper if the view is being passed a state property. Remaining in the *AddNewCar.swift* file, implement this subview as follows:

```
struct DataInput: View {

    var title: String
    @Binding var userInput: String

    var body: some View {
        VStack(alignment: HorizontalAlignment.leading) {
            Text(title)
                .font(.headline)
            TextField("Enter \(title)", text: $userInput)
                        .textFieldStyle(RoundedBorderTextFieldStyle())
        }
        .padding()
    }
}
```

With the subview added, declare the user interface layout for the main view as follows:

```
var body: some View {
```

```
        Form {
            Section(header: Text("Car Details")) {
                Image(systemName: "car.fill")
                    .resizable()
                    .aspectRatio(contentMode: .fit)
                    .padding()

                DataInput(title: "Model", userInput: $name)
                DataInput(title: "Description", userInput: $description)

                Toggle(isOn: $isHybrid) {
                        Text("Hybrid").font(.headline)
                }.padding()
            }

            Button(action: addNewCar) {
                Text("Add Car")
                }
            }
}
```

Note that two instances of the DataInput subview are included in the layout with an Image view, a Toggle, and a Button. The Button view is configured to call an action method named addNewCar when clicked. Within the body of the ContentView declaration, add this function now so that it reads as follows:

```
.
.
                Button(action: addNewCar) {
                    Text("Add Car")
                    }
                }
        }

        func addNewCar() {
            let newCar = Car(id: UUID().uuidString,
                        name: name, description: description,
                        isHybrid: isHybrid, imageName: "tesla_model_3" )

            carStore.cars.append(newCar)
        }
}
```

The new car function creates a new Car instance using the Swift *UUID()* method to generate a unique identifier for the entry and the content entered by the user. For simplicity, rather than add code to select a photo from the photo library the function reuses the tesla_model_3 image for new car entries. Finally, the new Car instance is appended to the carStore car array.

When rendered in the preview canvas, the AddNewCar view should match Figure 31-5 below:

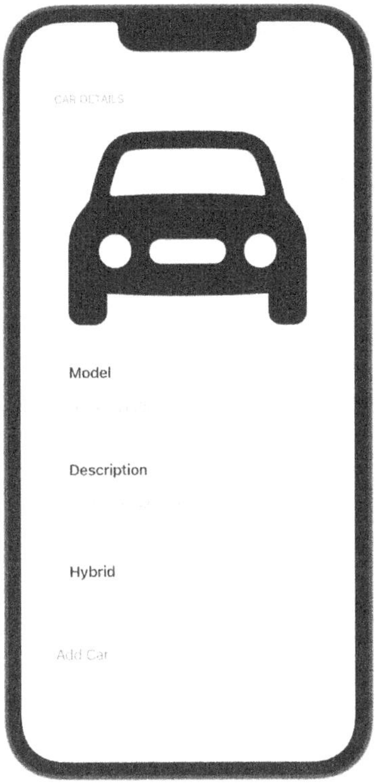

Figure 31-5

With this view completed, the next step is to modify the ContentView layout to include Add and Edit buttons.

31.11 Implementing Add and Edit Buttons

The Add and Edit buttons will be added to a navigation bar applied to the List view in the ContentView layout. The Navigation bar will also be used to display a title at the top of the list. These changes require the use of the *navigationBarTitle()* and *navigationBarItems()* modifiers as follows:

```
var body: some View {
    NavigationStack {
        List {
            ForEach (0..<carStore.cars.count, id: \.self) { i in
                NavigationLink(value: i) {
                    ListCell(car: carStore.cars[i])
                }
            }
        }
        .navigationDestination(for: Int.self) { i in
            CarDetail(selectedCar: carStore.cars[i])
        }
        .navigationBarTitle(Text("EV Cars"))
                .navigationBarItems(leading:
                NavigationLink(value: "Add Car") {
```

```
                    Text("Add")
                        .foregroundColor(.blue)
                }, trailing: EditButton())
    }
}
```

The Add button is configured to appear at the leading edge of the navigation bar and is implemented as a NavigationLink using a string value that reads "Add Car". We now need to add a second navigation destination modifier for this string-based link that displays the AddNewCar view:

```
NavigationStack {
    List {
        ForEach (0..<carStore.cars.count, id: \.self) { i in
            NavigationLink(value: i) {
                ListCell(car: carStore.cars[i])
            }
        }
    }
    .navigationDestination(for: Int.self) { i in
        CarDetail(selectedCar: carStore.cars[i])
    }
    .navigationDestination(for: String.self) { _ in
        AddNewCar(carStore: self.carStore)
    }
    .navigationBarTitle(Text("EV Cars"))
```

The Edit button, on the other hand, is positioned on the trailing edge of the navigation bar and is configured to display the built-in EditButton view. A preview of the modified layout at this point should match the following figure:

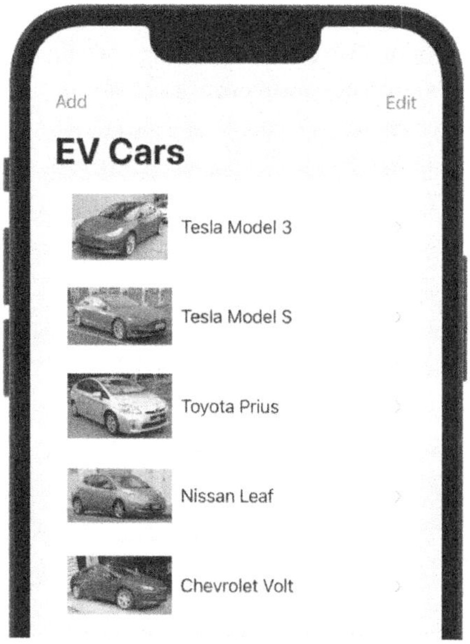

Figure 31-6

Using Live Preview mode, test that the Add button displays the new car screen and that entering new car details and clicking the Add Car button causes the new entry to appear in the list after tapping the back button to return to the content view screen. Ideally, the Add Car button should automatically return us to the content view without the need to use the back button. To implement this, we will need to use a navigation path.

31.12 Adding a Navigation Path

Begin by editing the *ContentView.swift* file, adding a NavigationPath declaration, and passing it through to the NavigationStack:

```
struct ContentView: View {

    @StateObject var carStore : CarStore = CarStore(cars: carData)
    @State private var stackPath = NavigationPath()

    var body: some View {
        NavigationStack(path: $stackPath) {
.
.
```

Having created a navigation path, we need to pass it to the AddNewCar view so that it can be used to return to the content view within the *addNewCar()* function. Edit the string-based *navigationDestination()* modifier to pass the path binding to the view:

```
.navigationDestination(for: String.self) { _ in
    AddNewCar(carStore: carStore: self.carStore, path: $stackPath)
}
```

Edit the *AddNewCar.swift* file to add the path binding parameter as follows:

```
struct AddNewCar: View {

    @StateObject var carStore : CarStore
    @Binding var path: NavigationPath
.
.
```

We also need to comment out the preview provider, since the view is now expecting to be passed a navigation view to which we do not have access within the live preview:

```
/*
struct AddNewCar_Previews: PreviewProvider {
    static var previews: some View {
        AddNewCar(carStore: CarStore(cars: carData))
    }
}
*/
```

The last task in this phase of the tutorial is to call *removeLast()* on the navigation path to pop the current view off the navigation stack and return to the content view:

```
func addNewCar() {
    let newCar = Car(id: UUID().uuidString,
                    name: name, description: description,
```

```
                    isHybrid: isHybrid, imageName: "tesla_model_3" )

    carStore.cars.append(newCar)
    path.removeLast()
}
```

Build and run the app on a device or simulator and test that the Add Car button returns to the content view when clicked.

31.13 Adding the Edit Button Methods

The final task in this tutorial is to add some action methods to be used by the EditButton view added to the navigation bar in the previous section. Because these actions are to be available for every row in the list, the actions must be applied to the list cells as follows:

```
var body: some View {
    NavigationStack(path: $stackPath) {
        List {
            ForEach (0..<carStore.cars.count, id: \.self) { i in
                NavigationLink(value: i) {
                    ListCell(car: carStore.cars[i])
                }
            }
            .onDelete(perform: deleteItems)
            .onMove(perform: moveItems)
        }
        .navigationDestination(for: Int.self) { i in
.
.
```

Next, add the *deleteItems()* and *moveItems()* functions within the scope of the body declaration:

```
.
.
            .navigationBarTitle(Text("EV Cars"))
                    .navigationBarItems(leading:
                    NavigationLink(value: "Add Car") {
                        Text("Add")
                            .foregroundColor(.blue)
                    }, trailing: EditButton())
        }
    }

    func deleteItems(at offsets: IndexSet) {
        carStore.cars.remove(atOffsets: offsets)
    }

    func moveItems(from source: IndexSet, to destination: Int) {
        carStore.cars.move(fromOffsets: source, toOffset: destination)
    }
```

```
}
```

In the case of the *deleteItems()* function, the offsets of the selected rows are provided and used to remove the corresponding elements from the car store array. The *moveItems()* function, on the other hand, is called when the user moves rows to a different location within the list. This function is passed source and destination values which are used to match the row position in the array.

Using Live Preview, click the Edit button and verify that it is possible to delete rows by tapping the red delete icon next to a row and to move rows by clicking and dragging on the three horizontal lines at the far-right edge of a row. In each case, the list contents should update to reflect the changes:

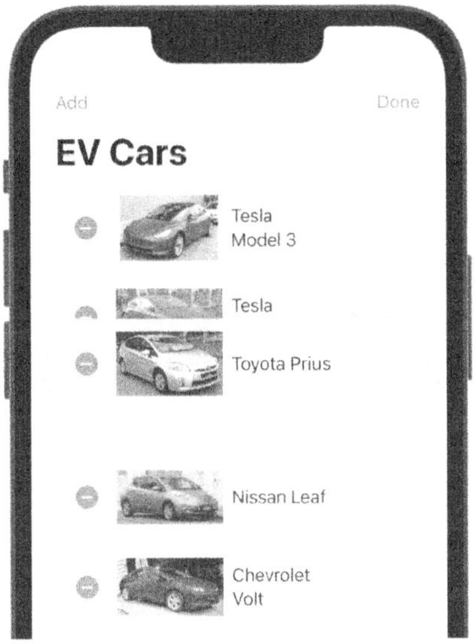

Figure 31-7

31.14 Summary

The main objective of this chapter has been to provide a practical example of using lists, navigation views, and navigation links within a SwiftUI project. This included the implementation of dynamic lists and list editing features. The chapter also served to reinforce topics covered in previous chapters including the use of observable objects, state properties, and property bindings. The chapter also introduced some additional SwiftUI features including the Form container view, navigation bar items, and the TextField view.

32. An Overview of Split View Navigation

The NavigationStack and NavigationLink views outlined in the previous chapters are ideal for adding navigation when each destination view needs to fill the entire device screen. While this is generally the preferred navigation paradigm when working on most iOS devices, it doesn't take advantage of larger display configurations available on the iPad or the iPhone Pro Max in landscape orientation. To take advantage of wider displays, SwiftUI includes the NavigationSplitView component which is designed to provide multicolumn-based navigation.

In this chapter, we will explain how to use NavigationSplitView in preparation for the next chapter titled *"A NavigationSplitView Tutorial"*.

32.1 Introducing NavigationSplitView

The purpose of NavigationSplitView is to provide multicolumn-based navigation on wide displays. It supports a maximum of three columns consisting of the sidebar (marked A in Figure 32-1), content (B), and detail (C) columns. A selection in one column controls the content displayed in the next column. The screen in Figure 32-1 shows the example app we will create in the next chapter. In this case, the app is running on an iPhone Pro Max in landscape orientation:

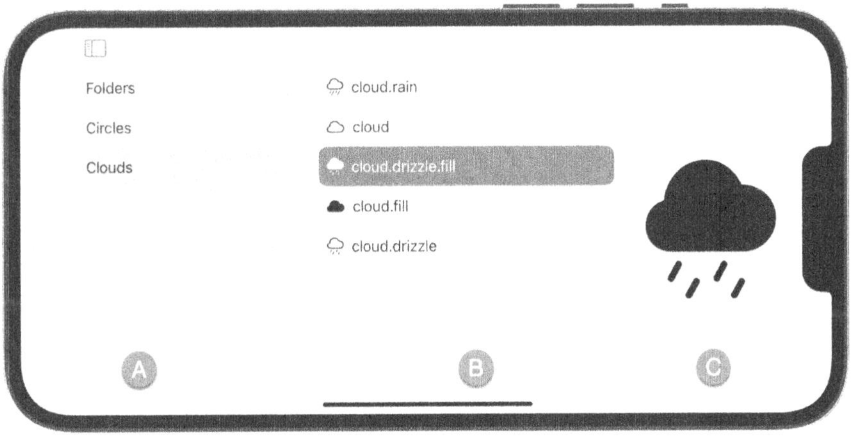

Figure 32-1

When a NavigationSplitView instance runs on narrower displays it behaves similarly to the NavigationStack where each destination view fully occupies the screen.

32.2 Using NavigationSplitView

NavigationSplitView uses a simple syntax that differs depending on whether you need two or three-column navigation. The following syntax is for two-column navigation, which consists of the sidebar and detail columns:

```
NavigationSplitView {
    // Sidebar List here
} detail: {
```

```
    // Detail view here
}
```

Three-column navigation consists of sidebar, content, and detail columns declared using the following syntax:

```
NavigationSplitView {
    // Sidebar List here
} content: {
    // Content List here
} detail: {
    // Detail view here
}
```

32.3 Handling List Selection

Both the sidebar and content columns will typically contain a List view from which the user will choose the content to be displayed in the next column. Selections made in a column are tracked by declaring a state variable and passing it to the List view via the *selection* parameter, for example:

```
@State private var colors = ["Red", "Green", "Blue"]
@State private var selectedColor: String?

var body: some View {
    NavigationSplitView {
        List(colors, id: \.self, selection: $selectedColor) { color in
            Text(color).tag(color)
        }
    } detail: {
        Text( selectedColor ?? "No color selected")
    }
}
```

In the code above, for example, the selection made within the List of color names controls the content displayed by the detail column via the *selectedColor* state variable. Note that the *tag()* modifier has been applied to the Text list item. This is used by SwiftUI to differentiate between selectable items in views such as List, Picker, and TabView.

32.4 NavigationSplitView Configuration

Several options are available to customize the appearance of a NavigationSplitView. For example, the width of an individual column can be controlled using the *navigationSplitViewColumnWidth()* modifier. In the following code the sidebar column has been assigned a fixed width of 100 points:

```
NavigationSplitView {
    List(colors, id: \.self, selection: $selectedColor) { color in
        Text(color).tag(color)
    }
    .navigationSplitViewColumnWidth(100)
} detail: {
    Text( selectedColor ?? "No color selected")
}
```

Style options can also be configured by applying the *navigationSplitViewStyle()* modifier to the NavigationSplitView parent declaration as follows:

```
NavigationSplitView {
    List(colors, id: \.self, selection: $selectedColor) { color in
        Text(color).tag(color)
    }
} detail: {
    Text( selectedColor ?? "No color selected")
}
.navigationSplitViewStyle(.automatic)
```

NavigationSplitView supports the following style options:

- **automatic** - This style allows the navigation view to decide how to present columns based on factors such as current content, screen size, and column selections.
- **balanced** - The balanced style reduces the width of the detail column when necessary to provide space for the sidebar and content columns.
- **prominentDetail** - This style prevents the size of the detail column from changing when the sidebar and content columns are added and removed from view. This style usually results in the sidebar and content columns overlapping the detail column.

32.5 Controlling Column Visibility

Column visibility can be controlled programmatically by passing an appropriately configured state value to NavigationSplitView via its columnVisibility initialization parameter. Changes to the state value will dynamically update the column visibility. Visibility options are provided by the NavigationSplitViewVisibility structure which includes the following options:

- **automatic** - Allows the navigation view to decide which columns should be visible based on the available screen space.
- **all** - Displays the sidebar, content, and detail columns.
- **doubleColumn** - In a two-column configuration, this setting displays the sidebar and detail columns. In a three-column configuration, only the content and detail columns will be visible.
- **detailOnly** - Only the detail column is visible.

The following code provides an example of setting column visibility based on a state variable set to *detailOnly*:

```
.
.
@State private var colors = ["Red", "Green", "Blue"]
@State private var selectedColor: String?
@State private var columnVisibility = NavigationSplitViewVisibility.detailOnly

var body: some View {
    NavigationSplitView(columnVisibility: $columnVisibility) {
        List(colors, id: \.self, selection: $selectedColor) { color in
            Text(color).tag(color)
        }
    } detail: {
```

```
            Text( selectedColor ?? "No color selected")
        }
        .navigationSplitViewStyle(.automatic)
}
```

32.6 Summary

The NavigationSplitView component allows you to build multicolumn-based navigation into your SwiftUI apps. When enough screen width is available, NavigationSplitView will display up to three columns consisting of sidebar, content, and detail columns. The sidebar and content panels contain List view items that, when selected, control the content in the next column. Selection handling is implemented by passing a state variable to the *selection* parameter of the column's List view. The column widths and style of a split navigation user interface can be configured using the *navigationSplitViewColumnWidth()* and *navigationSplitViewStyle()* modifiers. Several combinations of column visibility may be configured programmatically using the NavigationSplitView *columnVisibility* initialization parameter.

Chapter 33

33. A NavigationSplitView Tutorial

The previous chapter introduced us to the SwiftUI NavigationSplitView component and described how multicolumn navigation is implemented and configured. This chapter will take what we have learned about NavigationSplitView and use it to create an example iOS app project.

33.1 About the Project

This tutorial will create the three-column split navigation app illustrated in Figure 32-1 in the previous chapter. The sidebar column will list categories which, when selected, will update the content column to list icons belonging to the chosen category. The detail column will, in turn, display the currently selected icon from the content list.

33.2 Creating the NavSplitDemo Project

Launch Xcode and select the option to create a new Multiplatform App project named *NavSplitDemo*.

33.3 Adding the Project Data

Our first requirement is a class declaration we can use to store category names and corresponding icons. Right-click on the NavSplitDemo folder in the Project navigator, select the *New File...* menu option, and create a new Swift file named *IconCategory.swift*. With the file added to the project, modify it to declare a structure for storing each icon category:

```
import Foundation

struct IconCategory: Identifiable, Hashable {
    let id = UUID()
    var categoryName: String
    var images: [String]
}
```

Next, edit the *ContentView.swift* file and add a state array variable populated with categories and icon names:

```
import SwiftUI

struct ContentView: View {

    @State private var categories = [
        IconCategory(categoryName: "Folders", images: ["questionmark.folder.ar",
                                                        "questionmark.folder",
                                                        "questionmark.folder.fill.ar",
                                                        "folder.fill.badge.gear",
                                                        "questionmark.folder.fill"]),
        IconCategory(categoryName: "Circles", images: ["book.circle",
                                                        "books.vertical.circle",
                                                        "books.vertical.circle.fill",
                                                        "book.circle.fill",
```

```
                                                  "book.closed.circle"]),
        IconCategory(categoryName: "Clouds", images: ["cloud.rain",
                                                  "cloud",
                                                  "cloud.drizzle.fill",
                                                  "cloud.fill",
                                                  "cloud.drizzle"])
    ]
.
.
```

33.4 Creating the Navigation View

The next step is to replace the default view within the ContentView with a NavigationSplitView as outlined below. As the project requires three columns, we need to include the sidebar, content, and detail declarations:

```
.
.
var body: some View {
    NavigationSplitView {

    } content: {

    } detail: {

    }
}
.
.
```

33.5 Building the Sidebar Column

Now that we have added the NavigationSplitView we are ready to add the list of categories in the sidebar column. While doing this, we also need to add a state variable to store the currently selected item in the list. Remaining in the *ContentView.swift* file, make these changes as follows:

```
.
.
@State private var selectedCategory: IconCategory?

var body: some View {
    NavigationSplitView(columnVisibility: $columnVisibility) {
        List(categories, selection: $selectedCategory) { category in
            Text(category.categoryName).tag(category)
        }
    } content: {
.
.
```

The code we have added displays a List view where each item is a Text view displaying a category name from the categories array. The List is passed a reference to our selectedCategory state variable for storing the most recent item selection.

Check the Preview panel and verify that the sidebar appears as shown in Figure 33-1 below:

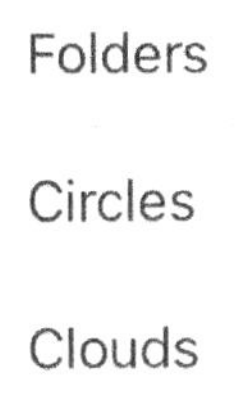

Figure 33-1

33.6 Adding the Content Column List

With the sidebar completed, we are ready to add a list within the content column. Since we also need to keep track of the currently selected icon name we will need another state variable. To avoid showing a blank column, we also need to add some code to display a message if the user has not yet made a category selection. We can do this by using an *if-let* statement to evaluate the selectedCategory state variable:

```
.
.
@State private var selectedCategory: IconCategory?
@State private var selectedImage: String?

var body: some View {
    NavigationSplitView {
        List(categories, selection: $selectedCategory) { category in
            Text(category.categoryName).tag(category)
        }
    } content: {
        if let selectedCategory {
            List(selectedCategory.images, id: \.self,
                               selection: $selectedImage) { image in
                HStack {
                    Image(systemName: image)
                    Text(image)
                }.tag(image)
            }
        } else {
            Text("Select a category")
        }
    } detail: {

    }
}
.
.
```

For each item in the list, we are using a horizontal stack containing the icon and name text. Select an iPad or iPhone Pro Max simulator or physical device as the run target and build and run the app. Once the app is running, rotate the device or simulator into landscape orientation. If the app is functioning as expected, selecting items from the sidebar should cause the content column to list the corresponding icon options as shown in Figure 33-2:

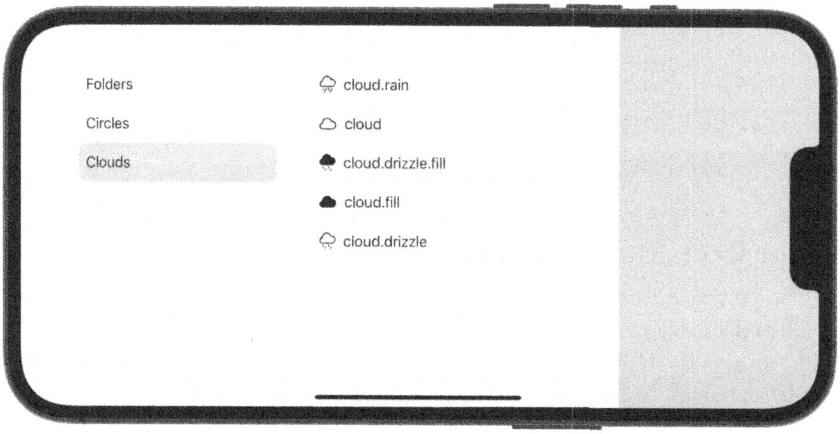

Figure 33-2

33.7 Adding the Detail Column

The detail column will display the selected icon in response to selections made within the content list. Locate the detail section within the NavigationSplitView declaration and modify it as follows, once again adding code to let the user know an icon needs to be selected:

```
NavigationSplitView {
    List(categories, selection: $selectedCategory) { category in
        Text(category.categoryName).tag(category)
    }
} content: {
.
.
} detail: {
    if let selectedImage {
        Image(systemName: selectedImage)
            .resizable()
            .aspectRatio(contentMode: .fit)
            .padding()
    } else {
        Text("Select an image")
    }
}
```

When the app is launched it will appear with only the detail column visible as shown in Figure 33-3:

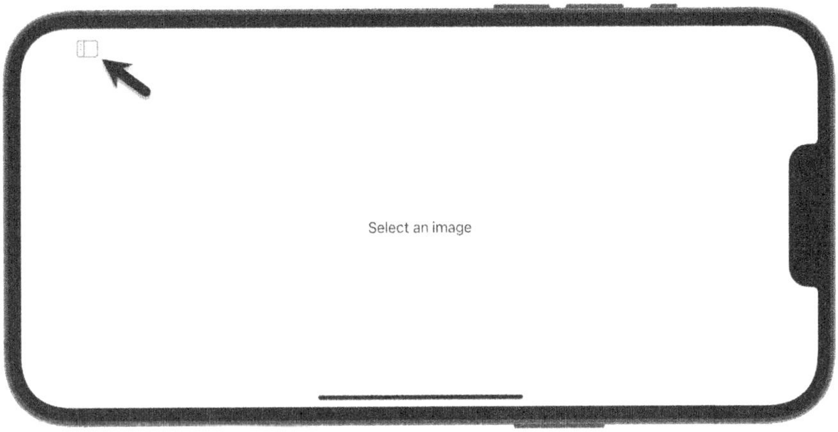

Figure 33-3

Clicking on the button marked by the arrow in the above figure will display the content column. Unfortunately, since we haven't yet made a category selection, this column only shows the "Select a category" message. Clicking the Back button will finally give us access to the sidebar column where we can begin to make selections. Once a category and icon have been selected we can see that the detail column is obscured by the sidebar and content panels. To view the entire icon image we have to click on the detail column to hide the other two columns. While this may be the desired behavior in some situations, this is the opposite of the experience we are looking for in our app so some additional configuration is required.

33.8 Configuring the Split Navigation Experience

The average user would probably find our split navigation implementation confusing. To make the app more intuitive, we need all three columns to be visible when the app first launches. We can achieve this by passing the *all* value to the columnVisibility parameter of the NavigationSplitView instance as follows:

```
.
.
@State private var selectedCategory: IconCategory?
@State private var selectedImage: String?
@State private var columnVisibility = NavigationSplitViewVisibility.all

var body: some View {
    NavigationSplitView(columnVisibility: $columnVisibility) {
        List(categories, selection: $selectedCategory) { category in
            Text(category.categoryName).tag(category)
        }
.
.
```

When we test the app, we will see all three columns but still have the problem that the detail view is obscured by the sidebar and content columns. The final change is to use the *navigationSplitViewStyle()* modifier to apply the balanced style:

```
.
.
            if let selectedImage {
```

```
                Image(systemName: selectedImage)
                    .resizable()
                    .aspectRatio(contentMode: .fit)
                    .padding()
            } else {
                Text("Select an image")
            }
        }
        .navigationSplitViewStyle(.balanced)
    }
}
.
.
```

With this final change applied, the running app should now match Figure 33-4:

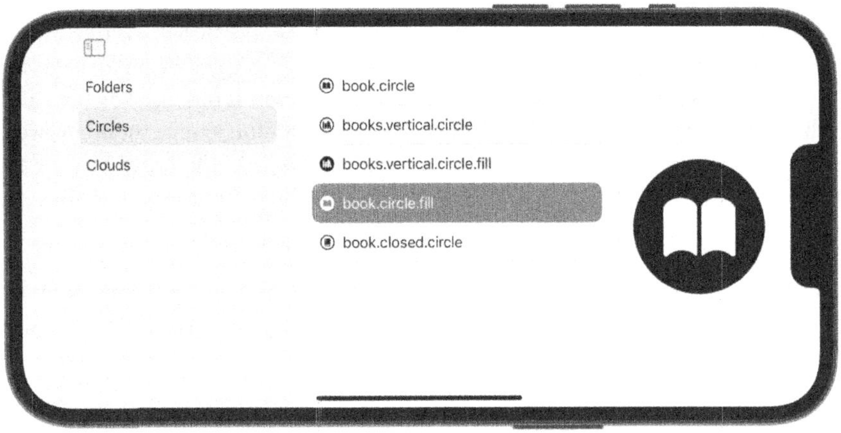

Figure 33-4

33.9 Summary

In this chapter, we created a SwiftUI-based app project that implements three-column navigation using the NavigationSplitView component. We also changed the default navigation behavior to match the requirements of our app.

34. An Overview of List, OutlineGroup and DisclosureGroup

The preceding chapters explored the use of the SwiftUI List view to display information to users in an ordered manner. Lists provide a way to present large amounts of information to the user in a navigable and scrollable format.

The features of the List covered so far, however, have not introduced any way to display hierarchical information within a list other than displaying an entirely new screen to the user in response to list item selections. A standard list also has the potential to overwhelm the user with options through which to scroll, with no way to hide sub-groups of items to ease navigation.

In this chapter, we will explore some features that address these issues, together with the OutlineGroup and DisclosureGroup views. Once these topics have been covered, the next chapter entitled *"A SwiftUI List, OutlineGroup and DisclosureGroup Tutorial"* will demonstrate the practical use of these views.

34.1 Hierarchical Data and Disclosures

In keeping with the automotive theme adopted in the previous chapter, consider an app required to present the user with the hierarchical data illustrated in Figure 34-1:

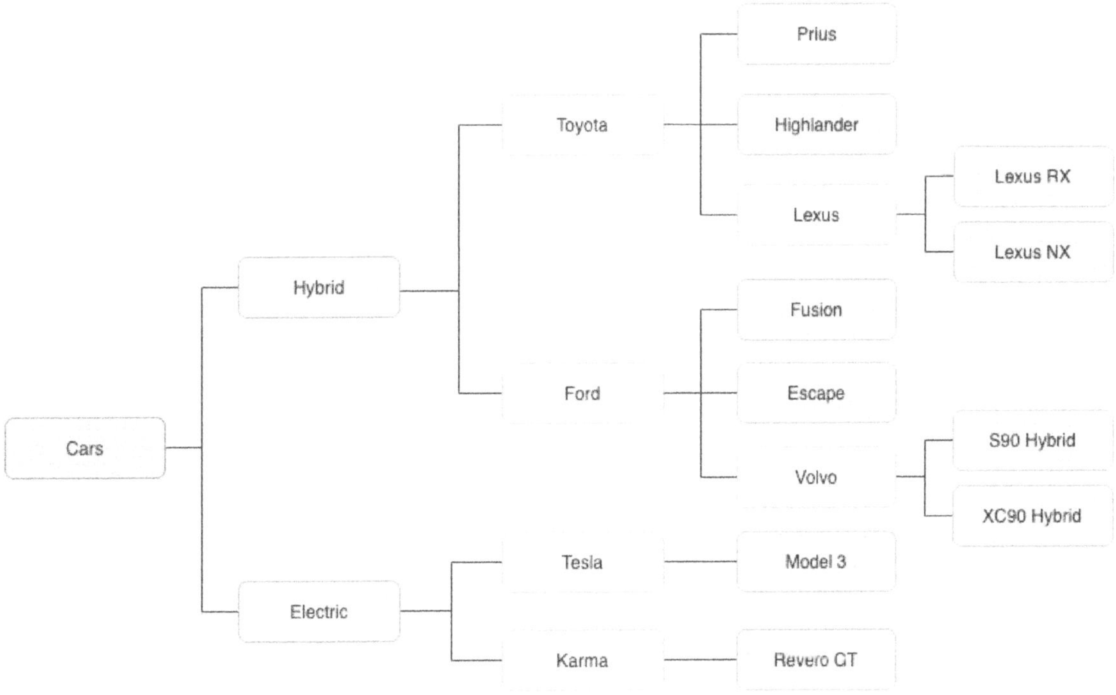

Figure 34-1

When designing such an app, one option would be to begin with a List containing only the two categories of cars

(Hybrid and Electric), presenting each subsequent layer of data on separate screens. A typical path through such a user interface might involve selecting the Hybrid category to navigate to a list containing the two hybrid car manufacturers, within which selecting Toyota would display a third screen containing the two hybrid models together with a selectable entry to display the hybrid models manufactured by Toyota's Lexus sub-brand. Having viewed the Lexus hybrid models, the user would then need to navigate back through multiple list levels to be able to navigate to view Tesla electric vehicles.

Clearly, a better option would be to display the information hierarchically within a single list, allowing the user to hide and show different sections of the hierarchy. Fortunately, this can be achieved using the List and OutlineGroup SwiftUI components.

34.2 Hierarchies and Disclosure in SwiftUI Lists

The previous chapter demonstrated the use of the List component to display so-called "flat", non-hierarchical data to the user. In fact, the List component can also present hierarchically structured data. It does this by traversing the data to identify the child elements in a data structure, and then presenting the resulting hierarchy visually. Figure 34-2 for example, shows the hierarchical data illustrated in Figure 34-1 above presented within a List view:

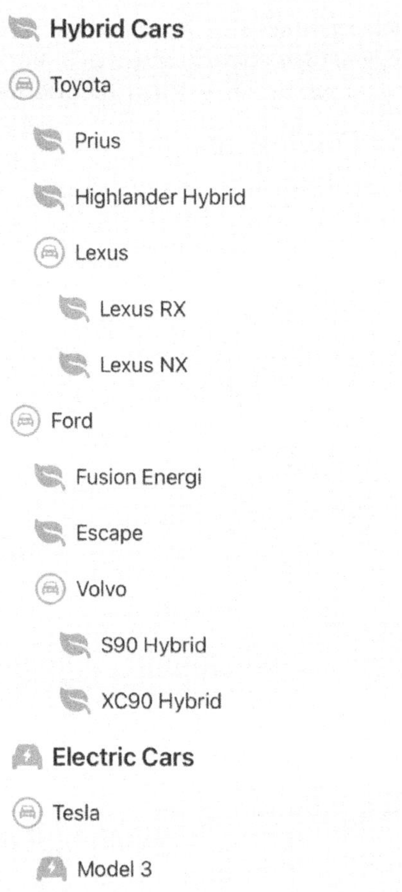

Figure 34-2

Clearly, this provides a better way to present the data to the user without having to traverse multiple depths of list navigation. Note also that disclosure controls are provided in the list to hide and show individual branches of data. Figure 34-3, for example, shows how the disclosure controls (highlighted) have been used to collapse the Toyota, Volvo, and electric car data branches:

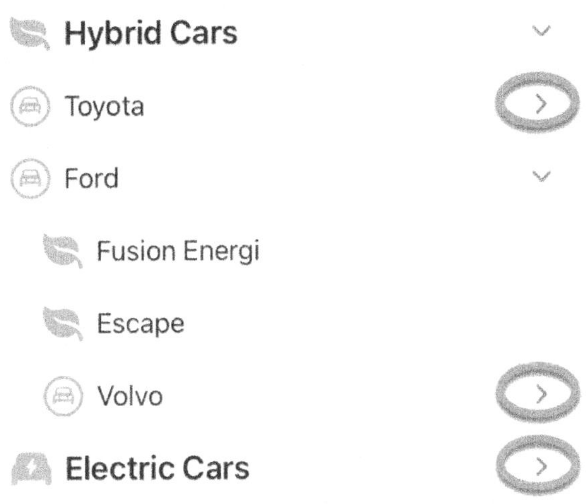

Figure 34-3

Clicking on a collapsed disclosure control will expand the corresponding section of the tree so that it is once again visible.

Assuming that the data to be displayed is correctly structured (an example data structure will be used in the chapter entitled *"A SwiftUI List, OutlineGroup and DisclosureGroup Tutorial"*), the above example was rendered with the following simple SwiftUI declaration:

```
struct ContentView: View {
    var body: some View {
        List(carItems, children: \.children) { item in
            HStack {
                Image(systemName: item.image)
                    .resizable()
                    .scaledToFit()
                    .frame(width: 25, height: 25)
                    .foregroundColor(.green)

                Text(item.name)
                    .font(.system(.title3, design: .rounded))
                    .bold()
            }
        }.listStyle(SidebarListStyle())
    }
}
```

All that was required to enable this behavior was to pass through the data structure (carItems in the above example) to the List view together with a keypath to the children and then iterate through each item.

34.3 Using OutlineGroup

Behind the scenes of the above example, the List view is making use of the OutlineGroup view. When used directly, OutlineGroup provides the same basic functionality such as automatically traversing the data tree structure and providing disclosure controls, but with greater control in terms of customizing the display of the data, particularly in terms of organizing data into groups.

Figure 34-4, for example, shows the same car data displayed using OutlineGroup within a List to categorize the data into sections titled Hybrid Cars and Electric cars:

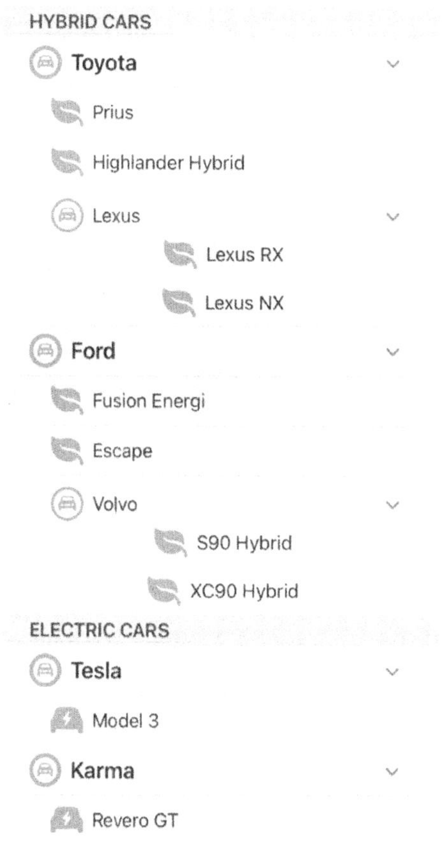

Figure 34-4

The SwiftUI declaration to create and implement the above display using the same car data reads as follows:

```
struct ContentView: View {
    var body: some View {
        List {
                ForEach(carItems) { carItem in
                    Section(header: Text(carItem.name)) {
                        OutlineGroup(carItem.children ?? [Car](),
                                     children: \.children) { child in

                            HStack {
                                Image(systemName: child.image)
```

```
                                    .resizable()
                                    .scaledToFit()
                                    .frame(width: 30, height: 30)
                                    .foregroundColor(.green)
                                Text(child.name)
                            }
                        }
                    }
                }
            }
    }
}
```

In the above example, the OutlineGroup is embedded within a List view. This is not a requirement for using OutlineGroup but results in a more visually pleasing result when the view is rendered.

34.4 Using DisclosureGroup

The disclosure behavior outlined in the previous sections is implemented in the background using the DisclosureGroup view which is also available for use directly in SwiftUI-based apps to allow the user to hide and show non-structured items in a layout. The DisclosureGroup view is particularly useful when used in conjunction with the Form view.

Consider, for example, the following Form based layout:

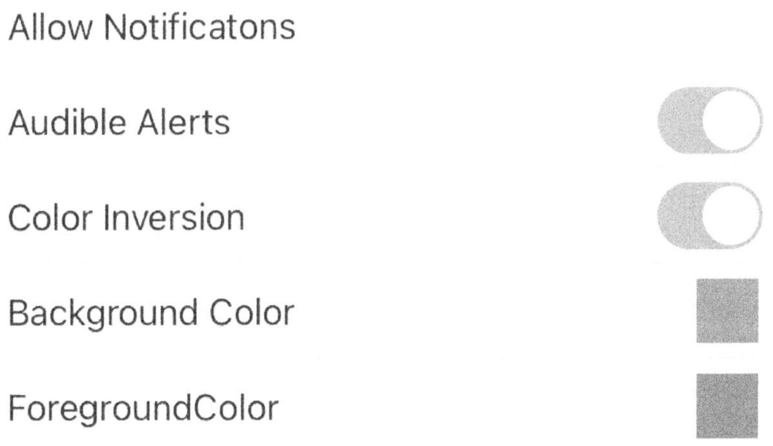

Figure 34-5

The above screen shows part of the settings screen for an app, the SwiftUI declaration for which reads as follows:

```
Form {
    Toggle("Allow Notifications", isOn: $stateOne)
        .padding(.leading)
        Toggle("Audible Alerts", isOn: $stateTwo)
            .padding(.leading)
        Toggle("Color Inversion", isOn: $stateThree)
            .padding(.leading)
```

```
        ColorControl(color: .red, label: "Background Color")
        ColorControl(color: .blue, label: "ForegroundColor")
}
```

The form has been implemented without consideration for grouping items into categories and, while this may be manageable with just five entries, this screen could become difficult to navigate with larger numbers of items.

Using DisclosureGroups, the form might be better organized as shown in Figure 34-6:

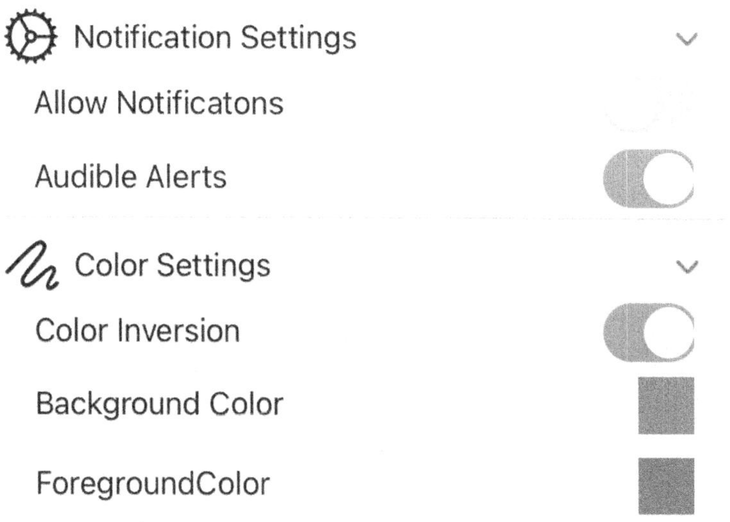

Figure 34-6

In this scenario, the form is divided into groups which can be expanded and collapsed using the embedded disclosure controls.

DisclosureGroups are declared using the following syntax:

```
DisclosureGroup(isExpanded: $controlsVisible) {
        // Content Views go here
        } label: {
            Label("Some Text", systemImage: "gear")
        }
```

Note that the DisclosureGroup accepts an optional trailing closure for declaring the label to appear above the content views. The above example uses a Label view, though this could be any combination of views. The Boolean isExpanded argument is also optional and can be used to control whether the group is expanded when first displayed.

The declaration for the form shown in Figure 34-5 above, might read as follows:

```
Form {
    DisclosureGroup {
        Toggle("Allow Notifications", isOn: $stateOne)
            .padding(.leading)
        Toggle("Audible Alerts", isOn: $stateTwo)
            .padding(.leading)
    } label: {
```

```
        Label("Notification Settings", systemImage: "gear")
    }
        DisclosureGroup {
            Toggle("Color Inversion", isOn: $stateThree)
                .padding(.leading)
            ColorControl(color: .red, label: "Background Color")
            ColorControl(color: .blue, label: "ForegroundColor")
        } label: {
            Label("Color Settings", systemImage: "scribble")
        }
}
```

34.5 Summary

This chapter has introduced the hierarchical data support and disclosure features of the List, OutlineGroup, and DisclosureGroup views included with SwiftUI. The List and OutlineGroup views allow hierarchical data to be displayed to the user with just a few lines of code with disclosure controls provided to allow the user to expand and collapse sections of the hierarchy. These disclosure controls are provided by the DisclosureGroup view which may also be used directly within your own SwiftUI view layouts.

Chapter 35

35. A SwiftUI List, OutlineGroup, and DisclosureGroup Tutorial

The previous chapter covered the List, OutlineGroup, and DisclosureGroup views and explored how these can be used to visually present hierarchical information within an app while allowing the user to selectively hide and display sections of that information.

This chapter will serve as a practical demonstration of these features in action through the creation of an example project.

35.1 About the Example Project

The project created in this chapter will recreate the user interface shown in Figure 34-4 in the previous chapter using the data represented in Figure 34-1. Initially, the project will use a List view to traverse and display the information in the car data structure. Next, the project will be modified to use the OutlineGroup within the List to display the information in groups using section headers. Finally, the project will be extended to use the DisclosureGroup view.

35.2 Creating the OutlineGroupDemo Project

Launch Xcode and select the option to create a new Multiplatform App project named *OutlineGroupDemo*.

35.3 Adding the Data Structure

The first step before a list can be displayed is to add the data structure that will form the basis of the user interface. Each row within the list will be represented by an instance of a structure named CarInfo designed to store the following information:

- **id** – A UUID to uniquely identify each CarInfo instance.
- **name** – A string value containing the name of the car type, manufacturer, or car model.
- **image** – A string referencing the SF Symbol image to be displayed.
- **children** – An array of CarInfo objects representing the children of the current CarInfo instance.

Within the project navigator panel, select the *ContentView.swift* file and modify it to add the CarInfo structure declaration as follows:

```
import SwiftUI

struct CarInfo: Identifiable {
    var id = UUID()
    var name: String
    var image: String
    var children: [CarInfo]?
}
```

```
struct ContentView: View {
    var body: some View {
        VStack {
            Image(systemName: "globe")
                .imageScale(.large)
                .foregroundColor(.accentColor)
            Text("Hello, world!")
        }
    }
}
.
.
```

Now that a structure has been defined, some data needs to be added to populate the CarInfo instances. As mentioned previously, this data structure is represented in Figure 34-1 in the previous chapter. Staying within the *ContentView.swift* file, add the data as a variable declaration as follows (to avoid typing in the structure, it can be cut and pasted from the *CarInfoData.swift* file located in the CarData directory of the code samples download):

```
.
.
struct CarInfo: Identifiable {
    var id = UUID()
    var name: String
    var image: String
    var children: [CarInfo]?
}

let carItems: [CarInfo] = [

    CarInfo(name: "Hybrid Cars", image: "leaf.fill", children: [
        CarInfo(name: "Toyota", image: "car.circle", children : [
            CarInfo(name: "Prius", image: "leaf.fill"),
            CarInfo(name: "Highlander Hybrid", image: "leaf.fill"),
            CarInfo(name: "Lexus", image: "car.circle", children: [
                    CarInfo(name: "Lexus RX", image: "leaf.fill"),
                    CarInfo(name: "Lexus NX", image: "leaf.fill")])
        ]),
        CarInfo(name: "Ford", image: "car.circle", children : [
            CarInfo(name: "Fusion Energi", image: "leaf.fill"),
            CarInfo(name: "Escape", image: "leaf.fill"),
            CarInfo(name: "Volvo", image: "car.circle", children: [
                    CarInfo(name: "S90 Hybrid", image: "leaf.fill"),
                    CarInfo(name: "XC90 Hybrid", image: "leaf.fill")])
        ]),
    ]),
```

```
    CarInfo(name: "Electric Cars", image: "bolt.car.fill", children: [
        CarInfo(name: "Tesla", image: "car.circle", children : [
            CarInfo(name: "Model 3", image: "bolt.car.fill")
        ]),
        CarInfo(name: "Karma", image: "car.circle", children : [
            CarInfo(name: "Revero GT", image: "bolt.car.fill")
        ])
    ])
]

struct ContentView: View {
    var body: some View {
        VStack {
.
.
        }
    }
}
.
.
```

35.4 Adding the List View

With the data structure added to the project, the next step is to modify the content view so that it uses a List configured to extract the structured data from the *carItems* array. Before doing that, however, we first need to design a custom view to be presented within each list cell. Add this view to the *ContentView.swift* file as follows:

```
struct CellView: View {

    var item: CarInfo

    var body: some View {
        HStack {
            Image(systemName: item.image)
                .resizable()
                .scaledToFit()
                .frame(width: 25, height: 25)
                .foregroundColor(.green)
            Text(item.name)
        }
    }
}
```

The above view expects to be passed a CarInfo instance before constructing a horizontal stack displaying the image and a Text view containing the name of the current item. In the case of the image, it is scaled and the foreground is changed to green.

Next, edit the ContentView structure and replace the default "Hello, world!" Text view so that the declaration reads as follows:

```
.
.
struct ContentView: View {
    var body: some View {
        List(carItems, children: \.children) { item in
            CellView(item: item)
        }
    }
}
.
.
```

35.5 Testing the Project

Test the progress so far by referring to the preview canvas and switching into Live Preview mode. On launching, the two top-level categories will be listed with disclosure controls available:

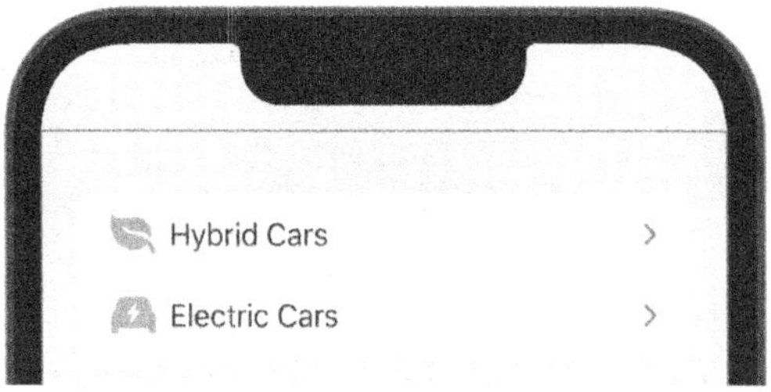

Figure 35-1

Using the disclosure controls, navigate through the levels to make sure that the view is working as expected:

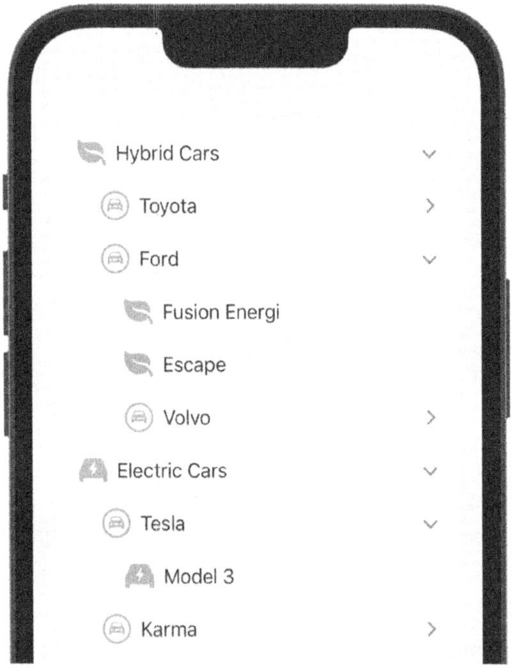

Figure 35-2

35.6 Using the Sidebar List Style

The List instance above is displayed using the default list style. When working with hierarchical lists it is worthwhile noting that a List style is available for this specific purpose in the form of the SidebarListSyle. To see this in action, add a modifier to the List view as follows:

```
struct ContentView: View {
    var body: some View {
        List(carItems, children: \.children) { item in
            CellView(item: item)
        }
        .listStyle(SidebarListStyle())
    }
}
```

When previewed, the list will now appear as shown in Figure 35-3, providing a cleaner and more ordered layout than that provided by the default style:

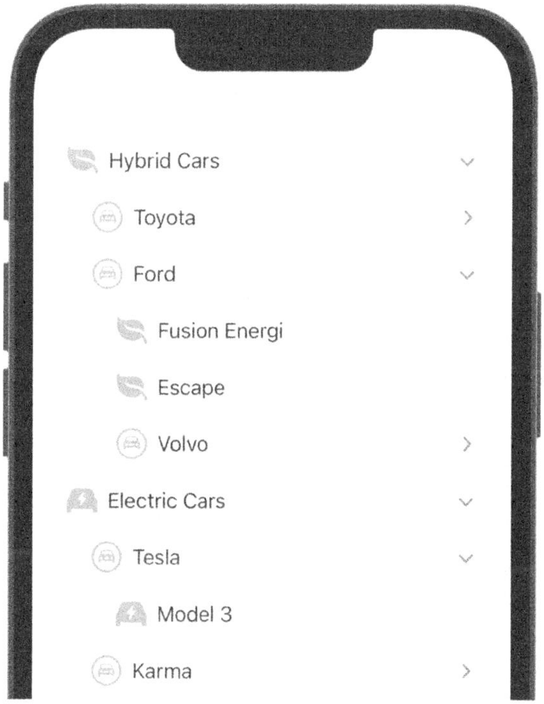

Figure 35-3

35.7 Using OutlineGroup

Now that we've seen the use of the List view to display hierarchical data, the project will be modified to make use of the OutlineGroup view within a list to divide the list into groups, each with a section header.

Once again working within the *ContentView.swift* file, modify the ContentView declaration so that it reads as follows:

```
struct ContentView: View {
    var body: some View {
        List {
```

```
                ForEach(carItems) { carItem in
                    Section(header: Text(carItem.name)) {
                        OutlineGroup(carItem.children ?? [CarInfo](),
                                    children: \.children) { child in

                            CellView(item: child)
                        }

                    }
                }
            }
            .listStyle(InsetListStyle())
    }
}
```

The above declaration takes the first entry in the data structure (in this case "Hybrid Cars") and assigns it as the title of a Section view. The OutlineGroup then iterates through all of the children of the Hybrid Cars entry. Once all of the children have been processed, the "Electric Cars" item is used as the title for another Section before iterating through all the electric car children.

When reviewed using Live Preview, the app should behave as before, with the exception that the information is now grouped into headed sections as shown in Figure 35-4, noting that this time the List is configured with the InsetListStyle modifier:

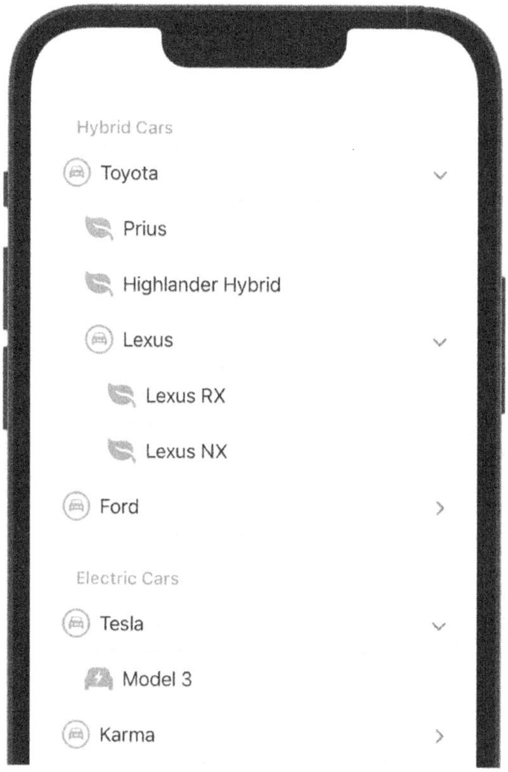

Figure 35-4

35.8 Working with DisclosureGroups

The DisclosureGroup view will be demonstrated within a new SwiftUI View file. To add this view, right-click on the Shared folder in the project navigator panel and select the *New File…* menu option. In the new file template dialog, select the SwiftUI View file option, click Next and name the file *SettingsView* before clicking on the Create button.

With the *SettingsView.swift* file loaded into the editor, make the following additions to add some custom views and state properties that will be used to simulate settings controls:

```
import SwiftUI

struct SettingsView: View {

    @State private var hybridState: Bool = false
    @State private var electricState: Bool = true
    @State private var fuelCellState: Bool = false
    @State private var inversionState: Bool = true
.
.
struct ColorControl: View {

    var color: Color
    var label: String

    var body: some View {
        HStack {
            Text(label)
            Spacer()
            Rectangle()
                .fill(color)
                .frame(width: 30, height: 30)
        }
        .padding(.leading)
        .scaledToFill()
    }
}

struct ToggleControl: View {
    var title: String
    @State var state: Bool

    var body: some View {
        Toggle(title, isOn: $state)
            .padding(.leading)
    }
}
```

Next, modify the body of the SettingsView structure to add a Form view containing the settings controls:

```
struct SettingsView: View {

    @State private var hybridState: Bool = false
    @State private var electricState: Bool = true
    @State private var fuelCellState: Bool = false
    @State private var inversionState: Bool = true

    var body: some View {

        Form {
            ToggleControl(title: " Hybrid Cars", state: hybridState)
            ToggleControl(title: " Electric Cars", state: electricState)
            ToggleControl(title: " Fuel Cell Cars", state: fuelCellState)

            ColorControl(color: .red, label: "Background Color")
            ColorControl(color: .blue, label: "ForegroundColor")
            ToggleControl(title: "Color Inversion",
                                          state: inversionState)
        }
    }
}
```

When reviewed in the preview canvas, the user interface layout should appear as shown in Figure 35-5:

Figure 35-5

With the initial steps of the settings form designed, the next step is to organize the form into groups with titles and disclosure controls. To achieve this, modify the Form view declaration as follows:

```
var body: some View {

    Form {
        DisclosureGroup {
            ToggleControl(title: "Hybrid Cars", state: hybridState)
            ToggleControl(title: "Electric Cars", state: electricState)
```

```
            ToggleControl(title: "Fuel Cell Cars", state: fuelCellState)
        } label : {
            Label("Categories Filters", systemImage: "car.2.fill")
        }

        DisclosureGroup {
            ColorControl(color: .red, label: "Background Color")
            ColorControl(color: .blue, label: "ForegroundColor")
            ToggleControl(title: "Color Inversion",
                                              state: inversionState)
        } label : {
            Label("Color Settings", systemImage: "scribble.variable")
        }
    }
}
```

With the form separated into disclosure groups, the view should appear in the preview canvas as follows:

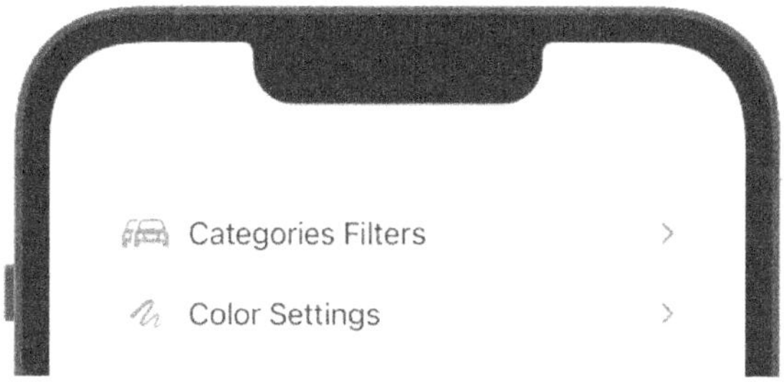

Figure 35-6

Switch into Live Preview mode and verify that the disclosure controls can be used to expand and collapse the two groups of settings:

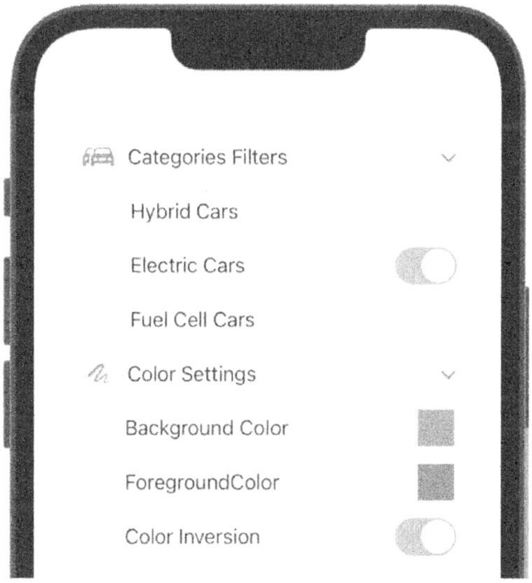

Figure 35-7

By default, disclosure groups are initially collapsed when displayed. To configure a group to appear in expanded mode, simply pass through a Boolean value to the DisclosureGroup declaration. The following code changes, for example, will cause the Category Filters section of the settings form to expand on initialization:

```
.
.
@State private var filtersExpanded: Bool = true

var body: some View {

    Form {
        DisclosureGroup(isExpanded: $filtersExpanded) {
            ToggleControl(title: "Hybrid Cars", state: hybridState)
            ToggleControl(title: "Electric Cars", state: electricState)
            ToggleControl(title: "Fuel Cell Cars", state: fuelCellState)
        } label : {
            Label("Categories Filters", systemImage: "car.2.fill")
        }
.
.
```

Using Live Preview once again, make sure that the category filters group is expanded when the user interface first appears.

35.9 Summary

The List and OutlineGroup views provide an easy way to group and display hierarchical information to users with minimal coding. The DisclosureGroup view is used by these views to allow users to expand and collapse sections of information, and may also be used directly in your own SwiftUI declarations. This chapter has demonstrated these views in action within an example project.

Chapter 36

36. Building SwiftUI Grids with LazyVGrid and LazyHGrid

In previous chapters, we have looked at using stacks, lists, and outline groups to present information to the user. None of these solutions, however, are particularly useful for displaying content in a grid format. SwiftUI also includes three views to display multi-column grids within a user interface layout in the form of LazyVGrid, LazyHGrid, and GridItem.

This chapter will introduce these views and demonstrate how, when combined with the ScrollView, they can be used to build scrolling horizontal and vertical grid layouts.

36.1 SwiftUI Grids

SwiftUI grids provide a way to display information in a multicolumn layout oriented either horizontally or vertically. When embedded in a ScrollView instance, the user will be able to scroll through the grid if it extends beyond the visible screen area of the device in which the app is running.

As the names suggest, the LazyVGrid and LazyHGrid views only create items to be displayed within the grid when they are about to become visible to the user and then discard those items from memory as they scroll out of view (a concept covered previously in the chapter entitled *"SwiftUI Stacks and Frames"*). This allows scrollable grids of potentially infinite numbers of items to be constructed without adversely impacting app performance.

The syntax for declaring a vertical grid is as follows:

```
LazyVGrid(columns: [GridItem], alignment: <horizontal alignment>,
                    spacing: CGFloat?, pinnedViews: <views>) {
    // Content Views
}
```

In the above syntax, only the *columns* argument is mandatory and takes the form of an array of GridItem instances.

Similarly, a horizontal grid would be declared as follows where, once again, all arguments are optional except for the *rows* argument:

```
LazyHGrid(rows: [GridItem], alignment: <vertical alignment>,
                    spacing: CGFloat?, pinnedViews: <views>) {
    // Content Views
}
```

36.2 GridItems

Each row or column in a grid layout is represented by an instance of the GridItem view. In other words, a GridItem instance represents each row in a LazyHGrid layout and each column when using the LazyVGrid view. The GridItem view defines the properties of the row or column in terms of sizing behavior, spacing, and alignment. The GridItem view also provides control over the number of rows or columns displayed within a grid and the minimum size to which an item may be reduced to meet those constraints.

GridItems are declared using the following syntax:

```
GridItem(sizing, spacing: CGFloat?, alignment: <alignment>)
```

The sizing argument is of type GridItemSize and must be declared as one of the following:

- **flexible()** – The number of rows or columns in the grid will be dictated by the number of GridItem instances in the array passed to LazyVGrid or LazyHGrid view.
- **adaptive(minimum: CGFloat)** – The size of the row or column is adjusted to fit as many items as possible into the available space. The minimum size to which the item may be reduced can be specified using the optional minimum argument.
- **fixed(size: CGFloat)** – Specifies a fixed size for the item.

Note that the GridItems in an array can use a mixture of the above settings, for example, to make the first column a fixed width with the remaining items configured to fit as many columns as possible into the remaining available space.

Since grids in SwiftUI are best explored visually, the remainder of this chapter will create a project demonstrating many of the features of LazyVGrid, LazyHGrid, and GridItem.

36.3 Creating the GridDemo Project

Launch Xcode and select the option to create a new Multiplatform App project named *GridDemo*. Once the project has been created, edit the *ContentView.swift* file to add a custom view to act as grid cell content together with an array of colors to make the grid more visually appealing:

```
import SwiftUI

struct ContentView: View {

    private var colors: [Color] = [.blue, .yellow, .green]
.
.
    struct CellContent: View {
        var index: Int
        var color: Color

        var body: some View {
            Text("\(index)")
                .frame(minWidth: 50, maxWidth: .infinity, minHeight: 100)
                .background(color)
                .cornerRadius(8)
                .font(.system(.largeTitle))
        }
    }
.
.
```

36.4 Working with Flexible GridItems

As previously discussed, if all of the GridItems contained in the array passed to a LazyVGrid view are declared as flexible, the number of GridItems in the array will dictate the number of columns included in the grid.

To see this in action, begin by editing the *ContentView.swift* file once again and declaring an array of three GridItems as follows:

```
struct ContentView: View {

    private var colors: [Color] = [.blue, .yellow, .green]
    private var gridItems = [GridItem(.flexible()),
                             GridItem(.flexible()),
                             GridItem(.flexible())]
.
.
```

Next, edit the body declaration to declare a vertical grid containing 9 instances of the custom CellContent custom view (numbered from 0 to 8), as follows:

```
var body: some View {

    LazyVGrid(columns: gridItems, spacing: 5) {
            ForEach((0...8), id: \.self) { index in
                CellContent(index: index,
                       color: colors[index % colors.count])

            }
        }
        .padding(5)
    }
}
```

With the changes made, refer to the preview canvas where the grid should appear as shown in Figure 36-1 below:

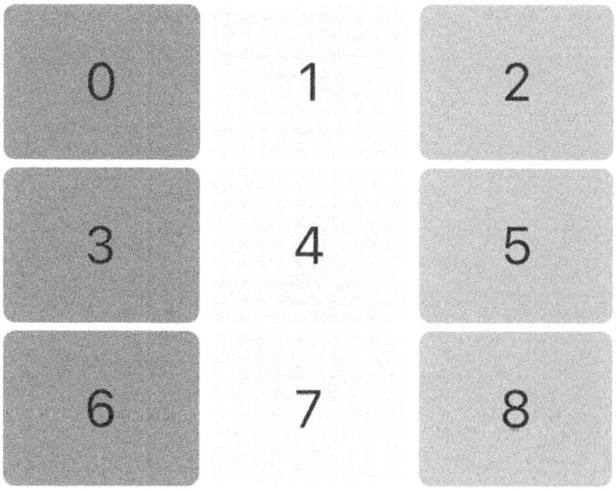

Figure 36-1

Clearly, the grid has been populated with three columns as expected. To add a column, simply place another GridItem into the array. It is worth noting at this point that flexible mode is the default setting for the GridItem view, so the flexible declaration can be omitted if desired:

```
private var gridItems = [GridItem(), GridItem(), GridItem(), GridItem()]
```

When previewed, the grid will appear with four columns as shown in Figure 36-2:

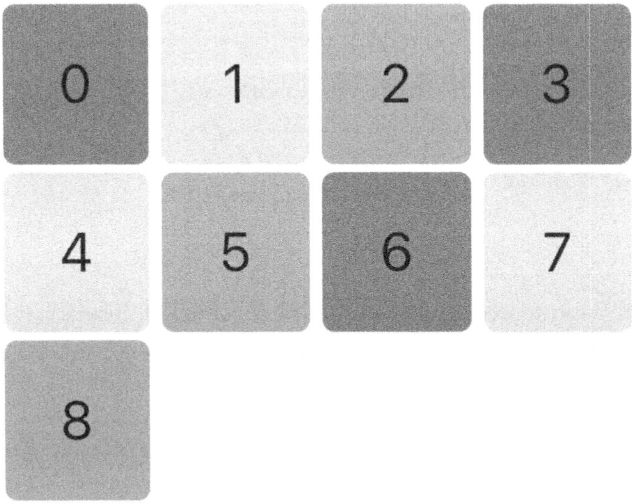

Figure 36-2

36.5 Adding Scrolling Support to a Grid

The above example grids contained a small number of items that were able to fit entirely within the viewing area of the device. A greater number of items will invariably cause the grid to extend beyond the available screen area. Try, for example, increasing the number of items in the ForEach loop of the body view declaration from 8 to 99 as follows:

```
var body: some View {

    LazyVGrid(columns: gridItems, spacing: 5) {
            ForEach((0...99), id: \.self) { index in
                CellContent(index: index,
                        color: colors[index % colors.count])
            }
        }
        .padding(5)
    }
}
```

When the grid is now previewed, it will appear as shown in Figure 36-3:

Figure 36-3

It is clear from the preview that the grid is now too tall to fit entirely on the screen. The screen also has the grid centered vertically so that the cells from the middle of the grid are visible instead of starting at the first row. It is also not possible to scroll up and down to view the rest of the grid. All of these issues can be addressed simply by embedding the LazyVGrid in a ScrollView as follows:

```
var body: some View {

    ScrollView {
        LazyVGrid(columns: gridItems, spacing: 5) {
                ForEach((0...99), id: \.self) { index in
```

```
                    CellContent(index: index,
                                color: colors[index % colors.count])
                }
            }
            .padding(5)
        }
    }
}
```

The top of the grid will now be visible within the preview and, if Live Preview is selected, it will be possible to scroll vertically through the grid.

36.6 Working with Adaptive GridItems

So far, we have seen how the flexible GridItem size setting allows us to define how many columns or rows appear in a grid. The adaptive setting, however, configures the grid view to automatically display as many rows or columns as it can fit into the space occupied by the view. To use adaptive sizing, modify the *gridItems* array to contain a single adaptive item as follows:

```
private var gridItems = [GridItem(.adaptive(minimum: 50))]
```

This change will result in the grid displaying as many columns as possible with the restriction that the column width cannot be less than 50dp. The following figure demonstrates a partial example of this change as it appears on an iPhone 11 in portrait orientation:

Figure 36-4

Figure 36-5, on the other hand, shows the same grid on an iPhone 13 in landscape orientation. Note that the grid has automatically adapted the number of columns to occupy the wider viewing area:

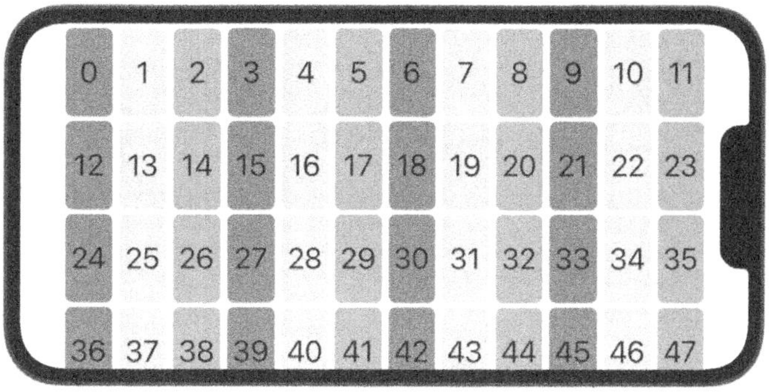

Figure 36-5

36.7 Working with Fixed GridItems

The GridItem fixed size setting allows rows or columns to be set at a specific size. When using only fixed GridItems in the array passed to the grid view, the number of GridItems will dictate the number of rows or columns. For example, the following array, when passed to a LazyVGrid view, will display a grid containing a single column with a width of 100dp.

```
private var gridItems = [GridItem(.fixed(100))]
```

The following array, on the other hand, will display a three-column grid with the columns sized at 75dp, 125dp, and 175dp respectively:

```
private var gridItems = [GridItem(.fixed(75)), GridItem(.fixed(125)),
                         GridItem(.fixed(175))]
```

When rendered, the grid will appear as shown in Figure 36-6:

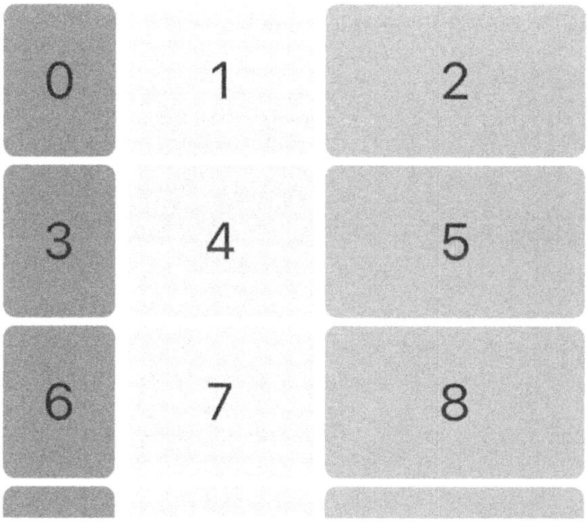

Figure 36-6

When working with grids it is also possible to combine GridItem sizing configurations. The following array, for example, will display the first column of each row with a fixed width with the second and third columns sized equally to occupy the remaining space:

```
private var gridItems = [GridItem(.fixed(85)), GridItem(),
                         GridItem()]
```

When rendered, the grid will appear as illustrated in Figure 36-7 below:

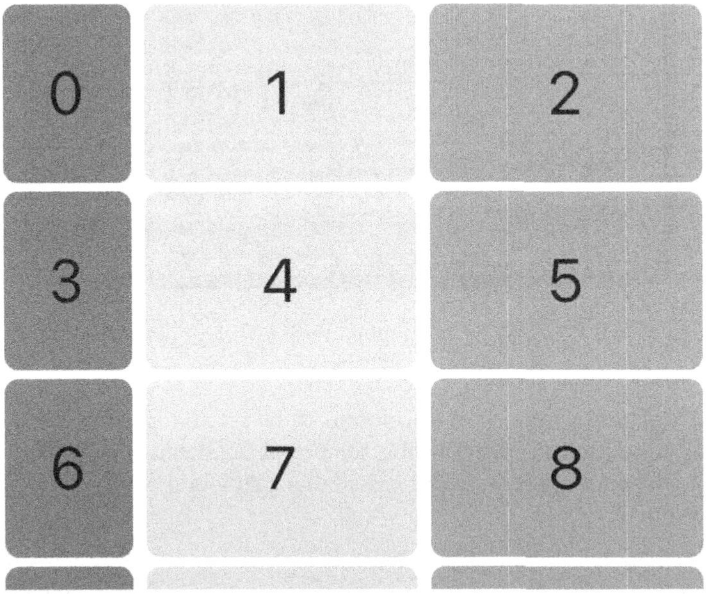

Figure 36-7

Similarly, the following array uses a combination of fixed and adaptive sizing:

```
private var gridItems = [GridItem(.fixed(100)),
                         GridItem(.adaptive(minimum: 50))]
```

This will result in the first column of each row appearing with a fixed size, with the remainder of the row filled with as many columns as possible subject to the minimum width restriction:

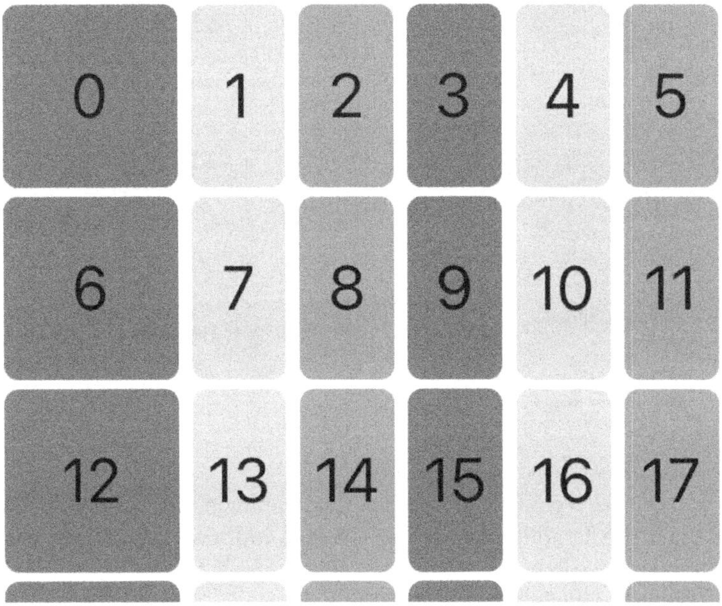

Figure 36-8

36.8 Using the LazyHGrid View

Horizontal grids work in much the same way as vertically oriented grids with the exception that the configuration is based on rows instead of columns, and that the fixed, minimum, and maximum values relate to row height instead of column width. Also, when scrolling is required the grid should be embedded in a horizontal ScrollView instance. The following declaration, for example, places a LazyHGrid within a horizontal ScrollView using adaptive sizing on all rows:

```
struct ContentView: View {

    private var colors: [Color] = [.blue, .yellow, .green]
    private var gridItems = [GridItem(.adaptive(minimum: 50))]

    var body: some View {

        ScrollView(.horizontal) {
            LazyHGrid(rows: gridItems, spacing: 5) {
                    ForEach((0...99), id: \.self) { index in
                        CellContent(index: index,
                                    color: colors[index % colors.count])
                    }
                }
                .padding(5)
            }
        }
}

struct CellContent: View {
    var index: Int
    var color: Color

    var body: some View {
        Text("\(index)")
            .frame(minWidth: 75, minHeight: 50, maxHeight: .infinity)
            .background(color)
            .cornerRadius(8)
            .font(.system(.largeTitle))
    }
}
```

When previewed, the above declaration will display the grid shown in Figure 36-9 including the ability to scroll horizontally:

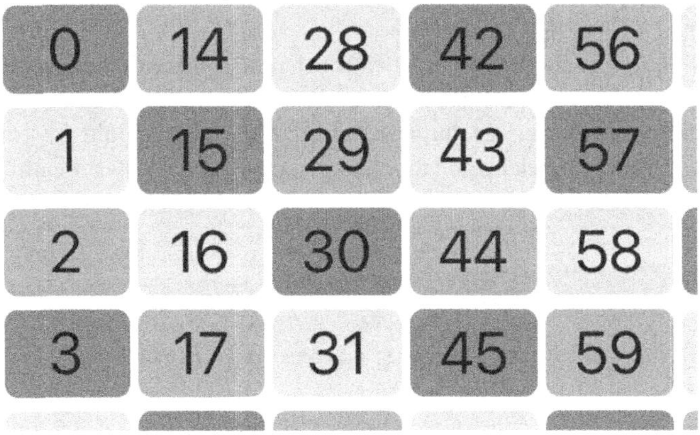

Figure 36-9

The following GridItem array, on the other hand, mixes fixed height with adaptive sizing to increase the height of the first and last grid rows:

```
private var gridItems = [GridItem(.fixed(150)),
     GridItem(.adaptive(minimum: 50)), GridItem(.fixed(150))]
```

When tested, the grid will appear as shown in Figure 36-10 below:

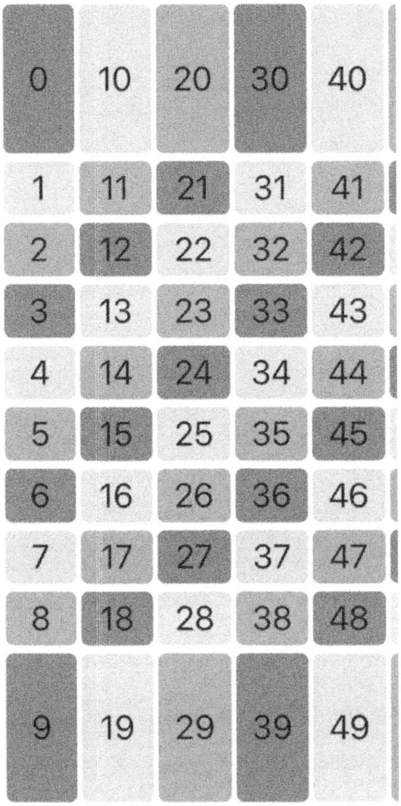

Figure 36-10

As a final example, consider the following GridItem array:

```
private var gridItems = [GridItem(.fixed(150)),
              GridItem(.flexible(minimum: 50)), GridItem(.fixed(150))]
```

When executed, the grid consists of fixed height first and last rows, while the middle row will size to fill the available remaining height:

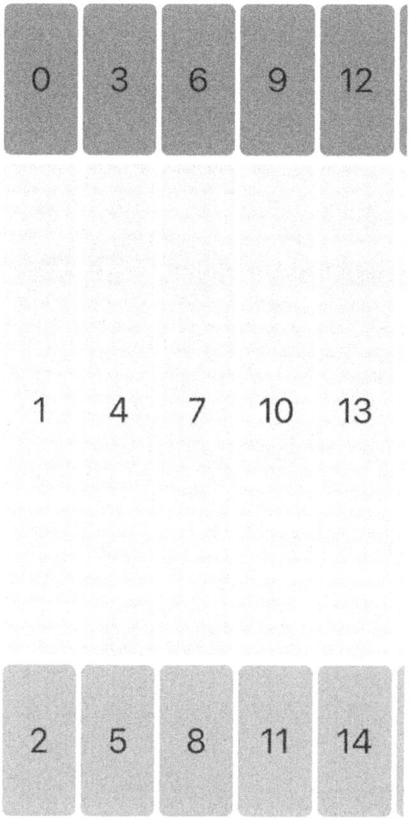

Figure 36-11

36.9 Summary

Grid-style layouts in SwiftUI are implemented using the LazyHGrid and LazyVGrid views which are designed to organize instances of the GridItem view. The LazyHGrid and LazyVGrid views are passed an array of GridItem views configured to define how the rows and columns of the grid are to be sized together with the content views to be displayed in the grid cells. Wrapping a grid in a ScrollView instance will add scrolling behavior to grids that extend beyond the visible area of the parent view.

Chapter 37

37. Building SwiftUI Grids with Grid and GridRow

The previous chapter introduced the LazyHGrid, LazyVGrid, and GridItem views and explored how they can be used to create scrollable multicolumn layouts. While these views can handle large numbers of rows, they lack flexibility, particularly in terms of grid cell arrangement and positioning.

In this chapter, we will work with two grid layout views (Grid and GridRow) that were introduced in iOS 16. While lacking support for large grid layouts, these two views provide several features that are not available when using the lazy grid views including column spanning cells, empty cells, and a range of alignment and spacing options.

37.1 Grid and GridRow Views

A grid layout is defined using the Grid view with each row represented by a GridRow child, and direct child views of a GridRow instance represent the column cells in that row.

The syntax for declaring a grid using Grid and GridRow is as follows:

```
Grid {

    GridRow {
        // Cell views here
    }

    GridRow {
        // Cell views here
    }
.
.
}
```

37.2 Creating the GridRowDemo Project

Launch Xcode and select the option to create a new Multiplatform App project named *GridRowDemo*. Once the project is ready, edit the *ContentView.swift* file to add a custom view to be used as the content for the grid cells in later examples:

```
struct CellContent: View {

    var index: Int
    var color: Color

    var body: some View {
        Text("\(index)")
```

```
            .frame(minWidth: 50, maxWidth: .infinity, minHeight: 100)
            .background(color)
            .cornerRadius(8)
            .font(.system(.largeTitle))
    }
}
```

37.3 A Simple Grid Layout

As a first step, we will create a simple grid 5 x 3 grid by modifying the body of the ContentView structure in the *ContentView.swift* file as follows:

```
struct ContentView: View {
    var body: some View {

        Grid {
            GridRow {
                ForEach(1...5, id: \.self) { index in
                    CellContent(index: index, color: .red)
                }
            }

            GridRow {
                ForEach(6...10, id: \.self) { index in
                    CellContent(index: index, color: .blue)
                }
            }

            GridRow {
                ForEach(11...15, id: \.self) { index in
                    CellContent(index: index, color: .green)
                }
            }
        }
        .padding()
    }
}
```

The above example consists of a Grid view parent containing three GridRow children. Each GridRow contains a ForEach loop that generates three CellContent views. After making these changes, the layout should appear within the Preview panel as shown in Figure 37-1:

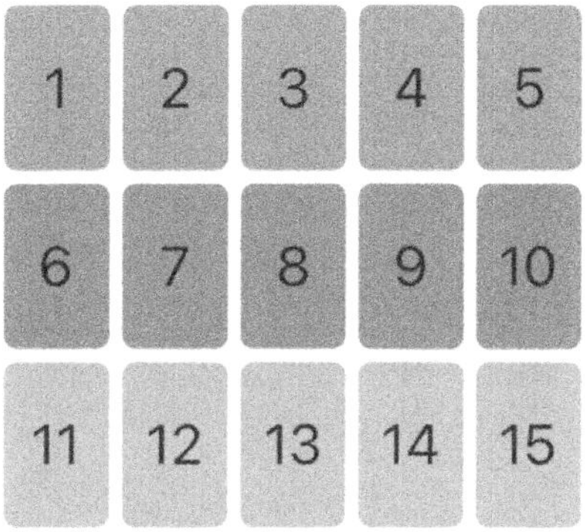

Figure 37-1

37.4 Non-GridRow Children

So far in this chapter, we have implied that the direct children of a Grid view must be GridRows. While this is the most common use of the Grid view, it is also possible to include children outside the scope of a GridRow. Grid children not contained within a GridRow will expand to occupy an entire row within the grid layout.

The following changes, for example, add a fourth row to the grid containing a single CellContent view that fills the row:

```
struct ContentView: View {
    var body: some View {
        Grid {
            GridRow {
                ForEach(1...5, id: \.self) { index in
                    CellContent(index: index, color: .red)
                }
            }

            GridRow {
                ForEach(6...10, id: \.self) { index in
                    CellContent(index: index, color: .blue)
                }
            }

            GridRow {
                ForEach(11...15, id: \.self) { index in
                    CellContent(index: index, color: .green)
                }
            }

            CellContent(index: 16, color: .blue)
        }
        .padding()
    }
}
```

Within the Preview panel, the grid should appear as shown in Figure 37-2 below:

Figure 37-2

37.5 Automatic Empty Grid Cells

When creating grids, we generally assume that each row must contain the same number of columns. This is not, however, a requirement when using the Grid and GridRow views. When the Grid view is required to display rows containing different cell counts, it will automatically add empty cells to shorter rows so that they match the longest row. To experience this in our example, change the ForEach loop ranges as follows:

```
.
.
GridRow {
    ForEach(1...5, id: \.self) { index in
        CellContent(index: index, color: .red)
    }
}

GridRow {
    ForEach(6...8, id: \.self) { index in
        CellContent(index: index, color: .blue)
    }
}

GridRow {
    ForEach(11...12, id: \.self) { index in
        CellContent(index: index, color: .green)
    }
}
.
.
```

When the grid is rendered, it will place empty cells within the rows containing fewer cells as shown in Figure 37-3:

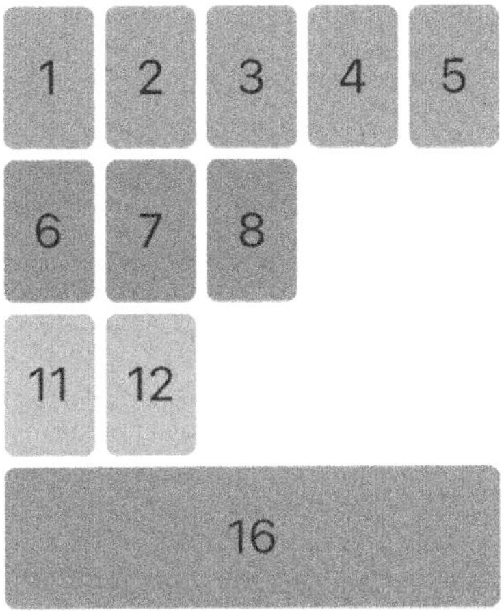

Figure 37-3

37.6 Adding Empty Cells

In addition to allowing GridRow to add empty cells, you can also insert empty cells into fixed positions in a grid layout. Empty cells are represented by a Color view configured with the "clear" color value. Applying the *gridCellUnsizedAxes()* modifier to the Color view ensures that the empty cell matches the default height and width of the occupied cells. Modify the first grid row in our example so that even-numbered columns contain empty cells:

```
GridRow {
    ForEach(1...5, id: \.self) { index in
        if (index % 2 == 1) {
            CellContent(index: index, color: .red)
        } else {
            Color.clear
                .gridCellUnsizedAxes([.horizontal, .vertical])
        }
    }
}
```

Refer to the Live Preview to verify that the empty cells appear in the first row of the grid as illustrated in Figure 37-4:

Figure 37-4

37.7 Column Spanning

A key feature of Grid and GridRow is the ability for a single cell to span a specified number of columns. We can achieve this by applying the *gridCellColumns()* modifier to individual content cell views within GridRow declarations. Add another row to the grid containing two cells configured to span two and three columns respectively:

```
.
.
CellContent(index: 16, color: .blue)

GridRow {
    CellContent(index: 17, color: .orange)
        .gridCellColumns(2)
    CellContent(index: 18, color: .indigo)
        .gridCellColumns(3)
}
.
.
```

The layout will now appear as shown below:

Figure 37-5

37.8 Grid Alignment and Spacing

Spacing between rows and columns can be applied using the Grid view's verticalSpacing and horizontalSpacing parameters, for example:

```
Grid(horizontalSpacing: 30, verticalSpacing: 0) {
    GridRow {
        ForEach(1...5, id: \.self) { index in
.
.
```

The above changes increase the spacing between columns while removing the spacing between rows so that the grid appears as shown in the figure below:

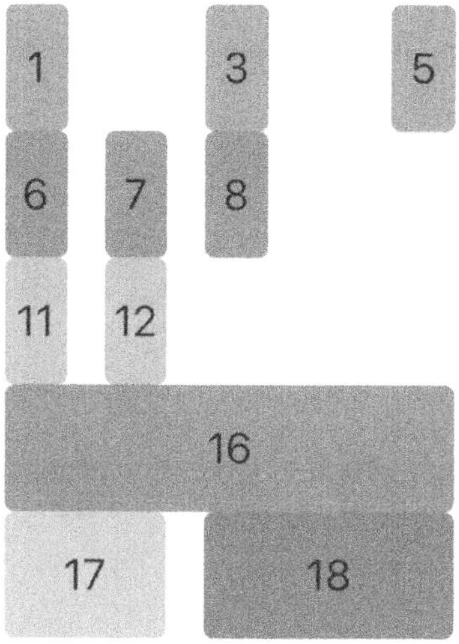

Figure 37-6

We designed the CellContent view used throughout this chapter to fill the available space within a grid cell. As this makes it impossible to see changes in alignment, we need to add cells containing content that will demonstrate alignment settings. Begin by inserting two new rows at the top of the grid as outlined below. Also, remove the code that placed empty cells in the row containing cells 1 through 5 so that all cells are displayed:

```
struct ContentView: View {
    var body: some View {
        Grid {

            GridRow {
                CellContent(index: 0, color: .orange)
                Image(systemName: "record.circle.fill")
                Image(systemName: "record.circle.fill")
                Image(systemName: "record.circle.fill")
                CellContent(index: 0, color: .yellow)

            }
            .font(.largeTitle)

            GridRow {
                CellContent(index: 0, color: .orange)
                Image(systemName: "record.circle.fill")
                Image(systemName: "record.circle.fill")
                Image(systemName: "record.circle.fill")
                CellContent(index: 0, color: .yellow)

            }
            .font(.largeTitle)
```

```
            GridRow {
                ForEach(1...5, id: \.self) { index in
                        CellContent(index: index, color: .red)
                }
            }
.
.
```

After making these changes, refer to the preview and verify that the top three rows of the grid match that shown in Figure 37-7:

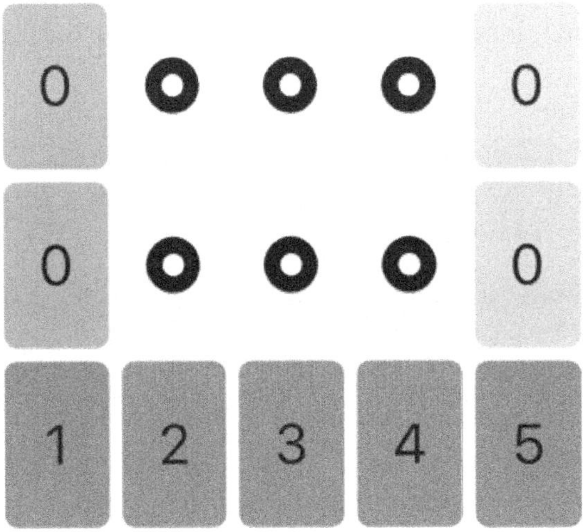

Figure 37-7

We can see from the positioning of the circle symbols that the Grid and GridRow views default to centering content within grid cells. The default alignment for all cells within a grid can be changed by assigning one of the following values to the alignment parameter of the Grid view:

- .trailing
- .leading
- .top
- .bottom
- .topLeading
- .topTrailing
- .bottomLeading
- .bottomTrailing
- .center

Cell content can also be aligned with the baselines of text contained in adjoining cells using the following alignment values:

- .centerFirstTextBaseline
- .centerLastTextBaseline
- .leadingFirstTextBaseline
- .leadingLastTextBaseline
- .trailingFirstTextBaseline
- .trailingLastTextBaseline

Modify the Grid declaration in the example code so that all content is aligned at the leading top of the containing cell:

```
struct ContentView: View {
    var body: some View {
        Grid(alignment: .topLeading) {
.
.
```

Review the preview panel and confirm that the positioning of the circle symbols matches the layout shown in Figure 37-8:

Figure 37-8

It is also possible to override the default vertical alignment setting on individual rows using the alignment property of the GridRow view. The following code modifications, for example, change the second row of symbols to use bottom alignment:

```
struct ContentView: View {
    var body: some View {
        Grid(alignment: .topLeading) {

        GridRow(alignment: .bottom) {
            CellContent(index: 0, color: .orange)
            Image(systemName: "record.circle.fill")
            Image(systemName: "record.circle.fill")
            Image(systemName: "record.circle.fill")
            CellContent(index: 0, color: .yellow)
```

```
        }
        .font(.largeTitle)
.
.
```

The circles in the first row are now positioned along the bottom of the row while the second row continues to adopt the default alignment specified by the parent grid view:

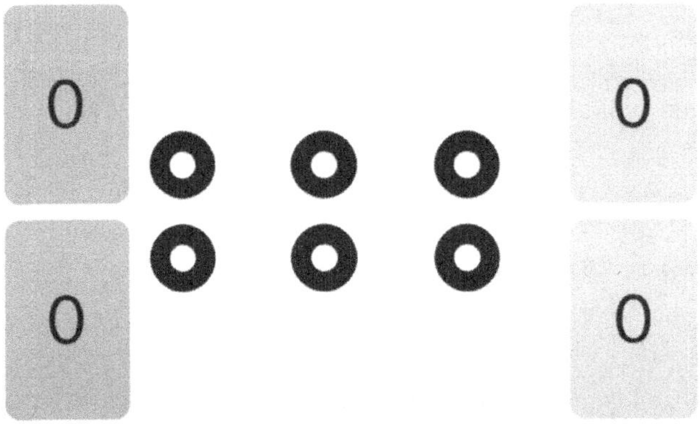

Figure 37-9

Note that GridRow alignment will only adjust the vertical positioning of cell content. As illustrated above, the first row of circles has continued to use the leading alignment applied to the parent Grid view.

Horizontal content alignment for the cells in individual columns can be changed by applying the *gridColumnAlignment()* modifier to any cell within the corresponding column. The following code change, for example, applies trailing alignment to the second grid column:

```
struct ContentView: View {
    var body: some View {
        Grid(alignment: .topLeading) {

        GridRow(alignment: .bottom) {
            CellContent(index: 0, color: .orange)
            Image(systemName: "record.circle.fill")
                .gridColumnAlignment(.trailing)
            Image(systemName: "record.circle.fill")
            Image(systemName: "record.circle.fill")
            CellContent(index: 0, color: .yellow)

        }
        .font(.largeTitle)
.
.
```

When previewed, the first grid rows will appear as illustrated in Figure 37-10:

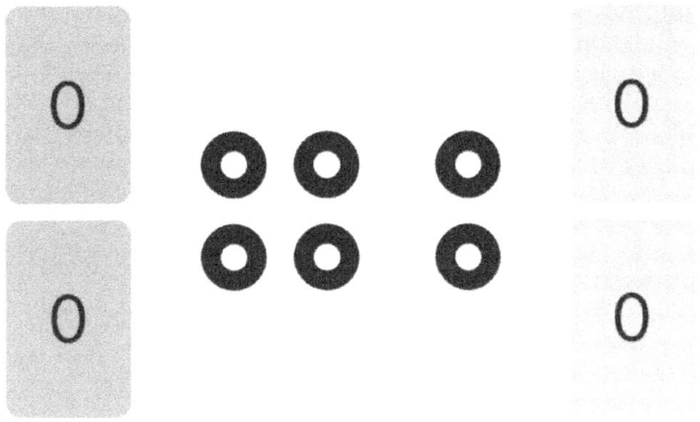

Figure 37-10

Finally, you can override content alignment in an individual cell using the *gridCellAnchor()* modifier as follows:

```
Grid(alignment: .topLeading) {

GridRow(alignment: .bottom) {
    CellContent(index: 0, color: .orange)
    Image(systemName: "record.circle.fill")
        .gridColumnAlignment(.trailing)
    Image(systemName: "record.circle.fill")
        .gridCellAnchor(.center)
    Image(systemName: "record.circle.fill")
        .gridCellAnchor(.top)
    CellContent(index: 0, color: .yellow)
}
.font(.largeTitle)
```

Once the preview updates to reflect the above changes, the circle symbol rows should appear as shown below:

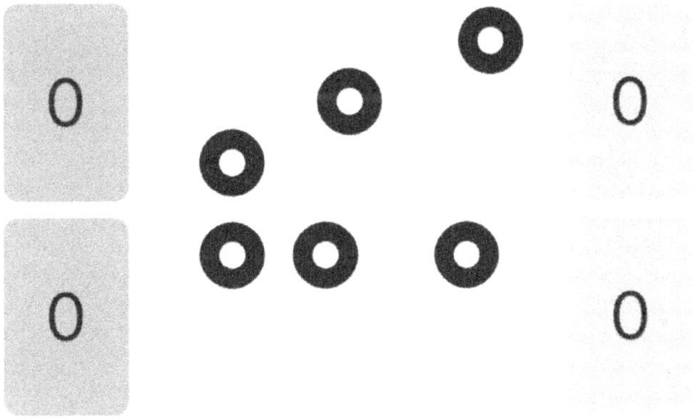

Figure 37-11

37.9 Summary

The Grid and GridRow views combine to provide highly flexible grid layout options when working with SwiftUI. While these views are unsuitable for displaying scrolling grids containing a large number of views, they have several advantages over the LazyVGrid and LazyHGrid views covered in the previous chapter. Particular strengths include the ability for a single cell to span multiple columns, support for empty cells, automatic addition of empty cells to maintain matching column counts, and the ability to adjust content alignment at the grid, row, and individual cell levels.

Chapter 38

38. Building Tabbed and Paged Views in SwiftUI

The SwiftUI TabView component allows the user to navigate between different child views either by selecting tab items located in a tab bar or, when using the page view tab style, by making swiping motions. This chapter will demonstrate how to implement a TabView-based interface in a SwiftUI app.

38.1 An Overview of SwiftUI TabView

Tabbed views are created in SwiftUI using the TabView container view and consist of a range of child views which represent the screens through which the user will navigate.

By default, the TabView presents a tab bar at the bottom of the layout containing the tab items used to navigate between the child views. A tab item is applied to each content view using a modifier and can be customized to contain Text and Image views (other view types are not supported in tab items).

The currently selected tab may also be controlled programmatically by adding tags to the tab items.

Figure 38-1 shows an example TabView layout:

Figure 38-1

38.2 Creating the TabViewDemo App

Launch Xcode and select the option to create a new Multiplatform App project named *TabViewDemo*.

38.3 Adding the TabView Container

With the *ContentView.swift* file loaded into the code editor, delete the default body content and add a TabView as follows:

```
import SwiftUI

struct ContentView: View {

    var body: some View {
        TabView {

        }
    }
}
```

38.4 Adding the Content Views

Next, add three content views to the layout. For the purposes of this example, Text views will be used, but in practice, these are likely to be more complex views consisting of stack layouts (note the addition of a font modifier to increase the size of the content text):

```
var body: some View {
    TabView {
        Text("First Content View")
        Text("Second Content View")
        Text("Third Content View")
    }
    .font(.largeTitle)
}
```

38.5 Adding View Paging

If the app were to be previewed at this point, the first view would appear but there would be no way to navigate to the other views. One way to implement navigation is to apply PageTabViewStyle to the TabView. This will allow the user to move between the three views by making left and right swiping motions on the screen. To apply this style, add the *tabViewStyle()* modifier to the TabView as follows:

```
var body: some View {
    TabView {
        Text("First Content View")
        Text("Second Content View")
        Text("Third Content View")
    }
    .font(.largeTitle)
    .tabViewStyle(PageTabViewStyle())
}
```

With the changes made, use Live Preview to test the view and verify that swiping left and right moves between the views.

38.6 Adding the Tab Items

As currently implemented, there is no visual indication to the user that more views are available other than the first view. An alternative to the page view style is to implement the TabView with a tab bar located along the bottom edge of the screen. Since no tab items have been added, the tab bar is currently empty. Clearly, the next step is to apply a tab item to each content view using the *tabItem()* modifier. In this example, each tab item will contain a Text and an Image view:

```
var body: some View {
    TabView {
        Text("First Content View")
            .tabItem {
                Image(systemName: "1.circle")
                Text("Screen One")
            }
        Text("Second Content View")
            .tabItem {
                Image(systemName: "2.circle")
                Text("Screen Two")
            }
        Text("Third Content View")
            .tabItem {
                Image(systemName: "3.circle")
                Text("Screen Three")
            }
    }
    .font(.largeTitle)
    .tabViewStyle(PageTabViewStyle())
}
```

Note also that the PageTabViewStyle modifier must be removed when using the tab bar, otherwise the tab bar will not appear.

With the changes made, verify that the tab items now appear in the tab bar before using Live Preview to test that clicking on a tab item displays the corresponding content view. The completed app should resemble that illustrated in Figure 38-1 above.

38.7 Adding Tab Item Tags

To control the currently selected tab in code, a tag needs to be added to each tab item and a state property declared to store the current selection as follows:

```
struct ContentView: View {

    @State private var selection = 1

    var body: some View {
        TabView() {
            Text("First Content View")
                .tabItem {
                    Image(systemName: "1.circle")
```

```
                    Text("Screen One")
                }.tag(1)
            Text("Second Content View")
                .tabItem {
                    Image(systemName: "2.circle")
                    Text("Screen Two")
                }.tag(2)
            Text("Third Content View")
                .tabItem {
                    Image(systemName: "3.circle")
                    Text("Screen Three")
                }.tag(3)
        }
        .font(.largeTitle)
    }
}
```

Next, bind the current selection value of the TabView to the selection state property:

```
var body: some View {
    TabView(selection: $selection) {
        Text("First Content View")
            .tabItem {
.
.
```

Any changes to the selection state property to a different value within the tag range (in this case a value between 1 and 3) elsewhere in the view will now cause the tabbed view to switch to the corresponding content view.

Test this behavior by changing the value assigned to the selection state property while the app is running in Live Preview mode.

38.8 Summary

The SwiftUI TabView container provides a mechanism via which the user can navigate between content views by selecting tabs in a tab bar or, when using the page view style, making swiping motions. When using the tab bar, the TabView is implemented by declaring child content views and assigning a tab item to each view. The tab items appear in the tab bar and can be constructed from a Text view, an Image view, or a combination of Text and Image views.

To control the current selection of a TabView programmatically, each tab item must be assigned a tag containing a unique value, binding the TabView current selection value to a state property.

Chapter 39

39. Building Context Menus in SwiftUI

A context menu in SwiftUI is a menu of options that appears when the user performs a long press over a view on which a menu has been configured. Each menu item will typically contain a Button view configured to perform an action when selected, together with a Text view and an optional Image view.

This chapter will work through the creation of an example app that makes use of a context menu to perform color changes on a view.

39.1 Creating the ContextMenuDemo Project

Launch Xcode and select the option to create a new Multiplatform App project named *ContextMenuDemo*.

39.2 Preparing the Content View

A context menu may be added to any view within a layout, but for the purposes of this example, a Text view will be used. Within Xcode, load the *ContentView.swift* file into the editor, add some state properties to store the foreground and background color values, and use these to control the color settings of a Text view. Also, use the *font()* modifier to increase the text font size:

```
import SwiftUI

struct ContentView: View {

    @State private var foregroundColor: Color = Color.black
    @State private var backgroundColor: Color = Color.white

    var body: some View {

        Text("Hello, world!")
            .padding()
            .font(.largeTitle)
            .foregroundColor(foregroundColor)
            .background(backgroundColor)
    }
.
.
```

39.3 Adding the Context Menu

Context menus are added to views in SwiftUI using the *contextMenu()* modifier and declaring the views that are to serve as menu items. Add menu items to the context menu by making the following changes to the body view of the *ContentView.swift* file:

```
var body: some View {
```

```
    Text("Hello, world!")
        .font(.largeTitle)
        .padding()
        .foregroundColor(foregroundColor)
        .background(backgroundColor)
        .contextMenu {
            Button(action: {

            }) {
                Text("Normal Colors")
                Image(systemName: "paintbrush")
            }

            Button(action: {

            }) {
                Text("Inverted Colors")
                Image(systemName: "paintbrush.fill")
            }
        }
}
```

Finally, add code to the two button actions to change the values assigned to the foreground and background state properties:

```
var body: some View {

    Text("Hello, world!")
        .font(.largeTitle)
        .padding()
        .foregroundColor(foregroundColor)
        .background(backgroundColor)

        .contextMenu {
            Button(action: {
                self.foregroundColor = .black
                self.backgroundColor = .white
            }) {
                Text("Normal Colors")
                Image(systemName: "paintbrush")
            }

            Button(action: {
                self.foregroundColor = .white
                self.backgroundColor = .black
            }) {
```

```
                Text("Inverted Colors")
                Image(systemName: "paintbrush.fill")
            }
    }
}
```

39.4 Testing the Context Menu

Use Live Preview mode to test the view and perform a long press on the Text view. After a short delay the context menu should appear resembling Figure 39-1 below:

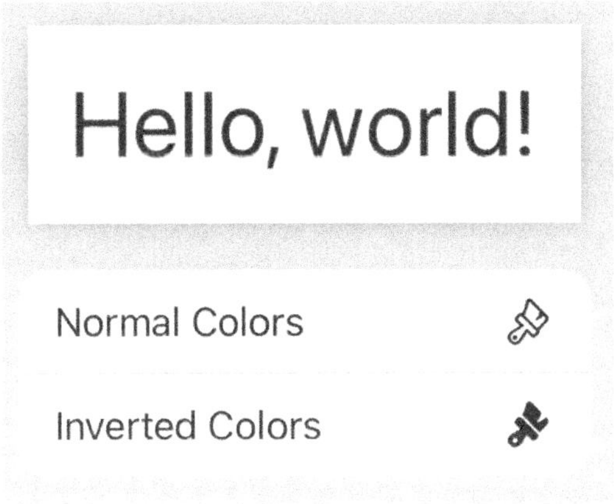

Figure 39-1

Select the Inverted Colors option to dismiss the menu and invert the colors on the Text view:

Figure 39-2

39.5 Summary

Context menus appear when a long press gesture is performed over a view in a layout. A context menu can be added to any view type and is implemented using the *contextMenu()* modifier. The menu is comprised of menu items which usually take the form of Button views configured with an action together with a Text view and an optional Image view.

Chapter 40

40. Basic SwiftUI Graphics Drawing

The goal of this chapter is to introduce SwiftUI 2D drawing techniques. In addition to a group of built-in shape and gradient drawing options, SwiftUI also allows custom drawing to be performed by creating entirely new views that conform to the Shape and Path protocols.

40.1 Creating the DrawDemo Project

Launch Xcode and select the option to create a new Multiplatform App named *DrawDemo*.

40.2 SwiftUI Shapes

SwiftUI includes a set of five pre-defined shapes that conform to the Shape protocol which can be used to draw circles, rectangles, rounded rectangles, and ellipses. Within the DrawDemo project, open the *ContentView.swift* file and add a single rectangle:

```
struct ContentView: View {
    var body: some View {
        Rectangle()
}
```

By default, a shape will occupy all the space available to it within the containing view and will be filled with the foreground color of the parent view (by default this will be black). Within the preview canvas, a black rectangle will fill the entire safe area of the screen.

The color and size of the shape may be adjusted using the *fill()* modifier and by wrapping it in a frame. Delete the Rectangle view and replace it with the declaration which draws a red-filled 200x200 circle:

```
Circle()
    .fill(.red)
    .frame(width: 200, height: 200)
```

When previewed, the above circle will appear as illustrated in Figure 40-1:

Figure 40-1

To draw an unfilled shape with a stroked outline, the *stroke()* modifier can be applied, passing through an optional line width value. By default, a stroked shape will be drawn using the default foreground color which may be altered using the *foregroundColor()* modifier. Remaining in the *ContentView.swift* file, replace the circle with the following:

```
Capsule()
    .stroke(lineWidth: 10)
    .foregroundColor(.blue)
    .frame(width: 200, height: 100)
```

Note that the frame for the above Capsule shape is rectangular. A Capsule contained in a square frame simply draws a circle. The above capsule declaration appears as follows when rendered:

Figure 40-2

The stroke modifier also supports different style types using a StrokeStyle instance. The following declaration, for example, draws a rounded rectangle using a dashed line:

```
RoundedRectangle(cornerRadius: CGFloat(20))
    .stroke(style: StrokeStyle(lineWidth: 8, dash: [CGFloat(10)]))
    .foregroundColor(.blue)
    .frame(width: 200, height: 100)
```

The above shape will be rendered as follows:

Figure 40-3

By providing additional dash values to a *StrokeStyle()* instance and adding a dash phase value, a range of different dash effects can be achieved, for example:

```
Ellipse()
    .stroke(style: StrokeStyle(lineWidth: 20,
```

```
            dash: [CGFloat(10), CGFloat(5), CGFloat(2)],
            dashPhase: CGFloat(10)))
    .foregroundColor(.blue)
    .frame(width: 250, height: 150)
```

When run or previewed, the above declaration will draw the following ellipse:

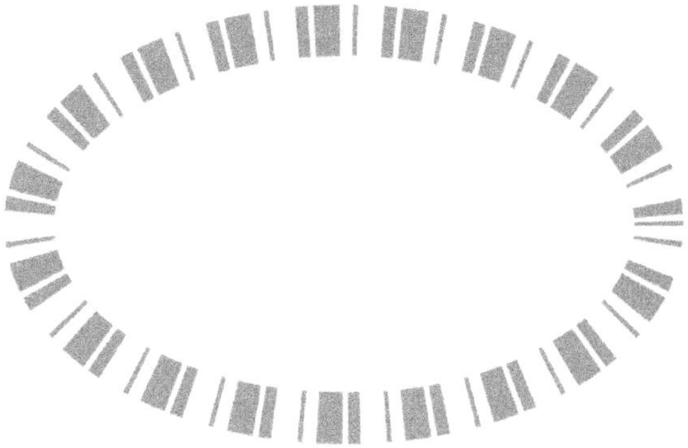

Figure 40-4

40.3 Using Overlays

When drawing a shape, it is not possible to combine the fill and stroke modifiers to render a filled shape with a stroked outline. This effect can, however, be achieved by overlaying a stroked view on top of the filled shape, for example:

```
Ellipse()
    .fill(.red)
    .overlay(Ellipse()
        .stroke(.blue, lineWidth: 10))
    .frame(width: 250, height: 150)
```

The above example draws a red-filled ellipse with a blue stroked outline as illustrated in Figure 40-5:

Figure 40-5

40.4 Drawing Custom Paths and Shapes

The shapes used so far in this chapter are essentially structure objects that conform to the Shape protocol. To conform with the shape protocol, a structure must implement a function named *path()* which accepts a rectangle in the form of a CGRect value and returns a Path object that defines what is to be drawn in that rectangle.

A Path instance provides the outline of a 2D shape by specifying coordinate points and defining the lines drawn between those points. Lines between points in a path can be drawn using straight lines, cubic and quadratic Bézier curves, arcs, ellipses, and rectangles.

In addition to being used in a custom shape implementation, paths may also be drawn directly within a view. Try modifying the *ContentView.swift* file so that it reads as follows:

```
struct ContentView: View {
    var body: some View {
        Path { path in
            path.move(to: CGPoint(x: 10, y: 0))
            path.addLine(to: CGPoint(x: 10, y: 350))
            path.addLine(to: CGPoint(x: 300, y: 300))
            path.closeSubpath()
        }
    }
}
```

A path begins with the coordinates of the start point using the *move()* method. Methods are then called to add additional lines between coordinates. In this case, the *addLine()* method is used to add straight lines. Lines may be drawn in a path using the following methods. In each case, the drawing starts at the current point in the path and ends at the specified endpoint:

- **addArc** – Adds an arc based on radius and angle values.
- **addCurve** – Adds a cubic Bézier curve using the provided end and control points.
- **addLine** – Adds a straight line ending at the specified point.
- **addLines** – Adds straight lines between the provided array of endpoints.
- **addQuadCurve** – Adds a quadratic Bézier curve using the specified control and endpoints.
- **closeSubPath** – Closes the path by connecting the endpoint to the start point.

A full listing of the line drawing methods and supported arguments can be found online at:

https://developer.apple.com/documentation/swiftui/path

When rendered in the preview canvas, the above path will appear as shown in Figure 40-6:

Figure 40-6

The custom drawing may also be adapted by applying modifiers, for example with a green fill color:

```
Path { path in
    path.move(to: CGPoint(x: 10, y: 0))
    path.addLine(to: CGPoint(x: 10, y: 350))
    path.addLine(to: CGPoint(x: 300, y: 300))
    path.closeSubpath()
}
.fill(.green)
```

Although it is possible to draw directly within a view, it generally makes more sense to implement custom shapes as reusable components. Within the *ContentView.swift* file, implement a custom shape as follows:

```
struct MyShape: Shape {
    func path(in rect: CGRect) -> Path {
        var path = Path()

        path.move(to: CGPoint(x: rect.minX, y: rect.minY))
        path.addQuadCurve(to: CGPoint(x: rect.minX, y: rect.maxY),
            control: CGPoint(x: rect.midX, y: rect.midY))
        path.addLine(to: CGPoint(x: rect.minX, y: rect.maxY))
        path.addLine(to: CGPoint(x: rect.maxX, y: rect.maxY))
        path.closeSubpath()
        return path
    }
}
```

The custom shape structure conforms to the Shape protocol by implementing the required *path()* function. The CGRect value passed to the function is used to define the boundaries into which a triangle shape is drawn, with one of the sides drawn using a quadratic curve.

Now that the custom shape has been declared, it can be used in the same way as the built-in SwiftUI shapes, including the use of modifiers. To see this in action, change the body of the main view to read as follows:

```
struct ContentView: View {
    var body: some View {
        MyShape()
            .fill(.red)
            .frame(width: 360, height: 350)
    }
}
```

When rendered, the custom shape will appear in the designated frame as illustrated in Figure 40-7 below:

Figure 40-7

40.5 Color Gradients and Shadows

A standard gradient effect can be added to any color choice by applying *.gradient* to the color declaration, for example:

```
Circle()
    .fill(.blue.gradient)
    .frame(width: 200, height: 200)
```

Similarly, shadow effects can be applied to color renderings using the *shadow()*, *drop()*, and *inner()* modifiers. The following example applies a drop shadow effect to a blue circle using black as the shadow color and a radius of 10 points:

```
Circle()
    .fill(.blue.shadow(.drop(color: .black, radius: 10)))
    .frame(width: 200, height: 200)
```

The following example, on the other hand, draws a white inner shadow on a black circle using a 15-point radius:

```
Circle()
    .fill(.blue.shadow(.inner(color: .white, radius: 15)))
    .frame(width: 200, height: 200)
```

Figure 40-8 illustrates how these effects appear when rendered on the screen:

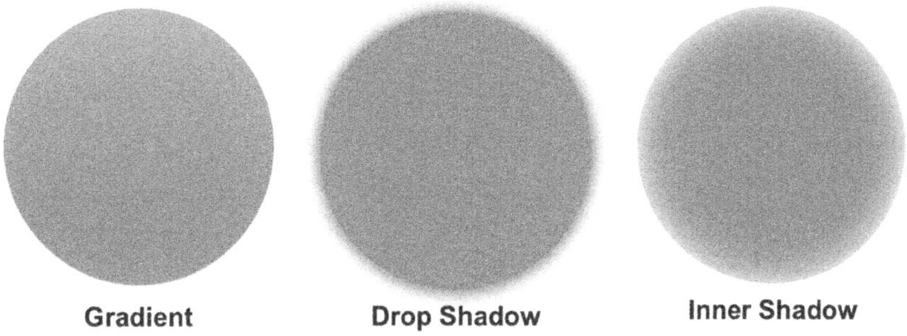

Figure 40-8

40.6 Drawing Gradients

For more advanced requirements, SwiftUI provides support for drawing gradients including linear, angular (conic), and radial gradients. In each case, the gradient is provided with a Gradient object initialized with an array of colors to be included in the gradient and values that control how the gradient is rendered.

The following declaration, for example, generates a radial gradient consisting of five colors applied as the fill pattern for a Circle:

```
struct ContentView: View {

    let colors = Gradient(colors: [Color.red, Color.yellow,
                   Color.green, Color.blue, Color.purple])

    var body: some View {
            Circle()
                .fill(RadialGradient(gradient: colors,
                     center: .center,
                     startRadius: CGFloat(0),
                     endRadius: CGFloat(300)))
    }
}
```

When rendered the above gradient will appear as follows:

Figure 40-9

The following declaration, on the other hand, generates an angular gradient with the same color range:

```
Circle()
    .fill(AngularGradient(gradient: colors, center: .center))
```

The angular gradient will appear as illustrated in the following figure:

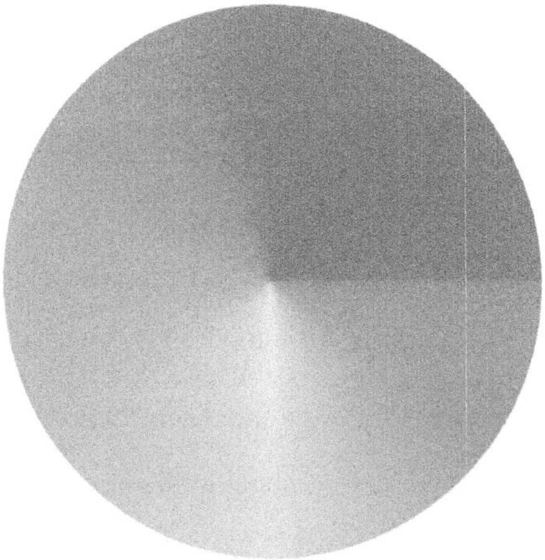

Figure 40-10

Similarly, a LinearGradient running diagonally would be implemented as follows:

```
Rectangle()
    .fill(LinearGradient(gradient: colors,
                         startPoint: .topLeading,
                           endPoint: .bottomTrailing))
    .frame(width: 360, height: 350)
```

The above linear gradient will be rendered as follows:

Figure 40-11

The final step in the DrawingDemo project is to apply gradients for the fill and background modifiers for our MyShape instance as follows:

```
MyShape()
    .fill(RadialGradient(gradient: colors,
```

```
                              center: .center,
                         startRadius: CGFloat(0),
                           endRadius: CGFloat(300)))
    .background(LinearGradient(gradient: Gradient(colors:
                                [Color.black, Color.white]),
                          startPoint: .topLeading,
                            endPoint: .bottomTrailing))
    .frame(width: 360, height: 350)
```

With the gradients added, the MyShape rendering should match the figure below:

Figure 40-12

40.7 Summary

SwiftUI includes a built-in set of views that conform to the Shape protocol for drawing standard shapes such as rectangles, circles, and ellipses. Modifiers can be applied to these views to control stroke, fill, and color properties.

Custom shapes are created by specifying paths that consist of sets of points joined by straight or curved lines. SwiftUI also includes support for drawing radial, linear, and angular gradient patterns.

Chapter 41

41. SwiftUI Animation and Transitions

This chapter is intended to provide an overview and examples of animating views and implementing transitions within a SwiftUI app. Animation can take a variety of forms including the rotation, scaling, and motion of a view on the screen.

Transitions, on the other hand, define how a view will appear as it is added to or removed from a layout, for example, whether a view slides into place when it is added, or shrinks from view when it is removed.

41.1 Creating the AnimationDemo Example Project

To try out the examples in this chapter, create a new Multiplatform App Xcode project named *AnimationDemo*.

41.2 Implicit Animation

Many of the built-in view types included with SwiftUI contain properties that control the appearance of the view such as scale, opacity, color, and rotation angle. Properties of this type are *animatable*, in that the change from one property state to another can be animated instead of occurring instantly. One way to animate these changes to a view is to use the *animation()* modifier (a concept referred to as *implicit animation* because the animation is implied for any modifiers applied to the view that precede the animation modifier).

To experience basic animation using this technique, modify the *ContentView.swift* file in the AnimationDemo project so that it contains a Button view configured to rotate in 60-degree increments each time it is tapped:

```
struct ContentView : View {

    @State private var rotation: Double = 0

    var body: some View {
       Button(action: {
           self.rotation =
                  (self.rotation < 360 ? self.rotation + 60 : 0)
           }) {
           Text("Click to animate")
               .rotationEffect(.degrees(rotation))
       }
    }
}
```

When tested using Live Preview, each click causes the Button view to rotate as expected, but the rotation is immediate. Similarly, when the rotation reaches a full 360 degrees, the view rotates counter-clockwise 360 degrees, but so quickly the effect is not visible. These effects can be slowed down and smoothed out by adding the *animation()* modifier with an optional animation curve to control the timing of the animation:

```
var body: some View {
```

```
    Button(action: {
        self.rotation =
                (self.rotation < 360 ? self.rotation + 60 : 0)
    }) {
        Text("Click to Animate")
            .rotationEffect(.degrees(rotation))
            .animation(.linear, value: rotation)
    }
}
```

The optional animation curve defines the linearity of the animation timeline. This setting controls whether the animation is performed at a constant speed or whether it starts slow and speeds up. SwiftUI provides the following basic animation curves:

- **linear** – The animation is performed at a constant speed for the specified duration and is the option declared in the above code example.
- **easeOut** – The animation starts fast and slows as the end of the sequence approaches.
- **easeIn** – The animation sequence starts slow and speeds up as the end approaches.
- **easeInOut** – The animation starts slow, speeds up, and then slows down again.

The value parameter tells the animation function which value is being used to control the animation which, in this case, is our *rotation* variable.

Preview the animation once again and note that the rotation now animates smoothly. When defining an animation, the duration may also be specified. Change the animation modifier so that it reads as follows:

```
.animation(.linear(duration: 1), value: rotation)
```

Now the animation will be performed more slowly each time the Button is clicked.

As previously mentioned, an animation can apply to more than one modifier. The following changes, for example, animate both rotation and scaling effects:

```
.
.
@State private var scale: CGFloat = 1

var body: some View {
    Button(action: {
         self.rotation =
                (self.rotation < 360 ? self.rotation + 60 : 0)
         self.scale = (self.scale < 2.8 ? self.scale + 0.3 : 1)
    }) {
        Text("Click to Animate")
         .scaleEffect(scale)
         .rotationEffect(.degrees(rotation))
         .animation(.linear(duration: 1), value: rotation)
    }
}
```

These changes will cause the button to increase in size with each rotation, then scale back to its original size during the return rotation.

Figure 41-1

A variety of spring effects may also be added to the animation using the *spring()* modifier, for example:

```
Text("Click to Animate")
    .scaleEffect(scale)
    .rotationEffect(.degrees(rotation))
    .animation(.spring(response: 1, dampingFraction: 0.2, blendDuration: 0),
                         value: rotation)
```

This will cause the rotation and scale effects to go slightly beyond the designated setting, then bounce back and forth before coming to rest at the target angle and scale.

When working with the *animation()* modifier, it is important to be aware that the animation is only implicit for modifiers that are applied before the animation modifier itself. In the following implementation, for example, only the rotation effect is animated since the scale effect is applied after the animation modifier:

```
Text("Click to Animate")
    .rotationEffect(.degrees(rotation))
    .scaleEffect(scale)
    .animation(.spring(response: 1, dampingFraction: 0.2, blendDuration: 0),
                         value: rotation)
    .scaleEffect(scale)
```

41.3 Repeating an Animation

By default, an animation will be performed once each time it is initiated. An animation may, however, be configured to repeat one or more times. In the following example, the animation is configured to repeat a specific number of times:

```
.animation(Animation.linear(duration: 1).repeatCount(10), value: rotation)
```

Each time an animation repeats, it will perform the animation in reverse as the view returns to its original state. If the view is required to instantly revert to its original appearance before repeating the animation, the autoreverses parameter must be set to false:

```
.animation(Animation.linear(duration: 1).repeatCount(10,
       autoreverses: false), value: rotation)
```

An animation may also be configured to repeat indefinitely using the *repeatForever()* modifier as follows:

```
.repeatForever(autoreverses: true))
```

41.4 Explicit Animation

As previously discussed, implicit animation using the *animation()* modifier implements animation on any of the animatable properties on a view that appear before the animation modifier. SwiftUI provides an alternative approach referred to as *explicit animation* which is implemented using the *withAnimation()* closure. When using explicit animation, only the property changes that take place within the *withAnimation()* closure will be animated. To experience this in action, modify the example so that the rotation effect is performed within a *withAnimation()* closure and remove the *animation()* modifier:

```
var body: some View {
    Button(action: { withAnimation(.linear (duration: 2)) {
            self.rotation =
                (self.rotation < 360 ? self.rotation + 60 : 0)
        }
        self.scale = (self.scale < 2.8 ? self.scale + 0.3 : 1)
    }) {

        Text("Click to Animate")
            .rotationEffect(.degrees(rotation))
            .scaleEffect(scale)
            .animation(.linear(duration: 1), value: rotation)
    }
}
```

With the changes made, preview the layout and note that only the rotation is now animated and that the changes to the scale of the text occur instantly. By using explicit animation, animation can be limited to specific properties of a view without having to worry about the ordering of modifiers.

Explicit animation is also useful for quickly adding basic animation effects to changes in state. Simple animation effects are easily added to an app with just a call to *withAnimation()*. The following changes to the *ContentView.swift* file, for example, animate the foreground color change of a circle each time it is tapped:

```
struct ContentView: View {
.
.
    @State private var redCircle = false

    var body: some View {
        Circle()
            .fill(redCircle ? .red : .blue)
            .frame(width: 200, height: 200)
                .onTapGesture {
                    withAnimation {
                        redCircle.toggle()
                    }
                }
    }
}
```

41.5 Animation and State Bindings

Animations may also be applied to state property bindings such that any view changes that occur as a result of that state value changing will be animated. If the state of a Toggle view causes one or more other views to become visible to the user, for example, applying an animation to the binding will cause the appearance and disappearance of all those views to be animated.

Within the *ContentView.swift* file, implement the following layout which consists of a VStack, Toggle view, and two Text views. The Toggle view is bound to a state property named *visible*, the value of which is used to control which of the two Text views is visible at one time:

```
.
.
@State private var visibility = false

var body: some View {
   VStack {
         Toggle(isOn: $visibility) {
            Text("Toggle Text Views")
         }
         .padding()

         if visibility {
             Text("Hello World")
                 .font(.largeTitle)
         }

         if !visibility {
             Text("Goodbye World")
                 .font(.largeTitle)
         }
    }
}
.
.
```

When previewed, switching the toggle on and off will cause one or other of the Text views to appear instantly. To add an animation to this change, simply apply a modifier to the state binding as follows:

```
.
.
var body: some View {
   VStack {
       Toggle(isOn: $visibility.animation(.linear(duration: 5))) {
           Text("Toggle Text Views")
       }
       .padding()
.
.
```

Now when the toggle is switched, one Text view will gradually fade from view as the other gradually fades in (unfortunately, at the time of writing this and other transition effects were only working when running on a simulator or physical device). The same animation will also be applied to any other views in the layout where the appearance changes as a result of the current state of the *visibility* property.

41.6 Automatically Starting an Animation

So far in this chapter, all the animations have been triggered by an event such as a button click. Often an animation will need to start without user interaction, for example when a view is first displayed to the user. Since an animation is triggered each time an animatable property of a view changes, this can be used to automatically start an animation when a view appears.

To see this technique in action, modify the example *ContentView.swift* file as follows:

```
struct ContentView : View {

    @State private var rotation: Double = 0

    var body: some View {

        ZStack {
            Circle()
                .stroke(lineWidth: 2)
                .foregroundColor(Color.blue)
                .frame(width: 360, height: 360)

            Image(systemName: "forward.fill")
               .font(.largeTitle)
               .offset(y: -180)
        }
    }
}
```

The content view uses a ZStack to overlay an Image view over a circle drawing where the offset of the Image view has been adjusted to position the image on the circumference of the circle. When previewed, the view should match that shown in Figure 41-2:

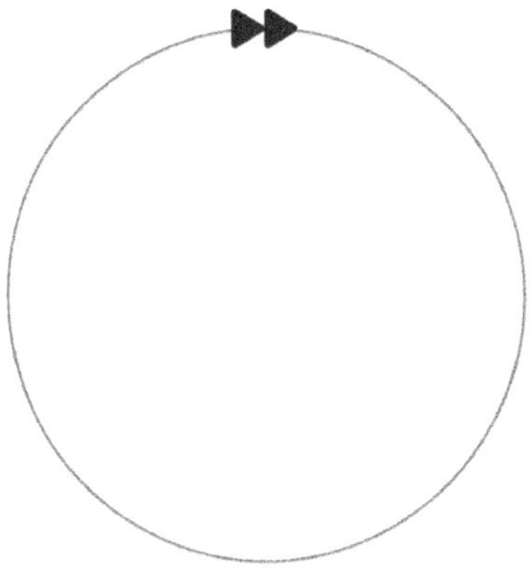

Figure 41-2

Adding a rotation effect to the Image view will give the appearance that the arrows are following the circle. Add this effect and an animation to the Image view as follows:

```
Image(systemName: "forward.fill")
   .font(.largeTitle)
   .offset(y: -180)
   .rotationEffect(.degrees(rotation))
   .animation(Animation.linear(duration: 5)
               .repeatForever(autoreverses: false), value: rotation)
```

As currently implemented the animation will not trigger when the view is tested in a Live Preview. This is because no action is taking place to change an animatable property, thereby initiating the animation.

This can be solved by making the angle of rotation subject to a Boolean state property, and then toggling that property when the ZStack first appears via the *onAppear()* modifier. In terms of implementing this behavior for our circle example, the content view declarations need to read as follows:

```
import SwiftUI

struct ContentView : View {

    @State private var rotation: Double = 0
    @State private var isSpinning: Bool = true

    var body: some View {

       ZStack {
            Circle()
                .stroke(lineWidth: 2)
                .foregroundColor(Color.blue)
                .frame(width: 360, height: 360)

            Image(systemName: "forward.fill")
               .font(.largeTitle)
               .offset(y: -180)
               .rotationEffect(.degrees(rotation))
               .animation(Animation.linear(duration: 5)
                           .repeatForever(autoreverses: false),
                                value: rotation)
       }
       .onAppear() {
          self.isSpinning.toggle()
          rotation = isSpinning ? 0 : 360
       }
    }
}
```

When SwiftUI initializes the content view, but before it appears on the screen, the isSpinning state property will be set to false and, based on the ternary operator, the rotation angle set to zero. After the view has appeared, however, the *onAppear()* modifier will toggle the isSpinning state property to true which will, in turn, cause the ternary operator to change the rotation angle to 360 degrees. As this is an animatable property, the animation modifier will activate and animate the rotation of the Image view through 360 degrees. Since this animation has been configured to repeat indefinitely, the image will continue to move around the circle.

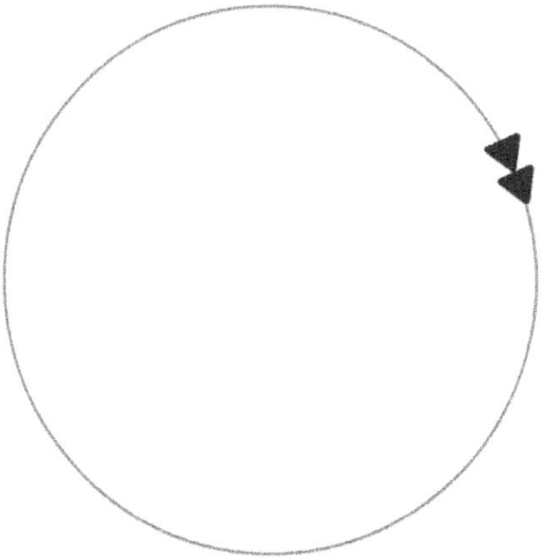

Figure 41-3

41.7 SwiftUI Transitions

A transition occurs in SwiftUI whenever a view is made visible or invisible to the user. To make this process more visually appealing than having the view instantly appear and disappear, SwiftUI allows these transitions to be animated in several ways using either individual effects or by combining multiple effects.

Begin by implementing a simple layout consisting of a Toggle button and a Text view. The toggle is bound to a state property which is then used to control whether the text view is visible. To make the transition more noticeable, animation has been applied to the state property binding:

```
struct ContentView : View {

    @State private var isButtonVisible: Bool = true

    var body: some View {
       VStack {
            Toggle(isOn:$isButtonVisible.animation(
                                   .linear(duration: 2))) {
                Text("Show/Hide Button")
            }
            .padding()

            if isButtonVisible {
                Button(action: {}) {
                    Text("Example Button")
                }
                .font(.largeTitle)
            }
        }
    }
```

```
}
```

After making the changes, use the Live Preview or a device or simulator to switch the toggle button state and note that the Text view fades in and out of view as the state changes (keeping in mind that some effects may not work in the Live Preview). This fading effect is the default transition used by SwiftUI. This default can be changed by passing a different transition to the *transition()* modifier, for which the following options are available:

- **scale** – The view increases in size as it is made visible and shrinks as it disappears.
- **slide** – The view slides in and out of view.
- **move(edge: edge)** – As the view is added or removed it does so by moving either from or toward the specified edge.
- **opacity** – The view retains its size and position while fading from view (the default transition behavior).

To configure the Text view to slide into view, change the example as follows:

```
if isButtonVisible {
    Button(action: {}) {
        Text("Example Button")
    }
    .font(.largeTitle)
    .transition(.slide)
}
```

Alternatively, the view can be made to shrink from view and then grow in size when inserted and removed:

```
.transition(.scale)
```

The *move()* transition can be used as follows to move the view toward a specified edge of the containing view. In the following example, the view moves from bottom to top when disappearing and from top to bottom when appearing:

```
.transition(.move(edge: .top))
```

When previewing the above move transition, you may have noticed that after completing the move, the Button disappears instantly. This somewhat jarring effect can be improved by combining the move with another transition.

41.8 Combining Transitions

SwiftUI transitions are combined using an instance of AnyTransition together with the *combined(with:)* method. To combine, for example, movement with opacity, a transition could be configured as follows:

```
.transition(AnyTransition.opacity.combined(with: .move(edge: .top)))
```

When the above example is implemented, the Text view will include a fading effect while moving.

To remove clutter from layout bodies and to promote re-usability, transitions can be implemented as extensions to the AnyTransition class. The above combined transition, for example, can be implemented as follows:

```
extension AnyTransition {
    static var fadeAndMove: AnyTransition {
        AnyTransition.opacity.combined(with: .move(edge: .top))
    }
}
```

When implemented as an extension, the transition can simply be passed as an argument to the *transition()*

modifier, for example:

```
.transition(.fadeAndMove)
```

41.9 Asymmetrical Transitions

By default, SwiftUI will simply reverse the specified insertion transition when removing a view. To specify a different transition for adding and removing views, the transition can be declared as being asymmetric. The following transition, for example, uses the scale transition for view insertion and sliding for removal:

```
.transition(.asymmetric(insertion: .scale, removal: .slide))
```

41.10 Summary

This chapter has explored the implementation of animation when changes are made to the appearance of a view. In the case of implicit animation, changes to a view caused by modifiers can be animated through the application of the *animated()* modifier. Explicit animation allows only specified properties of a view to be animated in response to appearance changes. Animation may also be applied to state property bindings such that any view changes that occur as a result of that state value changing will be animated.

A transition occurs when a view is inserted into, or removed from, a layout. SwiftUI provides several options for animating these transitions including fading, scaling, and sliding. SwiftUI also provides the ability to both combine transitions and define asymmetric transitions where different animation effects are used for insertion and removal of a view.

Chapter 42

42. Working with Gesture Recognizers in SwiftUI

The term *gesture* is used to describe an interaction between the touch screen and the user which can be detected and used to trigger an event in the app. Drags, taps, double taps, pinching, rotation motions, and long presses are all considered to be gestures in SwiftUI.

The goal of this chapter is to explore the use of SwiftUI gesture recognizers within a SwiftUI-based app.

42.1 Creating the GestureDemo Example Project

To try out the examples in this chapter, create a new Multiplatform App Xcode project named *GestureDemo*.

42.2 Basic Gestures

Gestures performed within the bounds of a view can be detected by adding a gesture recognizer to that view. SwiftUI provides recognizers for tap, long press, rotation, magnification (pinch), and drag gestures.

A gesture recognizer is added to a view using the *gesture()* modifier, passing through the gesture recognizer to be added.

In the simplest form, a recognizer will include one or more action callbacks containing the code to be executed when a matching gesture is detected on the view. The following example adds a tap gesture detector to an Image view and implements the *onEnded* callback containing the code to be performed when the gesture is completed successfully:

```
struct ContentView: View {
    var body: some View {
        Image(systemName: "hand.point.right.fill")
            .gesture(
                TapGesture()
                    .onEnded { _ in
                        print("Tapped")
                    }
            )
    }
}
```

Run the app on a device or emulator and test the above view declaration, noting the appearance of the "Tapped" message in the debug console panel when the image is clicked.

When working with gesture recognizers, it is usually preferable to assign the recognizer to a variable and then reference that variable in the modifier. This makes for tidier view body declarations and encourages reuse:

```
var body: some View {

    let tap = TapGesture()
```

```
                .onEnded { _ in
                print("Tapped")
            }

    return Image(systemName: "hand.point.right.fill")
        .gesture(tap)
}
```

When using the tap gesture recognizer, the number of taps required to complete the gesture may also be specified. The following, for example, will only detect double taps:

```
let tap = TapGesture(count: 2)
                .onEnded { _ in
                print("Tapped")
            }
```

The long press gesture recognizer is used in a similar way and is designed to detect when a view is touched for an extended length of time. The following declaration detects when a long press is performed on an Image view using the default time duration:

```
var body: some View {

    let longPress = LongPressGesture()
        .onEnded { _ in
            print("Long Press")
        }

    return Image(systemName: "hand.point.right.fill")
        .gesture(longPress)
}
```

To adjust the duration necessary to qualify as a long press, simply pass through a minimum duration value (in seconds) to the *LongPressGesture()* call. It is also possible to specify a maximum distance from the view from which the point of contact with the screen can move outside of the view during the long press. If the touch moves beyond the specified distance, the gesture will cancel and the onEnded action will not be called:

```
let longPress = LongPressGesture(minimumDuration: 10,
                                       maximumDistance: 25)
    .onEnded { _ in
        print("Long Press")
    }
```

A gesture recognizer can be removed from a view by passing a nil value to the *gesture()* modifier:

```
.gesture(nil)
```

42.3 The onChange Action Callback

In the previous examples, the onEnded action closure was used to detect when a gesture completes. Many of the gesture recognizers (except for TapGesture) also allow the addition of an onChange action callback. The onChange callback will be called when the gesture is first recognized, and each time the underlying values of the gesture change, up until the point that the gesture ends.

The onChange action callback is particularly useful when used with gestures involving motion across the device display (as opposed to taps and long presses). The magnification gesture, for example, can be used to detect the movement of touches on the screen.

```
struct ContentView: View {

    var body: some View {

        let magnificationGesture =
                    MagnificationGesture(minimumScaleDelta: 0)
            .onEnded { _ in
                print("Gesture Ended")
            }

        return Image(systemName: "hand.point.right.fill")
            .resizable()
            .font(.largeTitle)
            .gesture(magnificationGesture)
            .frame(width: 100, height: 90)
    }
}
```

The above implementation will detect a pinching motion performed over the Image view but will only report the detection after the gesture ends. Within the preview canvas, pinch gestures can be simulated by holding down the keyboard Option key while clicking in the Image view and dragging.

To receive notifications for the duration of the gesture, the onChanged callback action can be added:

```
let magnificationGesture =
                    MagnificationGesture(minimumScaleDelta: 0)
    .onChanged( { _ in
        print("Magnifying")
    })
    .onEnded { _ in
        print("Gesture Ended")
    }
```

Now when the gesture is detected, the onChanged action will be called each time the values associated with the pinch operation change. Each time the onChanged action is called, it will be passed a MagnificationGesture. Value instance which contains a CGFloat value representing the current scale of the magnification.

With access to this information about the magnification gesture scale, interesting effects can be implemented such as configuring the Image view to resize in response to the gesture:

```
struct ContentView: View {

    @State private var magnification: CGFloat = 1.0

    var body: some View {

        let magnificationGesture =
                MagnificationGesture(minimumScaleDelta: 0)
```

```
            .onChanged({ value in
                self.magnification = value
            })
            .onEnded({ _ in
                print("Gesture Ended")
            })

        return Image(systemName: "hand.point.right.fill")
            .resizable()
            .font(.largeTitle)
            .scaleEffect(magnification)
            .gesture(magnificationGesture)
            .frame(width: 100, height: 90)
    }
}
```

42.4 The updating Callback Action

The *updating* callback action is like *onChanged* with the exception that it works with a special property wrapper named @GestureState. GestureState is like the standard @State property wrapper but is designed exclusively for use with gestures. The key difference, however, is that @GestureState properties automatically reset to the original state when the gesture ends. As such, the updating callback is ideal for storing transient state that is only needed while a gesture is being performed.

Each time an updating action is called, it is passed the following three arguments:

- DragGesture.Value instance containing information about the gesture.
- A reference to the @GestureState property to which the gesture has been bound.
- A Transaction object containing the current state of the animation corresponding to the gesture.

The DragGesture.Value instance is particularly useful and contains the following properties:

- **location (CGPoint)** - The current location of the drag gesture.
- **predictedEndLocation (CGPoint)** – Predicted final location, based on the velocity of the drag if dragging stops.
- **predictedEndTranslation (CGSize)** - A prediction of what the final translation would be if dragging stopped now based on the current drag velocity.
- **startLocation (CGPoint)** - The location at which the drag gesture started.
- **time (Date)** – The time stamp of the current drag event.
- **translation (CGSize)** - The total translation from the start of the drag gesture to the current event (essentially the offset from the start position to the current drag location).

Typically, a drag gesture updating callback will extract the translation value from the DragGesture.Value object and assign it to a @GestureState property and will typically resemble the following:

```
let drag = DragGesture()
    .updating($offset) { dragValue, state, transaction in
        state = dragValue.translation
```

```
    }
```

The following example adds a drag gesture to an Image view and then uses the updating callback to keep a @ GestureState property updated with the current translation value. An *offset()* modifier is applied to the Image view using the @GestureState offset property. This has the effect of making the Image view follow the drag gesture as it moves across the screen.

```
struct ContentView: View {

    @GestureState private var offset: CGSize = .zero

    var body: some View {

        let drag = DragGesture()
            .updating($offset) { dragValue, state, transaction in
                state = dragValue.translation
            }

        return Image(systemName: "hand.point.right.fill")
            .font(.largeTitle)
            .offset(offset)
            .gesture(drag)
    }
}
```

If it is not possible to drag the image this may be because of a problem with the live view in the current Xcode 14 release. The example should work if tested on a simulator or physical device. Note that once the drag gesture ends, the Image view returns to the original location. This is because the offset gesture property was automatically reverted to its original state when the drag ended.

42.5 Composing Gestures

So far in this chapter, we have looked at adding a single gesture recognizer to a view in SwiftUI. Though a less common requirement, it is also possible to combine multiple gestures and apply them to a view. Gestures can be combined so that they are detected simultaneously, in sequence, or exclusively. When gestures are composed simultaneously, both gestures must be detected at the same time for the corresponding action to be performed. In this case, if sequential gestures, the first gesture must be completed before the second gesture will be detected. For exclusive gestures, the detection of one gesture will be treated as all gestures being detected.

Gestures are composed using the *simultaneously()*, *sequenced()* and *exclusively()* modifiers. The following view declaration, for example, composes a simultaneous gesture consisting of a long press and a drag:

```
struct ContentView: View {

    @GestureState private var offset: CGSize = .zero
    @GestureState private var longPress: Bool = false

    var body: some View {

        let longPressAndDrag = LongPressGesture(minimumDuration: 1.0)
            .updating($longPress) { value, state, transition in
```

```
                state = value
            }
            .simultaneously(with: DragGesture())
            .updating($offset) { value, state, transaction in
                state = value.second?.translation ?? .zero
             }

            return Image(systemName: "hand.point.right.fill")
                .foregroundColor(longPress ? Color.red : Color.blue)
                .font(.largeTitle)
                .offset(offset)
                .gesture(longPressAndDrag)
    }
}
```

In the case of the following view declaration, a sequential gesture is configured which requires the long press gesture to be completed before the drag operation can begin. When executed, the user will perform a long press on the image until it turns green, at which point the drag gesture can be used to move the image around the screen.

```
struct ContentView: View {

    @GestureState private var offset: CGSize = .zero
    @State private var dragEnabled: Bool = false

    var body: some View {

        let longPressBeforeDrag = LongPressGesture(minimumDuration: 2.0)
            .onEnded( { _ in
                self.dragEnabled = true
            })
            .sequenced(before: DragGesture())
            .updating($offset) { value, state, transaction in

                switch value {

                    case .first(true):
                        print("Long press in progress")

                    case .second(true, let drag):
                        state = drag?.translation ?? .zero

                    default: break
                }
            }
            .onEnded { value in
                self.dragEnabled = false
```

```
            }

            return Image(systemName: "hand.point.right.fill")
                .foregroundColor(dragEnabled ? Color.green : Color.blue)
                .font(.largeTitle)
                .offset(offset)
                .gesture(longPressBeforeDrag)
    }
}
```

42.6 Summary

Gesture detection can be added to SwiftUI views using gesture recognizers. SwiftUI includes recognizers for drag, pinch, rotate, long press, and tap gestures. Gesture detection notification can be received from the recognizers by implementing onEnded, updated and onChange callback methods. The updating callback works with a special property wrapper named @GestureState. A GestureState property is like the standard state property wrapper but is designed exclusively for use with gestures and automatically resets to its original state when the gesture ends. Gesture recognizers may be combined so that they are recognized simultaneously, sequentially or exclusively.

Chapter 43

43. Creating a Customized SwiftUI ProgressView

The SwiftUI ProgressView, as the name suggests, provides a way to visually indicate the progress of a task within an app. An app might, for example, need to display a progress bar while downloading a large file. This chapter will work through an example project demonstrating how to implement a ProgressView-based interface in a SwiftUI app including linear, circular, and indeterminate styles in addition to creating your own custom progress views.

43.1 ProgressView Styles

The ProgressView can be displayed in three different styles. The linear style displays progress in the form of a horizontal line as shown in Figure 43-1 below:

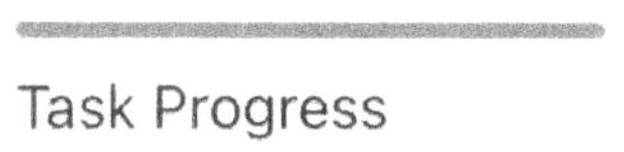

Figure 43-1

Alternatively, progress may be displayed using the circular style as shown in Figure 43-2:

Figure 43-2

Finally, for indeterminate progress, the spinning animation shown in Figure 43-3 below is used. This style is useful for indicating to the user that progress is being made on a task when the percentage of work completed is unknown.

Figure 43-3

As we will see later in the chapter, it is also possible to design a custom style by creating declarations conforming to the ProgressViewStyle protocol.

43.2 Creating the ProgressViewDemo Project

Launch Xcode and create a new project named *ProgressViewDemo* using the Multiplatform App template.

43.3 Adding a ProgressView

The content view for this example app will consist of a ProgressView and a Slider. The Slider view will serve as a way to change the value of a State property variable, such that changes to the slider position will be reflected by the ProgressView.

Edit the *ContentView.swift* file and modify the view as follows:

```
struct ContentView: View {

    @State private var progress: Double = 1.0

    var body: some View {

        VStack {
            ProgressView("Task Progress", value: progress, total: 100)
                .progressViewStyle(LinearProgressViewStyle())
            Slider(value: $progress, in: 1...100, step: 0.1)
        }
        .padding()
    }
}
```

Note that the ProgressView is passed a string to display as the title, a value indicating the current progress, and a total used to define when the task is complete. Similarly, the Slider is configured to adjust the *progress* state property between 1 and 100 in increments of 0.1.

Use Live Preview to test the view and verify that the progress bar moves in unison with the slider:

Figure 43-4

The color of the progress line may be changed using the tint argument as follows:

```
ProgressView("Task Progress", value: progress, total: 100)
    .progressViewStyle(LinearProgressViewStyle(tint: Color.red))
```

43.4 Using the Circular ProgressView Style

To display a circular ProgressView, the *progressViewStyle()* modifier needs to be called and passed an instance of CircularProgressViewStyle as follows:

```
struct ContentView: View {

    @State private var progress: Double = 1.0
```

```
    var body: some View {

        VStack {
            ProgressView("Task Progress", value: progress, total: 100)
                .progressViewStyle(CircularProgressViewStyle())
            Slider(value: $progress, in: 1...100, step: 0.1)
        }
        .padding()
    }
}
```

When the app is now previewed, the progress will be shown using the circular style. Note that a bug in all versions of iOS up to and including iOS 16 causes the circular style to appear using the intermediate style. This bug has been reported to Apple and will hopefully be resolved in a future release. In the meantime, the behavior can be tested by targeting macOS instead of iOS when running the app.

Although the *progressViewStyle()* modifier was applied directly to the ProgressView in the above example, it may also be applied to a container view such as VStack. When used in this way, the style will be applied to all child ProgressView instances. In the following example, therefore, all three ProgressView instances will be displayed using the circular style:

```
VStack {
    ProgressView("Task 1 Progress", value: progress, total: 100)
    ProgressView("Task 2 Progress", value: progress, total: 100)
    ProgressView("Task 3 Progress", value: progress, total: 100)
}
.progressViewStyle(CircularProgressViewStyle())
```

43.5 Declaring an Indeterminate ProgressView

The indeterminate ProgressView displays the spinning indicator shown previously in Figure 43-3 and is declared using the ProgressView without including a value binding to indicate progress:

```
ProgressView()
```

If required, text may be assigned to appear alongside the view:

```
ProgressView("Working...")
```

43.6 ProgressView Customization

The appearance of a ProgressView may be changed by declaring a structure conforming to the ProgressViewStyle protocol and passing an instance through to the *progressViewStyle()* modifier.

To conform with the ProgressViewStyle protocol, the style declaration must be structured as follows:

```
struct MyCustomProgressViewStyle: ProgressViewStyle {
    func makeBody(configuration: Configuration) -> some View {
        ProgressView(configuration)
            // Modifiers here to customize the view
    }
}
```

The structure contains a *makeBody()* method which is passed the configuration information for the ProgressView on which the custom style is being applied. One option is to simply return a modified ProgressView instance. The following style, for example, applies accent color and shadow effects to the ProgressView:

```
import SwiftUI

struct ContentView: View {

    @State private var progress: Double = 1.0

    var body: some View {

        VStack {
            ProgressView("Task Progress", value: progress, total: 100)
                .progressViewStyle(ShadowProgressViewStyle())

            Slider(value: $progress, in: 1...100, step: 0.1)
        }
        .padding()
    }
}

struct ShadowProgressViewStyle: ProgressViewStyle {
    func makeBody(configuration: Configuration) -> some View {
        ProgressView(configuration)
            .accentColor(.red)
            .shadow(color: Color(red: 0, green: 0.7, blue: 0),
                    radius: 5.0, x: 2.0, y: 2.0)
            .progressViewStyle(LinearProgressViewStyle())
    }
}
.
.
```

The ProgressView will now appear with a green shadow with the progress line appearing in red. A closer inspection of the *makeBody()* method will reveal that it can return a View instance of any type, meaning that the method is not limited to returning a ProgressView instance. We could, for example, return a Text view as shown below. The Configuration instance passed to the *makeBody()* method contains a property named fractionComplete, we can use this to display the progress percentage in the Text view:

```
.
.
        VStack {
            ProgressView("Task Progress", value: progress, total: 100)
                .progressViewStyle(MyCustomProgressViewStyle())
.
.
    }
}
```

```
struct MyCustomProgressViewStyle: ProgressViewStyle {
    func makeBody(configuration: Configuration) -> some View {
        let percent = Int(configuration.fractionCompleted! * 100)
        return  Text("Task \(percent)% Complete")
    }
}
```

When previewed, the custom style will appear as shown in Figure 43-5:

Figure 43-5

In fact, custom progress views of any level of complexity may be designed using this technique. Consider, for example, the following custom progress view implementation:

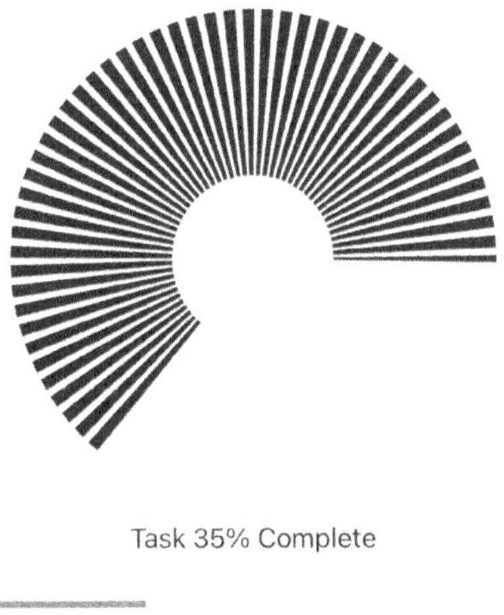

Figure 43-6

The above example was created using a Shape declaration to draw a dashed circular path based on the fractionComplete property:

```
struct MyCustomProgressViewStyle: ProgressViewStyle {
    func makeBody(configuration: Configuration) -> some View {

        let degrees = configuration.fractionCompleted! * 360
        let percent = Int(configuration.fractionCompleted! * 100)

        return VStack {
```

```
            MyCircle(startAngle: .degrees(1), endAngle: .degrees(degrees))
                .frame(width: 200, height: 200)
                .padding(50)
            Text("Task \(percent)% Complete")
        }
    }
}

struct MyCircle: Shape {
    var startAngle: Angle
    var endAngle: Angle

    func path(in rect: CGRect) -> Path {
        var path = Path()
        path.addArc(center: CGPoint(x: rect.midX, y: rect.midY),
                 radius: rect.width / 2, startAngle: startAngle,
                              endAngle: endAngle, clockwise: true)

        return path.strokedPath(.init(lineWidth: 100, dash: [5, 3],
                 dashPhase: 10))
    }
}
```

43.7 Summary

The SwiftUI ProgressView provides a way for apps to visually convey to the user the progress of a long-running task such as a large download transaction. ProgressView instances may be configured to display progress either as a straight bar or using a circular style, while the indeterminate style displays a spinning icon that indicates the task is running but without providing progress information. The prevailing style is assigned using the *progressViewStyle()* modifier which may be applied either to individual ProgressView instances or all of the instances within a container view such as a VStack.

By adopting the ProgressViewStyle protocol, custom progress view designs of almost any level of complexity can be created.

Chapter 44

44. Presenting Data with SwiftUI Charts

One of the best ways to present data is to do so in the form of a chart or graph. While it has always been possible, given sufficient time and skills, to generate charts in SwiftUI by writing your own data handling and drawing code, it was not until the introduction of the SwiftUI Charts API that it became a simple as writing a few lines of code. In this chapter, we will explore the more commonly used features of SwiftUI Charts before creating a project in the next chapter that will allow you to see Charts in action and experiment with the main features of this API.

44.1 Introducing SwiftUI Charts

SwiftUI Charts consists of views and modifiers that allow you to visually present data, typically with just a few lines of code. The API is highly configurable and includes options to present data in the form of area, line, point, rectangle, bar, and stacked bar graphs. The Chart view also includes the rule mark which draws a straight line between specified start and end coordinates. The top-level view in any chart implementation is the Chart view. Each data point within a Chart takes the form of a *mark* view. The type of mark view used will depend on the chart style. For example, a bar chart will be made up of instances of BarMark, while an area graph will contain AreaMark instances. The Charts API supports the following mark types:

- AreaMark
- BarMark
- LineMark
- PointMark
- RectangleMark
- RuleMark

Each mark must be initialized with x and y values, each of which is represented by an instance of the PlottableValue class. The following declaration, for example, creates an area chart consisting of three marks (note that the Charts library must be imported when working with this API):

```
.
.
import Charts
.
.
Chart {
    AreaMark(
        x: PlottableValue.value("Month", "Jan"),
        y: PlottableValue.value("Temp", 50)
    )
```

```
    AreaMark(
        x: PlottableValue.value("Month", "Feb"),
        y: PlottableValue.value("Temp", 43)
    )
    AreaMark(
        x: PlottableValue.value("Month", "Mar"),
        y: PlottableValue.value("Temp", 61)
    )
}
```

For tidier code, the *PlottableValue.value* declarations can be abbreviated to *.value*, for example:

```
AreaMark(
    x: .value("Month", "Jan"),
    y: .value("Temp", 50)
)
```

The above example will generate a chart matching that shown in Figure 44-1 below:

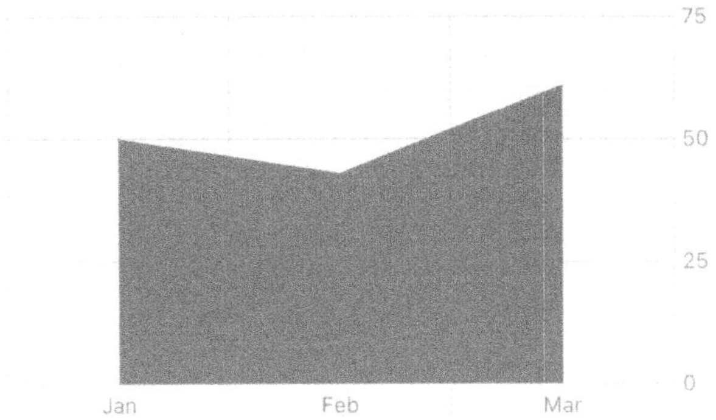

Figure 44-1

44.2 Passing Data to the Chart

In the previous example, we manually coded each point on the chart. It is more likely, however, that the data to be plotted exists outside of the chart. In this situation we can pass the data as a parameter to the Chart view as follows:

```
struct MonthlyTemp: Identifiable {
    var id = UUID()
    var month: String
    var degrees: Int
}

let tempData: [MonthlyTemp] = [
    MonthlyTemp(month: "Jan", degrees: 50),
    MonthlyTemp(month: "Feb", degrees: 43),
    MonthlyTemp(month: "Mar", degrees: 61)
]

Chart(tempData) { data in
```

```
    AreaMark(
        x: .value("Month", data.month),
        y: .value("Temp", data.degrees)
    )
}
```

The above code will create the same chart illustrated in Figure 44-1. A ForEach loop will produce the same result:

```
Chart {
    ForEach(tempData) { data in
        AreaMark(
            x: .value("Month", data.month),
            y: .value("Temp", data.degrees)
        )
    }
}
```

44.3 Combining Mark Types

So far in this chapter, we have only displayed data using one type of graph. We can display the same data in different ways within the same chart. In the following example, our temperature data appears in both rectangle and line format:

```
Chart(tempData) { data in
    RectangleMark(
        x: .value("Month", data.month),
        y: .value("Temp", data.degrees)
    )
    LineMark(
        x: .value("Month", data.month),
        y: .value("Temp", data.degrees)
    )
}
```

This code will generate the graph shown in Figure 44-2:

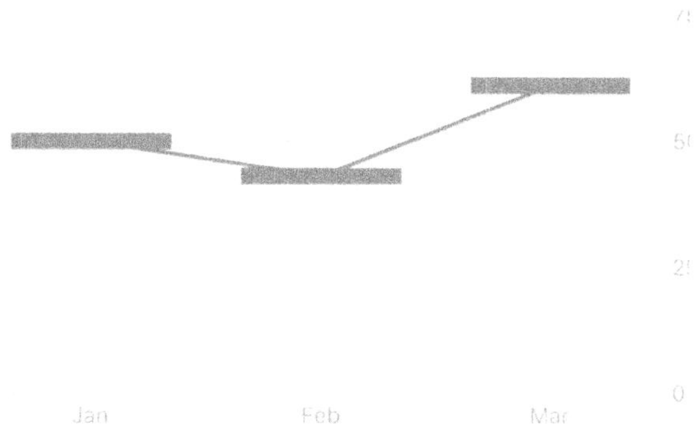

Figure 44-2

44.4 Filtering Data into Multiple Graphs

If the data contains information that allows it to be filtered into categories, the *foregroundStyle()* modifier can be used to generate multiple graphs within a single chart instance. Suppose, for example, that our temperature data includes values for more than one year. This data might be declared as follows:

```
struct MonthlyTemp: Identifiable {
    var id = UUID()
    var month: String
    var degrees: Int
    var year: String
}

let tempData: [MonthlyTemp] = [
    MonthlyTemp(month: "Jan", degrees: 50, year: "2021"),
    MonthlyTemp(month: "Feb", degrees: 43, year: "2021"),
    MonthlyTemp(month: "Mar", degrees: 61, year: "2021"),

    MonthlyTemp(month: "Jan", degrees: 30, year: "2022"),
    MonthlyTemp(month: "Feb", degrees: 38, year: "2022"),
    MonthlyTemp(month: "Mar", degrees: 29, year: "2022")
]
```

The only change required to the Chart code is to apply the *foregroundStyle()* modifier to the mark declaration and pass it a PlottableValue instance configured to separate the data by year:

```
Chart {
    ForEach(tempData) { data in
        LineMark(
            x: .value("Month", data.month),
            y: .value("Temp", data.degrees)
        )
        .foregroundStyle(by: .value("Year", data.year))
    }
}
```

The chart will now separate the data into two lines, each rendered in a different color. Note also that a scale appears at the bottom of the chart showing the correspondence between colors and years:

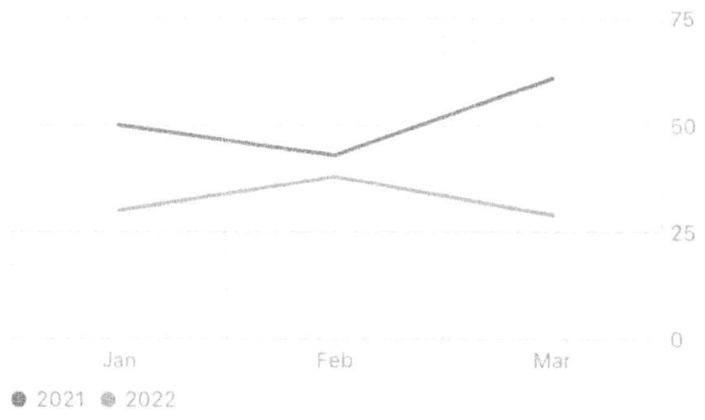

Figure 44-3

In addition to the line colors, we can also add symbols at each mark point to further differentiate the data categories. We do this by applying the *symbol()* modifier to the mark declaration passing as a parameter an appropriately configured PlottableValue instance as outlined above for the *foregroundStyle()* modifier:

```
Chart {
    ForEach(tempData) { data in
        LineMark(
            x: .value("Month", data.month),
            y: .value("Temp", data.degrees)
        )
        .foregroundStyle(by: .value("Year", data.year))
        .symbol(by: .value("Year", data.year))
    }
}
```

A close inspection of the two lines in our chart will show that the lines are using different symbols for the mark points:

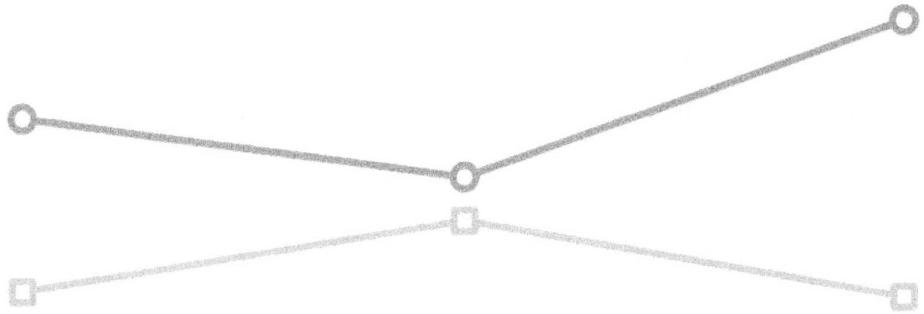

Figure 44-4

44.5 Changing the Chart Background

The background of the Chart view can be changed using the *chartPlotStyle()* modifier. This modifier is used with a trailing closure to which it passes a reference to the plot area on which the graph is being drawn. This reference may then be used to change properties such as the background color:

```
Chart {
.
.
}
.chartPlotStyle { plotArea in
    plotArea
        .background(.gray.opacity(0.3))
}
.
.
```

44.6 Changing the Interpolation Method

Interpolation refers to how lines are drawn to connect the data points in a graph. The interpolation method used by a chart can be changed by applying the *interpolationMethod()* modifier to mark declarations. The list of interpolation options is as follows:

- cardinal
- catmullRom
- linear
- monotone
- stepCenter
- stepEnd
- stepStart

The following code example configures our example chart to use stepStart interpolation:

```
Chart {
    ForEach(tempData) { data in
        LineMark(
            x: .value("Month", data.month),
            y: .value("Temp", data.degrees)
        )
        .interpolationMethod(.stepStart)
        .foregroundStyle(by: .value("Year", data.year))
        .symbol(by: .value("Year", data.year))
    }
}
```

The resulting chart using stepStart interpolation will appear as shown below:

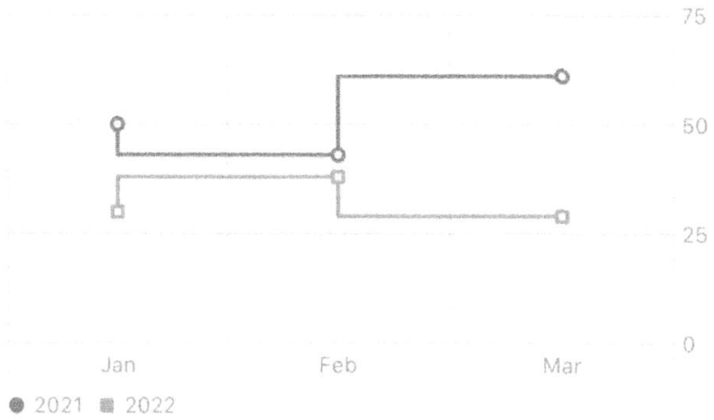

Figure 44-5

44.7 Summary

SwiftUI Charts provides an intuitive way to visualize data in the form of charts and graphs with minimal coding. This is achieved using a parent Chart view containing data points in the form of mark instances. Marks are available for several graph types including area, line, bar, plot, and rectangle. The x and y data for each mark is, in turn, contained within a PlottableValue instance. Graphs can be combined and configured using modifiers including changing the interpolation style and adding point symbol markers.

Chapter 45

45. A SwiftUI Charts Tutorial

This chapter will demonstrate the main features of the SwiftUI Charts in the form of a tutorial. Topics covered include creating a chart, displaying data from multiple data sources, and use of the style modifier.

The concept behind the tutorial is a chart that displays monthly unit sales data containing graphs for both online and retail sales channels.

45.1 Creating the ChartDemo Project

Launch Xcode and select the usual options to create a new multiplatform project named ChartDemo.

45.2 Adding the Project Data

The first requirement for handling the sales data is to declare a structure to store data for each month. Right-click on the ChartDemo folder in the Project Navigator panel, select the *New File...* menu option and create a new SwiftUI file named *SalesData.swift*. Edit the file and add the following struct declaration:

```
import Foundation

struct SalesInfo: Identifiable {
    var id = UUID()
    var month: String
    var total: Int
}
```

Remaining within the *SalesData.swift* file, add two arrays containing the retail and online sales data for January through July as follows:

```
.
.
var retailSales: [SalesInfo] = [
    .init(month: "Jan", total: 5),
    .init(month: "Feb", total: 7),
    .init(month: "March", total: 6),
    .init(month: "April", total: 5),
    .init(month: "May", total: 6),
    .init(month: "June", total: 3),
    .init(month: "July", total: 6)
]

var onlineSales: [SalesInfo] = [
    .init(month: "Jan", total: 2),
    .init(month: "Feb", total: 4),
    .init(month: "March", total: 5),
    .init(month: "April", total: 2),
    .init(month: "May", total: 4),
```

```
    .init(month: "June", total: 1),
    .init(month: "July", total: 4)
]
```

Our next requirement is a third array that combines the data from both sales channels. Each element in this third array will also need to include a label string that can be used later when the time comes to split the data into separate channel graphs. Add this array now within the *ContentView.swift* file. Now is also a good opportunity to import the Charts framework:

```
import SwiftUI
import Charts

struct ContentView: View {
    var body: some View {

        let sales = [ (channel: "Retail", data: retailSales),
                      (channel: "Online", data: onlineSales) ]
.
.
```

45.3 Adding the Chart View

The chart view is going to need to use nested ForEach loops. The outer loop will iterate through the channel entries in the *sales* array while the inner loop will iterate through the sales data for each channel. Start by adding the Chart view and the outer loop as follows:

```
struct ContentView: View {
    var body: some View {

        let sales = [ (channel: "Retail", data: retailSales),
                      (channel: "Online", data: onlineSales) ]

        Chart {
            ForEach(sales, id: \.channel) { channels in

            }
        }
        .frame(height: 250)
        .padding()
    }
}
```

The outer loop passes the set of channels to the inner loop where we can then iterate through the sales data. For each month in the data, the inner ForEach loop will need to add an AreaMark instance configured with the month name and sales total. Modify the Chart view declaration so that it reads as follows:

```
Chart {
    ForEach(sales, id: \.channel) { channels in
        ForEach(channels.data) { sales in
            AreaMark(
                x: .value("Month", sales.month),
```

```
                y: .value("Total", sales.total)
            )
        }
    }
}
.
.
```

Review the chart in the Preview panel where it should appear as shown in Figure 45-1 below:

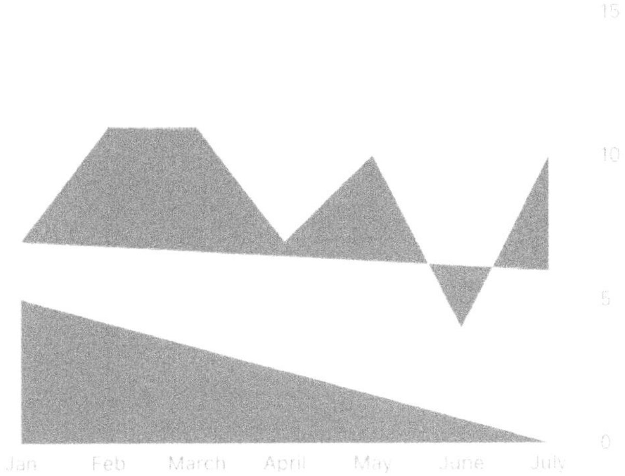

Figure 45-1

At this point, the chart is not appearing as intended because we have not taken any steps to separate the online and retail sales data. To divide the data into two graphs we will need to apply the *foregroundStyle()* modifier to the AreaMark declaration and configure it to filter the data based on the sales channel.

45.4 Creating Multiple Graphs

Edit the *ContentView.swift* file once again, locate the AreaMark instance, and apply the *foregroundStyle()* modifier:

```
Chart {
    ForEach(sales, id: \.channel) { channels in
        ForEach(channels.data) { sales in
            AreaMark(
                x: .value("Month", sales.month),
                y: .value("Total", sales.total)
            )
            .foregroundStyle(by: .value("Channel", channels.channel))
        }
    }
}
```

Preview the chart once again and confirm that it now appears correctly as shown in Figure 45-2:

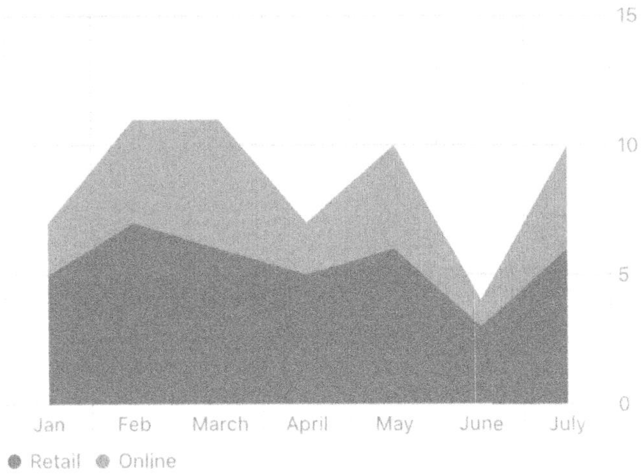

Figure 45-2

Now that the project is complete, take some time to experiment with the chart by adding symbols and using different mark types and interpolation methods. Figure 45-3, for example, shows the effect of replacing AreaMark with PointMark:

Figure 45-3

45.5 Summary

In this chapter, we have created a project that uses SwiftUI Charts to visualize two sets of data in the form of area graphs. Steps covered in the tutorial included the use of the Chart and AreaMark components and the use of the foreground style modifier.

46. An Overview of SwiftUI DocumentGroup Scenes

The chapter entitled *"SwiftUI Architecture"* introduced the concept of SwiftUI scenes and explained that the SwiftUI framework, in addition to allowing you to build your own scenes, also includes two pre-built scene types in the form of WindowGroup and DocumentGroup. So far, the examples in this book have made exclusive use of the WindowGroup scene. This chapter will introduce the DocumentGroup scene and explain how it can be used to build document-based apps in SwiftUI.

46.1 Documents in Apps

If you have used iOS for an appreciable amount of time, the chances are good that you will have encountered the built-in *Files* app. The Files app provides a way to browse, select and manage the Documents stored both on the local device file system and iCloud storage in addition to third-party providers such as Google Drive. Documents in this context can include just about any file type including plain text, image, data, and binary files. Figure 46-1 shows a typical browsing session within the iOS Files app:

Figure 46-1

The purpose of the DocumentGroup scene is to allow the same capabilities provided by the Files app to be built into SwiftUI apps, in addition to the ability to create new files.

Document support can be built into an app with relatively little work. Xcode includes a project template specifically for this task which performs much of the setup work for you. Before attempting to work with DocumentGroups, however, some basic concepts first need to be covered. A good way to traverse this learning curve is to review the Document App project template generated by Xcode.

46.2 Creating the DocDemo App

Begin by launching Xcode and creating a new project using the Multiplatform Document App template option as shown in Figure 46-2 below:

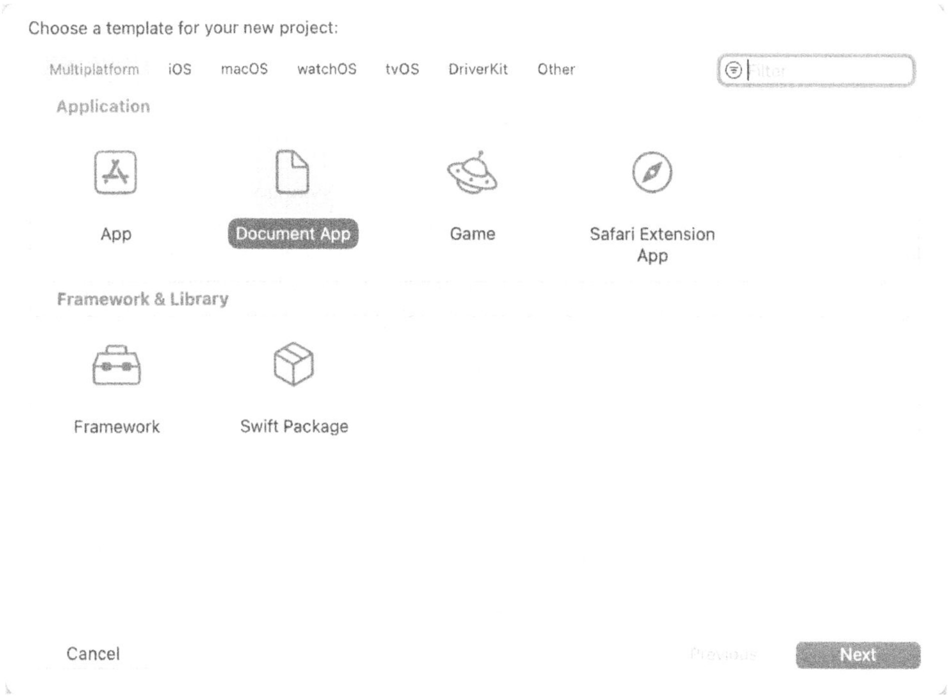

Figure 46-2

Click the Next button, name the project *DocDemo* and save the project to a suitable location.

46.3 The DocumentGroup Scene

The DocumentGroup scene contains most of the infrastructure necessary to provide app users with the ability to create, delete, move, rename and select files and folders from within an app. An initial document group scene is declared by Xcode within the *DocDemoApp.swift* file as follows:

```
import SwiftUI

@main
struct DocDemoApp: App {
    var body: some Scene {
        DocumentGroup(newDocument: DocDemoDocument()) { file in
            ContentView(document: file.$document)
        }
```

```
    }
}
```

As currently implemented, the first scene presented to the user when the app starts will be the DocumentGroup user interface which will resemble Figure 46-1 above. Passed through to the DocumentGroup is a DocDemoDocument instance which, along with some additional configuration settings, contains the code to create, read and write files. When a user either selects an existing file or creates a new one, the content view is displayed and passed the DocDemoDocument instance for the selected file from which the content may be extracted and presented to the user:

```
ContentView(document: file.$document)
```

The *DocDemoDocument.swift* file generated by Xcode is designed to support plain text files and may be used as the basis for supporting other file types. Before exploring this file in detail, we first need to understand file types.

46.4 Declaring File Type Support

A key step in implementing document support is declaring the file types that the app supports. The DocumentGroup user interface uses this information to ensure that only files of supported types are selectable when browsing. A user browsing documents in an app which only supports image files, for example, would see documents of other types (such as plain text) grayed out and unselectable within the document list. This can be separated into the following components:

46.4.1 Document Content Type Identifier

Defining the types of files supported by an app begins by declaring a *document content type identifier*. This is declared using *Uniform Type Identifier* (UTI) syntax which typically takes the form of a reverse domain name combined with a *common type identifier*. A document identifier for an app that supports plain text files, for example, might be declared as follows:

```
com.ebookfrenzy.plain-text
```

46.4.2 Handler Rank

The document content type may also declare a *handler rank* value. This value declares to the system how the app relates to the file type. If the app uses its own custom file type, this should be set to *Owner*. If the app is to be opened as the default app for files of this type, the value should be set to *Default*. If, on the other hand, the app can handle files of this type but is not intended to be the default handler a value of *Alternate* should be used. Finally, *None* should be used if the app is not to be associated with the file type.

46.4.3 Type Identifiers

Having declared a document content type identifier, this identifier must have associated with it a list of specific data types to which it conforms. This is achieved using *type identifiers*. These type identifiers can be chosen from an extensive list of built-in types provided by Apple and are generally prefixed with "public.". For example, the UTI for a plain text document is *public.plain-text*, while that for any type of image file is *public.image*. Similarly, if an app only supports JPEG image files, the *public.jpeg* UTI would be used.

Each of the built-in UTI types has associated with it a UTType equivalent which can be used when working with types programmatically. The *public.plain-text* UTI, for example, has a UTType instance named *plainText* while the UTType instance for *public.mpeg4move* is named *mpeg4Movie*. A full list of supported UTType declarations can be found at the following URL:

https://developer.apple.com/documentation/uniformtypeidentifiers/uttype/system_declared_types

46.4.4 Filename Extensions

In addition to declaring the type identifiers, filename extensions for which support is provided may also be specified (for example *.txt*, *.png*, *.doc*, *.mydata* etc.). Note that many of the built-in type identifiers are already configured to support associated file types. The *public.png* type, for example, is pre-configured to recognize *.png* filename extensions.

The extension declared here will also be appended to the filename of any new documents created by the app.

46.4.5 Custom Type Document Content Identifiers

When working with proprietary data formats (perhaps your app has its own database format), it is also possible to declare your own document content identifier without using one of the common identifiers. A document type identifier for a custom type might, therefore, be declared as follows:

```
com.ebookfrenzy.mydata
```

46.4.6 Exported vs. Imported Type Identifiers

When a built-in type is used (such as *plain.image*), it is said to be an *imported type identifier* (since it is imported into the app from the range of identifiers already known to the system). A custom type identifier, on the other hand, is described as an *exported type identifier* because it originates from within the app and is exported to the system so that the browser can recognize files of that type as being associated with the app.

46.5 Configuring File Type Support in Xcode

All of the above settings are configured within the project's *Info.plist* file. Although these changes can be made with the Xcode property list editor, a better option is to access the settings via the Xcode *Info* screen of the app target. To review the settings for the example project using this approach, select the DocDemo entry at the top of the project navigator window (marked A in Figure 46-3), followed by the DocDemo target (B) before clicking on the Info tab (C).

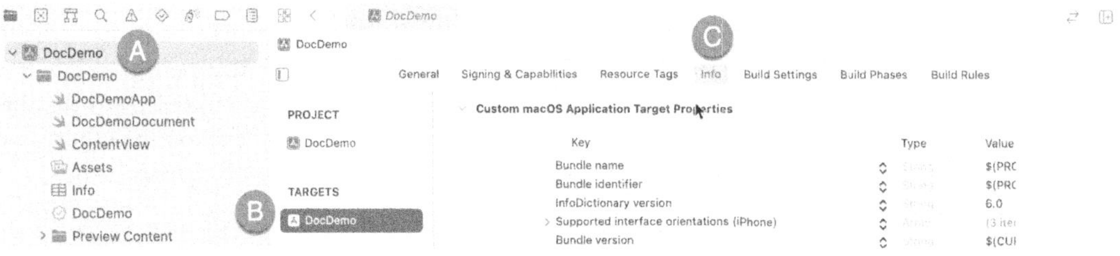

Figure 46-3

Scroll down to the *Document Types* section within the Info screen and note that Xcode has created a single document content type identifier set to *com.example.plain-text* with the handler rank set to *Default*:

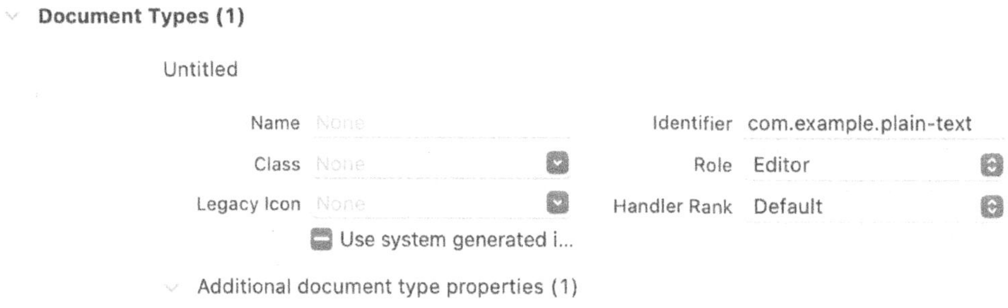

Figure 46-4

Next, scroll down to the *Imported Type Identifiers* section where we can see that our document content type identifier (*com.example.plain-text*) has been declared as conforming to the *public.plain-text* type with a single filename extension of *exampletext*:

Figure 46-5

Type identifiers for custom types are declared in the *Exported Type Identifiers* section of the Info screen. For example, a binary custom file might be declared as conforming to *public.data* while the file names for this type might have a *mydata* filename extension:

Figure 46-6

Note that in both cases, icons may be added to represent the files within the document browser user interface.

46.6 The Document Structure

When the example project was created, Xcode generated a file named *DocDemoDocument.swift*, an instance of which is passed to ContentView within the App declaration. As generated, this file reads as follows:

```
import SwiftUI
import UniformTypeIdentifiers

extension UTType {
    static var exampleText: UTType {
        UTType(importedAs: "com.example.plain-text")
    }
}

struct DocDemoDocument: FileDocument {
    var text: String

    init(text: String = "Hello, world!") {
        self.text = text
```

```
    }

    static var readableContentTypes: [UTType] { [.exampleText] }

    init(configuration: ReadConfiguration) throws {
        guard let data = configuration.file.regularFileContents,
              let string = String(data: data, encoding: .utf8)
        else {
            throw CocoaError(.fileReadCorruptFile)
        }
        text = string
    }

    func fileWrapper(configuration: WriteConfiguration) throws -> FileWrapper {
        let data = text.data(using: .utf8)!
        return .init(regularFileWithContents: data)
    }
}
```

The structure is based on the FileDocument class and begins by declaring a new UTType named exampleText which imports our *com.example.plain-text* identifier. This is then referenced in the readableContentTypes array to indicate which types of files can be opened by the app:

```
extension UTType {
    static var exampleText: UTType {
        UTType(importedAs: "com.example.plain-text")
    }
}
.
.
    static var readableContentTypes: [UTType] { [.exampleText] }
.
.
```

The structure also includes two initializers, the first of which will be called when the creation of a new document is requested by the user and simply configures a sample text string as the initial data:

```
init(text: String = "Hello, world!") {
    self.text = text
}
```

The second initializer, on the other hand, is called when the user opens an existing document and is passed a ReadConfiguration instance:

```
init(configuration: ReadConfiguration) throws {
    guard let data = configuration.file.regularFileContents,
          let string = String(data: data, encoding: .utf8)
    else {
        throw CocoaError(.fileReadCorruptFile)
    }
```

```
    text = string
}
```

The ReadConfiguration instance holds the content of the file in Data format which may be accessed via the *regularFileContents* property. Steps are then taken to decode this data and convert it to a String so that it can be displayed to the user. The exact steps to decode the data will depend on how the data was originally encoded within the *fileWrapper()* method. In this case, the method is designed to work with String data:

```
func fileWrapper(configuration: WriteConfiguration) throws -> FileWrapper {
    let data = text.data(using: .utf8)!
    return .init(regularFileWithContents: data)
}
```

The *fileWrapper()* method is passed a WriteConfiguration instance for the selected file and is expected to return a FileWrapper instance initialized with the data to be written. For the content to be written to the file it must first be converted to data and stored in a Data object. In this case, the text String value is simply encoded into data. The steps involved to achieve this in your own apps will depend on the type of content being stored in the document.

46.7 The Content View

As we have seen early in the chapter, the ContentView is passed an instance of the DocDemoDocument structure from within the App declaration:

```
ContentView(document: file.$document)
```

In the case of the DocDemo example, the ContentView binds to this property and references it as the content for a TextEditor view:

```
.
.
struct ContentView: View {
    @Binding var document: DocDemoDocument

    var body: some View {
        TextEditor(text: $document.text)
    }
}
.
.
```

When the view appears it will display the current string assigned to the text property of the document instance and, as the user edits the text, the changes will be stored. When the user navigates back to the document browser, a call to the *fileWrapper()* method will be triggered automatically and the changes saved to the document.

46.8 Running the Example App

Having explored the internals of the example DocDemo app, the final step is to experience the app in action. With this in mind, compile and run the app on a device or simulator and, once running, select the Browse tab located at the bottom of the screen:

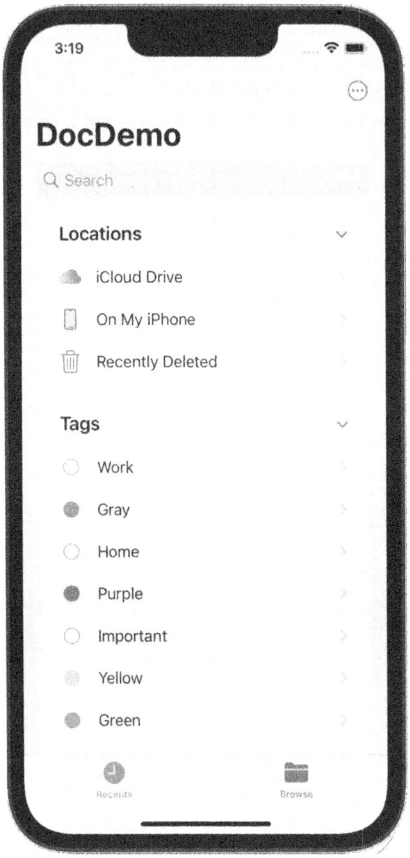

Figure 46-7

Navigate to a suitable location either on the device or within your iCloud storage and click on the *Create Document* entry as shown in Figure 46-8:

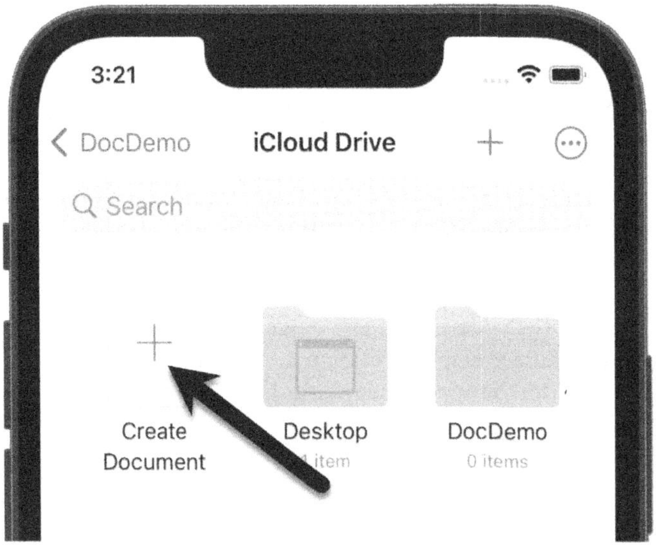

Figure 46-8

The new file will be created and the content loaded into the ContentView. Edit the sample text and return to the document browser where the document (named *untitled*) will now be listed. Open the document once again so that it loads into the ContentView and verify that the changes were saved.

46.9 Summary

The SwiftUI DocumentGroup scene allows the document browsing and management capabilities available within the built-in Files app to be integrated into apps with relatively little effort. The core element of DocumentGroup implementation is the document declaration which acts as the interface between the document browser and views that make up the app and is responsible for encoding and decoding document content. In addition, the *Info.plist* file for the app must include information about the types of files the app can to support.

Chapter 47

47. A SwiftUI DocumentGroup Tutorial

The previous chapter provided an introduction to the DocumentGroup scene type provided with SwiftUI and explored the architecture that makes it possible to add document browsing and management to apps.

This chapter will demonstrate how to take the standard Xcode Multiplatform Document App template and modify it to work with image files instead of plain text documents. Upon completion of the tutorial, the app will allow image files to be opened, modified using a sepia filter, and then saved back to the original file.

47.1 Creating the ImageDocDemo Project

Begin by launching Xcode and create a new project named *ImageDocDemo* using the Multiplatform Document App template.

47.2 Modifying the Info.plist File

Since the app will be working with image files instead of plain text, some changes need to be made to the type identifiers declared in the *Info.plist* file. To make these changes, select the ImageDocDemo entry at the top of the project navigator window (marked A in Figure 47-1), followed by the ImageDocDemo target (B) before clicking on the Info tab (C).

Figure 47-1

Scroll down to the *Document Types* section within the Info screen and change the *Identifier* field from com.example.plain-text to *com.ebookfrenzy.image*:

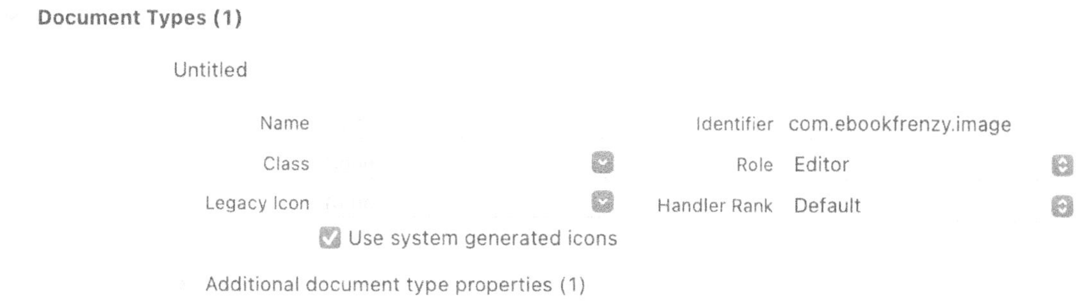

Figure 47-2

Next, locate the *Imported Type Identifiers* section and make the following changes:

- **Description** – Example Image
- **Identifier** - com.ebookfrenzy.image
- **Conforms To** – public.image
- **Extensions** - png

Once these changes have been made, the settings should match those shown in Figure 47-3:

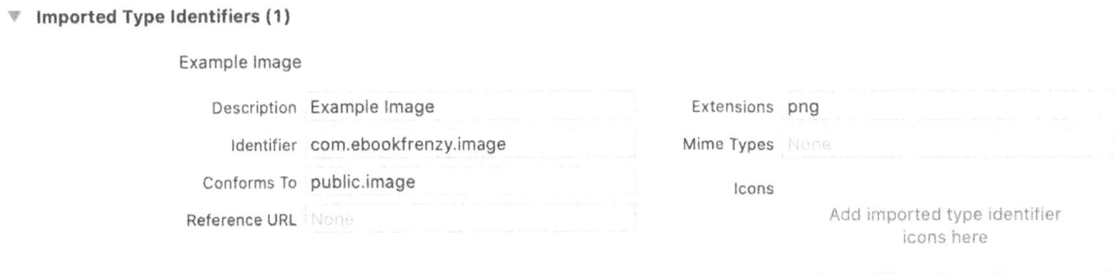

Figure 47-3

47.3 Adding an Image Asset

If the user decides to create a new document instead of opening an existing one, a sample image will be displayed from the project asset catalog. For this purpose, the *cascadefalls.png* file located in the *project_images* folder of the sample code archive will be added to the asset catalog. If you do not already have the source code downloaded, it can be downloaded from the following URL:

https://www.ebookfrenzy.com/retail/swiftui-ios16/

Once the image file has been located in a Finder window, select the *Assets* entry in the Xcode project navigator and drag and drop the image as shown in Figure 47-4:

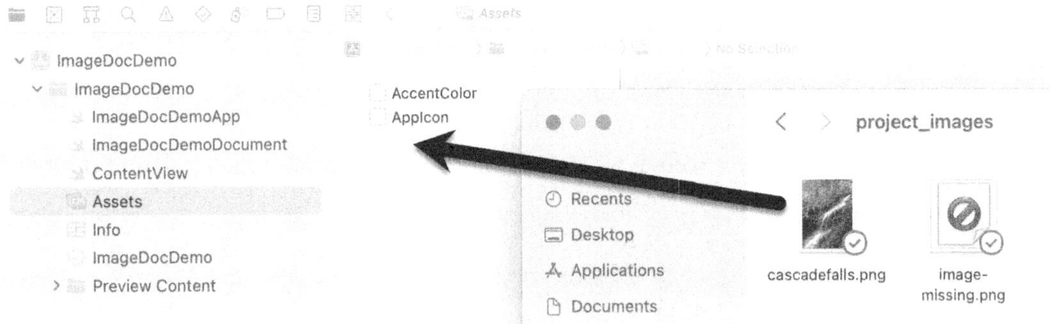

Figure 47-4

47.4 Modifying the ImageDocDemoDocument.swift File

Although we have changed the type identifiers to support images instead of plain text, the document declaration is still implemented for handling text-based content. Select the *ImageDocDemoDocument.swift* file to load it into the editor and begin by modifying the UTType extension so that it reads as follows:

```
extension UTType {
    static var exampleImage: UTType {
```

```
        UTType(importedAs: "com.ebookfrenzy.image")
    }
}
```

Next, locate the readableContentTypes variable and modify it to use the new UTType:

```
static var readableContentTypes: [UTType] { [.exampleImage] }
```

With the necessary type changes made, the next step is to modify the structure to work with images instead of string data. Remaining in the *ImageDocDemoDocument.swift* file, change the *text* variable from a string to an image and modify the first initializer to use the *cascadefalls* image:

```
.
.
struct ImageDocDemoDocument: FileDocument {

    var text: String
    var image: UIImage = UIImage()

    init(text: String = "Hello, world!") {
        if let image = UIImage(named: "cascadefalls") {
            self.image = image
        }
    }
.
.
```

Moving on to the second *init()* method, make the following modifications to decode image instead of string data:

```
init(configuration: ReadConfiguration) throws {
    guard let data = configuration.file.regularFileContents,
          let string = String(data: data, encoding: .utf8)
          let decodedImage: UIImage = UIImage(data: data)
    else {
        throw CocoaError(.fileReadCorruptFile)
    }
    text = string
    image = decodedImage
}
```

Finally, modify the *write()* method to encode the image to Data format so that it can be saved to the document:

```
func fileWrapper(configuration: WriteConfiguration) throws -> FileWrapper {
    let data = image.pngData()!
    return .init(regularFileWithContents: data)
}
```

47.5 Designing the Content View

Before performing some initial tests on the project so far, the content view needs to be modified to display an image instead of text content. We will also take this opportunity to add a Button view to the layout to apply the sepia filter to the image. Edit the *ContentView.swift* file and modify it so that it reads as follows:

```
import SwiftUI
```

```
struct ContentView: View {

    @Binding var document: ImageDocDemoDocument

    var body: some View {
        VStack {
            Image(uiImage: document.image)
                .resizable()
                .aspectRatio(contentMode: .fit)
                .padding()
            Button(action: {

            }, label: {
                Text("Filter Image")
            })
            .padding()
        }
    }
}
```

With the changes made, run the app on a device or simulator, use the browser to navigate to a suitable location, and then click on the Create Document item. The app will create a new image document containing the sample image from the asset catalog and then display it in the content view:

Figure 47-5

Tap the back arrow in the top left-hand corner to return to the browser where the new document should be listed with an icon containing a thumbnail image:

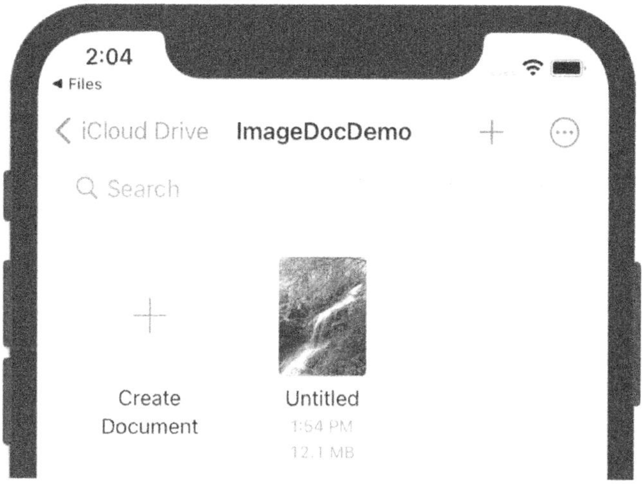

Figure 47-6

47.6 Filtering the Image

The final step in this tutorial is to apply the sepia filter to the image when the Button in the content view is tapped. This will make use of the CoreImage Framework and involves converting the UIImage to a CIImage and applying the sepia tone filter before being converted back to a UIImage. Edit the *ContentView.swift* file and make the following changes:

```
import SwiftUI
import CoreImage
import CoreImage.CIFilterBuiltins

struct ContentView: View {

    @Binding var document: ImageDocDemoDocument
    @State private var ciFilter = CIFilter.sepiaTone()

    let context = CIContext()

    var body: some View {
        VStack {
            Image(uiImage: document.image)
                .resizable()
                .aspectRatio(contentMode: .fit)
                .padding()
            Button(action: {
                filterImage()
            }, label: {
                Text("Filter Image")
            })
```

```
                .padding()
            }
        }

    func filterImage() {
        ciFilter.intensity = Float(1.0)

        let ciImage = CIImage(image: document.image)

        ciFilter.setValue(ciImage, forKey: kCIInputImageKey)

        guard let outputImage = ciFilter.outputImage else { return }

        if let cgImage = context.createCGImage(outputImage,
                                        from: outputImage.extent) {
            document.image = UIImage(cgImage: cgImage)
        }
    }
}
```

47.7 Testing the App

Run the app once again and either create a new image document or select the existing image to display the content view. Within the content view, tap the Filter Image button and wait while the sepia filter is applied to the image. Tap the back arrow to return to the browser where the thumbnail image will now appear in sepia tones. Select the image to load it into the content view and verify that the sepia changes were indeed saved to the document.

47.8 Summary

This chapter has demonstrated how to modify the Xcode Document App template to work with different content types. This involved changing the type identifiers, modifying the document declaration, and adapting the content view to handle image content.

48. An Introduction to Core Data and SwiftUI

A common requirement when developing iOS apps is to store data in some form of structured database. One option is to directly manage data using an embedded database system such as SQLite. While this is a perfectly good approach for working with SQLite in many cases, it does require knowledge of SQL and can lead to some complexity in terms of writing code and maintaining the database structure. This complexity is further compounded by the non-object-oriented nature of the SQLite API functions. In recognition of these shortcomings, Apple introduced the Core Data Framework. Core Data is essentially a framework that places a wrapper around the SQLite database (and other storage environments) enabling the developer to work with data in terms of Swift objects without requiring any knowledge of the underlying database technology.

We will begin this chapter by defining some of the concepts that comprise the Core Data model before providing an overview of the steps involved in working with this framework. Once these topics have been covered, the next chapter will work through a SwiftUI Core Data tutorial.

48.1 The Core Data Stack

Core Data consists of several framework objects that integrate to provide the data storage functionality. This stack can be visually represented as illustrated in Figure 48-1:

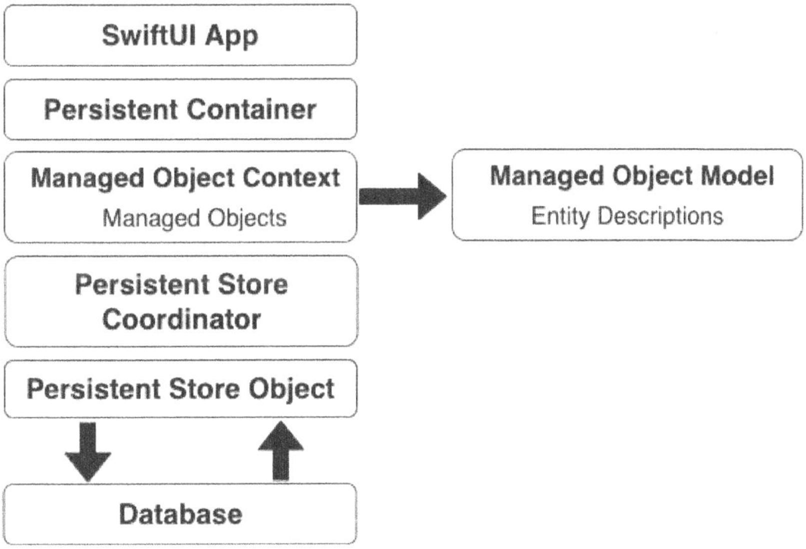

Figure 48-1

As we can see from Figure 48-1, the app sits on top of the stack and interacts with the managed data objects handled by the managed object context. Of particular significance in this diagram is the fact that although the lower levels in the stack perform a considerable amount of the work involved in providing Core Data functionality, the application code does not interact with them directly.

Before moving on to the more practical areas of working with Core Data it is important to spend some time explaining the elements that comprise the Core Data stack in a little more detail.

48.2 Persistent Container

The persistent container handles the creation of the Core Data stack and is designed to be easily subclassed to add additional application-specific methods to the base Core Data functionality. Once initialized, the persistent container instance provides access to the managed object context.

48.3 Managed Objects

Managed objects are the objects that are created by your application code to store data. A managed object may be thought of as a row or a record in a relational database table. For each new record to be added, a new managed object must be created to store the data. Similarly, retrieved data will be returned in the form of managed objects, one for each record matching the defined retrieval criteria. Managed objects are instances of the NSManagedObject class, or a subclass thereof. These objects are contained and maintained by the managed object context.

48.4 Managed Object Context

Core Data-based applications never interact directly with the persistent store. Instead, the application code interacts with the managed objects contained in the managed object context layer of the Core Data stack. The context maintains the status of the objects in relation to the underlying data store and manages the relationships between managed objects defined by the managed object model. All interactions with the underlying database are held temporarily within the context until the context is instructed to save the changes, at which point the changes are passed down through the Core Data stack and written to the persistent store.

48.5 Managed Object Model

So far we have focused on the management of data objects but have not yet looked at how the data models are defined. This is the task of the Managed Object Model which defines a concept referred to as entities.

Much as a class description defines a blueprint for an object instance, entities define the data model for managed objects. In essence, an entity is analogous to the schema that defines a table in a relational database. As such, each entity has a set of attributes associated with it that define the data to be stored in managed objects derived from that entity. For example, a Contacts entity might contain name, address, and phone number attributes.

In addition to attributes, entities can also contain relationships, fetched properties, persistent stores, and fetch requests:

- **Relationships** – In the context of Core Data, relationships are the same as those in other relational database systems in that they refer to how one data object relates to another. Core Data relationships can be one-to-one, one-to-many, or many-to-many.

- **Fetched property** – This provides an alternative to defining relationships. Fetched properties allow properties of one data object to be accessed from another data object as though a relationship had been defined between those entities. Fetched properties lack the flexibility of relationships and are referred to by Apple's Core Data documentation as "weak, one-way relationships" best suited to "loosely coupled relationships".

- **Fetch request** – A predefined query that can be referenced to retrieve data objects based on defined predicates. For example, a fetch request can be configured into an entity to retrieve all contact objects where the name field matches "John Smith".

48.6 Persistent Store Coordinator

The persistent store coordinator is responsible for coordinating access to multiple persistent object stores. As an iOS developer, you will never directly interact with the persistent store coordinator and will very rarely need to develop an application that requires more than one persistent object store. When multiple stores are required, the coordinator presents these stores to the upper layers of the Core Data stack as a single store.

48.7 Persistent Object Store

The term persistent object store refers to the underlying storage environment in which data are stored when using Core Data. Core Data supports three disk-based and one memory-based persistent store. Disk-based options consist of SQLite, XML, and binary. By default, iOS will use SQLite as the persistent store. In practice, the type of store being used is transparent to you as the developer. Regardless of your choice of persistent store, your code will make the same calls to the same Core Data APIs to manage the data objects required by your application.

48.8 Defining an Entity Description

Entity descriptions may be defined from within the Xcode environment. When a new project is created with the option to include Core Data, a template file will be created named *<entityname>.xcdatamodeld*. Xcode also provides a way to manually add entity description files to existing projects. Selecting this file in the Xcode project navigator panel will load the model into the entity editing environment as illustrated in Figure 48-2:

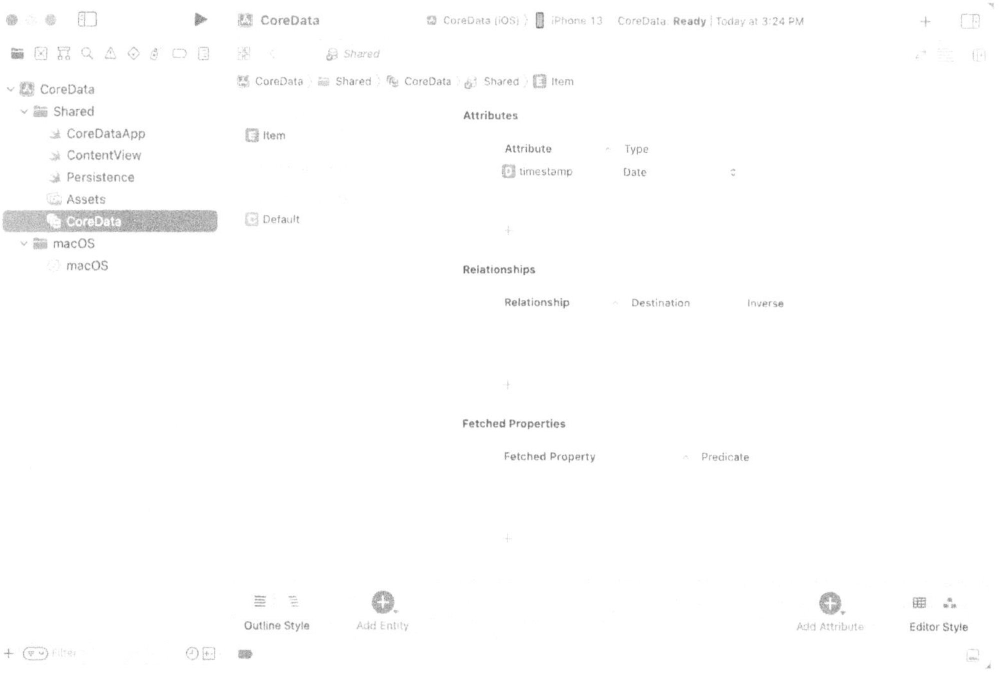

Figure 48-2

Create a new entity by clicking on the Add Entity button located in the bottom panel. The new entity will appear as a text box in the Entities list. By default, this will be named Entity. Double-click on this name to change it.

To add attributes to the entity, click on the Add Attribute button located in the bottom panel, or use the + button located beneath the Attributes section. In the Attributes panel, name the attribute and specify the type and any other options that are required.

Repeat the above steps to add more attributes and additional entities.

The Xcode entity editor also allows relationships to be established between entities. Assume, for example, two entities named Contacts and Sales. To establish a relationship between the two tables select the Contacts entity and click on the + button beneath the Relationships panel. In the detail panel, name the relationship, specify the destination as the Sales entity, and any other options that are required for the relationship. Once the relationship has been established it is, perhaps, best viewed graphically by selecting the *Table, Graph* option in the Editor Style control located in the bottom panel:

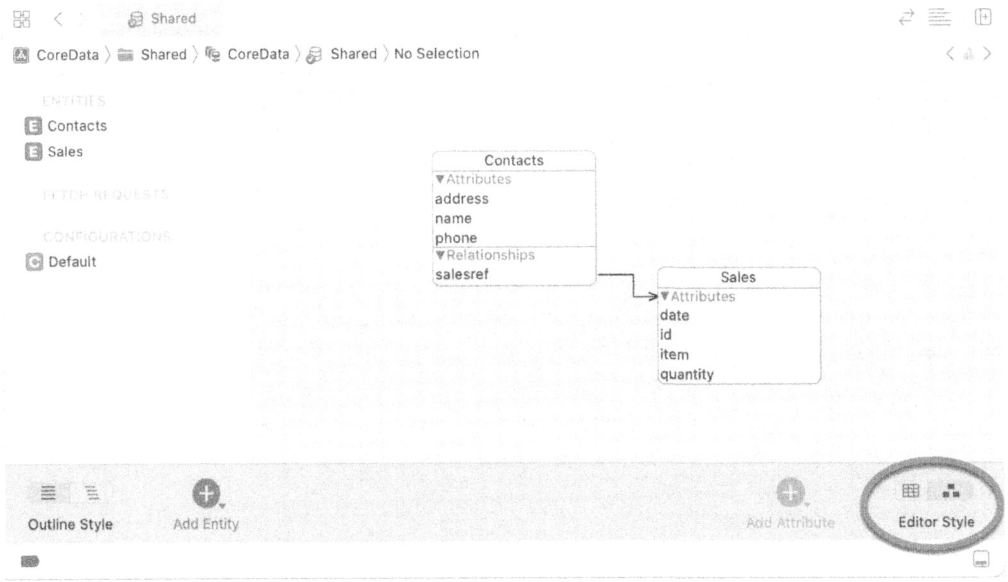

Figure 48-3

48.9 Initializing the Persistent Container

The persistent container is initialized by creating a new NSPersistentContainer instance, passing through the name of the model to be used, and then making a call to the *loadPersistentStores* method of that object as follows:

```
let persistentContainer: NSPersistentContainer

persistentContainer = NSPersistentContainer(name: "DemoData")
persistentContainer.loadPersistentStores { (storeDescription, error) in
    if let error = error as NSError? {
        fatalError("Container load failed: \(error)")
    }
}
```

48.10 Obtaining the Managed Object Context

Since many of the Core Data methods require the managed object context as an argument, the next step after defining entity descriptions often involves obtaining a reference to the context. This can be achieved by accessing the viewContext property of the persistent container instance:

```
let managedObjectContext = persistentContainer.viewContext
```

48.11 Setting the Attributes of a Managed Object

As previously discussed, entities and the managed objects from which they are instantiated contain data in the form of attributes. Once a managed object instance has been created as outlined above, those attribute values can be used to store the data before the object is saved. Assuming a managed object named *contact* with attributes named *name*, *address* and *phone* respectively, the values of these attributes may be set as follows before saving the object to storage:

```
contact.name = "John Smith"
contact.address = "1 Infinite Loop"
contact.phone = "555-564-0980"
```

48.12 Saving a Managed Object

Once a managed object instance has been created and configured with the data to be stored it can be saved to storage using the *save()* method of the managed object context as follows:

```
do {
    try viewContext.save()
} catch {
    let error = error as NSError
    fatalError("An error occured: \(error)")
}
```

48.13 Fetching Managed Objects

Once managed objects are saved into the persistent object store those objects and the data they contain will likely need to be retrieved. One way to fetch data from Core Data storage is to use the @FetchRequest property wrapper when declaring a variable in which to store the data. The following code, for example, declares a variable named *customers* which will be automatically updated as data is added to or removed from the database:

```
@FetchRequest(entity: Customer.entity(), sortDescriptors: [])
private var customers: FetchedResults<Customer>
```

The @FetchRequest property wrapper may also be configured to sort the fetched results. In the following example, the customer data stored in the *customers* variable will be sorted alphabetically in ascending order based on the *name* entity attribute:

```
@FetchRequest(entity: Customer.entity(),
        sortDescriptors: [NSSortDescriptor(key: "name", ascending: true)])
private var customers: FetchedResults<Customer>
```

48.14 Retrieving Managed Objects based on Criteria

The preceding example retrieved all of the managed objects from the persistent object store. More often than not only managed objects that match specified criteria are required during a retrieval operation. This is performed by defining a predicate that dictates criteria that a managed object must meet to be eligible for retrieval. For example, the following code configures a @FetchRequest property wrapper declaration with a predicate to extract only those managed objects where the name attribute matches "John Smith":

```
@FetchRequest(
  entity: Customer.entity(),
  sortDescriptors: [],
  predicate: NSPredicate(format: "name LIKE %@", "John Smith")
)
private var customers: FetchedResults<Customer>
```

The above example will maintain the *customers* variable so that it always contains the entries that match the specified predicate criteria. It is also possible to perform one-time fetch operations by creating NSFetchRequest instances, configuring them with the entity and predicate settings, and then passing them to the *fetch()* method of the managed object context. For example:

```
@State var matches: [Customer]?
let fetchRequest: NSFetchRequest<Product> = Product.fetchRequest()

fetchRequest.entity = Customer.entity()
fetchRequest.predicate = NSPredicate(
    format: "name LIKE %@", "John Smith"
)

matches = try? viewContext.fetch(fetchRequest)
```

48.15 Summary

The Core Data Framework stack provides a flexible alternative to directly managing data using SQLite or other data storage mechanisms. By providing an object-oriented abstraction layer on top of the data the task of managing data storage is made significantly easier for the SwiftUI application developer. Now that the basics of Core Data have been covered, the next chapter entitled *"A SwiftUI Core Data Tutorial"* will work through the creation of an example application.

Chapter 49

49. A SwiftUI Core Data Tutorial

Now that we have explored the concepts of Core Data it is time to put that knowledge to use by creating an example app project. In this project tutorial, we will be creating a simple inventory app that uses Core Data to persistently store the names and quantities of products. This will include the ability to add, delete, and search for database entries.

49.1 Creating the CoreDataDemo Project

Launch Xcode, select the option to create a new project, and choose the Multiplatform App template before clicking the Next button. On the project options screen, name the project CoreDataDemo and choose an organization identifier that will uniquely identify your app (this will be important when we add CloudKit support to the project in a later chapter).

Note that the options screen includes a *Use Core Data* setting as highlighted in Figure 49-1. This setting does the work of setting up the project for Core Data support and generates code to implement a simple app that demonstrates Core Data in action. Instead of using this template, this tutorial will take you through the steps of manually adding Core Data support to a project so that you have a better understanding of how Core Data works. For this reason, make sure the Use Core Data option is turned *off* before clicking the Next button:

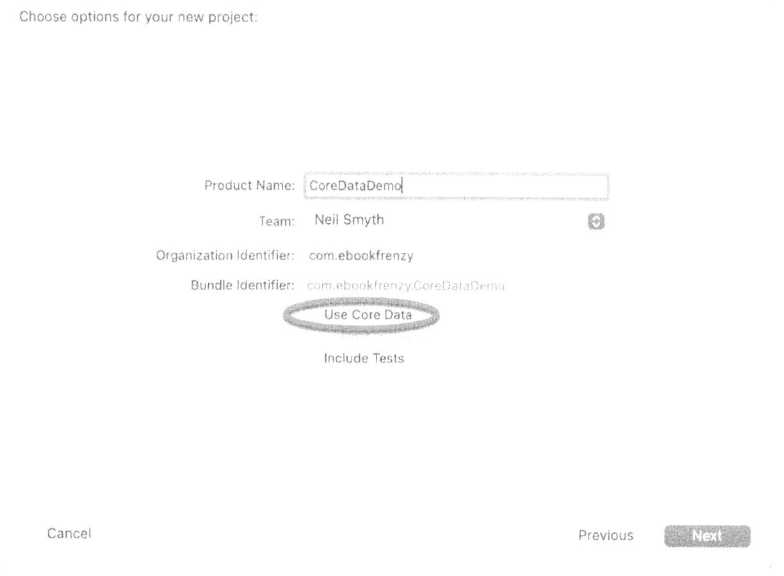

Figure 49-1

Select a suitable location in which to save the project before clicking on the Finish button.

49.2 Defining the Entity Description

For this example, the entity takes the form of a data model designed to hold the names and quantities that will make up the product inventory. Select the *File -> New -> File...* menu option and, within the template dialog, select the Data Model entry located in the Core Data section as shown in Figure 49-2, then click the Next button:

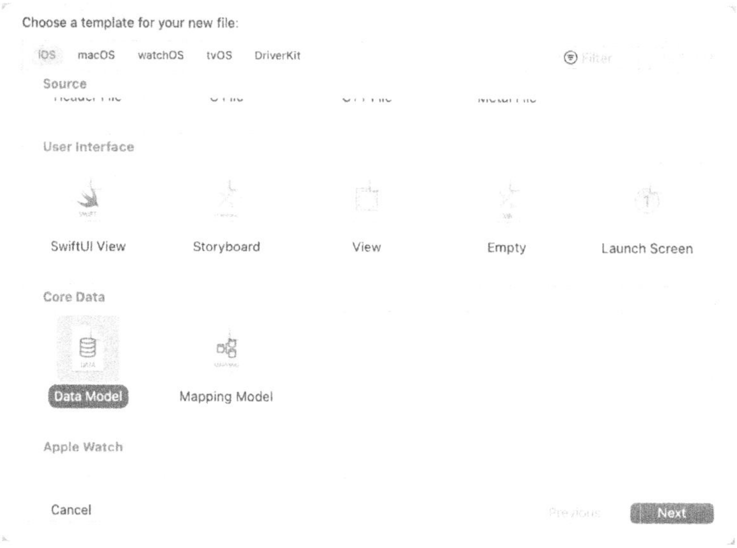

Figure 49-2

Name the file *Products* and click on the Create button to generate the file. Once the file has been created, it will appear within the entity editor as shown below:

Figure 49-3

To add a new entity to the model, click on the Add Entity button marked A in Figure 49-3 above. Xcode will add a new entity (named Entity) to the model and list it beneath the Entities heading (B). Click on the new entity and change the name to Product:

Figure 49-4

Now that the entity has been created, the next step is to add the name and quantity attributes. To add the first attribute, click on the + button located beneath the Attributes section of the main panel. Name the new attribute *name* and change the Type to String as shown in Figure 49-5:

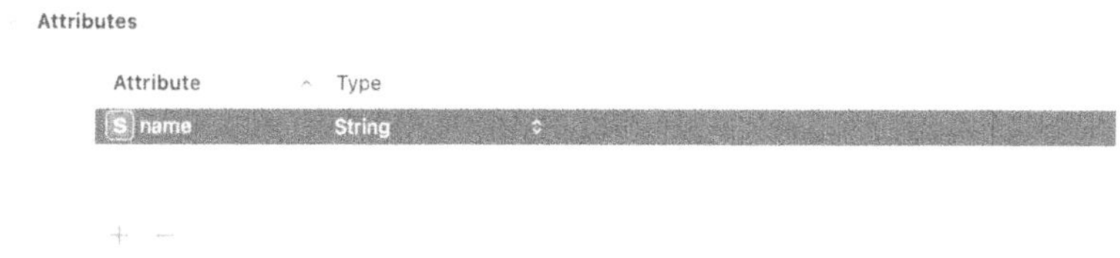

Figure 49-5

Repeat these steps to add a second attribute of type String named *quantity*. Upon completion of these steps, the attributes panel should match Figure 49-6:

Figure 49-6

49.3 Creating the Persistence Controller

The next requirement for our project is a persistence controller class in which to create and initialize an NSPersistentContainer instance. Select the *File -> New -> File...* menu option and, within the template dialog, select the Swift File template option and save it as *Persistence.swift*. With the new file loaded into the code editor, modify it so that it reads as follows:

```
import CoreData

struct PersistenceController {
    static let shared = PersistenceController()

    let container: NSPersistentContainer

    init() {
        container = NSPersistentContainer(name: "Products")

        container.loadPersistentStores { (storeDescription, error) in
            if let error = error as NSError? {
                fatalError("Container load failed: \(error)")
            }
        }
    }
}
```

49.4 Setting up the View Context

Now that we have created a persistent controller we can use it to obtain a reference to the view context. An ideal place to perform this task is within the *CoreDataDemoApp.swift* file. To make the context accessible to the views that will make up the app, we will insert it into the view hierarchy as an environment object as follows:

```
import SwiftUI

@main
struct CoreDataDemoApp: App {

    let persistenceController = PersistenceController.shared

    var body: some Scene {
        WindowGroup {
            ContentView()
                .environment(\.managedObjectContext,
                             persistenceController.container.viewContext)
        }
    }
}
```

49.5 Preparing the ContentView for Core Data

Before we start adding views to design the app user interface, the following initial changes are required within the *ContentView.swift* file:

```
import SwiftUI
import CoreData

struct ContentView: View {

    @State var name: String = ""
    @State var quantity: String = ""

    @Environment(\.managedObjectContext) private var viewContext

    @FetchRequest(entity: Product.entity(), sortDescriptors: [])
    private var products: FetchedResults<Product>

    var body: some View {
.
.
```

In addition to importing the CoreData library, we have also declared two state objects into which will be stored the product name and quantity as they are entered by the user. We have also gained access to the view context environment object that was created in the *CoreDataDemoApp.swift* file.

The @FetchRequest property wrapper is also used to declare a variable named *products* into which Core Data will store the latest product data stored in the database.

49.6 Designing the User Interface

With most of the preparatory work complete, we can now begin designing the layout of the main content view. Remaining in the *ContentView.swift* file, modify the body of the ContentView structure so that it reads as follows:

.

```
.
    var body: some View {
        NavigationView {
            VStack {
                TextField("Product name", text: $name)
                TextField("Product quantity", text: $quantity)

                HStack {
                    Spacer()
                    Button("Add") {

                    }
                    Spacer()
                    Button("Clear") {
                        name = ""
                        quantity = ""
                    }
                    Spacer()
                }
                .padding()
                .frame(maxWidth: .infinity)

                List {
                    ForEach(products) { product in
                        HStack {
                            Text(product.name ?? "Not found")
                            Spacer()
                            Text(product.quantity ?? "Not found")
                        }
                    }
                }
                .navigationTitle("Product Database")
            }
            .padding()
            .textFieldStyle(RoundedBorderTextFieldStyle())
        }
    }
.
.
```

The layout initially consists of two TextField views, two Buttons, and a List which should render within the preview canvas as follows.

Figure 49-7

49.7 Saving Products

More code changes are now required so that data entered into the product name and quantity text fields is saved by Core Data into persistent storage when the Add button is clicked. Edit the *ContentView.swift* file once again to add this functionality:

```
.
.
    var body: some View {
        NavigationView {
            VStack {
                TextField("Product name", text: $name)
                TextField("Product quantity", text: $quantity)

                HStack {
                    Spacer()
                    Button("Add") {
                        addProduct()
                    }
                    Spacer()
                    Button("Clear") {
                        name = ""
                        quantity = ""
                    }
.
.
            .padding()
            .textFieldStyle(RoundedBorderTextFieldStyle())
        }
    }

    private func addProduct() {
        withAnimation {
            let product = Product(context: viewContext)
```

```
            product.name = name
            product.quantity = quantity

            saveContext()
        }
    }

    private func saveContext() {
        do {
            try viewContext.save()
        } catch {
            let error = error as NSError
            fatalError("An error occurred: \(error)")
        }
    }
}
.
.
```

The first change configured the Add button to call a function named *addProduct()* which was declared as follows:

```
private func addProduct() {
    withAnimation {
        let product = Product(context: viewContext)
        product.name = name
        product.quantity = quantity

        saveContext()
    }
}
```

The *addProduct()* function creates a new Product entity instance and assigns the current content of the product name and quantity state properties to the corresponding entity attributes. A call is then made to the following *saveContext()* function:

```
private func saveContext() {
    do {
        try viewContext.save()
    } catch {
        let error = error as NSError
        fatalError("An error occurred: \(error)")
    }
}
```

The *saveContext()* function uses a "do.. try .. catch" construct to save the current viewContext to persistent storage. For testing purposes, a fatal error is triggered to terminate the app if the save action failed. More comprehensive error handling would typically be required for a production-quality app.

Saving the data will cause the latest data to be fetched and assigned to the *products* data variable. This, in turn, will cause the List view to update with the latest products. To make this update visually appealing, the code in the *addProduct()* function is placed in a *withAnimation* call.

49.8 Testing the addProduct() Function

Compile and run the app on a device or simulator, enter a few product and quantity entries, and verify that those entries appear in the List view as they are added. After entering information into the text fields, check that clicking on the Clear button clears the current entries.

At this point in the tutorial, the running app should resemble that shown in Figure 49-8 after some products have been added:

Figure 49-8

To make the list more organized, the product items need to be sorted in ascending alphabetical order based on the *name* attribute. To implement this, add a sort descriptor to the @FetchRequest definition as outlined below. This requires the creation of an NSSortDescriptor instance configured with the *name* attribute declared as the key and the ascending property set to true:

```
@FetchRequest(entity: Product.entity(),
        sortDescriptors: [NSSortDescriptor(key: "name", ascending: true)])
private var products: FetchedResults<Product>
```

When the app is now run, the list of products will be sorted in ascending alphabetic order.

49.9 Deleting Products

Now that the app has a mechanism for adding product entries to the database, we need a way to delete entries that are no longer needed. For this project, we will use the same steps demonstrated in the chapter entitled *"SwiftUI Lists and Navigation"*. This will allow the user to delete entries by swiping on the list item and tapping the delete button. Beneath the existing *addProduct()* function, add a new function named *deleteProduct()* that reads as follows:

```
private func deleteProducts(offsets: IndexSet) {
    withAnimation {
        offsets.map { products[$0] }.forEach(viewContext.delete)
            saveContext()
        }
}
```

When the method is called, it is passed a set of offsets within the List entries representing the positions of the items selected by the user for deletion. The above code loops through these entries calling the viewContext *delete()* function for each deleted item. Once the deletions are complete, the changes are saved to the database via a call to our *saveContext()* function.

Now that we have added the *deleteProduct()* function, the List view can be modified to call it via the *onDelete()* modifier:

```
.
.
        List {
            ForEach(products) { product in
                HStack {
                    Text(product.name ?? "Not found")
                    Spacer()
                    Text(product.quantity ?? "Not found")
                }
            }
            .onDelete(perform: deleteProducts)
        }
        .navigationTitle("Product Database")
.
.
```

Run the app and verify both that performing a leftward swipe on a list item reveals the delete option and that clicking it removes the item from the list.

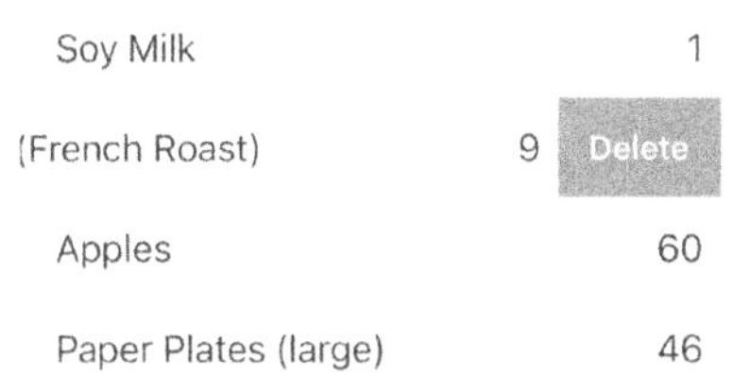

Figure 49-9

49.10 Adding the Search Function

The final feature to be added to the project will allow us to search the database for products that match the text entered into the name text field. The results will appear in a list contained within a second view named ResultsView. When it is called from ContentView, ResultsView will be passed the current value of the *name* state property and a reference to the viewContext object.

Begin by adding the ResultsView structure to the *ContentView.swift* file as follows:

```
struct ResultsView: View {

    var name: String
    var viewContext: NSManagedObjectContext
    @State var matches: [Product]?

    var body: some View {

        return VStack {
            List {
                ForEach(matches ?? []) { match in
                    HStack {
                        Text(match.name ?? "Not found")
                        Spacer()
                        Text(match.quantity ?? "Not found")
                    }
                }
            }
            .navigationTitle("Results")
        }
    }
}
```

In addition to the name and viewContext parameters, the declaration also includes a state property named *matches* into which will be placed the matching product search results which, in turn, will be displayed within the List view.

We now need to add some code to perform the search and will do so by applying a *task()* modifier to the VStack container view. This will ensure that searches are performed asynchronously and that all of the view's properties have been initialized before the search is executed:

```
.
.
    return VStack {
        List {

            ForEach(myMatches ?? []) { match in
                HStack {
                    Text(match.name ?? "Not found")
                    Spacer()
                    Text(match.quantity ?? "Not found")
                }
            }
        }
        .navigationTitle("Results")
```

```
    }
    .task {
        let fetchRequest: NSFetchRequest<Product> = Product.fetchRequest()

        fetchRequest.entity = Product.entity()
        fetchRequest.predicate = NSPredicate(
            format: "name CONTAINS %@", name
        )
        matches = try? viewContext.fetch(fetchRequest)
    }
.
.
```

So that the search finds all products that contain the specified text, the predicate is configured using the CONTAINS keyword. This provides more flexibility than performing exact match searches using the LIKE keyword by finding partial matches.

The code in the closure of the *task()* modifier obtains an NSFetchRequest instance from the Product entity and assigns it an NSPredicate instance configured to find matches between the *name* variable and the *name* product entity attribute. The fetch request is then passed to the *fetch()* method of the view context, and the results are assigned to the *matches* state object. This, in turn, will cause the List to be re-rendered with the matching products.

The last task before testing the search feature is to add a navigation link to ResultsView, keeping in mind that ResultsView is expecting to be passed the *name* state object and a reference to *viewContext*. This needs to be positioned between the Add and Clear buttons as follows:

```
.
.
   HStack {
        Spacer()
        Button("Add") {
            addProduct()
        }
        Spacer()
        NavigationLink(destination: ResultsView(name: name,
                           viewContext: viewContext)) {
            Text("Find")
        }
        Spacer()
        Button("Clear") {
            name = ""
            quantity = ""
        }
        Spacer()
    }
.
.
```

Check the preview canvas to confirm that the navigation link appears as shown in Figure 49-10:

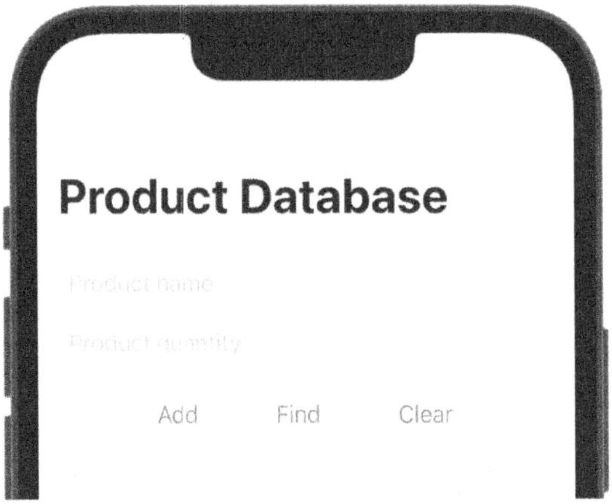

Figure 49-10

49.11 Testing the Completed App

Run the app once again and add some additional products, preferably with some containing the same word. Enter the common word into the name text field and click on the Find link. The ResultsView screen should appear with a list of matching items. Figure 49-11, for example, illustrates a search performed on the word "Milk":

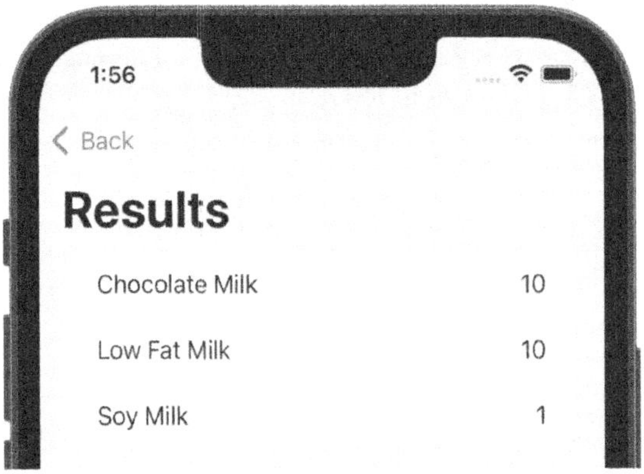

Figure 49-11

49.12 Summary

In this chapter, we have used Core Data to provide persistent database storage within an app project. Topics covered include the creation of a Core Data entity model and the configuration of entity attributes. Steps were also taken to initialize a persistent container from which we obtained the view context. The project also used the @FetchRequest property wrapper configured to store entries in alphabetical order and also made use of the view context to add, delete, and search for database entries. In implementing the search behavior, we used an NSFetchRequest instance configured with an NSPredicate object and passed that to the *fetch()* method of the view context to find matching results.

Chapter 50

50. An Overview of SwiftUI Core Data and CloudKit Storage

CloudKit provides a way for apps to store cloud-based databases using iCloud storage so that it is accessible across multiple devices, users, and apps.

Although initially provided with a dedicated framework that allows code to be written to directly create, manage and access iCloud-based databases, the recommended approach is now to use CloudKit in conjunction with Core Data.

This chapter will provide a high-level introduction to the various elements that make up CloudKit, and explain how those correspond to Core Data.

50.1 An Overview of CloudKit

The CloudKit Framework provides applications with access to the iCloud servers hosted by Apple and provides an easy-to-use way to store, manage and retrieve data and other asset types (such as large binary files, videos, and images) in a structured way. This provides a platform for users to store private data and access it from multiple devices, and also for the developer to provide data that is publicly available to all the users of an application.

The first step in learning to use CloudKit is to gain an understanding of the key components that constitute the CloudKit framework. Keep in mind that we won't be directly working with these components when using Core Data with CloudKit. We will, instead, continue to work with the Core Data elements covered in the previous chapters using a CloudKit enabled version of the Persistent Container. This container will handle all of the work of mapping these Core Data components to their equivalents within the CloudKit ecosystem.

While it is theoretically possible to implement CloudKit-based Core Data storage without this knowledge, this information will be useful when using the CloudKit Console. Basic knowledge of how CloudKit works will also be invaluable if you decide to explore more advanced topics in the future such as CloudKit sharing and subscriptions.

50.2 CloudKit Containers

Each CloudKit enabled application has at least one container on iCloud. The container for an application is represented in CloudKit by the CKContainer class and it is within these containers that the databases reside. Containers may also be shared between multiple applications. When working with Core Data, the container can be thought of as the equivalent of the Managed Object Model.

50.3 CloudKit Public Database

Each cloud container contains a single public database. This is the database into which is stored data that is needed by all users of an application. A map application, for example, might have a set of data about locations and routes that apply to all users of the application. This data would be stored within the public database of the application's cloud container.

50.4 CloudKit Private Databases

Private cloud databases are used to store data that is private to each specific user. Each cloud container, therefore, will contain one private database for each user of the application.

50.5 Data Storage Quotas

Data and assets stored in the public cloud database of an app count against the storage quota of the app. Anything stored in a private database, on the other hand, is counted against the iCloud quota of the corresponding user. Applications should, therefore, try to minimize the amount of data stored in private databases to avoid users having to unnecessarily purchase additional iCloud storage space.

At the time of writing, each application is provided with 1PB of free iCloud storage for public data for all of its users.

Apple also imposes limits on the volume of data transfers and the number of queries per second that are included in the free tier. While official documentation on these quotas and corresponding pricing is hard to find, it is unlikely that the average project will encounter these restrictions.

50.6 CloudKit Records

Data is stored in both the public and private databases in the form of records. Records are represented by the CKRecord class and are essentially dictionaries of key-value pairs where keys are used to reference the data values stored in the record. When stored is data via CloudKit using Core Data, these records are represented by Core Data Managed Objects.

The overall concept of an application cloud container, private and public databases, zones, and records can be visualized as illustrated in Figure 50-1:

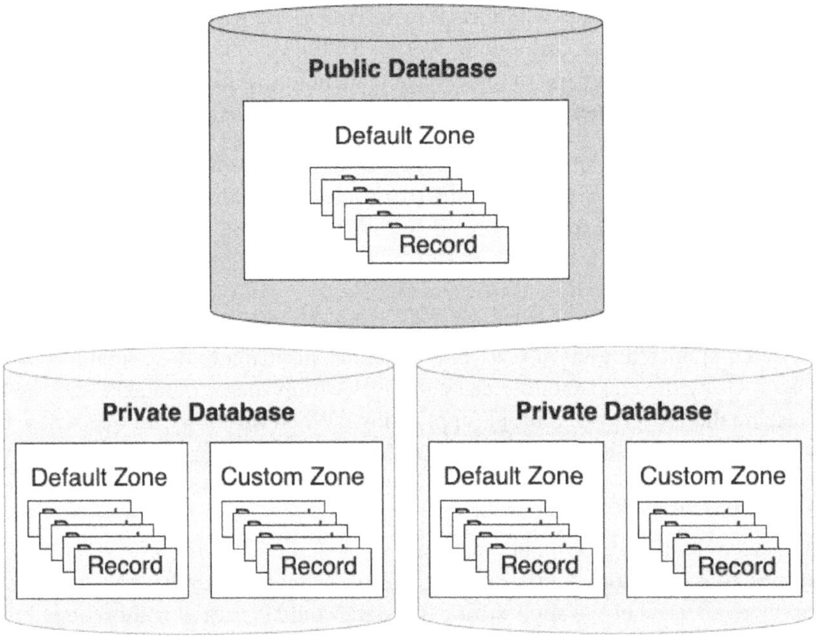

Figure 50-1

50.7 CloudKit Record IDs

Each CloudKit record has associated with it a unique record ID represented by the CKRecordID class. If a record ID is not specified when a record is first created, one is provided for it automatically by the CloudKit framework.

50.8 CloudKit References

CloudKit references are implemented using the CKReference class and provide a way to establish relationships between different records in a database. A reference is established by creating a CKReference instance for an originating record and assigning to it the record to which the relationship is to be targeted. The CKReference object is then stored in the originating record as a key-value pair field. A single record can contain multiple references to other records.

Once a record is configured with a reference pointing to a target record, that record is said to be owned by the target record. When the owner record is deleted, all records that refer to it are also deleted and so on down the chain of references (a concept referred to as cascading deletes).

50.9 Record Zones

CloudKit record zones (CKRecordZone) provide a mechanism for relating groups of records within a private database. Unless a record zone is specified when a record is saved to the cloud it is placed in the default zone of the target database. Custom zones can be added to private databases and used to organize related records and perform tasks such as writing to multiple records simultaneously in a single transaction. Each record zone has associated with it a unique record zone ID (CKRecordZoneID) which must be referenced when adding new records to a zone. All of the records within a public database are considered to be in the public default zone.

The CloudKit record zone translates to the Core Data persistent container. When working with Core Data in the previous chapter, persistent containers were created as instances of the NSPersistentContainer class. When integrating Core Data with CloudKit, however, we will be using the NSPersistentCloudKitContainer class instead. In terms of modifying code to use Core Data with CloudKit, this usually simply involves substituting NSPersistentCloudKitContainer for NSPersistentContainer.

50.10 CloudKit Console

The CloudKit Console is a web-based portal that provides an interface for managing the CloudKit options and storage for applications. The console can be accessed via the following URL:

https://icloud.developer.apple.com/dashboard/

Alternatively, the CloudKit Console can be accessed via the button located in the iCloud section of the Xcode *Signing & Capabilities* panel for a project as shown in Figure 50-2:

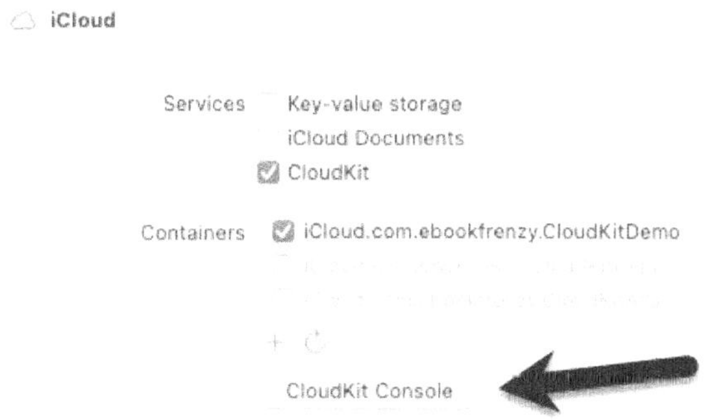

Figure 50-2

Access to the dashboard requires a valid Apple developer login and password and, once loaded into a browser window, will appear providing access to the CloudKit containers associated with your team account.

Once one or more containers have been created, the console provides the ability to view data, add, update, query, and delete records, modify the database schema, view subscriptions and configure new security roles. It also provides an interface for migrating data from a development environment over to a production environment in preparation for an application to go live in the App Store

The Logs and Telemetry options provide an overview of CloudKit usage by the currently selected container, including operations performed per second, average data request size and error frequency, and log details of each transaction.

In the case of data access through the CloudKit Console, it is important to be aware that private user data cannot be accessed using the dashboard interface. Only data stored in the public database and the private databases belonging to the developer account used to log in to the console can be viewed and modified.

50.11 CloudKit Sharing

Clearly, a CloudKit record contained within the public database of an app is accessible to all users of that app. Situations might arise, however, where a user wants to share with others specific records contained within a private database. This was made possible with the introduction of CloudKit sharing.

50.12 CloudKit Subscriptions

CloudKit subscriptions allow users to be notified when a change occurs within the cloud databases belonging to an installed app. Subscriptions use the standard iOS push notifications infrastructure and can be triggered based on a variety of criteria such as when records are added, updated, or deleted. Notifications can also be further refined using predicates so that notifications are based on data in a record matching certain criteria. When a notification arrives, it is presented to the user in the same way as other notifications through an alert or a notification entry on the lock screen.

50.13 Summary

This chapter has covered a number of the key classes and elements that make up the data storage features of the CloudKit framework. Each application has its own cloud container which, in turn, contains a single public cloud database in addition to one private database for each application user. Data is stored in databases in the form of records using key-value pair fields. Larger data such as videos and photos are stored as assets which, in turn, are stored as fields in records. Records stored in private databases can be grouped into record zones and records may be associated with each other through the creation of relationships. Each application user has an iCloud user id and a corresponding user record both of which can be obtained using the CloudKit framework. In addition, CloudKit user discovery can be used to obtain, subject to permission having been given, a list of IDs for those users in the current user's address book who have also installed and run the app.

Finally, the CloudKit Dashboard is a web-based portal that provides an interface for managing the CloudKit options and storage for applications.

Chapter 51

51. A SwiftUI Core Data and CloudKit Tutorial

Using the CoreDataDemo project created in the chapter entitled *"A SwiftUI Core Data Tutorial"*, this chapter will demonstrate how to add CloudKit support to an Xcode project and migrate from Core Data to CloudKit-based storage. This chapter assumes that you have read the chapter entitled *"An Introduction to Core Data and SwiftUI"*.

51.1 Enabling CloudKit Support

Begin by launching Xcode and opening the CoreDataDemo project. Once the project has loaded into Xcode, the first step is to add the iCloud capability to the app. Select the *CoreDataDemo* target located at the top of the Project Navigator panel (marked A in Figure 51-1) so that the main panel displays the project settings. From within this panel, select the *Signing & Capabilities* tab (B) followed by the CoreDataDemo target entry (C):

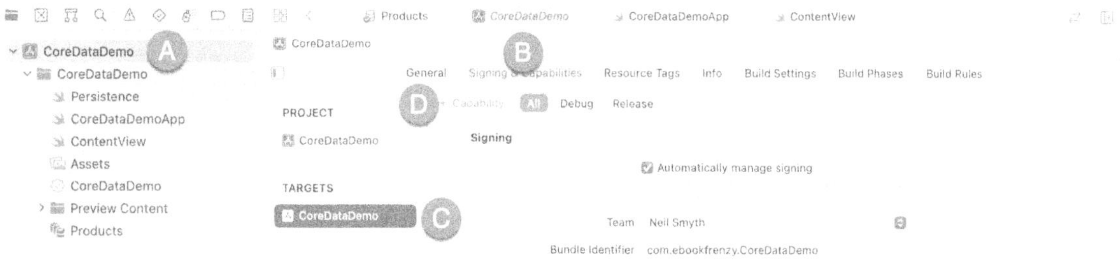

Figure 51-1

Click on the "+ Capability" button (D) to display the dialog shown in Figure 51-2. Enter *iCloud* into the filter bar, select the result and press the keyboard enter key to add the capability to the project:

Figure 51-2

If iCloud is not listed as an option, you will need to pay to join the Apple Developer program as outlined in the chapter entitled *"Joining the Apple Developer Program"*. If you are already a member, use the steps outlined in the chapter entitled *"Installing Xcode 14 and the iOS 16 SDK"* to ensure you have created a *Developer ID Application* certificate.

Within the iCloud entitlement settings, make sure that the CloudKit service is enabled before clicking on the "+" button indicated by the arrow in Figure 51-3 below to add an iCloud container for the project:

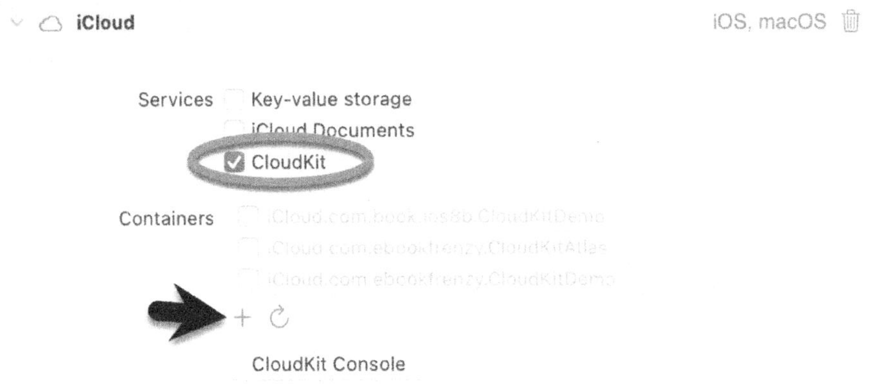

Figure 51-3

After clicking the "+" button, the dialog shown in Figure 51-4 will appear containing a text field into which you will need to enter the container identifier. This entry should uniquely identify the container within the CloudKit ecosystem, generally includes your organization identifier (as defined when the project was created), and should be set to something similar to *iCloud.com.yourcompany.CoreDataDemo*.

Figure 51-4

Once you have entered the container name, click the OK button to add it to the app entitlements. Returning to the *Signing & Capabilities* screen, make sure that the new container is selected:

Figure 51-5

51.2 Enabling Background Notifications Support

When the app is running on multiple devices and a data change is made in one instance of the app, CloudKit will use remote notifications to notify other instances of the app to update to the latest data. To enable background notifications, repeat the above steps, this time adding the *Background Modes* entitlement. Once the entitlement has been added, review the settings and make sure that *Remote notifications* mode is enabled as highlighted in Figure 51-6:

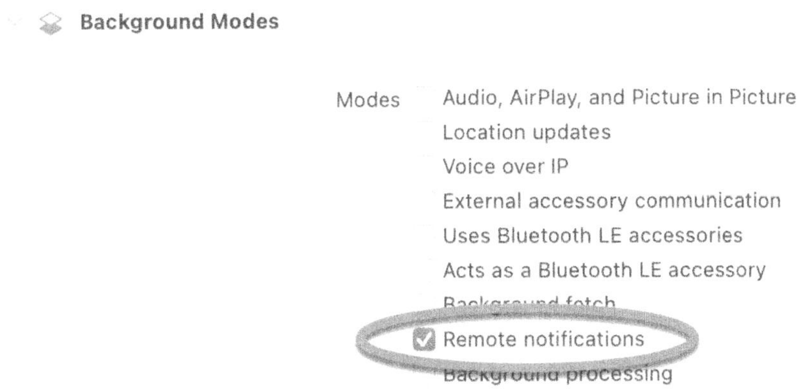

Figure 51-6

Now that the necessary entitlements have been enabled for the app, all that remains is to make some minor code changes to the project.

51.3 Switching to the CloudKit Persistent Container

Locate the *Persistence.swift* file in the project navigator panel and select it so that it loads into the code editor. Within the *init()* function, change the container creation call from NSPersistentContainer to NSPersistentCloudKitContainer as follows:

```
.
.
let container: NSPersistentCloudKitContainer
.
.
init() {
    container = NSPersistentCloudKitContainer(name: "Products")

    container.loadPersistentStores { (storeDescription, error) in
        if let error = error as NSError? {
            fatalError("Container load failed: \(error)")
        }
    }
}
```

Since multiple instances of the app could potentially change the same data at the same time, we also need to define a merge policy to make sure that conflicting changes are handled as follows:

```
init() {
    container = NSPersistentCloudKitContainer(name: "Products")
```

```
    container.loadPersistentStores { (storeDescription, error) in
        if let error = error as NSError? {
            fatalError("Container load failed: \(error)")
        }
    }
    container.viewContext.automaticallyMergesChangesFromParent = true
}
```

51.4 Testing the App

CloudKit storage can be tested on either physical devices, simulators, or a mixture of both. All test devices and simulators must be signed in to iCloud using your Apple developer account and have the iCloud Drive option enabled. Once these requirements have been met, run the CoreDataDemo app and add some product entries. Next, run the app on another device or simulator and check that the newly added products appear. This confirms that the data is being stored and retrieved from iCloud.

With both app instances running, enter a new product in one instance and check that it appears in the other. Note that a bug in the simulator means that you may need to place the app in the background and then restore it before the new data will appear.

51.5 Reviewing the Saved Data in the CloudKit Console

Once some product entries have been added to the database, return to the *Signing & Capabilities* screen for the project (Figure 51-1) and click on the CloudKit Console button. This will launch the default web browser on your system and load the CloudKit Dashboard portal. Enter your Apple developer login and password and, once the dashboard has loaded, the home screen will provide the range of options illustrated in Figure 51-7:

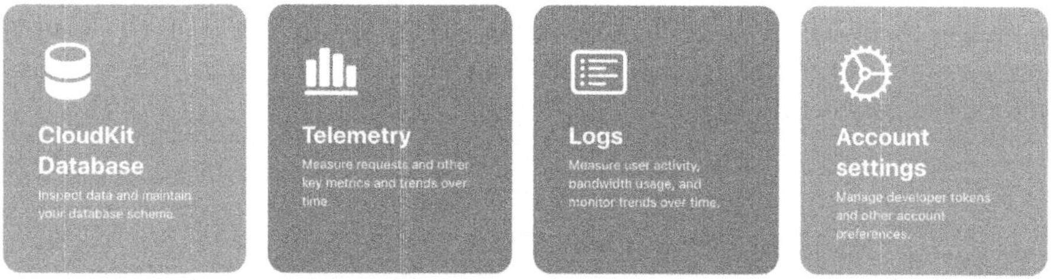

Figure 51-7

Select the CloudKit Database option and, on the resulting web page, select the container for your app from the drop-down menu (marked A in Figure 51-8 below). Since the app is still in development and has not been published to the App Store, make sure that menu B is set to Development and not Production:

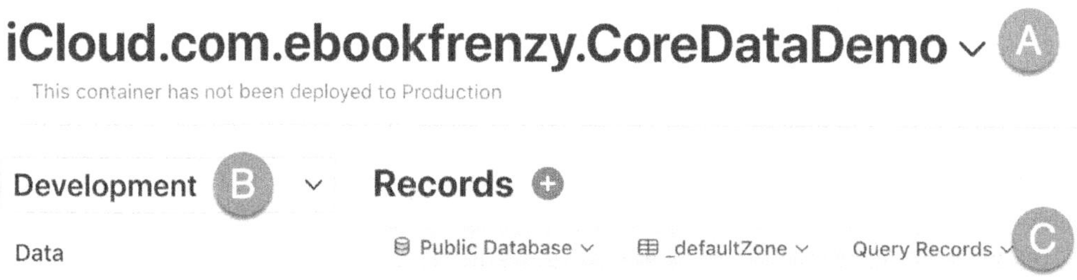

Figure 51-8

Next, we can query the records stored in the app container's private database. Set the row of menus (C) to *Private Database*, *com.apple.coredata.cloudkit.zone*, and *Query Records* respectively. Finally, set the Record Type menu to *CD_Product* and the *Fields* menu to All:

Figure 51-9

Clicking on the Query Records button should display a list of all the product items saved in the database as illustrated in Figure 51-10:

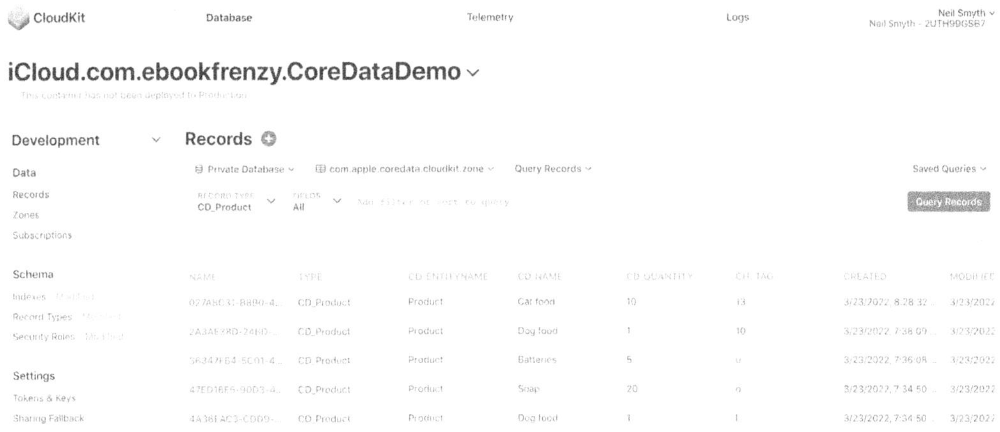

Figure 51-10

If, instead of a list of database entries, you see a message which reads "Field 'recordName' is not marked queryable", follow the steps in the next section.

51.6 Fixing the recordName Problem

When attempting to query the database, the error message shown below may appear instead of the query results:

Figure 51-11

To resolve this problem, select the Indexes option in the navigation panel (marked A in Figure 51-12) followed by CD_Product record type (B):

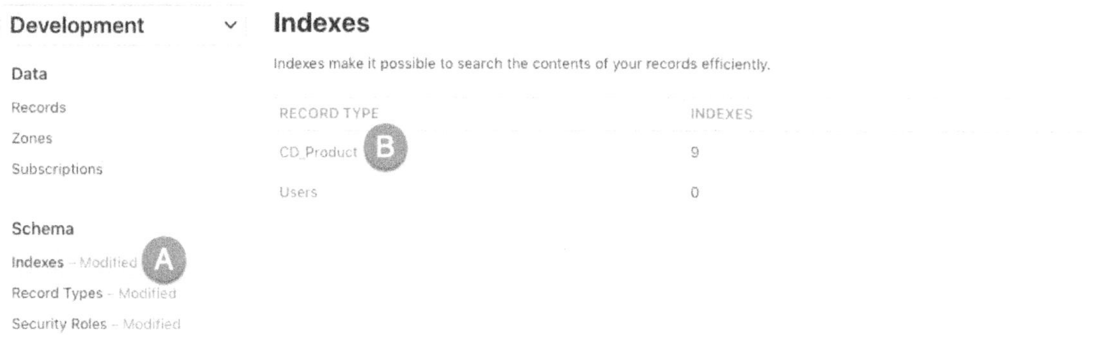

Figure 51-12

Within the list of indexes for the CD_Product record type, click on the Add Basic Index button located at the bottom of the list:

Figure 51-13

Within the new index row, select the recordName field and set the index type to Queryable:

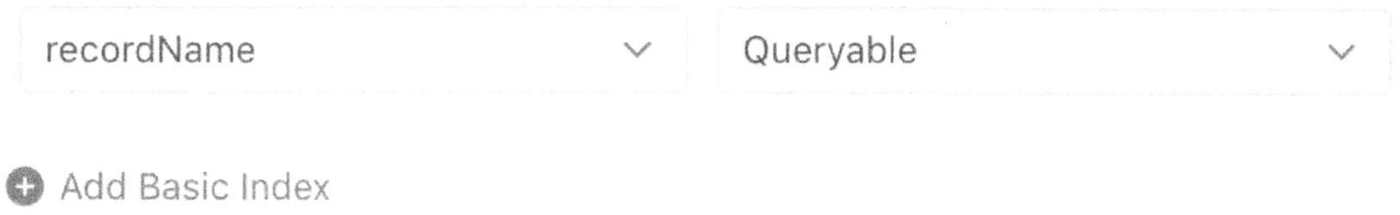

Figure 51-14

After adding the new index, click on the Save Changes button at the top of the index list before returning to the Records screen. Repeat the steps to configure and perform the query. Instead of the error message, the database records should now be listed.

51.7 Filtering and Sorting Queries

The queries we have been running so far are returning all of the records in the database. Queries may also be performed based on sorting and filtering criteria by clicking in the "Add filter or sort to query" field. Clicking in this field will display a menu system that will guide you through setting up the criteria. In Figure 51-15, for example, the menu system is being used to set up a filtered query based on the *CD_name* field:

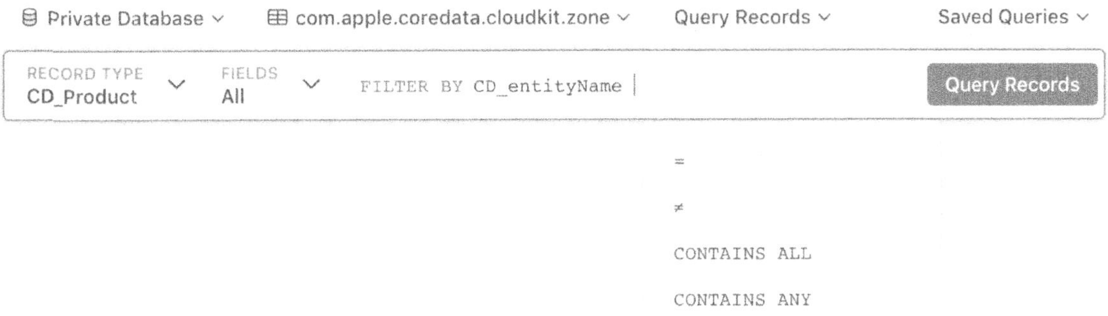

Figure 51-15

Similarly, Figure 51-16 shows the completed filter and query results:

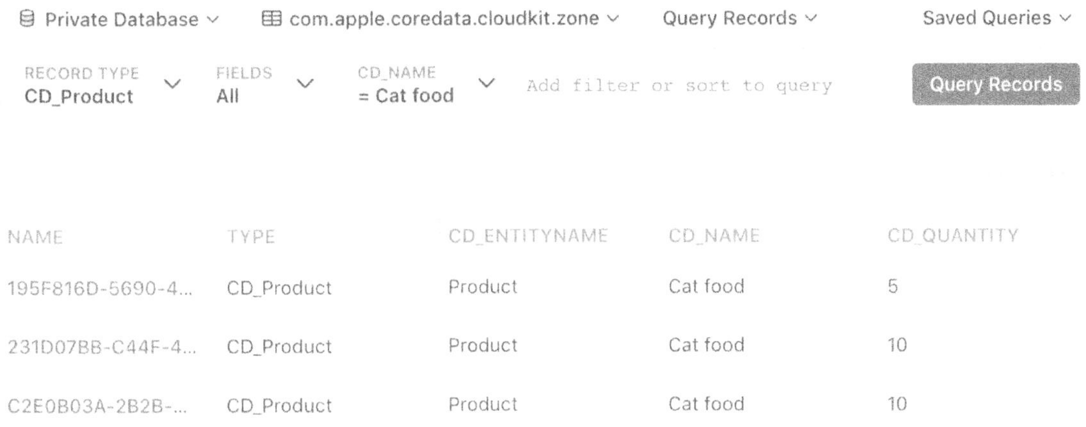

Figure 51-16

The same technique can be used to sort the results in ascending or descending order. You can also combine multiple criteria in a single query. To edit or remove a query criterion, left-click on it and select the appropriate menu option.

51.8 Editing and Deleting Records

In addition to querying the records in the database, the CloudKit Console also allows records to be edited and deleted. To edit or delete a record, locate it in the query list and click on the entry in the name column as highlighted below:

Figure 51-17

Once the record has been selected, the Record Details panel shown in Figure 51-18 will appear. In addition to displaying detailed information about the record, this panel also allows the record to be modified or deleted.

Figure 51-18

51.9 Adding New Records

To add a new record to a database, click on the "+" located at the top of the query results list and select the Create New Record option:

Figure 51-19

When the New Record panel appears (Figure 51-20) enter the new data before clicking the Save button:

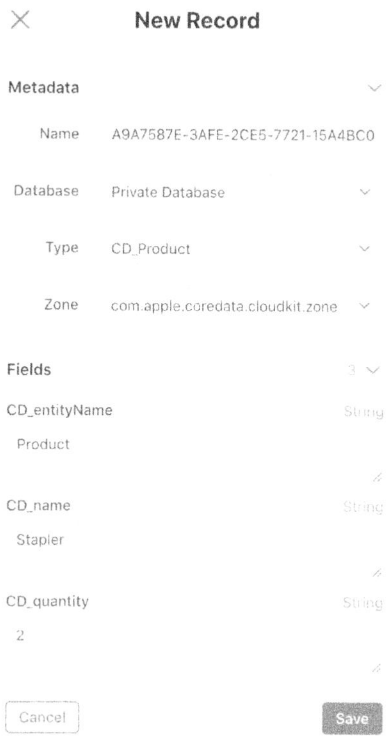

Figure 51-20

51.10 Viewing Telemetry Data

To view telemetry data, select the Telemetry tab at the top of the console as indicated in Figure 51-21, or by selecting the home screen Telemetry option (Figure 51-7):

Figure 51-21

Within the telemetry screen, select the container, environment, timescale, and database type options:

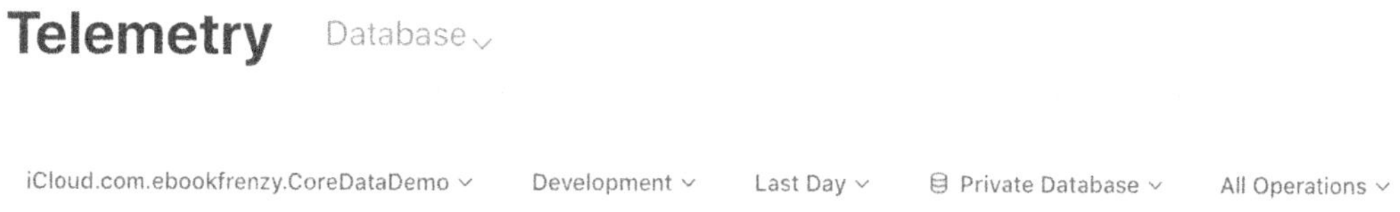

Figure 51-22

Hovering the mouse pointer over a graph will display a key explaining the metric represented by the different line colors:

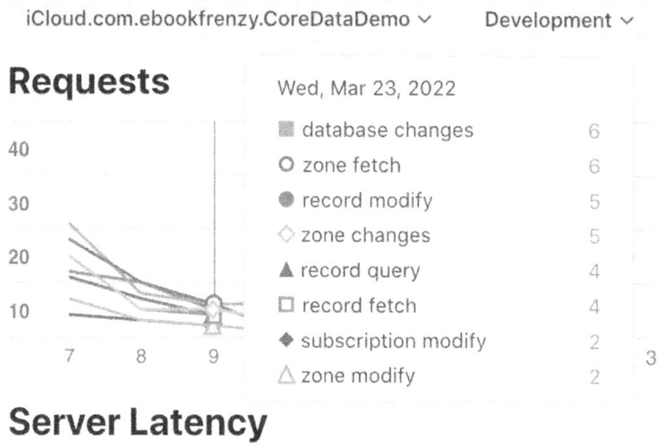

Figure 51-23

The console also provides a menu to display data for different operation types:

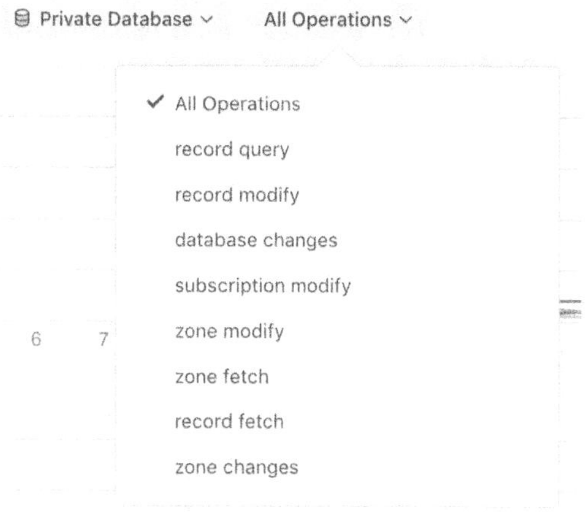

Figure 51-24

By default, telemetry data is displayed for database activity. This can be changed to display data relating to notifications or database usage using the menu shown in Figure 51-25:

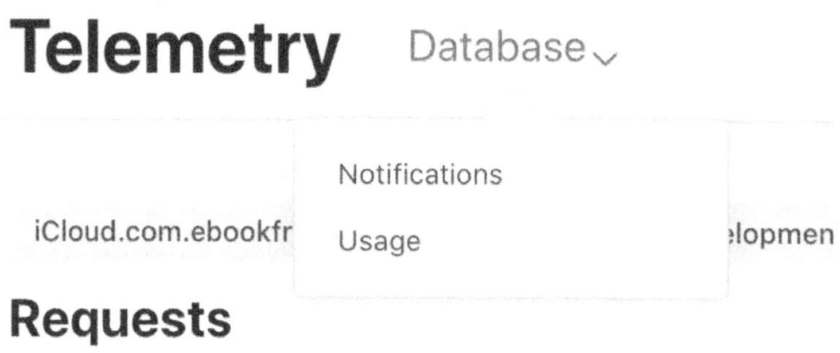

Figure 51-25

51.11 Summary

The first step in adding CloudKit support to an Xcode SwiftUI project is to add the iCloud capability, enabling both the CloudKit service and remote notifications, and configuring a container to store the databases associated with the app. The migration from Core Data to CloudKit is simply a matter of changing the code to use NSPersistentCloudKitContainer instead of NSPersistentContainer and re-building the project.

CloudKit databases can be queried, modified, managed, and monitored from within the CloudKit Console.

Chapter 52

52. An Introduction to SiriKit

Although Siri has been part of iOS for a number of years, it was not until the introduction of iOS 10 that some of the power of Siri was made available to app developers through SiriKit. Initially limited to particular categories of app, SiriKit has since extended to allow Siri functionality to be built into apps of any type.

The purpose of SiriKit is to allow key areas of application functionality to be accessed via voice commands through the Siri interface. An app designed to send messages, for example, may be integrated into Siri to allow messages to be composed and sent using voice commands. Similarly, a time management app might use SiriKit to allow entries to be made in the Reminders app.

This chapter will provide an overview of SiriKit and outline the ways in which apps are configured to integrate SiriKit support.

52.1 Siri and SiriKit

Most iOS users will no doubt be familiar with Siri, Apple's virtual digital assistant. Pressing and holding the home button, or saying "Hey Siri" launches Siri and allows a range of tasks to be performed by speaking in a conversational manner. Selecting the playback of a favorite song, asking for turn-by-turn directions to a location or requesting information about the weather are all examples of tasks that Siri can perform in response to voice commands.

When an app integrates with SiriKit, Siri handles all of the tasks associated with communicating with the user and interpreting the meaning and context of the user's words. Siri then packages up the user's request into an *intent* and passes it to the iOS app. It is then the responsibility of the iOS app to verify that enough information has been provided in the intent to perform the task and to instruct Siri to request any missing information. Once the intent contains all of the necessary data, the app performs the requested task and notifies Siri of the results. These results will be presented either by Siri or within the iOS app itself.

52.2 SiriKit Domains

When initially introduced, SiriKit could only be used with apps to perform tasks that fit into narrowly defined categories, also referred to as *domains*. With the release of iOS 10, Siri could only be used by apps when performing tasks that fit into one or more of the following domains:

- Messaging
- Notes and Lists
- Payments
- Visual Codes
- Photos
- Workouts
- Ride Booking
- CarPlay

- Car Commands
- VoIP Calling
- Restaurant Reservations
- Media

If your app fits into one of these domains then this is still the recommended approach to performing Siri integration. If, on the other hand, your app does not have a matching domain, SiriKit can now be integrated using custom Siri Shortcuts.

52.3 Siri Shortcuts

Siri Shortcuts allow frequently performed activities within an app to be stored as a shortcut and triggered via Siri using a pre-defined phrase. If a user regularly checked a specific stock price within a financial app, for example, that task could be saved as a shortcut and performed at any time via Siri voice command without the need to manually launch the app. Although lacking the power and flexibility of SiriKit domain-based integration, Siri Shortcuts provide a way for key features to be made accessible via Siri for apps that would otherwise be unable to provide any Siri integration.

An app can provide an "Add to Siri" button that allows a particular task to be configured as a shortcut. Alternatively, an app can make shortcut suggestions by *donating* actions to Siri. The user can review any shortcut suggestions within the Shortcuts app and choose those to be added as shortcuts.

Based on user behavior patterns, Siri will also suggest shortcuts to the user in the Siri Suggestions and Search panel that appears when making a downward swiping motion on the device home screen.

Siri Shortcuts will be covered in detail in the chapters entitled *"An Overview of Siri Shortcut App Integration"* and *"A SwiftUI Siri Shortcut Tutorial"*. Be sure to complete this chapter before looking at the Siri Shortcut chapters. Much of the content in this chapter applies equally to SiriKit domains and Siri Shortcuts.

52.4 SiriKit Intents

Each domain allows a predefined set of tasks, or intents, to be requested by the user for fulfillment by an app. An intent represents a specific task of which Siri is aware and for which SiriKit expects an integrated iOS app to be able to perform. The Messaging domain, for example, includes intents for sending and searching for messages, while the Workout domain contains intents for choosing, starting and finishing workouts. When the user makes a request of an app via Siri, the request is placed into an intent object of the corresponding type and passed to the app for handling.

In the case of Siri Shortcuts, a SiriKit integration is implemented by using a custom intent combined with an intents definition file describing how the app will interact with Siri.

52.5 How SiriKit Integration Works

Siri integration is performed via the iOS extension mechanism. Extensions are added as targets to the app project within Xcode in the same way as other extension types. SiriKit provides two types of extension, the key one being the Intents Extension. This extension contains an *intent handler* which is subclassed from the INExtension class of the Intents framework and contains the methods called by Siri during the process of communicating with the user. It is the responsibility of the intent handler to verify that Siri has collected all of the required information from the user, and then to execute the task defined in the intent.

The second extension type is the UI Extension. This extension is optional and comprises a storyboard file and a subclass of the IntentViewController class. When provided, Siri will use this UI when presenting information to the user. This can be useful for including additional information within the Siri user interface or for bringing the branding and theme of the main iOS app into the Siri environment.

When the user makes a request of an app via Siri, the first method to be called is the *handler(forIntent:)* method of the intent handler class contained in the Intents Extension. This method is passed the current intent object and returns a reference to the object that will serve as the intent handler. This can either be the intent handler class itself or another class that has been configured to implement one or more intent handling protocols.

The intent handler declares the types of intent it is able to handle and must then implement all of the protocol methods required to support those particular intent types. These methods are then called as part of a sequence of phases that make up the intent handling process as illustrated in Figure 52-1:

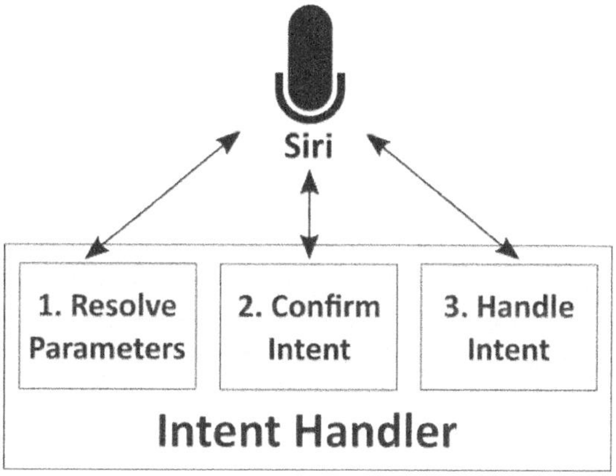

Figure 52-1

The first step after Siri calls the handler method involves calls to a series of methods to resolve the parameters associated with the intent.

52.6 Resolving Intent Parameters

Each intent domain type has associated with it a group of parameters that are used to provide details about the task to be performed by the app. While many parameters are mandatory, some are optional. The intent to send a message must, for example, contain a valid recipient parameter in order for a message to be sent. A number of parameters for a Photo search intent, on the other hand, are optional. A user might, for example, want to search for photos containing particular people, regardless of the date that the photos were taken.

When working with Siri domains, Siri knows all of the possible parameters for each intent type, and for each parameter Siri will ask the app extension's intent handler to *resolve* the parameter via a corresponding method call. If Siri already has a parameter, it will ask the intent handler to verify that the parameter is valid. If Siri does not yet have a value for a parameter it will ask the intent handler if the parameter is required. If the intent handler notifies Siri that the parameter is not required, Siri will not ask the user to provide it. If, on the other hand, the parameter is needed, Siri will ask the user to provide the information.

Consider, for example, a photo search app called CityPicSearch that displays all the photos taken in a particular city. The user might begin by saying the following:

"Hey Siri. Find photos using CityPicSearch."

From this sentence, Siri will infer that a photo search using the CityPicSearch app has been requested. Siri will know that CityPicSearch has been integrated with SiriKit and that the app has registered that it supports the InSearchForPhotosIntent intent type. Siri also knows that the InSearchForPhotosIntent intent allows photos to be searched for based on date created, people in the photo, the location of the photo and the photo album in which the photo resides. What Siri does not know, however, is which of these parameters the CityPicSearch app actually needs to perform the task. To find out this information, Siri will call the resolve method for each of these parameters on the app's intent handler. In each case the intent handler will respond indicating whether or not the parameter is required. In this case, the intent handler's *resolveLocationCreated* method will return a status indicating that the parameter is mandatory. On receiving this notification, Siri will request the missing information from the user by saying:

"Find pictures from where?"

The user will then provide a location which Siri will pass to the app by calling *resolveLocationCreated* once again, including the selection in the intent object. The app will verify the validity of the location and indicate to Siri that the parameter is valid. This process will repeat for each parameter supported by the intent type until all necessary parameter requirements have been satisfied.

Techniques are also available to assist Siri and the user clarify ambiguous parameters. The intent handler can, for example, return a list of possible options for a parameter which will then be presented to the user for selection. If the user were to ask an app to send a message to "John", the *resolveRecipients* method would be called by Siri. The method might perform a search of the contacts list and find multiple entries where the contact's first name is John. In this situation the method could return a list of contacts with the first name of John. Siri would then ask the user to clarify which "John" is the intended recipient by presenting the list of matching contacts.

Once the parameters have either been resolved or indicated as not being required, Siri will call the *confirm* method of the intent handler.

52.7 The Confirm Method

The confirm method is implemented within the extension intent handler and is called by Siri when all of the intent parameters have been resolved. This method provides the intent handler with an opportunity to make sure that it is ready to handle the intent. If the confirm method reports a ready status, Siri calls the *handle* method.

52.8 The Handle Method

The *handle* method is where the activity associated with the intent is performed. Once the task is completed, a response is passed to Siri. The form of the response will depend on the type of activity performed. For example, a photo search activity will return a count of the number of matching photos, while a send message activity will indicate whether the message was sent successfully.

The handle method may also return a *continueInApp* response. This tells Siri that the remainder of the task is to be performed within the main app. On receiving this response, Siri will launch the app, passing in an NSUserActivity object. NSUserActivity is a class that enables the status of an app to be saved and restored. In iOS 10 and later, the NSUserActivity class has an additional property that allows an NSInteraction object to be stored along with the app state. Siri uses this *interaction* property to store the NSInteraction object for the session and passes it to the main iOS app. The interaction object, in turn, contains a copy of the intent object which the app can extract to continue processing the activity. A custom NSUserActivity object can be created by the extension and passed to the iOS app. Alternatively, if no custom object is specified, SiriKit will create one by default.

A photo search intent, for example, would need to use the *continueInApp* response and user activity object so that photos found during the search can be presented to the user (SiriKit does not currently provide a mechanism for displaying the images from a photo search intent within the Siri user interface).

It is important to note that an intent handler class may contain more than one handle method to handle different intent types. A messaging app, for example, would typically have different handler methods for send message and message search intents.

52.9 Custom Vocabulary

Clearly Siri has a broad knowledge of vocabulary in a wide range of languages. It is quite possible, however, that your app or app users might use certain words or terms which have no meaning or context for Siri. These terms can be added to your app so that they are recognized by Siri. These custom vocabulary terms are categorized as either *user-specific* or *global.*

User specific terms are terms that only apply to an individual user. This might be a photo album with an unusual name or the nicknames the user has entered for contacts in a messaging app. User specific terms are registered with Siri from within the main iOS app (not the extension) at application runtime using the *setVocabularyStrings(oftype:)* method of the NSVocabulary class and must be provided in the form of an ordered list with the most commonly used terms listed first. User-specific custom vocabulary terms may only be specified for contact and contact group names, photo tag and album names, workout names and CarPlay car profile names. When calling the *setVocabularyStrings(oftype:)* method with the ordered list, the category type specified must be one of the following:

- contactName
- contactGroupName
- photoTag
- photoAlbumName
- workoutActivityName
- carProfileName

Global vocabulary terms are specific to your app but apply to all app users. These terms are supplied with the app bundle in the form of a property list file named *AppInventoryVocabulary.plist.* These terms are only applicable to work out and ride sharing names.

52.10 The Siri User Interface

Each SiriKit domain has a standard user interface layout that is used by default to convey information to the user during the Siri integration. The Ride Booking extension, for example, will display information such as the destination and price. These default user interfaces can be customized by adding an intent UI app extension to the project. This topic is covered in the chapter entitled *"Customizing the SiriKit Intent User Interface"*. In the case of a Siri Shortcut, the same technique can be used to customize the user interface that appears within Siri when the shortcut is used.

52.11 Summary

SiriKit brings some of the power of Siri to third-party apps, allowing the functionality of an app to be accessed by the user using the Siri virtual assistant interface. Siri integration was originally only available when performing tasks that fall into narrowly defined domains such as messaging, photo searching and workouts. This has now been broadened to provide support for apps of just about any type. Siri integration uses the standard iOS extensions mechanism. The Intents Extension is responsible for interacting with Siri, while the optional UI Extension provides a way to control the appearance of any results presented to the user within the Siri environment.

All of the interaction with the user is handled by Siri, with the results structured and packaged into an intent. This intent is then passed to the intent handler of the Intents Extension via a series of method calls designed to verify that all the required information has been gathered. The intent is then handled, the requested task performed and the results presented to the user either via Siri or the main iOS app.

Chapter 53

53. A SwiftUI SiriKit Messaging Extension Tutorial

The previous chapter covered much of the theory associated with integrating Siri into an iOS app. This chapter will review the example Siri messaging extension that is created by Xcode when a new Intents Extension is added to a project. This will not only show a practical implementation of the topics covered in the previous chapter, but will also provide some more detail on how the integration works. The next chapter will cover the steps required to make use of a UI Extension within an app project.

53.1 Creating the Example Project

Begin by launching Xcode and creating a new Multiplatform App project named *SiriDemo*.

53.2 Enabling the Siri Entitlement

Once the main project has been created the Siri entitlement must be enabled for the project. Select the *SiriDemo* target located at the top of the Project Navigator panel (marked A in Figure 51-1) so that the main panel displays the project settings. From within this panel, select the *Signing & Capabilities* tab (B) followed by the SiriDemo target entry (C):

Figure 53-1

Click on the "+ Capability" button (D) to display the dialog shown in Figure 51-2. Enter *Siri* into the filter bar, select the result and press the keyboard enter key to add the capability to the project:

Figure 53-2

If Siri is not listed as an option, you will need to pay to join the Apple Developer program as outlined in the chapter entitled *"Joining the Apple Developer Program"*. If you are already a member, use the steps outlined in the chapter entitled *"Installing Xcode 14 and the iOS 16 SDK"* to ensure you have created a *Developer ID Application* certificate.

53.3 Seeking Siri Authorization

In addition to enabling the Siri entitlement, the app must also seek authorization from the user to integrate the app with Siri. This is a two-step process which begins with the addition of an entry to the *Info.plist* file of the iOS app target for the NSSiriUsageDescription key with a corresponding string value explaining how the app makes use of Siri.

With the SiriDemo target still selected in the project navigator panel, select the *Info* tab within main panel as shown in Figure 53-3:

Figure 53-3

Once selected, locate the bottom entry in the list of properties and hover the mouse pointer over the item. When the plus button appears, click on it to add a new entry to the list. From within the drop-down list of available keys, locate and select the *Privacy – Siri Usage Description* option as shown in Figure 53-4:

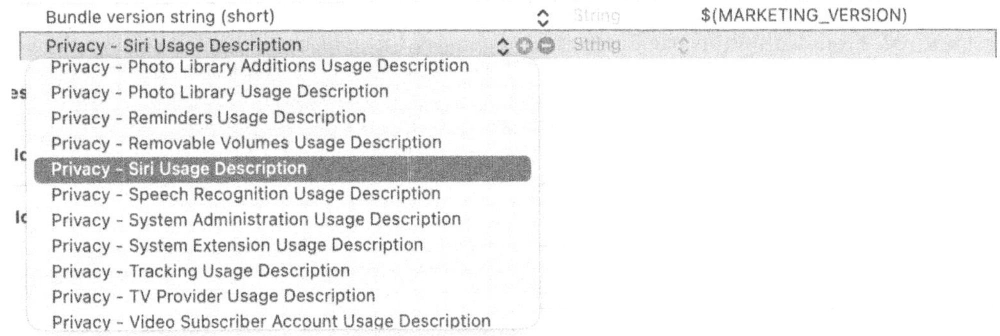

Figure 53-4

Within the value field for the property, enter a message to display to the user when requesting permission to use speech recognition. For example:

```
Siri support is used to send and review messages.
```

In addition to adding the Siri usage description key, a call also needs to be made to the *requestSiriAuthorization()* class method of the INPreferences class. Ideally, this call should be made the first time that the app runs, not only so that authorization can be obtained, but also so that the user learns that the app includes Siri support. For the purposes of this project, the call will be made within the *onChange()* modifier based on the scenePhase changes within the app declaration located in the *SiriDemoApp.swift* file as follows:

```
import SwiftUI
import Intents

@main
struct SiriDemoApp: App {

    @Environment(\.scenePhase) private var scenePhase
```

```
    var body: some Scene {
        WindowGroup {
            ContentView()
        }
        .onChange(of: scenePhase) { phase in
            INPreferences.requestSiriAuthorization({status in
                // Handle errors here
            })
        }
    }
}
```

Before proceeding, compile and run the app on an iOS device or simulator. When the app loads, a dialog will appear requesting authorization to use Siri. Select the OK button in the dialog to provide authorization.

53.4 Adding the Intents Extension

The next step is to add the Intents Extension to the project ready to begin the SiriKit integration. Select the Xcode *File -> New -> Target...* menu option, select the iOS tab at the top of the dialog, and add an Intents Extension to the project. Name the product *SiriDemoIntent,* set the Starting Point menu to *Messaging* and make sure that the *Include UI Extension* option is turned off (this will be added in the next chapter) before clicking on the *Finish* button. When prompted to do so, activate the build scheme for the Intents Extension.

53.5 Supported Intents

In order to work with Siri, an extension must specify the intent types it is able to support. These declarations are made in the *Info.plist* files of the extension folders. Within the Project Navigator panel, select the *Info* entry located in the *SiriDemoIntent* folder and unfold the *NSExtension -> NSExtensionAttributes - IntentsSupported* section. This will show that the *IntentsSupported* key has been assigned an array of intent class names:

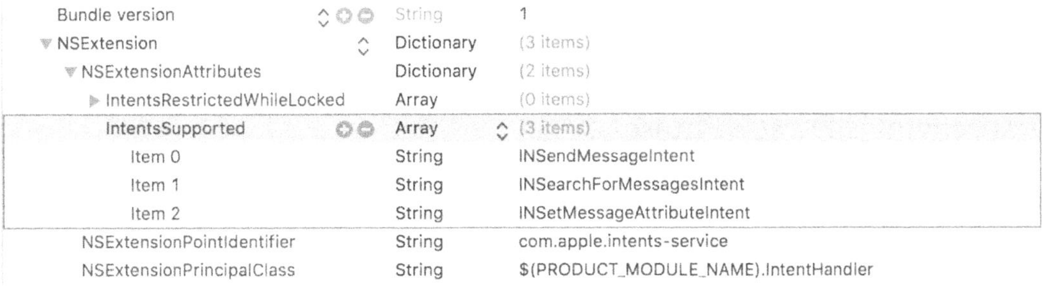

Figure 53-5

Note that entries are available for intents that are supported and intents that are supported but restricted when the lock screen is enabled. It might be wise, for example, for a payment based intent to be restricted when the screen is locked. As currently configured, the extension supports all of the messaging intent types without restrictions. To support a different domain, change these intents or add additional intents accordingly. For example, a photo search extension might only need to specify *INSearchForPhotosIntent* as a supported intent.

When the Intents UI Extension is added in the next chapter, it too will contain an *Info.plist* file with these supported intent value declarations. Note that the intents supported by the Intents UI Extension can be a subset of those declared in the UI Extension. This allows the UI Extension to be used only for certain intent types.

53.6 Trying the Example

Before exploring the structure of the project it is worth running the app and experiencing the Siri integration. The example simulates searching for and sending messages, so can be safely used without any messages actually being sent.

Make sure that the *SiriDemoIntent* option is selected as the run target in the toolbar as illustrated in Figure 53-6 and click on the run button.

Figure 53-6

When prompted, select Siri as the app within which the extension is to run. When Siri launches experiment with phrases such as the following:

"Send a message with SiriDemo."

"Send a message to John with SiriDemo."

"Use SiriDemo to say Hello to John and Kate."

"Find Messages with SiriDemo."

If Siri indicates that SiriDemo has not yet been set up, exit the Siri session, locate the SiriDemo app on the device and launch it manually. Once the app has launched, press and hold the home or power button to relaunch Siri and try the above phrases again.

In each case, all of the work involved in understanding the phrases and converting them into structured representations of the request is performed by Siri. All the intent handler needs to do is work with the resulting intent object.

53.7 Specifying a Default Phrase

A useful option when repeatedly testing SiriKit behavior is to configure a phrase to be passed to Siri each time the app is launched from within Xcode. This avoids having to repeatedly speak to Siri each time the app is re-launched. To specify the test phrase, select the SiriDemoIntent run target in the Xcode toolbar and select *Edit scheme...* from the resulting menu as illustrated in Figure 53-7:

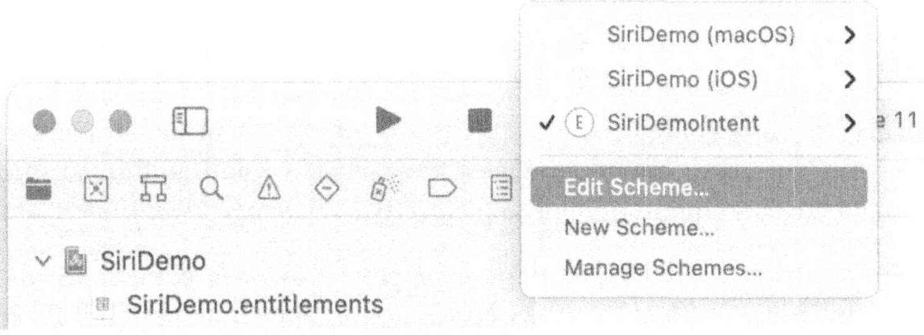

Figure 53-7

In the scheme panel, select the Run entry in the left-hand panel followed by the *Info* tab in the main panel. Within the Info settings, enter a query phrase into the *Siri Intent Query* text box before closing the panel:

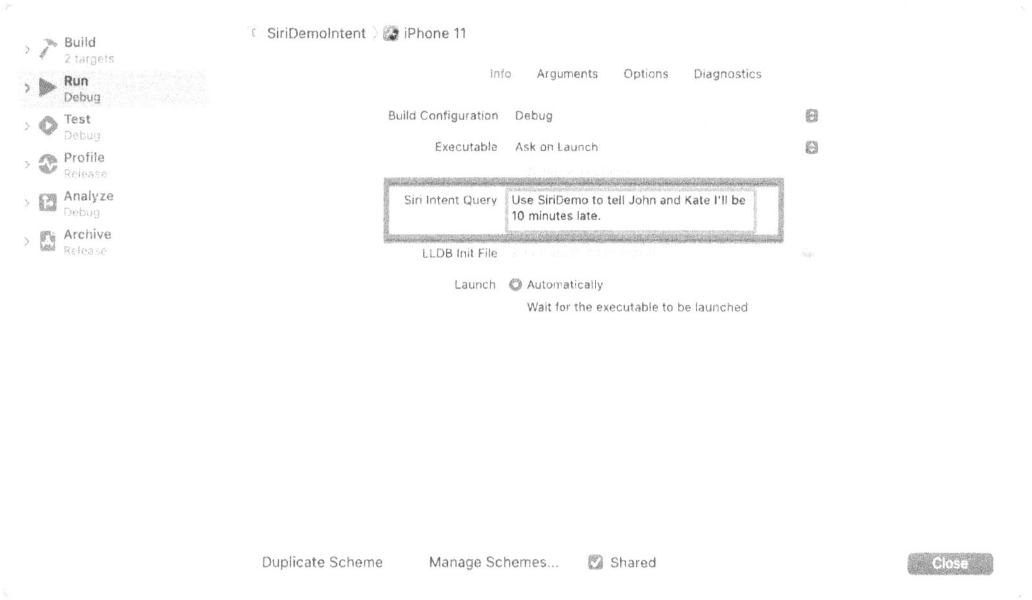

Figure 53-8

Run the extension once again and note that the phrase is automatically passed to Siri to be handled:

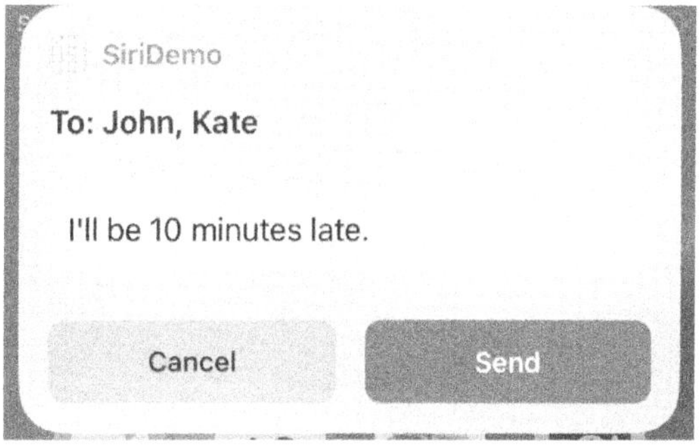

Figure 53-9

53.8 Reviewing the Intent Handler

The Intent Handler is declared in the *IntentHandler.swift* file in the *SiriDemoIntent* folder. Load the file into the editor and note that the class declares that it supports a range of intent handling protocols for the messaging domain:

```
class IntentHandler: INExtension, INSendMessageIntentHandling, 
  INSearchForMessagesIntentHandling, INSetMessageAttributeIntentHandling {
.
.
}
```

The above declaration declares the class as supporting all three of the intents available in the messaging domain. As an alternative to listing all of the protocol names individually, the above code could have achieved the same result by referencing the *INMessagesDomainHandling* protocol which encapsulates all three protocols.

If this template were to be re-purposed for a different domain, these protocol declarations would need to be replaced. For a payment extension, for example, the declaration might read as follows:

```
class IntentHandler: INExtension, INSendPaymentIntentHandling,
    INRequestPaymentIntent {
.
.
}
```

The class also contains the *handler* method, resolution methods for the intent parameters and the *confirm* method. The *resolveRecipients* method is of particular interest since it demonstrates the use of the resolution process to provide the user with a range of options from which to choose when a parameter is ambiguous.

The implementation also contains multiple handle methods for performing tasks for message search, message send and message attribute change intents. Take some time to review these methods before proceeding.

53.9 Summary

This chapter has provided a walk-through of the sample messaging-based extension provided by Xcode when creating a new Intents Extension. This has highlighted the steps involved in adding both Intents and UI Extensions to an existing project, and enabling and seeking SiriKit integration authorization for the project. The chapter also outlined the steps necessary for the extensions to declare supported intents and provided an opportunity to gain familiarity with the methods that make up a typical intent handler. The next chapter will outline the mechanism for implementing and configuring a UI Extension.

Chapter 54

54. An Overview of Siri Shortcut App Integration

When SiriKit was first introduced with iOS 10, an app had to fit neatly into one of the SiriKit domains covered in the chapter entitled *"An Introduction to SiriKit"* in order to integrate with Siri. In iOS 12, however, SiriKit was extended to allow an app of any type to make key features available for access via Siri voice commands, otherwise known as Siri Shortcuts. This chapter will provide a high level overview of Siri Shortcuts and the steps involved in turning app features into Siri Shortcuts.

54.1 An Overview of Siri Shortcuts

A Siri shortcut is essentially a commonly used feature of an app that can be invoked by the user via a chosen phrase. The app for a fast-food restaurant might, for example, allow the user to order a favorite lunch item by simply using the phrase "Order Lunch" from within Siri. Once a shortcut has been configured, iOS learns the usage patterns of the shortcut and will begin to place that shortcut in the Siri Suggestions area on the device at appropriate times of the day. If the user uses the lunch ordering shortcut at lunch times on weekdays, the system will suggest the shortcut at that time of day.

A shortcut can be configured within an app by providing the user with an Add to Siri button at appropriate places in the app. Our hypothetical restaurant app might, for example, include an Add to Siri button on the order confirmation page which, when selected, will allow the user to add that order as a shortcut and provide a phrase to Siri with which to launch the shortcut (and order the same lunch) in future.

An app may also suggest (a concept referred to as *donating*) a feature or user activity as a possible shortcut candidate which the user can then turn into a shortcut via the iOS Shortcuts app.

As with the SiriKit domains, the key element of a Siri Shortcut is an intent extension. Unlike domain based extensions such as messaging and photo search, which strictly define the parameters and behavior of the intent, Siri shortcut intents are customizable to meet the specific requirements of the app. A restaurant app, for example would include a custom shortcut intent designed to handle information such as the menu items ordered, the method of payment and the pick-up or delivery location. Unlike SiriKit domain extensions, however, the parameters for the intent are stored when the shortcut is created and are not requested from the user by Siri when the shortcut is invoked. A shortcut to order the user's usual morning coffee, for example, will already be configured with the coffee item and pickup location, both of which will be passed to the intent handler by Siri when the shortcut is triggered.

The intent will also need to be configured with custom responses such as notifying the user through Siri that the shortcut was successfully completed, a particular item in an order is currently unavailable or that the pickup location is currently closed.

The key component of a Siri Shortcut in terms of specifying the parameters and responses is the *SiriKit Intent Definition* file.

54.2 An Introduction to the Intent Definition File

When a SiriKit extension such as a Messaging Extension is added to an iOS project, it makes use of a pre-defined *system intent* provided by SiriKit (in the case of a Messaging extension, for example, this might involve the

INSendMessageIntent). In the case of Siri shortcuts, however, a custom intent is created and configured to fit with the requirements of the app. The key to creating a custom intent lies within the Intent Definition file.

An Intent Definition file can be added to an Xcode project by selecting the Xcode *File -> New -> File…* menu option and choosing the *SiriKit Intent Definition File* option from the *Resource* section of the template selection dialog.

Once created, Xcode provides an editor specifically for adding and configuring custom intents (in fact the editor may also be used to create customized variations of the system intents such as the Messaging, Workout and Payment intents). New intents are added by clicking on the '+' button in the lower left corner of the editor window and making a selection from the menu:

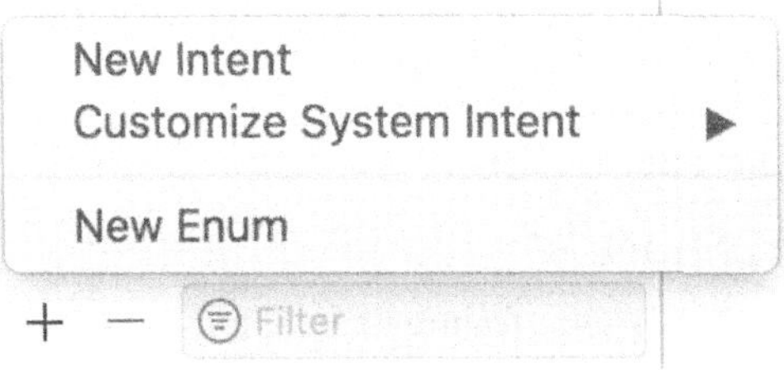

Figure 54-1

Selecting the *Customize System Intent* option will provide a list of system intents from which to choose while the *New Intent* option creates an entirely new intent with no pre-existing configuration settings. Once a new custom intent has been created, it appears in the editor as shown in Figure 54-2:

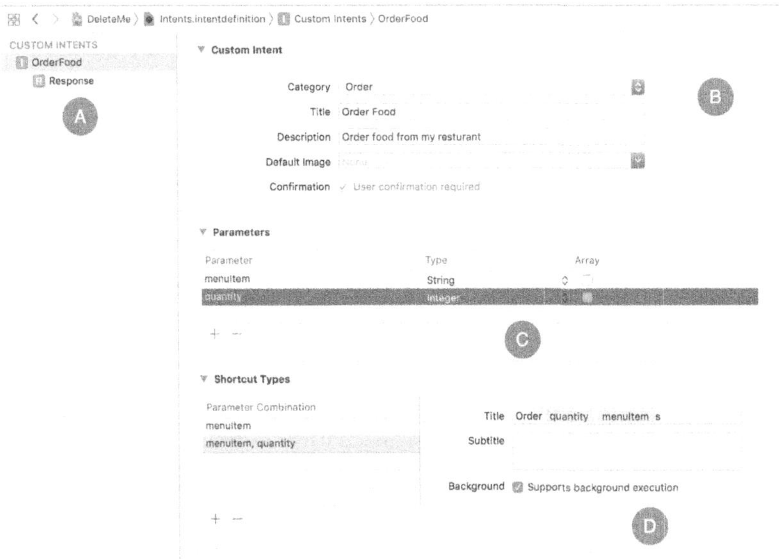

Figure 54-2

The section marked A in the above figure lists the custom intents contained within the file. The Custom Intent section (B) is where the category of the intent is selected from a list of options including categories such as order, buy, do, open, search etc. Since this example is an intent for ordering food, the category is set to Order. This section also includes the title of the intent, a description and an optional image to include with the shortcut. A checkbox is also provided to require Siri to seek confirmation from the user before completing the shortcut. For some intent categories such as buying and ordering this option is mandatory.

The parameters section (C) allows the parameters that will be passed to the intent to be declared. If the custom intent is based on an existing SiriKit system intent, this area will be populated with all of the parameters the intent is already configured to handle and the settings cannot be changed. For a new custom intent, as many parameters as necessary may be declared and configured in terms of name, type and whether or not the parameter is an array.

Finally, the Shortcut Types section (D) allows different variations of the shortcut to be configured. A shortcut type is defined by the combination of parameters used within the shortcut. For each combination of parameters that the shortcut needs to support, settings are configured including the title of the shortcut and whether or not the host app can perform the associated task in the background without presenting a user interface. Each intent can have as many parameter combinations as necessary to provide a flexible user shortcut experience.

The Custom Intents panel (A) also lists a Response entry under the custom intent name. When selected, the editor displays the screen shown in Figure 54-3:

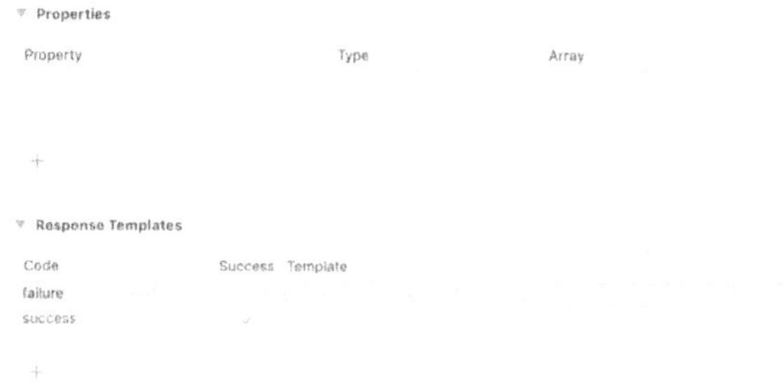

Figure 54-3

Keep in mind that a Siri shortcut involves a two-way interaction between Siri and the user and that to maintain this interaction Siri needs to know how to respond to the user based on the results of the intent execution. This is defined through a range of *response templates* which define the phrases to be spoken by Siri when the intent returns specific codes. These response settings also allow parameters to be configured for inclusion in the response phrases. A restaurant app might, for example, have a response code named *failureStoreClosed* which results in Siri responding with the phrase "We are sorry, we cannot complete your cheeseburger order because the store is closed.", and a success response code with the phrase "Your order of two coffees will be ready for pickup in 20 minutes".

Once the Intent Definition file has been configured, Xcode will automatically generate a set of class files ready for use within the intent handler code of the extension.

54.3 Automatically Generated Classes

The purpose of the Intent Definition file is to allow Xcode to generate a set of classes that will be used when implementing the shortcut extension. Assuming that a custom intent named OrderFood was added to the definition file, the following classes would be automatically generated by Xcode:

- **OrderFoodIntent** – The intent object that encapsulates all of the parameters declared in the definition file. An instance of this class will be passed by Siri to the *handler()*, *handle()* and *confirm()* methods of the extension intent handler configured with the appropriate parameter values for the current shortcut.

- **OrderIntentHandling** – Defines the protocol to which the intent handler must conform in order to be able to fully handle food ordering intents.

- **OrderIntentResponse** – A class encapsulating the response codes, templates and parameters declared for the intent in the Intent Definition file. The intent handler will use this class to return response codes and parameter values to Siri so that the appropriate response can be communicated to the user.

Use of these classes within the intent handler will be covered in the next chapter entitled *"A SwiftUI Siri Shortcut Tutorial"*.

54.4 Donating Shortcuts

An app typically donates a shortcut when a common action is performed by the user. This donation does not automatically turn the activity into a shortcut, but includes it as a suggested shortcut within the iOS Shortcuts app. A donation is made by calling the *donate()* method of an INInteraction instance which has been initialized with a shortcut intent object. For example:

```
let intent = OrderFoodIntent()

intent.menuItem = "Cheeseburger"
intent.quantity = 1
intent.suggestedInvocationPhrase = "Order Lunch"

let interaction = INInteraction(intent: intent, response: nil)

interaction.donate { (error) in
    if error != nil {
        // Handle donation failure
    }
}
```

54.5 The Add to Siri Button

The Add to Siri button allows a shortcut to be added to Siri directly from within an app. This involves writing code to create an INUIAddVoiceShortcutButton instance, initializing it with a shortcut intent object with shortcut parameters configured and then adding it to a user interface view. A target method is then added to the button to be called when the button is clicked.

As of iOS 16, the Add to Siri button has not been integrated directly into SwiftUI, requiring the integration of UIKit into the SwiftUI project.

54.6 Summary

Siri shortcuts allow commonly performed tasks within apps to be invoked using Siri via a user provided phrase. When added, a shortcut contains all of the parameter values needed to complete the task within the app together with templates defining how Siri should respond based on the status reported by the intent handler. A shortcut is implemented by creating a custom intent extension and configuring an Intent Definition file containing all of the information regarding the intent, parameters and responses. From this information, Xcode generates all of the class files necessary to implement the shortcut. Shortcuts can be added to Siri either via an Add to Siri button within the host app, or by the app donating suggested shortcuts. A list of donated shortcuts can be found in the iOS Shortcuts app.

Chapter 55

55. A SwiftUI Siri Shortcut Tutorial

As previously discussed, the purpose of Siri Shortcuts is to allow key features of an app to be invoked by the user via Siri by speaking custom phrases. This chapter will demonstrate how to integrate shortcut support into an existing iOS app, including the creation of a custom intent and intent UI, the configuration of a SiriKit Intent Definition file and outline the code necessary to handle the intents, provide responses and donate shortcuts to Siri.

55.1 About the Example App

The project used as the basis for this tutorial is an app which simulates the purchasing of financial stocks and shares. The app is named *ShortcutDemo* and can be found in the sample code download available at the following URL:

https://www.ebookfrenzy.com/retail/swiftui-ios16/

The app consists of a "Buy" screen into which the stock symbol and quantity are entered and the purchase initiated, and a "History" screen consisting of a List view listing all previous transactions. Selecting an entry in the transaction history displays a third screen containing details about the corresponding stock purchase.

55.2 App Groups and UserDefaults

Much about the way in which the app has been constructed will be familiar from techniques outlined in previous chapters of the book. The project also makes use of app storage in the form of UserDefaults and the @AppStorage property wrapper, concepts which were introduced in the chapter entitled *"SwiftUI Data Persistence using AppStorage and SceneStorage"*. The ShortcutDemo app uses app storage to store an array of objects containing the symbol, quantity and time stamp data for all stock purchase transactions. Since this is a test app that needs to store minimal amounts of data, this storage is more than adequate. In a real-world environment, however, a storage system capable of handling larger volumes of data such as SQLite, CoreData or iCloud storage would need to be used.

In order to share the UserDefaults data between the app and the SiriKit intents extension, the project also makes use of *App Groups*. App Groups allow apps to share data with other apps and targets within the same app group. App Groups are assigned a name (typically similar to group.com.yourdomain.myappname) and are enabled and configured within the Xcode project *Signing & Capabilities* screen.

55.3 Preparing the Project

Once the ShortcutDemo project has been downloaded and opened within Xcode, some configuration changes need to be made before the app can be compiled and run. Begin by selecting the ShortcutDemo target at the top of the project navigator panel (marked A in Figure 55-1) followed by the ShortcutDemo entry in the Targets list (B). Select the *Signing & Capabilities* tab (C) and choose your developer ID from the Team menu in the Signing section (D):

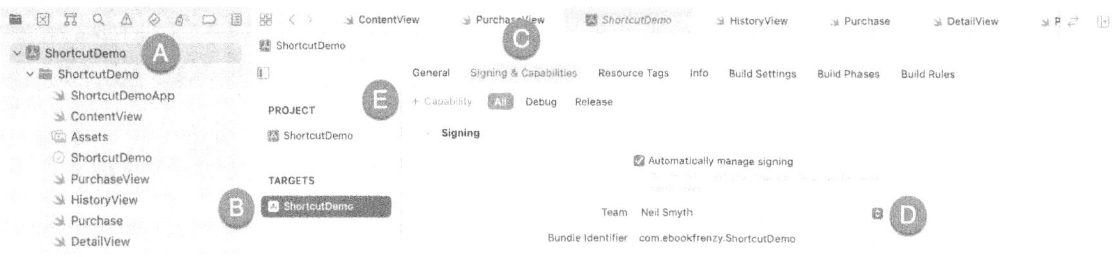

Figure 55-1

Next, click the "+ Capability" button (E) and double-click on the App Groups entry in the resulting dialog to add the capability to the project. Once added, click on the '+' button located beneath the list of App Groups (as indicated in Figure 55-2):

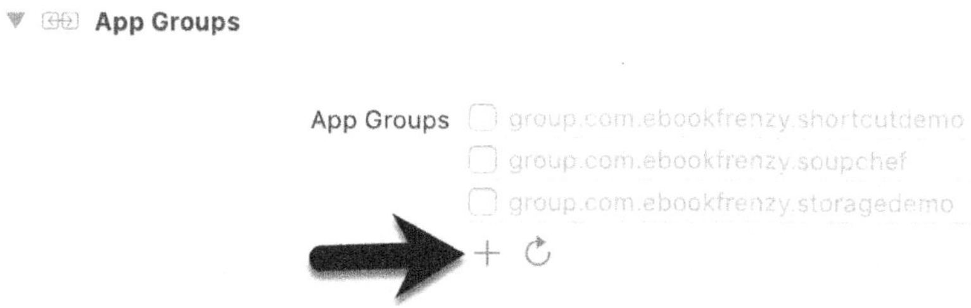

Figure 55-2

In the resulting panel, provide a name for the app group container that will be unique to your project (for example group.com.<your domain name>.shortcutdemo). Once a name has been entered, click on the OK button to add it to the project entitlements file (*ShortcutDemo.entitlements*) and make sure that its toggle button is enabled.

Now that the App Group container has been created, the name needs to be referenced in the project code. Edit the *PurchaseStore.swift* file and replace the placeholder text in the following line of code with your own App Group name:

```
@AppStorage("demostorage", store: UserDefaults(
    suiteName: "YOUR APP GROUP NAME HERE")) var store: Data = Data()
```

55.4 Running the App

Run the app on a device or simulator and enter a stock symbol and quantity (for example 100 shares of TSLA and 20 GE shares) and click on the *Purchase* button. Assuming the transaction is successful, select the *History* tab at the bottom of the screen and confirm that the transactions appear in the list as shown in Figure 55-3:

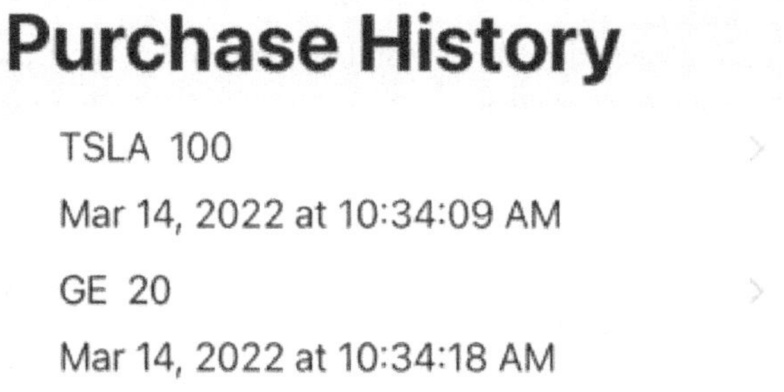

Figure 55-3

If the purchased stocks do not appear in the list, switch between the Buy and History screens once more at which point the items should appear (this is a bug in SwiftUI which has been reported to Apple but not yet fixed). Select a transaction from the list to display the Detail screen for that purchase:

Figure 55-4

With the app installed, configured and running, the next step is to begin integrating shortcut support into the project.

55.5 Enabling Siri Support

To add the Siri entitlement, return to the *Signing & Capabilities* screen, click on the "+ Capability" button to display the capability selection dialog, enter *Siri* into the filter bar and double-click on the result to add the capability to the project.

55.6 Seeking Siri Authorization

In addition to enabling the Siri entitlement, the app must also seek authorization from the user to integrate the app with Siri. This is a two-step process which begins with the addition of an entry to the *Info.plist* file of the iOS app target for the NSSiriUsageDescription key with a corresponding string value explaining how the app makes use of Siri.

Select the ShortcutDemo target at the top of the project navigator panel (marked A in Figure 55-5) and the ShortcutDemo entry in the Targets list (B), followed by the Info tab (C):

Figure 55-5

Locate the bottom entry in the list of target properties and hover the mouse pointer over the item. When the plus button appears, click on it to add a new entry to the list. From within the drop-down list of available keys, locate and select the *Privacy - Siri Usage Description* option as shown in Figure 55-6:

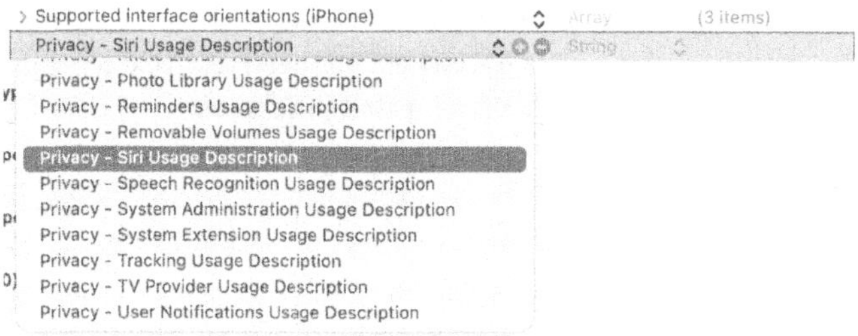

Figure 55-6

Within the value field for the property, enter a message to display to the user when requesting permission to use speech recognition. For example:

```
Siri support is used to suggest shortcuts
```

In addition to adding the Siri usage description key, a call also needs to be made to the *requestSiriAuthorization* class method of the INPreferences class. Ideally, this call should be made the first time that the app runs, not only so that authorization can be obtained, but also so that the user learns that the app includes Siri support. For the purposes of this project, the call will be made within the *onChange()* modifier based on the scenePhase changes within the app declaration located in the *ShortcutDemoApp.swift* file as follows:

```
import SwiftUI
import Intents

@main
struct ShortcutDemoApp: App {

    @Environment(\.scenePhase) private var scenePhase

    var body: some Scene {
        WindowGroup {
            ContentView()
        }
        .onChange(of: scenePhase) { phase in
                INPreferences.requestSiriAuthorization({status in
                // Handle errors here
            })
        }
    }
}
```

Before proceeding, compile and run the app on an iOS device or simulator. When the app loads, a dialog will appear requesting authorization to use Siri. Select the OK button in the dialog to provide authorization.

55.7 Adding the Intents Extension

To add shortcut support, an intents extension will be needed for the Siri shortcuts associated with this app. Select the *File -> New -> Target...* menu option, followed by the Intents Extension option and click on the Next button. On the options screen, enter *ShortcutDemoIntent* into the product name field, change the Starting Point to *None* and make sure that the *Include UI Extension* option is enabled before clicking on the Finish button:

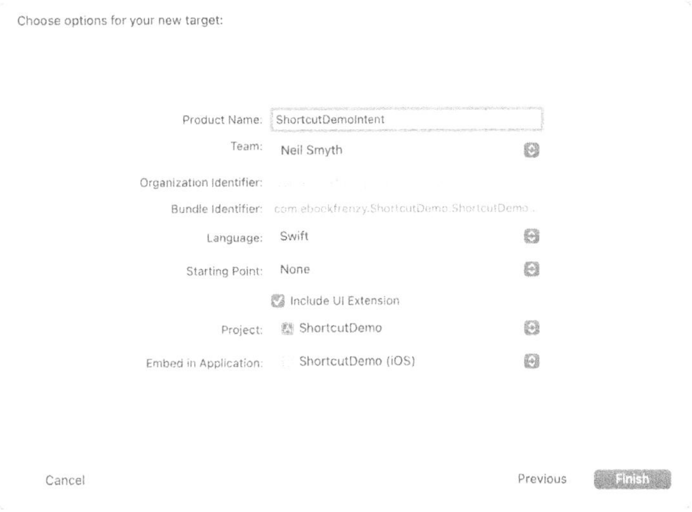

Figure 55-7

If prompted to do so, activate the ShortcutDemoIntent target scheme.

55.8 Adding the SiriKit Intent Definition File

Now that the intent extension has been added to the project, the SiriKit Intent Definition file needs to be added so that the intent can be configured. Right-click on the ShortcutDemo folder in the project navigator panel and select *New File…* from the menu. In the template selection dialog scroll down to the *Resource* section and select the *SiriKit Intent Definition File* template followed by the Next button:

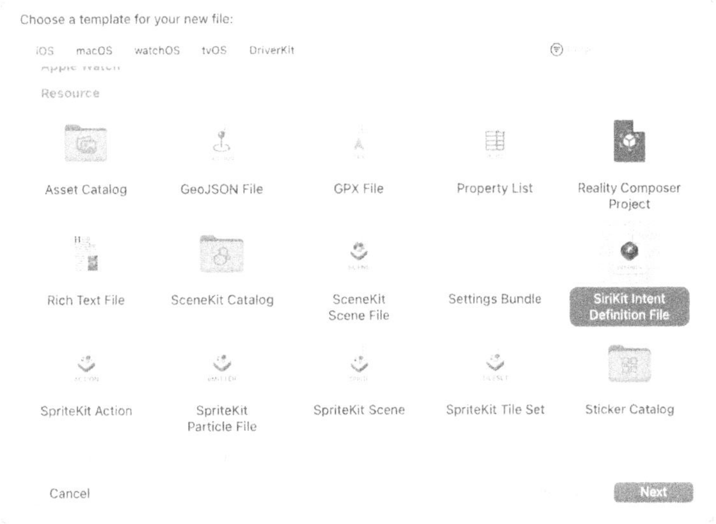

Figure 55-8

Keep the default name of *Intents* in the Save As: field, but make sure that the file is available to all of the targets in the project by enabling all of the options in the Targets section of the dialog before clicking on the Create button:

Figure 55-9

55.9 Adding the Intent to the App Group

The purchase history data will be shared between the main app and the intent using app storage. This requires that the App Group capability be added to the ShortcutDemoIntent target and enabled for the same container name as that used by the ShortcutDemo target. To achieve this, select the ShortcutDemo item at the top of the project navigator panel, switch to the *Signing & Capabilities* panel, select the ShortcutDemoIntent entry in the list of targets and add the App Group capability. Once added, make sure that the App Group name used by the ShortcutDemo target is selected:

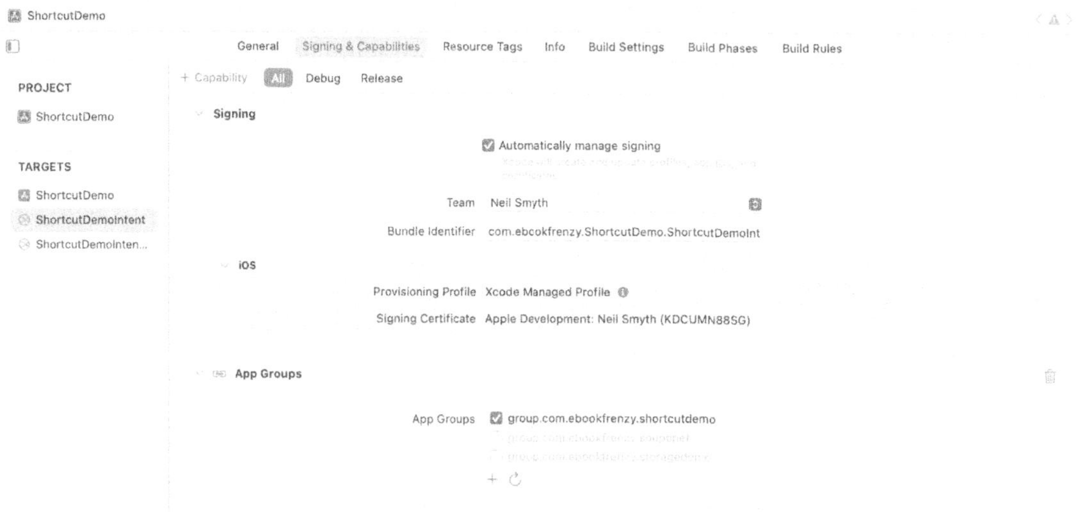

Figure 55-10

55.10 Configuring the SiriKit Intent Definition File

Locate the *Intents.intentdefinition* file (listed as Intents in the project navigator) and select it to load it into the editor:

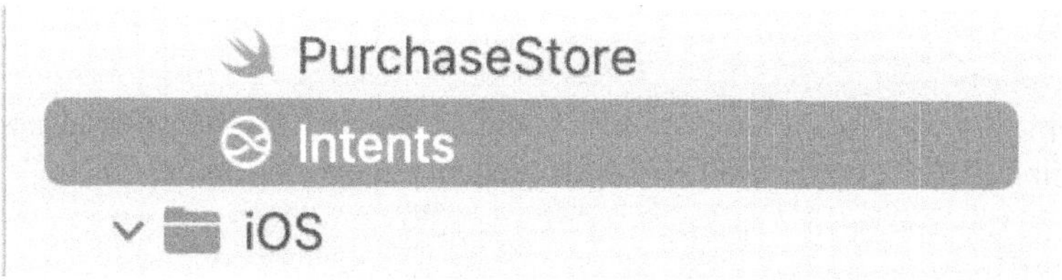

Figure 55-11

The file is currently empty, so add a new intent by clicking on the '+' button in the lower left-hand corner of the editor panel and selecting the *New Intent* menu option:

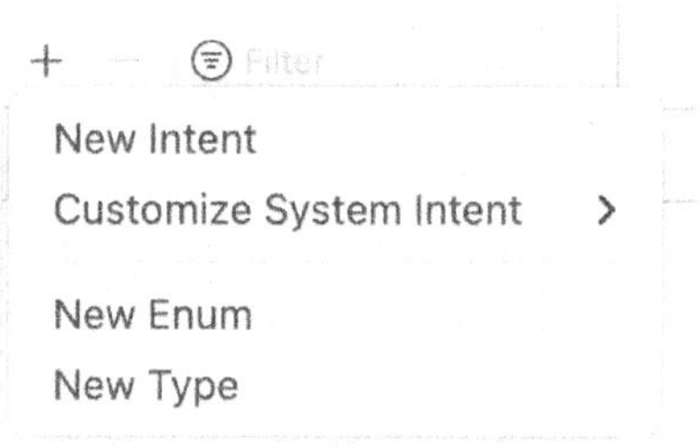

Figure 55-12

In the Custom Intents panel, rename the new intent to *BuyStock* as shown in Figure 55-13:

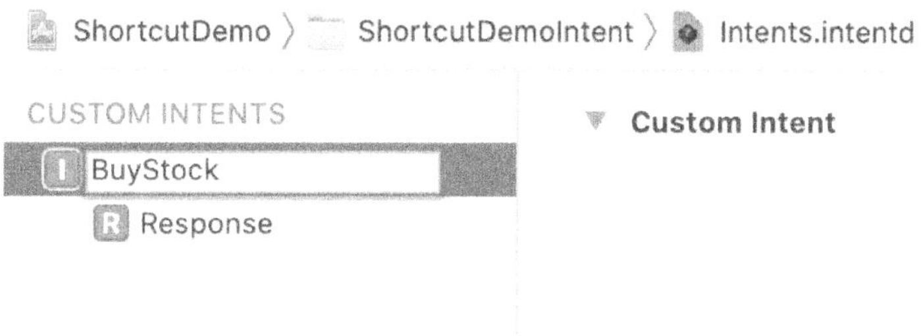

Figure 55-13

Next, change the Category setting in the Custom Intent section of the editor from "Do" to "Buy", enter "ShortcutDemo" and "Buy stocks and shares" into the *Title* and *Description* fields respectively, and enable both the *Configurable in Shortcuts* and *Siri Suggestions* options. Since this is a buy category intent, the *User confirmation required* option is enabled by default and cannot be disabled:

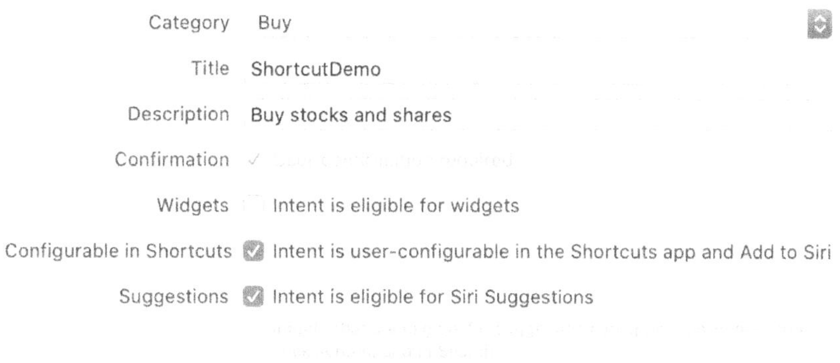

Figure 55-14

55.11 Adding Intent Parameters

In order to complete a purchase, the intent is going to need two parameters in the form of the stock symbol and quantity. Remaining within the Intent Definition editor, use the '+' button located beneath the Parameters section to add a parameter named *symbol* with the type set to *String*, the display name set to "Symbol", and both the Configurable and Resolvable options enabled. Within the Siri Dialog section, enter "Specify a stock symbol" into the Prompt field:

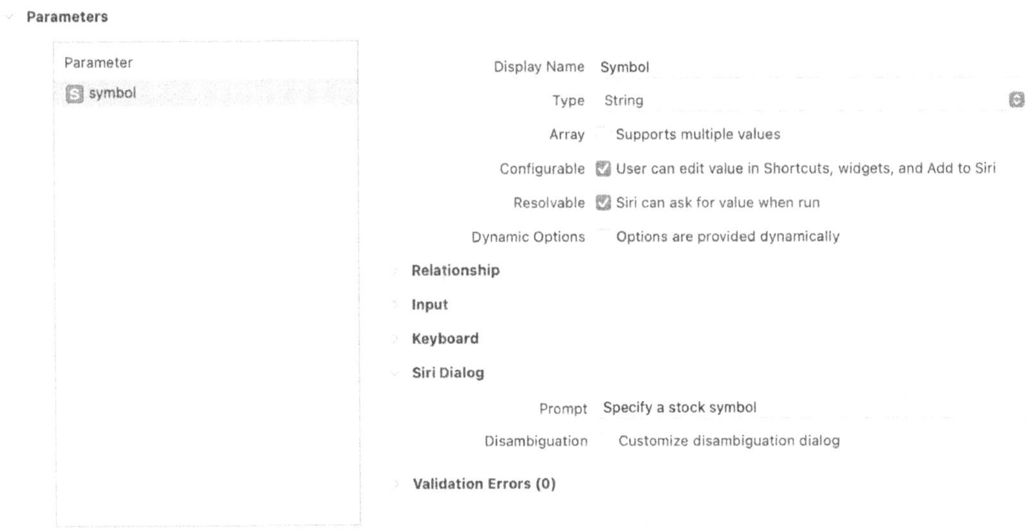

Figure 55-15

Repeat the above steps to add a *quantity* parameter to the intent, setting the prompt to "Specify a quantity to purchase".

55.12 Declaring Shortcut Combinations

A shortcut intent can be configured to handle different combinations of intent parameters. Each unique combination of parameters defines a *shortcut combination*. For each combination, the intent needs to know the phrase that Siri will speak when interacting with the user which can contain embedded parameters. These need to be configured both for shortcut suggestions and for use within the Shortcuts apps so that the shortcuts can be selected manually by the user. For this example, the only combination required involves both the symbol and quantity which will have been added automatically within the *Supported Combinations* panel of the *Shortcuts app* section of the intents configuration editor screen.

Within the Supported Combinations panel, select the symbol, quantity parameter combination and begin typing into the Summary field. Type the word "Buy" followed by the first few letters of the word "quantity". Xcode will notice that this could be a reference to the quantity parameter name and suggests it as an option to embed the parameter into the phrase as shown in Figure 55-16:

Figure 55-16

Select the parameter from the suggestion to embed it into the phrase, then continue typing so that the message reads "Buy quantity shares of symbol" where "symbol" is also an embedded parameter:

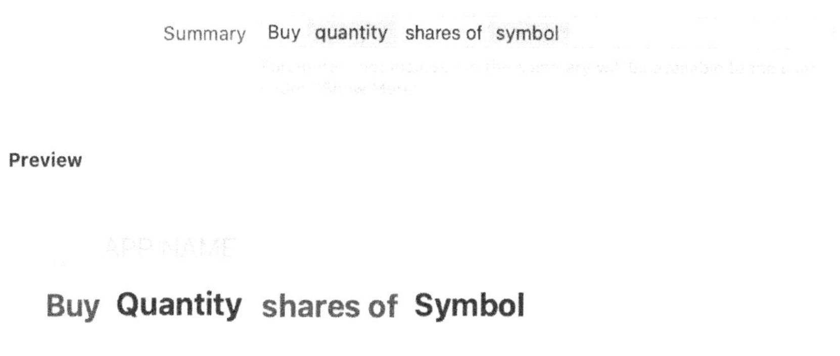

Figure 55-17

These combination settings will have been automatically duplicated under the Suggestions heading. The *Supports background execution* for suggestions defines whether or not the app can handle the shortcut type in the background without having to be presented to the user for additional input. Make sure this option is enabled for this shortcut combination.

55.13 Configuring the Intent Response

The final area to be addressed within the Intent Definition file is the response handling. To view these settings, select the *Response* entry located beneath the *BuyStock* intent in the Custom Intents panel:

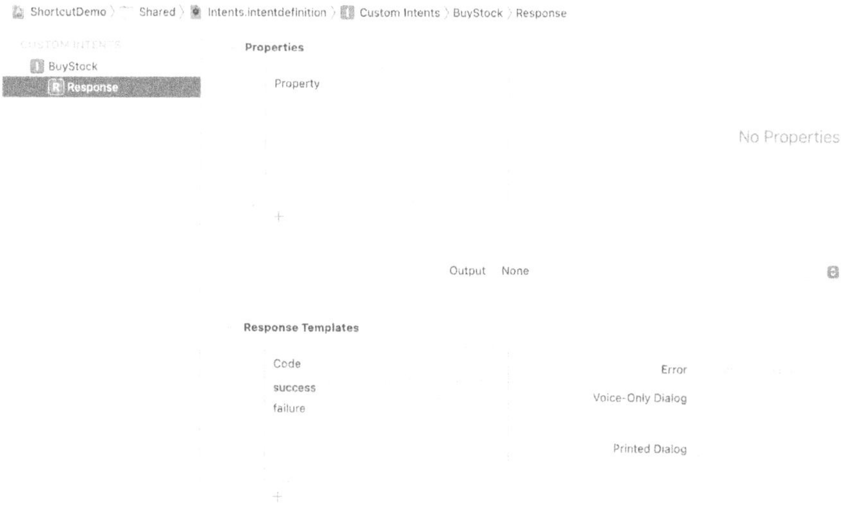

Figure 55-18

The first task is to declare the properties that will be included in the response phrases. As with the intent configuration, add both the symbol and quantity parameters configured as Strings.

Next, select the *success* entry in the response templates code list:

Figure 55-19

Enter the following message into the Voice-Only Dialog field (making sure to insert the parameters for the symbol and quantity using the same technique used above the combination summary settings):

```
Successfully purchased quantity symbol shares
```

Repeat this step to add the following template text to the failure code:

```
Sorry, could not purchase quantity shares of symbol
```

Behind the scenes, Xcode will take the information provided within the Intent Definition file and automatically generate new classes named BuyStockIntentHandling, BuyStockIntent and BuyStockIntentResponse, all of which will be used in the intent handling code. To make sure these files are generated before editing the code, select the *Product -> Clean Builder Folder* menu option followed by *Product -> Build.*

55.14 Configuring Target Membership

Many of the classes and targets in the project are interdependent and need to be accessible to each other during both compilation and execution. To allow this access, a number of classes and files within the project need specific target membership settings. While some of these settings will have set up correctly by default, others may need to be set up manually before testing the app. Begin by selecting the *IntentHandler.swift* file (located in the ShortcutDemoIntent folder) in the project navigator panel and display the File Inspector (*View -> Inspectors -> File*). In the file inspector panel, locate the Target Membership section and make sure that all targets are enabled as shown in Figure 55-20:

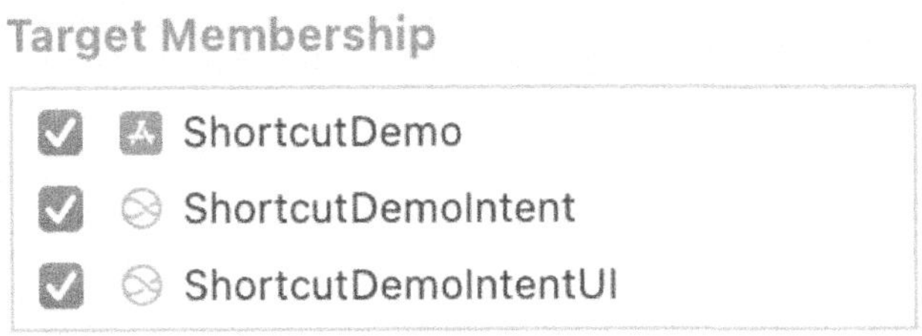

Figure 55-20

Repeat these steps for the *Purchase.swift*, *PurchaseData.swift* and *PurchaseStore.swift* files located in the Shared folder.

55.15 Modifying the Intent Handler Code

Now that the intent definition is complete and the classes have been auto-generated by Xcode, the intent handler needs to be modified to implement the BuyStockIntentHandling protocol.

Edit the *IntentHandler.swift* file and make the following changes:

```
import Intents
```

```
class IntentHandler: INExtension, BuyStockIntentHandling {

    override func handler(for intent: INIntent) -> Any {

        guard intent is BuyStockIntent else {
            fatalError("Unknown intent type: \(intent)")
        }

        return self
    }

    func handle(intent: BuyStockIntent,
        completion: @escaping (BuyStockIntentResponse) -> Void) {

    }
}
```

The *handler()* method simply checks that the intent type is recognized and, if so, returns itself as the intent handler.

Next, add the resolution methods for the two supported parameters:

```
.
.
    func resolveSymbol(for intent: BuyStockIntent, with completion: @escaping 
(INStringResolutionResult) -> Void) {

        if let symbol = intent.symbol {
            completion(INStringResolutionResult.success(with: symbol))
        } else {
            completion(INStringResolutionResult.needsValue())
        }
    }

    func resolveQuantity(for intent: BuyStockIntent, with completion: @escaping 
(INStringResolutionResult) -> Void) {
        if let quantity = intent.quantity {
            completion(INStringResolutionResult.success(with: quantity))
        } else {
            completion(INStringResolutionResult.needsValue())
        }
    }
.
.
```

Code now needs to be added to the *handle()* method to perform the stock purchase. Since this will need access to the user defaults app storage, begin by making the following changes (replacing the placeholder text with your app group name):

```
import Intents
import SwiftUI

class IntentHandler: INExtension, BuyStockIntentHandling {

    @AppStorage("demostorage", store: UserDefaults(
      suiteName: "YOUR APP GROUP NAME HERE"))
    var store: Data = Data()
    var purchaseData = PurchaseData()
.
.
```

Before modifying the *handle()* method, add the following method to the *IntentHandler.swift* file which will be called to save the latest purchase to the app storage:

```
func makePurchase(symbol: String, quantity: String) -> Bool {

    var result: Bool = false
    let decoder = JSONDecoder()

    if let history = try? decoder.decode(PurchaseData.self,
                                              from: store) {
        purchaseData = history
        result = purchaseData.saveTransaction(symbol: symbol,
                                         quantity: quantity)
    }
    return result
}
```

The above method uses a JSON decoder to decode the data contained within the app storage (for a reminder about encoding and decoding app storage data, refer to the chapter entitled *"SwiftUI Data Persistence using AppStorage and SceneStorage"*). The result of this decoding is a PurchaseData instance, the *saveTransaction()* method of which is called to save the current purchase.

Next, modify the *handle()* method as follows:

```
func handle(intent: BuyStockIntent,
   completion: @escaping (BuyStockIntentResponse) -> Void) {

    guard let symbol = intent.symbol,
          let quantity = intent.quantity
       else {
          completion(BuyStockIntentResponse(code: .failure,
                 userActivity: nil))
          return
    }

    let result = makePurchase(symbol: symbol, quantity: quantity)
```

```
    if result {
        completion(BuyStockIntentResponse.success(quantity: quantity,
                                 symbol: symbol))
    } else {
        completion(BuyStockIntentResponse.failure(quantity: quantity,
                                 symbol: symbol))
    }
}
```

When called, the method is passed a BuyStockIntent intent instance and completion handler to be called when the purchase is completed. The method begins by extracting the symbol and quantity parameter values from the intent object:

```
guard let symbol = intent.symbol,
      let quantity = intent.quantity
   else {
      completion(BuyStockIntentResponse(code: .failure,
                   userActivity: nil))
      return
}
```

These values are then passed through to the *makePurchase()* method to perform the purchase transaction. Finally, the result returned by the *makePurchase()* method is used to select the appropriate response to be passed to the completion handler. In each case, the appropriate parameters are passed to the completion handler for inclusion in the response template:

```
let result = makePurchase(symbol: symbol, quantity: quantity)

if result {
    completion(BuyStockIntentResponse.success(quantity: quantity,
                            symbol: symbol))
} else {
    completion(BuyStockIntentResponse.failure(quantity: quantity,
                            symbol: symbol))
}
```

55.16 Adding the Confirm Method

To fully conform with the BuyStockIntentHandling protocol, the IntentHandler class also needs to contain a *confirm()* method. As outlined in the SiriKit introductory chapter, this method is called by Siri to check that the handler is ready to handle the intent. All that is needed for this example is for the *confirm()* method to provide Siri with a ready status as follows:

```
public func confirm(intent: BuyStockIntent,
    completion: @escaping (BuyStockIntentResponse) -> Void) {

    completion(BuyStockIntentResponse(code: .ready, userActivity: nil))
}
```

55.17 Donating Shortcuts to Siri

Each time the user successfully completes a stock purchase within the main app the action needs to be donated to Siri as a potential shortcut. The code to make these donations should now be added to the *PurchaseView.swift* file in a method named *makeDonation()*, which also requires that the Intents framework be imported:

```
import SwiftUI
import Intents

struct PurchaseView: View {
.
.
        .onAppear() {
            purchaseData.refresh()

        }
    }

    func makeDonation(symbol: String, quantity: String) {
        let intent = BuyStockIntent()

        intent.quantity = quantity
        intent.symbol = symbol
        intent.suggestedInvocationPhrase = "Buy \(quantity) \(symbol)"

        let interaction = INInteraction(intent: intent, response: nil)

        interaction.donate { (error) in
            if error != nil {
                if let error = error as NSError? {
                    print(
                     "Donation failed: %@" + error.localizedDescription)
                }
            } else {
                print("Successfully donated interaction")
            }
        }
    }
.
.
}
```

The method is passed string values representing the stock and quantity of the purchase. A new BuyStockIntent instance is then created and populated with both these values and a suggested activation phrase containing both the quantity and symbol. Next, an INInteraction object is created using the BuyStockIntent instance and the *donate()* method of the object called to make the donation. The success or otherwise of the donation is then output to the console for diagnostic purposes.

The donation will only be made after a successful purchase has been completed, so add the call to *makeDonation()* after the *saveTransaction()* call in the *buyStock()* method:

```
private func buyStock() {
    if (symbol == "" || quantity == "") {
        status = "Please enter a symbol and quantity"
    } else {
        if purchaseData.saveTransaction(symbol: symbol,
                                        quantity: quantity) {
            status = "Purchase completed"
            makeDonation(symbol: symbol, quantity: quantity)
        }
    }
}
```

55.18 Testing the Shortcuts

Before running and testing the app, some settings on the target device or simulator need to be changed in order to be able to fully test the shortcut functionality. To enable these settings, open the Settings app on the device or simulator on which you intend to test the app, select the Developer option and locate and enable the *Display Recent Shortcuts* and *Display Donations on Lock Screen* options as shown in Figure 55-21:

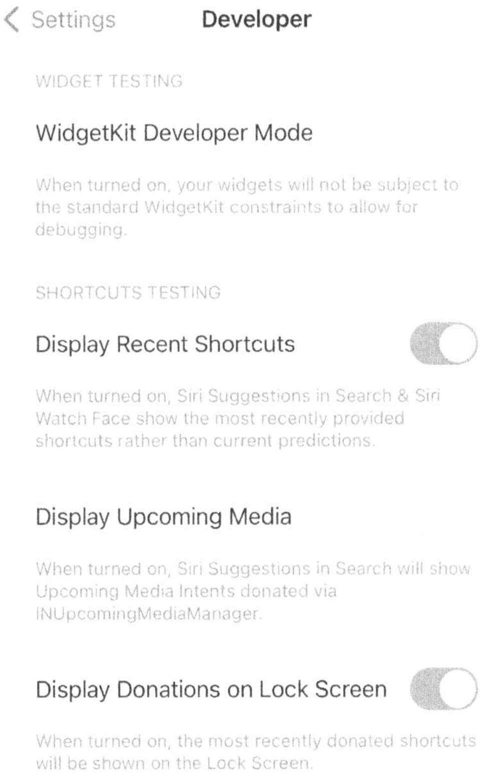

Figure 55-21

These settings will ensure that newly donated shortcuts always appear in Siri search and on the lock screen rather than relying on Siri to predict when the shortcuts should be suggested to the user.

With the settings changed, run the ShortcutDemo app target (it may be necessary to change the run target from ShortcutDemoIntentUI) and make a stock purchase (for example buy 100 IBM shares). After the purchase is complete, check the Xcode console to verify that the "Successfully donated interaction" message appeared.

Next, locate the built-in iOS Shortcuts app on the device home screen as highlighted in Figure 55-22 below and tap to launch it:

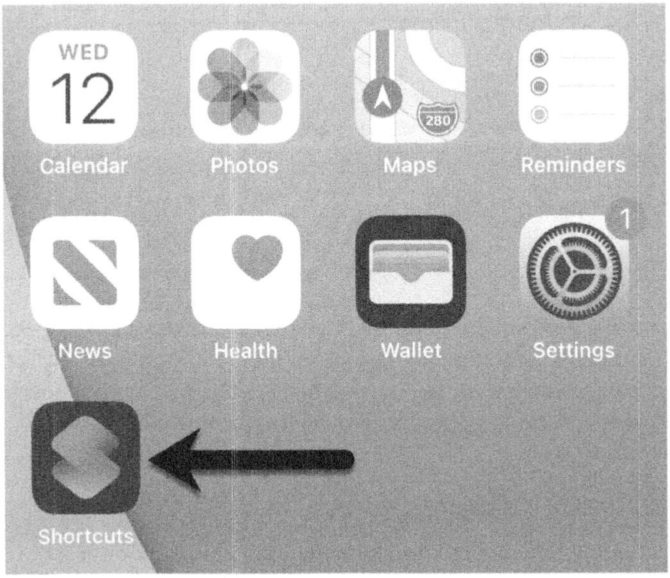

Figure 55-22

Within the Shortcuts app, select the Gallery tab where the donated shortcut should appear as shown in Figure 55-23 below:

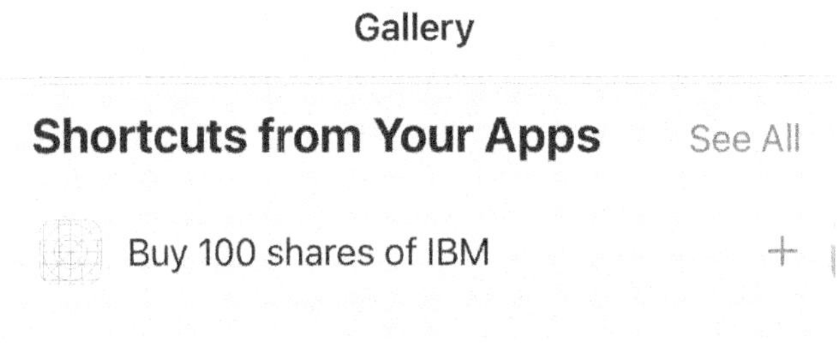

Figure 55-23

Click on the '+' button to the right of the shortcut title to display the Add to Siri screen (Figure 55-24). Note that "Buy 100 IBM" is suggested as configured when the donation was made in the *makeDonation()* method. Change this by clicking on the Change Voice Phrase button and record the following phrase (Siri has difficulty distinguishing between "buy" and "by"):

"Purchase 100 IBM"

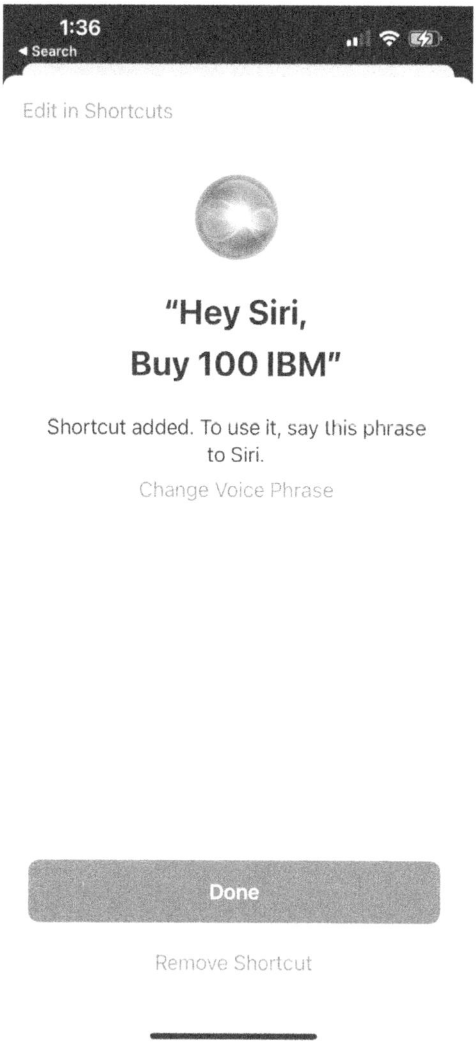

Figure 55-24

Select the My Shortcuts tab and verify that the new shortcut has been added:

Figure 55-25

Press and hold the Home button to launch Siri and speak the shortcut phrase. Siri will seek confirmation that the purchase is to be made:

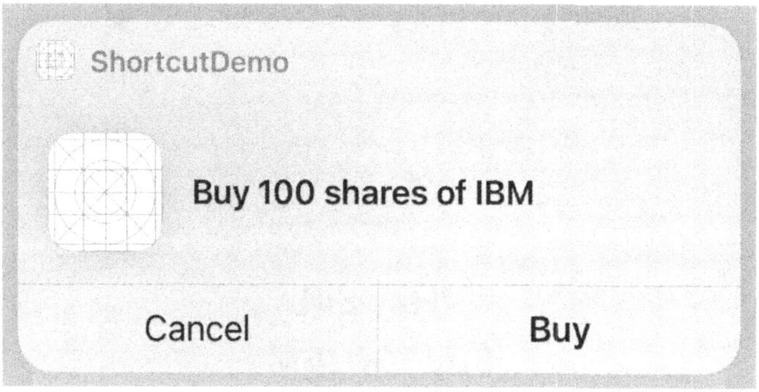

Figure 55-26

After completing the purchase, Siri will use the success response template declared in the Intent Definition file to confirm that the transaction was successful:

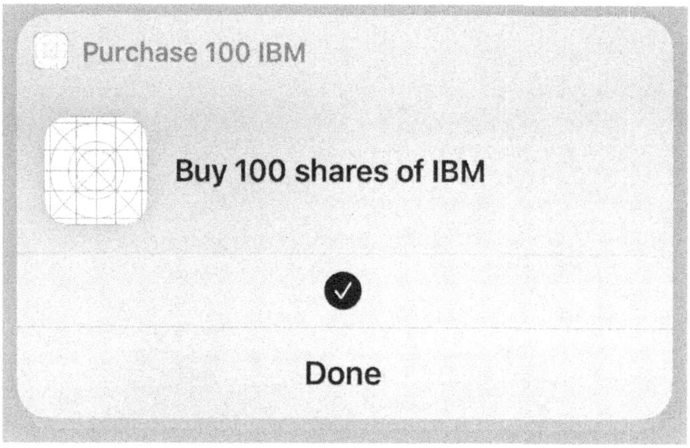

Figure 55-27

After making a purchase using the shortcut, open the ShortcutDemo app and verify that the transaction appears in the transaction history.

55.19 Summary

This chapter has provided a practical demonstration of how to integrate Siri shortcut support into a SwiftUI app. This included the creation and configuration of an Intent Definition file, the addition of a custom intent extension and the implementation of intent handling code.

Chapter 56

56. Building Widgets with SwiftUI and WidgetKit

Widgets allow small amounts of app content to be displayed alongside the app icons that appear on the device home screen pages, the Today view, and the macOS Notification Center. Widgets are built using SwiftUI in conjunction with the WidgetKit Framework.

The focus of this chapter is to provide a high-level outline of the various components that make up a widget before exploring widget creation in practical terms in the chapters that follow.

56.1 An Overview of Widgets

Widgets are intended to provide users with "at a glance" views of important, time-sensitive information relating to your app. When a widget is tapped by the user, the corresponding app is launched, taking the user to a specific screen where more detailed information may be presented. Widgets are intended to display information that updates based on a timeline, ensuring that only the latest information is displayed to the user. A single app can have multiple widgets displaying different information.

Widgets are available in three *size families* (small, medium, and large), of which at least one size must be supported by the widget, and can be implemented such that the information displayed is customizable by the user.

Widgets are selected from the widget gallery and positioned by the user on the device home screens. To conserve screen space, iOS allows widgets to be stacked, providing the user the ability to flip through each widget in the stack with a swiping gesture. A widget can increase the probability of moving automatically to the top of the stack by assigning a relevancy score to specific timeline entries. The widget for a weather app might, for example, assign high relevancy to a severe weather warning in the hope that WidgetKit will move it to the top of the stack, thereby increasing the likelihood that the user will see the information.

56.2 The Widget Extension

A widget is created by adding a *widget extension* to an existing app. A widget extension consists of a Swift file, an optional *intent definition* file (required if the widget is to be user configurable), an asset catalog, and an *Info.plist* file.

The widget itself is declared as a structure conforming to the Widget protocol, and it is within this declaration that the basic configuration of the widget is declared. The body of a typical widget declaration will include the following items:

- **Widget kind** – Identifies the widget within the project. This can be any String value that uniquely identifies the widget within the project.
- **Widget Configuration** – A declaration that conforms to the WidgetConfiguration protocol. This includes a reference to the *provider* of the timeline containing the information to be displayed, the widget display name and description, and the size families supported by the widget. WidgetKit supports two types of widget configuration referred to as *static configuration* and *intent configuration*.
- **Entry View** – A reference to the SwiftUI View containing the layout that is to be presented to the user when

the widget is displayed. This layout is populated with content from individual *timeline entries* at specific points in the *widget timeline*.

In addition to the widget declaration, the extension must also include a placeholder View defining the layout to be displayed to the user while the widget is loading and gathering data. This may either be declared manually, or configured to be generated automatically by WidgetKit based on the entry view included in the Widget view declaration outlined above.

56.3 Widget Configuration Types

When creating a widget, the choice needs to be made as to whether it should be created using the static or intent configuration model. These two options can be summarized as follows:

- **Intent Configuration** – Used when it makes sense for the user to be able to configure aspects of the widget. For example, allowing the user to select the news publications from which headlines are to be displayed within the widget.

- **Static Configuration** – Used when the widget does not have any user configurable properties.

When the Intent Configuration option is used, the configuration options to be presented to the user are declared within a SiriKit intent definition file.

The following is an example widget entry containing a static configuration designed to support both small and medium size families:

```
@main
struct SimpleWidget: Widget {
    private let kind: String = "SimpleWidget"

    public var body: some WidgetConfiguration {
        StaticConfiguration(kind: kind, provider: Provider(),
                 placeholder: PlaceholderView()) { entry in
            SimpleWidgetEntryView(entry: entry)
        }
        .configurationDisplayName("A Simple Weather Widget")
        .description("This is an example widget.")
        .supportedFamilies([.systemSmall, .systemMedium])
    }
}
```

The following listing, on the other hand, declares a widget using the intent configuration:

```
@main
struct SimpleWidget: Widget {
    private let kind: String = "SimpleWidget"

    public var body: some WidgetConfiguration {
        IntentConfiguration(kind: kind,
             intent: LocationSelectionIntent.self, provider: Provider(),
               placeholder: PlaceholderView()) { entry in
            SimpleWidgetEntryView(entry: entry)
        }
```

```
        .configurationDisplayName("Weather Fun")
        .description("Learning about weather in real-time.")
    }
}
```

The primary difference in the above declaration is that it uses IntentConfiguration instead of StaticConfiguration which, in turn, includes a reference to a SiriKit intent definition. The absence of the supported families modifier in the above example indicates to WidgetKit that the widget supports all three sizes. Both examples include a widget entry view.

56.4 Widget Entry View

The widget entry view is simply a SwiftUI View declaration containing the layout to be displayed by the widget. Conditional logic (for example *if* or *switch* statements based on the *widgetFamily* environment property) can be used to present different layouts subject to the prevailing size family.

Except for tapping to open the corresponding app, widgets are non-interactive. As such, the entry view will typically consist of display-only views (in other words no buttons, sliders, or toggles).

When WidgetKit creates an instance of the entry view, it passes it a *widget timeline entry* containing the data to be displayed on the views that make up the layout. The following view declaration is designed to display city name and temperature values:

```
struct SimpleWidgetEntryView : View {
    var entry: Provider.Entry

    var body: some View {
        VStack {
            Text("City: \(entry.city)")
            Text("Temperature: \(entry.temperature)")
        }
    }
}
```

56.5 Widget Timeline Entries

The purpose of a widget is to display different information at specific points in time. The widget for a calendar app, for example, might change throughout the day to display the user's next upcoming appointment. The content to be displayed at each point in the timeline is contained within *widget entry* objects conforming to the TimelineEntry protocol. Each entry must, at a minimum, include a Date object defining the point in the timeline at which the data in the entry is to be displayed, together with any data that is needed to fully populate the widget entry view at the specified time. The following is an example of a timeline entry declaration designed for use with the above entry view:

```
struct WeatherEntry: TimelineEntry {
    var date: Date
    let city: String
    let temperature: Int
}
```

If necessary, the Date object can simply be a placeholder to be updated with the actual time and date when the entry is added to a timeline.

56.6 Widget Timeline

The widget timeline is simply an array of widget entries that defines the points in time that the widget is to be updated, together with the content to be displayed at each time point. Timelines are constructed and returned to WidgetKit by a *widget provider*.

56.7 Widget Provider

The widget provider is responsible for providing the content that is to be displayed on the widget and must be implemented to conform to the TimelineProvider protocol. At a minimum, it must implement the following methods:

- **getSnapshot()** – The *getSnapshot()* method of the provider will be called by WidgetKit when a single, populated widget timeline entry is required. This snapshot is used within the widget gallery to show an example of how the widget would appear if the user added it to the device. Since real data may not be available at the point that the user is browsing the widget gallery, the entry returned should typically be populated with sample data.

- **getTimeline()** - This method is responsible for assembling and returning a Timeline instance containing the array of widget timeline entries that define how and when the widget content is to be updated together with an optional *reload policy* value.

The following code excerpt declares an example timeline provider:

```
struct Provider: TimelineProvider {
    public typealias Entry = SimpleEntry

    public func getSnapshot(with context: Context,
              completion: @escaping (SimpleEntry) -> ()) {

        // Construct a single entry using sample content
        let entry = SimpleEntry(date: Date(), city: "London",
                                 temperature: 89)
        completion(entry)
    }

    public func getTimeline(with context: Context,
                  completion: @escaping (Timeline<Entry>) -> ()) {
        var entries: [SimpleEntry] = []

        // Construct timeline array here

        let timeline = Timeline(entries: entries, policy: .atEnd)
        completion(timeline)
    }
}
```

56.8 Reload Policy

When a widget is displaying entries from a timeline, WidgetKit needs to know what action to take when it reaches the end of the timeline. The following predefined reload policy options are available for use when the provider returns a timeline:

- **atEnd** – At the end of the current timeline, WidgetKit will request a new timeline from the provider. This is the default behavior if no reload policy is specified.
- **after(Date)** – WidgetKit will request a new timeline after the specified date and time.
- **never** – The timeline is not reloaded at the end of the timeline.

56.9 Relevance

As previously mentioned, iOS allows widgets to be placed in a stack in which only the uppermost widget is visible. While the user can scroll through the stacked widgets to decide which is to occupy the topmost position, this presents the risk that an important update may not be seen by the user in time to act on the information.

To address this issue, WidgetKit is allowed to move a widget to the top of the stack if the information it contains is considered to be of relevance to the user. This decision is based on a variety of factors such as previous behavior of the user (for example checking a bus schedule widget at the same time every day) together with a relevance score assigned by the widget to a particular timeline entry.

Relevance is declared using a TimelineEntryRelevance structure. This contains a relevancy score and a time duration for which the entry is relevant. The score can be any floating point value and is measured relative to all other timeline entries generated by the widget. For example, if most of the relevancy scores in the timeline entries range between 0.0 and 10.0, a relevancy score of 20.0 assigned to an entry may cause the widget to move to the top of the stack. The following code declares two relevancy entries:

```
let lowScore = TimelineEntryRelevance(score: 0.0, duration: 0)
let highScore = TimelineEntryRelevance(score: 10.0, duration: 0)
```

If relevancy is to be included in an entry, it must appear after the date entry, for example:

```
struct WeatherEntry: TimelineEntry {
    var date: Date
    var relevance: TimelineEntryRelevance?
    let city: String
    let temperature: Int
}
.
.
let entry1 = WeatherEntry(date: Date(), relevance: lowScore, city: "London", 
temperature: 87)

let entry2 = WeatherEntry(date: Date(), relevance: highScore, city: "London", 
temperature: 87)
```

56.10 Forcing a Timeline Reload

When a widget is launched, WidgetKit requests a timeline containing the timepoints and content to display to the user. Under normal conditions, WidgetKit will not request another timeline update until the end of the timeline is reached, and then only if required by the reload policy.

Situations may commonly arise, however, where the information in a timeline needs to be updated. A user might, for example, add a new appointment to a calendar app that requires a timeline update. Fortunately, the widget can be forced to request an updated timeline by making a call to the *reloadTimelines()* method of the WidgetKit WidgetCenter instance, passing through the widget's *kind* string value (defined in the widget configuration as outlined earlier in the chapter). For example:

```
WidgetCenter.shared.reloadTimelines(ofKind: "My Kind")
```

Alternatively, it is also possible to trigger a timeline reload for all the active widgets associated with an app as follows:

```
WidgetCenter.shared.reloadAllTimelines()
```

56.11 Widget Sizes

As previously discussed, widgets can be displayed in small, medium, and large sizes. The widget declares which sizes it supports by applying the *supportedFamilies()* modifier to the widget configuration as follows:

```
@main
struct SimpleWidget: Widget {
    private let kind: String = "SimpleWidget"

    public var body: some WidgetConfiguration {
        IntentConfiguration(kind: kind,
             intent: LocationSelectionIntent.self, provider: Provider(),
               placeholder: PlaceholderView()) { entry in
            SimpleWidgetEntryView(entry: entry)
        }
        .configurationDisplayName("Weather Fun")
        .description("Learning about weather in real-time.")
        .supportedFamilies([.systemSmall, .systemMedium])
    }
}
```

The following figure shows the built-in iOS Calendar widget in small, medium, and large formats:

Figure 56-1

56.12 Widget Placeholder

As previously mentioned, the widget extension must provide a placeholder. This is the view that is displayed to the user while the widget is initializing and takes the form of the widget entry view without any data or information. Consider the following example widget:

Figure 56-2

The above example, of course, shows the widget running after it has received timeline data to be displayed. During initialization, however, the placeholder view resembling Figure 56-3 would be expected to be displayed:

Figure 56-3

Fortunately, SwiftUI includes the *redacted(reason:)* modifier which may be applied to an instance of the widget entry view to act as a placeholder. The following is an example of a placeholder view declaration for a widget extension using the *redacted()* modifier (note that the reason is set to *placeholder*):

```
struct PlaceholderView : View {
    var body: some View {
        SimpleWidgetEntryView()
            .redacted(reason: .placeholder)
    }
}
```

56.13 Summary

Widgets allow apps to present important information to the user directly on the device home screen without the need to launch the app. Widgets are implemented using the WidgetKit Framework and take the form of extensions added to the main app. Widgets are driven by timelines which control the information to be displayed to the user and when it is to appear. Widgets can support small, medium, and large formats and may be designed to be configurable by the user. When adding widgets to the home screen, the user has the option to place them into a stack. By adjusting the relevance of a timeline entry, a widget can increase the chances of being moved to the top of the stack.

Chapter 57

57. A SwiftUI WidgetKit Tutorial

From the previous chapter we now understand the elements that make up a widget and the steps involved in creating one. In this, the first of a series of tutorial chapters dedicated to WidgetKit, we will begin the process of creating an app which includes a widget extension. On completion of these tutorials, a functioning widget will have been created, including widget design and the use of timelines, support for different size families, deep links, configuration using intents and basic intelligence using SiriKit donations and relevance.

57.1 About the WidgetDemo Project

The project created in this tutorial can be thought of as the early prototype of a weather app designed to teach children about weather storms. The objective is to provide the user with a list of severe weather systems (tropical storms, thunderstorms etc.) and, when a storm type is selected, display a second screen providing a description of the weather system.

A second part of the app is intended to provide real-time updates on severe weather occurring in different locations around the world. When a storm is reported, a widget will be updated with information about the type and location of the storm, together with the prevailing temperature. When the widget is tapped by the user, the app will open the screen containing information about that storm category.

Since this app is an early prototype, however, it will only provide weather updates from two cities, and that data will be simulated rather than obtained from a real weather service. The app will be functional enough, however, to demonstrate how to implement the key features of WidgetKit.

57.2 Creating the WidgetDemo Project

Launch Xcode and select the option to create a new Multiplatform App project named *WidgetDemo*.

57.3 Building the App

Before adding the widget extension to the project, the first step is to build the basic structure of the app. This will consist of a List view populated with some storm categories which, when selected, will appear in a detail screen.

The detail screen will be declared in a new SwiftUI View file named *WeatherDetailView.swift*. Within the project navigator panel, right-click on the WidgetDemo folder and select the *New File...* menu option. In the resulting dialog, select the SwiftUI View template option and click on the Next button. Name the file *WeatherDetailView.swift* before creating the file.

With the *WeatherDetailView.swift* file selected, modify the view declaration so that it reads as follows (we will be declaring the WeatherType struct in the next step):

```
import SwiftUI

struct WeatherDetailView: View {

    var weather: WeatherType

    var body: some View {
        VStack {
```

```
            Image(systemName: weather.icon)
                .resizable()
                    .scaledToFit()
                    .frame(width: 150.0, height: 150.0)
            Text(weather.name)
                .padding()
                .font(.title)
            Text("If this were a real weather app, a description of \(weather.
name) would appear here.")
                .padding()
            Spacer()
        }
    }
}

struct WeatherDetailView_Previews: PreviewProvider {
    static var previews: some View {
        let weather = WeatherType(name: "Thunder Storms", icon: "cloud.bolt")
        WeatherDetailView(weather: weather)
    }
}
```

When rendered, the above view should appear in the preview canvas as shown in Figure 57-1 below:

Figure 57-1

Next, select the *ContentView.swift* file and modify it to add a structure to hold the currently selected weather selection and a List view embedded in a NavigationStack as follows:

```
import SwiftUI

struct WeatherType: Hashable {
    var name: String
    var icon: String
}
```

```
struct ContentView: View {
    var body: some View {

        NavigationStack {
            List {
                NavigationLink(value: WeatherType(name: "Hail Storm",
                                                  icon: "cloud.hail")) {
                    Label("Hail Storm", systemImage: "cloud.hail")
                }

                NavigationLink(value: WeatherType(name: "Thunder Storm",
                                                  icon: "cloud.bolt.rain")) {
                    Label("Thunder Storm", systemImage: "cloud.bolt.rain")
                }

                NavigationLink(value: WeatherType(name: "Tropical Storm",
                                                  icon: "tropicalstorm")) {
                    Label("Tropical Storm", systemImage: "tropicalstorm")
                }

            }
            .navigationDestination(for: WeatherType.self) { weather in
                WeatherDetailView(weather: weather)
            }
            .navigationTitle("Severe Weather")
        }
    }
}
.
.
```

Once the changes are complete, make sure that the layout matches that shown in Figure 57-2:

Figure 57-2

Using Live Preview, make sure that selecting a weather type displays the detail screen populated with the correct storm name and image.

57.4 Adding the Widget Extension

The next step in the project is to add the widget extension by selecting the *File -> New -> Target…* menu option. From within the target template panel, select the Widget Extension option as shown in Figure 57-3 before clicking on the Next button:

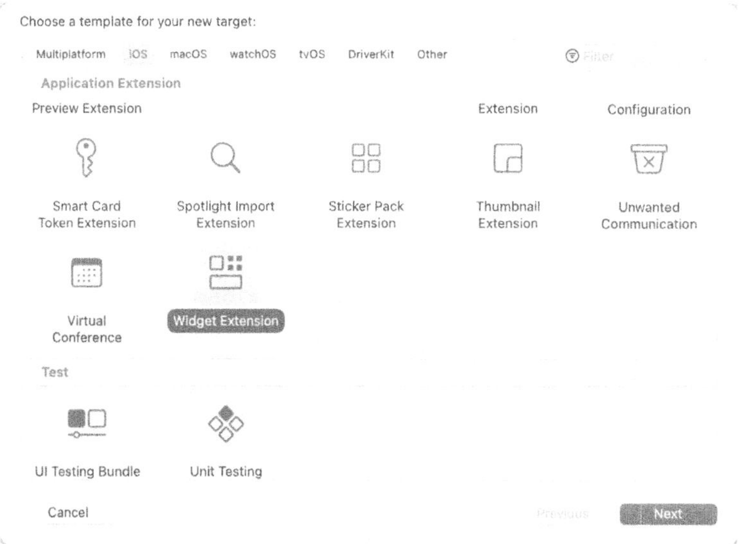

Figure 57-3

On the subsequent screen, enter WeatherWidget into the product name field. When the widget is completed, the user will be able to select the geographical location for which weather updates are to be displayed. To make this possible the widget will need to use the intent configuration type. Before clicking on the Finish button, therefore, make sure that the *Include Configuration Intent* option is selected as shown in Figure 57-4:

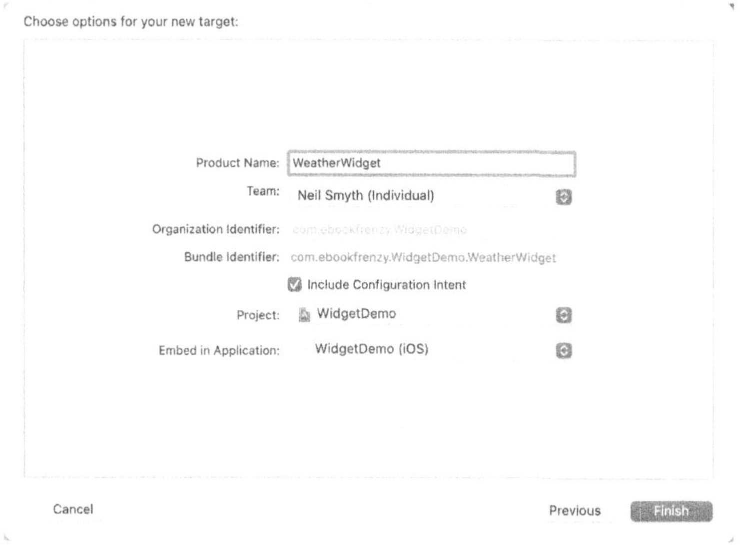

Figure 57-4

When prompted, click on the Activate button to activate the extension within the project scheme. This will ensure that the widget is included in the project build process:

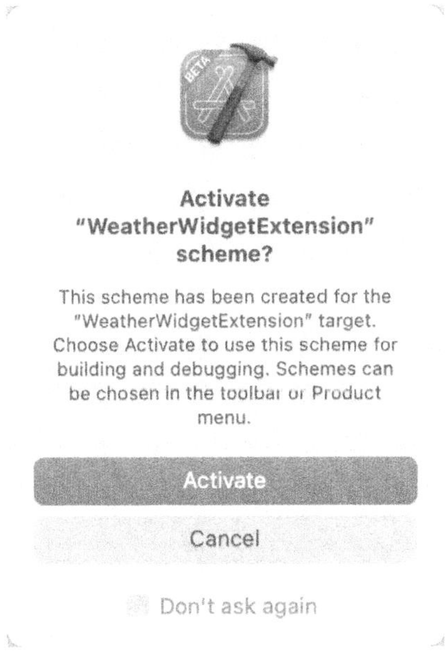

Figure 57-5

Once the extension has been added, refer to the project navigator panel, where a new folder containing the widget extension will have been added as shown in Figure 57-6:

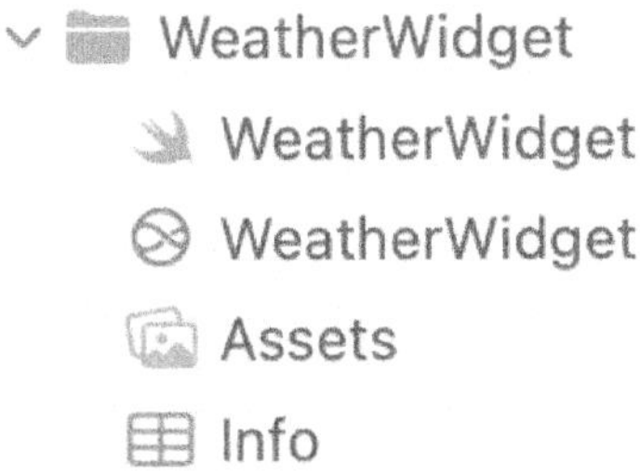

Figure 57-6

57.5 Adding the Widget Data

Now that the widget extension has been added to the project, the next step is to add some data and data structures that will provide the basis for the widget timeline. Begin by right-clicking on the WidgetDemo folder in the project navigator and selecting the *New File...* menu option.

From the template selection panel, select the *Swift File* entry, click on the Next button and name the file *WeatherData.swift*. Before clicking on the Create button, make sure that the WeatherWidgetExtension entry is enabled in the Targets section of the panel as shown in Figure 57-7 so that the file will be accessible to the extension:

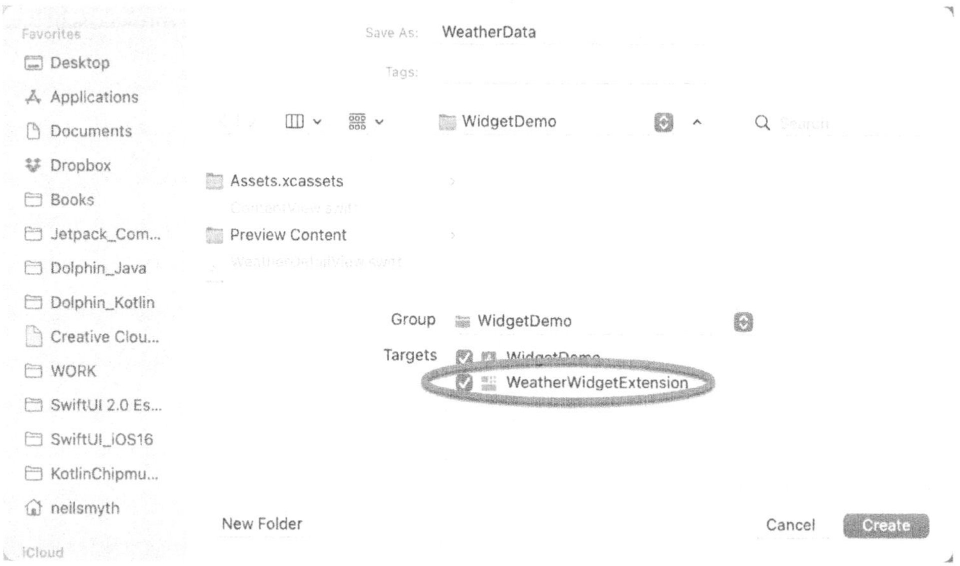

Figure 57-7

As outlined in the previous chapter, each point in the widget timeline is represented by a widget timeline entry instance. Instances of this structure contain the date and time that the entry is to be presented by the widget, together with the data to be displayed. Within the *WeatherData.swift* file, add a TimelineEntry structure as follows (noting that the WidgetKit framework also needs to be imported):

```
import Foundation
import WidgetKit

struct WeatherEntry: TimelineEntry {
    var date: Date
    let city: String
    let temperature: Int
    let description: String
    let icon: String
    let image: String
}
```

57.6 Creating Sample Timelines

Since this prototype app does not have access to live weather data, the timelines used to drive the widget content will contain sample weather entries for two cities. Remaining within the *WeatherData.swift* file, add these timeline declarations as follows:

```
.
.
let londonTimeline = [
    WeatherEntry(date: Date(), city: "London", temperature: 87,
          description: "Hail Storm", icon: "cloud.hail",
                image: "hail"),
    WeatherEntry(date: Date(), city: "London", temperature: 92,
          description: "Thunder Storm", icon: "cloud.bolt.rain",
```

```
                image: "thunder"),
    WeatherEntry(date: Date(), city: "London", temperature: 95,
          description: "Hail Storm", icon: "cloud.hail",
                image: "hail")
]

let miamiTimeline = [
    WeatherEntry(date: Date(), city: "Miami", temperature: 81,
          description: "Thunder Storm", icon: "cloud.bolt.rain",
                image: "thunder"),
    WeatherEntry(date: Date(), city: "Miami", temperature: 74,
          description: "Tropical Storm", icon: "tropicalstorm",
                image: "tropical"),
    WeatherEntry(date: Date(), city: "Miami", temperature: 72,
          description: "Thunder Storm", icon: "cloud.bolt.rain",
                image: "thunder")
]
```

Note that the timeline entries are populated with the current date and time via a call to the Swift *Date()* method. These values will be replaced with more appropriate values by the provider when the timeline is requested by WidgetKit.

57.7 Adding Image and Color Assets

Before moving to the next step of the tutorial, some image and color assets need to be added to the asset catalog of the widget extension.

Begin by selecting the *Assets* item located in the WeatherWidget folder in the project navigator panel as highlighted in Figure 57-8:

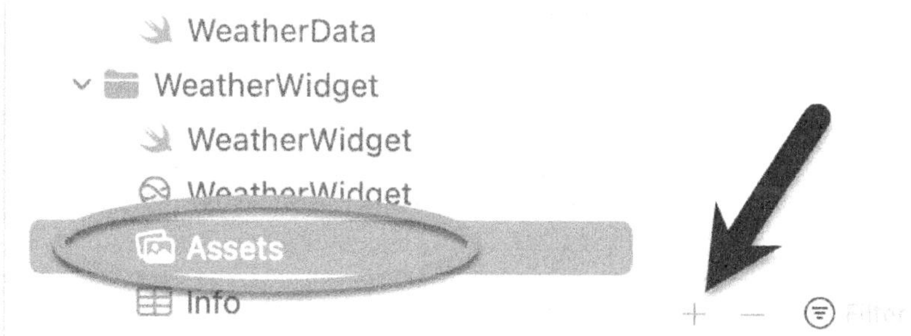

Figure 57-8

Add a new entry to the catalog by clicking on the button indicated by the arrow in Figure 57-8 above. In the resulting menu, select the *Color Set* option. Click on the new Color entry and change the name to weatherBackgroundColor. With this new entry selected, click on the *Any Appearance* block in the main panel as shown in Figure 57-9:

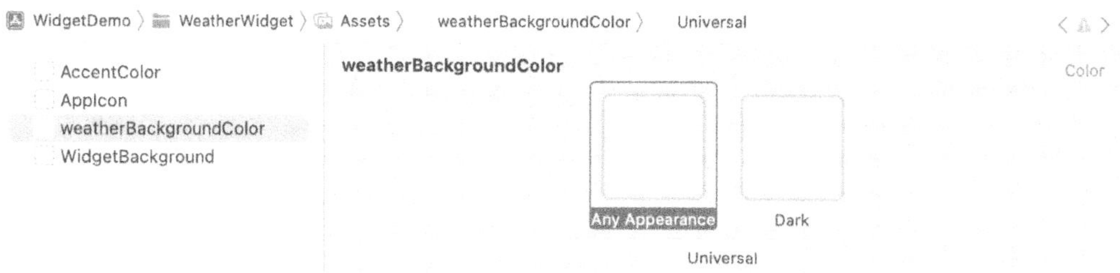

Figure 57-9

Referring to the Color section of the attributes inspector panel, set Content to *Display P3*, Input Method to *8-bit Hexadecimal* and the Hex field to *#4C5057*:

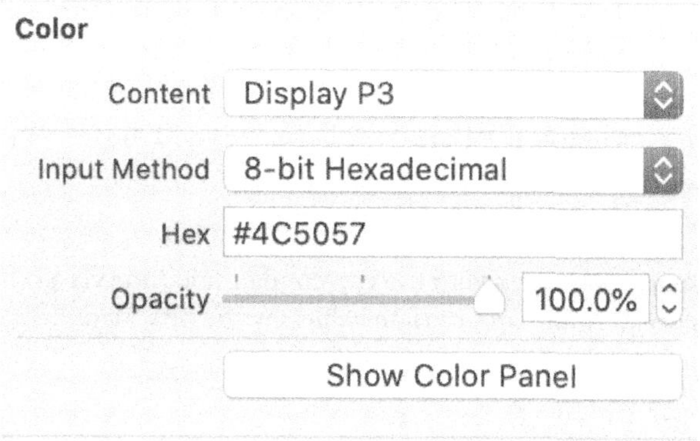

Figure 57-10

Select the Dark Appearance and make the same attribute changes, this time setting the Hex value to *#3A4150.*

Next, add a second Color Set asset, name it weatherInsetColor and use #4E7194 for the Any Appearance color value and *#7E848F* for the Dark Appearance.

The images used by this project can be found in the *weather_images* folder of the sample code download available from the following URL:

https://www.ebookfrenzy.com/retail/swiftui-ios16/

Once the source archive has been downloaded and unpacked, open a Finder window, navigate to the *weather_images* folder and select, drag and drop the images on to the left-hand panel of the Xcode asset catalog screen as shown in Figure 57-11:

Figure 57-11

57.8 Designing the Widget View

Now that the widget entry has been created and used as the basis for some sample timeline data, the widget view needs to be designed. When the widget extension was added to the project, a template widget entry view was included in the *WeatherWidget.swift* file which reads as follows:

```
struct WeatherWidgetEntryView : View {
    var entry: Provider.Entry

    var body: some View {
        Text(entry.date, style: .time)
    }
}
```

As currently implemented, the view is passed a widget entry from which the date value is extracted and displayed on a Text view.

Modify the view structure so that it reads as follows, keeping in mind that it will result in syntax errors appearing in the editor. These will be resolved later in the tutorial:

```
struct WeatherWidgetEntryView: View {
    var entry: Provider.Entry

    var body: some View {
        ZStack {
            Color("weatherBackgroundColor")
            WeatherSubView(entry: entry)
        }
    }
}

struct WeatherSubView: View {

    var entry: WeatherEntry

    var body: some View {

        VStack {
            VStack {
                Text("\(entry.city)")
                    .font(.title)
                Image(systemName: entry.icon)
                    .font(.largeTitle)
                Text("\(entry.description)")
                    .frame(minWidth: 125, minHeight: nil)
            }
            .padding(.bottom, 2)
            .background(ContainerRelativeShape()
                        .fill(Color("weatherInsetColor")))
```

```
                Label("\(entry.temperature)°F", systemImage: "thermometer")
            }
            .foregroundColor(.white)
            .padding()
        }
}
```

Since we have changed the view, the preview provider declaration will also need to be changed as follows:

```
struct WeatherWidget_Previews: PreviewProvider {
    static var previews: some View {

        WeatherWidgetEntryView(entry: WeatherEntry(date: Date(),
                     city: "London", temperature: 89,
              description: "Thunder Storm",
                     icon: "cloud.bolt.rain", image: "thunder"))
            .previewContext(WidgetPreviewContext(family: .systemSmall))
    }
}
```

Once all of the necessary changes have eventually been made to the *WeatherWidget.swift* file, the above preview provider will display a preview canvas configured for the widget small family size.

57.9 Modifying the Widget Provider

When the widget extension was added to the project, Xcode added a widget provider to the *WeatherWidget.swift* file. This declaration now needs to be modified to make use of the WeatherEntry structure declared in the *WeatherData.swift* file. The first step is to modify the *getSnapshot()* method to use WeatherEntry and to return an instance populated with sample data:

```
.
.
struct Provider: IntentTimelineProvider {
    func getSnapshot(for configuration: ConfigurationIntent, with context: Context, 
completion: @escaping (WeatherEntry) -> ()) {

        let entry = WeatherEntry(date: Date(), city: "London",
                    temperature: 89, description: "Thunder Storm",
                         icon: "cloud.bolt.rain", image: "thunder")
        completion(entry)
    }
.
.
```

Next, the *getTimeline()* method needs to be modified to return an array of timeline entry objects together with a reload policy value. Since user configuration has not yet been added to the widget, the *getTimeline()* method will be configured initially to return the timeline for London:

```
struct Provider: IntentTimelineProvider {
.
.
    func getTimeline(for configuration: ConfigurationIntent, with context: Context,
```

```
completion: @escaping (Timeline<Entry>) -> ()) {

        var entries: [WeatherEntry] = []
        var eventDate = Date()
        let halfMinute: TimeInterval = 30

        for var entry in londonTimeline {
            entry.date = eventDate
            eventDate += halfMinute
            entries.append(entry)
        }
        let timeline = Timeline(entries: entries, policy: .never)
        completion(timeline)
    }
}
```

The above code begins by declaring an array to contain the WeatherEntry instances before creating variables designed to represent the current event time and a 30 second time interval respectively.

A loop then iterates through the London timeline declared in the *WeatherData.swift* file, setting the eventDate value as the date and time at which the event is to be displayed by the widget. A 30 second interval is then added to the eventDate ready for the next event. Finally, the modified event is appended to the entries array. Once all of the events have been added to the array, it is used to create a Timeline instance with a reload policy of *never* (in other words WidgetKit will not ask for a new timeline when the first timeline ends). The timeline is then returned to WidgetKit via the completion handler.

This implementation of the *getTimeline()* method will result in the widget changing content every 30 seconds until the final entry in the London timeline array is reached.

57.10 Configuring the Placeholder View

The Final task before previewing the widget is to make sure that the placeholder view has been implemented. Xcode will have already created a *placeholder()* method for this purpose within the *WeatherWidget.swift* file which reads as follows:

```
func placeholder(in context: Context) -> SimpleEntry {
   SimpleEntry(date: Date(), configuration: ConfigurationIntent())
}
```

This method now needs to be modified so that it returns a WeatherWidget instance populated with some sample data as follows:

```
func placeholder(in context: Context) -> WeatherEntry {
    WeatherEntry(date: Date(), city: "London",
                        temperature: 89, description: "Thunder Storm",
                            icon: "cloud.bolt.rain", image: "thunder")
}
```

57.11 Previewing the Widget

Using the preview canvas, verify that the widget appears as shown in Figure 57-12 below:

Figure 57-12

Next, test the widget on a device or simulator by changing the active scheme in the Xcode toolbar to the WeatherWidgetExtension scheme before clicking on the run button:

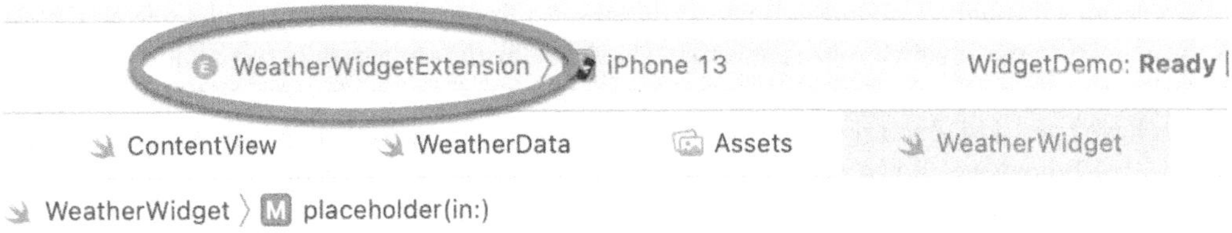

Figure 57-13

After a short delay, the widget will appear on the home screen and cycle through the different weather events at 30 second intervals:

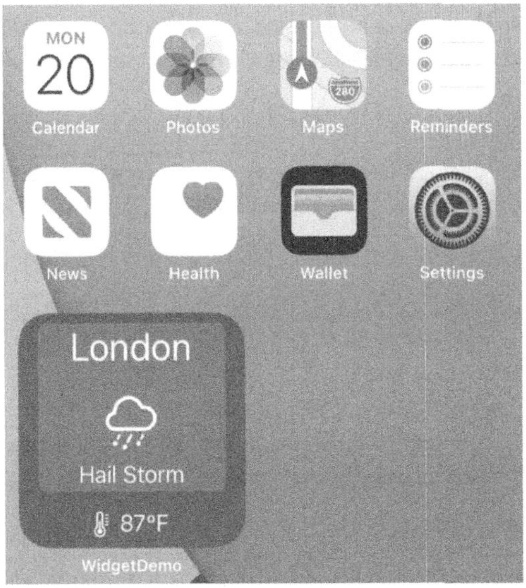

Figure 57-14

57.12 Summary

The example project created in this chapter has demonstrated how to use WidgetKit to create a widget extension for an iOS app. This included the addition of the extension to the project, the design of the widget view and entry together with the implementation of a sample timeline. The widget created in this chapter, however, has not been designed to make use of the different widget size families supported by WidgetKit, a topic which will be covered in the next chapter.

Chapter 58

58. Supporting WidgetKit Size Families

In the chapter titled *"Building Widgets with SwiftUI and WidgetKit"*, we learned that a widget is able to appear in small, medium and large sizes. The project created in the previous chapter included a widget view designed to fit within the small size format. Since the widget did not specify the supported sizes, it would still be possible to select a large or medium sized widget from the gallery and place it on the home screen. In those larger formats, however, the widget content would have filled only a fraction of the available widget space. If larger widget sizes are to be supported, the widget should be designed to make full use of the available space.

In this chapter, the WidgetDemo project created in the previous chapter will be modified to add support for the medium widget size.

58.1 Supporting Multiple Size Families

Begin by launching Xcode and loading the WidgetDemo project from the previous chapter. As outlined above, this phase of the project will add support for the medium widget size (though these steps apply equally to adding support for the large widget size).

In the absence of specific size configuration widgets are, by default, configured to support all three size families. To restrict a widget to specific sizes, the *supportedFamilies()* modifier must be applied to the widget configuration.

To restrict the widget to only small and medium sizes for the WidgetDemo project, edit the *WeatherWidget.swift* file and modify the WeatherWidget declaration to add the modifier. Also take this opportunity to modify the widget display name and description:

```
@main
struct WeatherWidget: Widget {
    private let kind: String = "WeatherWidget"

    public var body: some WidgetConfiguration {
        IntentConfiguration(kind: kind, intent: ConfigurationIntent.self, provider: 
Provider(), placeholder: PlaceholderView()) { entry in
            WeatherWidgetEntryView(entry: entry)
        }
        .configurationDisplayName("My Weather Widget")
        .description("A demo weather widget.")
        .supportedFamilies([.systemSmall, .systemMedium])
    }
}
```

To preview the widget in medium format, edit the preview provider to add an additional preview, embedding both in a Group:

```
struct WeatherWidget_Previews: PreviewProvider {
    static var previews: some View {
```

```
        Group {
            WeatherWidgetEntryView(entry: WeatherEntry(date: Date(),
                  city: "London", temperature: 89,
                  description: "Thunder Storm", icon: "cloud.bolt.rain",
                        image: "thunder"))
                .previewContext(WidgetPreviewContext(
                                          family: .systemSmall))

            WeatherWidgetEntryView(entry: WeatherEntry(date: Date(),
                  city: "London", temperature: 89,
                  description: "Thunder Storm", icon: "cloud.bolt.rain",
                        image: "thunder"))
                .previewContext(WidgetPreviewContext(
                                          family: .systemMedium))
        }
    }
}
```

When the preview canvas updates, it will now include the widget rendered in medium size as shown in Figure 58-1:

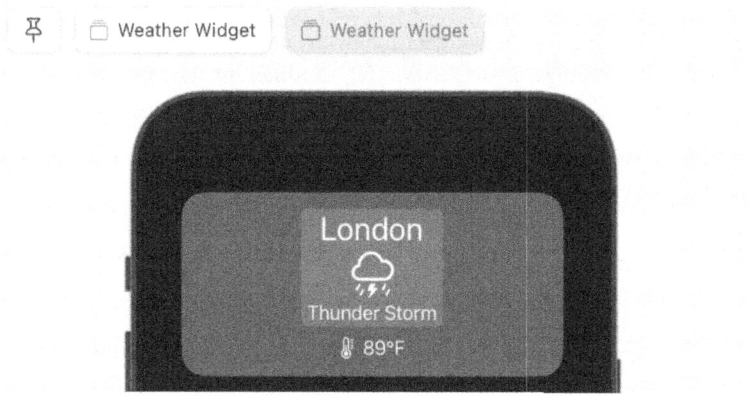

Figure 58-1

Clearly the widget is not taking advantage of the additional space offered by the medium size. To address this shortcoming, some changes to the widget view need to be made.

58.2 Adding Size Support to the Widget View

The changes made to the widget configuration mean that the widget can be displayed in either small or medium size. To make the widget adaptive, the widget view needs to identify the size in which it is currently being displayed. This can be achieved by accessing the widgetFamily property of the SwiftUI environment. Remaining in the *WeatherWidget.swift* file, locate and edit the WeatherWidgetEntryView declaration to obtain the widget family setting from the environment:

```
struct WeatherWidgetEntryView: View {
    var entry: Provider.Entry
```

```
    @Environment(\.widgetFamily) var widgetFamily
.
.
```

Next, embed the subview in a horizontal stack and conditionally display the image for the entry if the size is medium:

```
struct WeatherWidgetEntryView : View {
    var entry: Provider.Entry

    @Environment(\.widgetFamily) var widgetFamily

    var body: some View {

        ZStack {
            Color("weatherBackgroundColor")

            HStack {
                WeatherSubView(entry: entry)
                if widgetFamily == .systemMedium {
                    Image(entry.image)
                        .resizable()
                }
            }
        }
    }
}
```

When previewed, the medium sized version of the widget should appear as shown in Figure 58-2:

Figure 58-2

To test the widget on a device or simulator, run the extension as before and, once the widget is installed and running, perform a long press on the home screen background. After a few seconds have elapsed, the screen will change as shown in Figure 58-3:

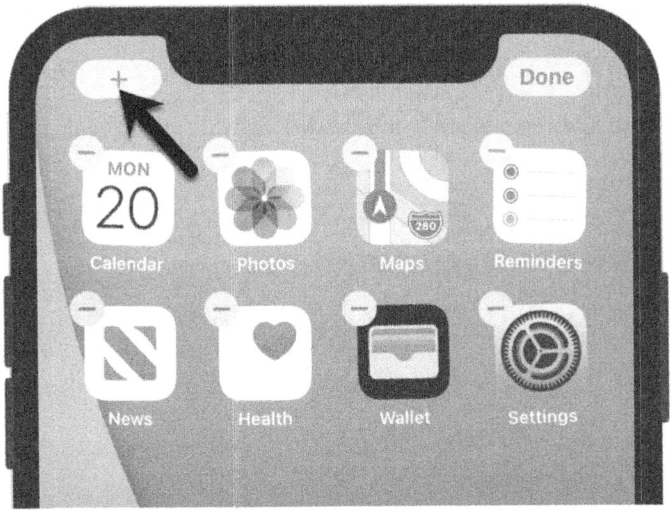

Figure 58-3

Click on the '+' button indicated by the arrow in the above figure to display the widget gallery and scroll down the list of widgets until the WidgetDemo entry appears:

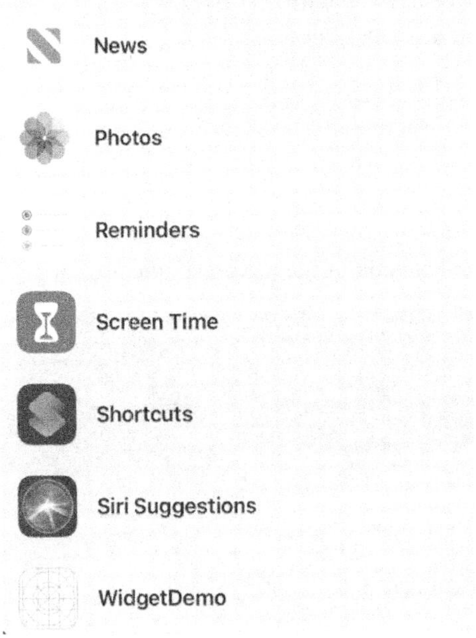

Figure 58-4

Select the WidgetDemo entry to display the widget size options. Swipe to the left to display the medium widget size as shown in Figure 58-5 before tapping on the Add Widget button:

Figure 58-5

On returning to the home screen, click on the Done button located in the top right-hand corner of the home screen to commit the change. The widget will appear as illustrated in Figure 58-6 and update as the timeline progresses:

Figure 58-6

58.3 Summary

WidgetKit supports small, medium and large widget size families and, by default, a widget is assumed to support all three formats. In the event that a widget only supports specific sizes, WidgetKit needs to be notified using a widget configuration modifier.

To fully support a size format, a widget should take steps to detect the current size and provide a widget entry layout which makes use of the available space allocated to the widget on the device screen. This involves accessing the SwiftUI environment widgetFamily property and using it as the basis for conditional layout declarations within the widget view.

Now that widget size family support has been added to the project, the next chapter will add some interactive support to the widget in the form of deep linking into the companion app and widget configuration.

59. A SwiftUI WidgetKit Deep Link Tutorial

WidgetKit deep links allow the individual views that make up the widget entry view to open different screens within the companion app when tapped. In addition to the main home screen, the WidgetDemo app created in the preceding chapters contains a detail screen to provide the user with information about different weather systems. As currently implemented, however, tapping the widget always launches the home screen of the companion app, regardless of the current weather conditions.

The purpose of this chapter is to implement deep linking on the widget so that tapping the widget opens the appropriate weather detail screen within the app. This will involve some changes to both the app and widget extension.

59.1 Adding Deep Link Support to the Widget

Deep links allow specific areas of an app to be presented to the user based on the opening of a URL. The WidgetDemo app used in the previous chapters consists of a list of severe storm types. When a list item is selected, the app navigates to a details screen where additional information about the selected storm is displayed. In this tutorial, changes will be made to both the app and widget to add deep link support. This means, for example, that when the widget indicates that a thunder storm is in effect, tapping the widget will launch the app and navigate to the thunder storm detail screen.

The first step in adding deep link support is to modify the WeatherEntry structure to include a URL for each timeline entry. Edit the *WeatherData.swift* file and modify the structure so that it reads as follows:

```
.
.
struct WeatherEntry: TimelineEntry {
    var date: Date
    let city: String
    let temperature: Int
    let description: String
    let icon: String
    let image: String
    let url: URL?
}
.
.
```

Next, add some constants containing the URLs which will be used to identify the storm types that the app knows about:

```
.
.
let hailUrl = URL(string: "weatherwidget://hail")
```

```
let thunderUrl = URL(string: "weatherwidget://thunder")
let tropicalUrl = URL(string: "weatherwidget://tropical")
.
.
```

The last remaining change to the weather data is to include the URL within the sample timeline entries:

```
.
.
let londonTimeline = [
    WeatherEntry(date: Date(), city: "London", temperature: 87,
          description: "Hail Storm", icon: "cloud.hail",
                image: "hail", url: hailUrl),
    WeatherEntry(date: Date(), city: "London", temperature: 92,
          description: "Thunder Storm", icon: "cloud.bolt.rain",
                image: "thunder", url: thunderUrl),
    WeatherEntry(date: Date(), city: "London", temperature: 95,
          description: "Hail Storm", icon: "cloud.hail",
                image: "hail", url: hailUrl)
]

let miamiTimeline = [
    WeatherEntry(date: Date(), city: "Miami", temperature: 81,
          description: "Thunder Storm", icon: "cloud.bolt.rain",
                image: "thunder", url: thunderUrl),
    WeatherEntry(date: Date(), city: "Miami", temperature: 74,
          description: "Tropical Storm", icon: "tropicalstorm",
                image: "tropical", url: tropicalUrl),
    WeatherEntry(date: Date(), city: "Miami", temperature: 72,
          description: "Thunder Storm", icon: "cloud.bolt.rain",
                image: "thunder", url: thunderUrl)
]
.
.
```

With the data modified to include deep link URLs, the widget declaration now needs to be modified to match the widget entry structure. First, the *placeholder()* and *getSnapshot()* methods of the provider will need to return an entry that includes the URL. Edit the *WeatherWidget.swift* file, locate these methods within the IntentTimelineProvider structure and modify them as follows:

```
struct Provider: IntentTimelineProvider {
   func placeholder(in context: Context) -> WeatherEntry {

        WeatherEntry(date: Date(), city: "London",
                              temperature: 89, description: "Thunder Storm",
                                   icon: "cloud.bolt.rain", image: "thunder",
                                        url: thunderUrl)
     }
```

```
    func getSnapshot(for configuration: ConfigurationIntent, with context: Context,
completion: @escaping (WeatherEntry) -> ()) {

        let entry = WeatherEntry(date: Date(), city: "London",
                      temperature: 89, description: "Thunder Storm",
                        icon: "cloud.bolt.rain", image: "thunder",
                         url: thunderUrl)
        completion(entry)
    }
.
.
```

Repeat this step for both declarations in the preview provider:

```
struct WeatherWidget_Previews: PreviewProvider {
    static var previews: some View {

        Group {
            WeatherWidgetEntryView(entry: WeatherEntry(date: Date(),
                        city: "London", temperature: 89,
                 description: "Thunder Storm", icon: "cloud.bolt.rain",
                       image: "thunder", url: thunderUrl))
                .previewContext(WidgetPreviewContext(
                                      family: .systemSmall))

            WeatherWidgetEntryView(entry: WeatherEntry(date: Date(),
                        city: "London", temperature: 89,
                 description: "Thunder Storm", icon: "cloud.bolt.rain",
                       image: "thunder", url: thunderUrl))
                 .previewContext(WidgetPreviewContext(
                                      family: .systemMedium))
        }
    }
}
```

The final task within the widget code is to assign a URL action to the widget entry view. This is achieved using the *widgetUrl()* modifier, passing through the URL from the widget entry. Remaining in the *WeatherWidget.swift* file, locate the WeatherWidgetEntryView declaration and add the modifier to the top level ZStack as follows:

```
struct WeatherWidgetEntryView : View {
    var entry: Provider.Entry

    @Environment(\.widgetFamily) var widgetFamily

    var body: some View {
        ZStack {
            Color("weatherBackgroundColor")
            HStack {
                WeatherSubView(entry: entry)
```

```
                if widgetFamily == .systemMedium {
                    Image(entry.image)
                        .resizable()
                }
            }
        }
        .widgetURL(entry.url)
    }
}
```

With deep link support added to the widget the next step is to add support to the app.

59.2 Adding Deep Link Support to the App

When an app is launched via a deep link, it is passed a URL object which may be accessed via the top level view in the main content view. This URL can then be used to present different content to the user than would normally be displayed.

The first step in adding deep link support to the WidgetDemo app is to modify the *ContentView.swift* file to a navigation path to the NavigationStack as outlined below. This will allow us to navigate to the detail view when a selection is made within the widget:

```
import SwiftUI
.
.
struct ContentView: View {

    @State var path = NavigationPath()

    var body: some View {
        NavigationStack(path: $path) {
            List {
```

When a view is displayed as the result of a deep link, the URL used to launch the app can be identified using the *onOpenUrl()* modifier on the parent view. Modify the ContentView declaration to add the *onOpenUrl()* modifier as follows:

```
.
.
var body: some View {
    NavigationStack(path: $path) {
        List {
.
.
        }
        .navigationDestination(for: WeatherType.self) { weather in
            WeatherDetailView(weather: weather)
        }
        .navigationTitle("Severe Weather")
        .onOpenURL(perform: { (url) in
```

```
            if (!path.isEmpty) {
                path.removeLast(path.count)
            }

            if (url == hailUrl) {
                path.append(WeatherType(name: "Hail Storm",
                                        icon: "cloud.hail"))
            } else if (url == thunderUrl) {
                path.append(WeatherType(name: "Thunder Storm",
                                        icon: "cloud.bolt.rain"))
            } else if (url == tropicalUrl) {
                path.append(WeatherType(name: "Tropical Storm",
                                        icon: "tropicalstorm"))
            }
        })
    }
}
```

The code performs a comparison of the URL used to launch the app with each of the custom URLs supported by the widget. If a matching URL is found, a WeatherType instance is configured and appended to the navigation path. This, in turn, triggers the *navigationDestination()* modifier causing the WeatherDetailView to be displayed.

We have also added code that checks whether the navigation path is empty and, if necessary, removes any existing destinations. We are doing this because the app may already be displaying a detail view from a previous session when it is launched from the widget. If we append destinations to the non-empty path the user will have to navigate back through any previous views if they decide to return to the home screen.

59.3 Testing the Widget

After making the changes, run the app on a device or simulator and make sure that tapping the widget opens the app and displays the detail screen correctly configured for the current weather.

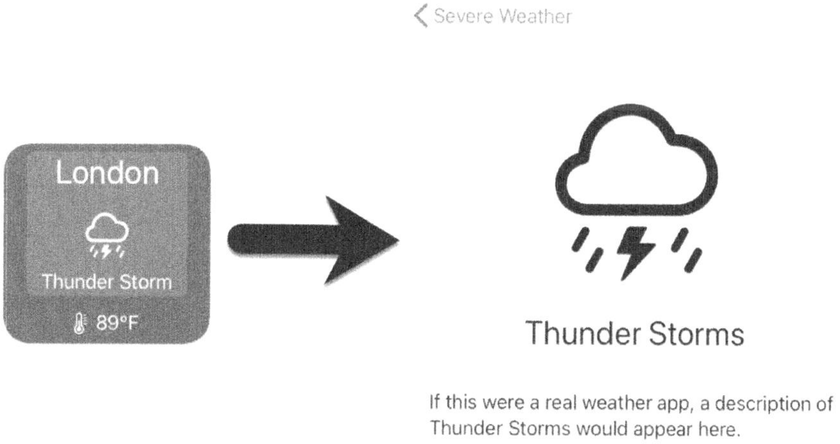

Figure 59-1

59.4 Summary

By default, a widget will launch the main view of the companion app when tapped by the user. This behavior can be enhanced by establishing deep links that take the user to specific areas of the app. This involves using the *widgetUrl()* modifier to assign destination URLs to the views in a widget entry layout. Within the app the *onOpenUrl()* modifier is then used to identify the URL used to launch the app and initiate navigation to the corresponding view.

Chapter 60

60. Adding Configuration Options to a WidgetKit Widget

The WidgetDemo app created in the preceding chapters is currently only able to display weather information for a single geographical location. Through the use of configuration intents, it is possible to make aspects of the widget user configurable. In this chapter we will enhance the widget extension so that the user can choose to view the weather for different cities. This will involve some minor changes to the weather data, the modification of the SiriKit intent definition and updates to the widget implementation.

60.1 Modifying the Weather Data

Before adding configuration support to the widget, an additional structure needs to be added to the widget data to provide a way to associate cities with weather timelines. Add this structure by modifying the *WeatherData.swift* file as follows:

```
import Foundation
import WidgetKit

struct LocationData: Identifiable {

    let city: String
    let timeline: [WeatherEntry]

    var id: String {
        city
    }

    static let london = LocationData(city: "London",
                                 timeline: londonTimeline)
    static let miami = LocationData(city: "Miami",
                                timeline: miamiTimeline)

    func hash(into hasher: inout Hasher) {
        hasher.combine(city)
    }
}
.
.
```

60.2 Configuring the Intent Definition

The next step is to configure the intent definition which will be used to present the user with widget configuration choices. When the WeatherWidget extension was added to the project, the "Include Configuration Intent" option was enabled, causing Xcode to generate a definition file named *WeatherWidget.intentdefinition* located in the WeatherWidget project folder as highlighted in Figure 60-1 below:

Figure 60-1

Select this file to load it into the intent definition editor where it will appear as shown in Figure 60-2:

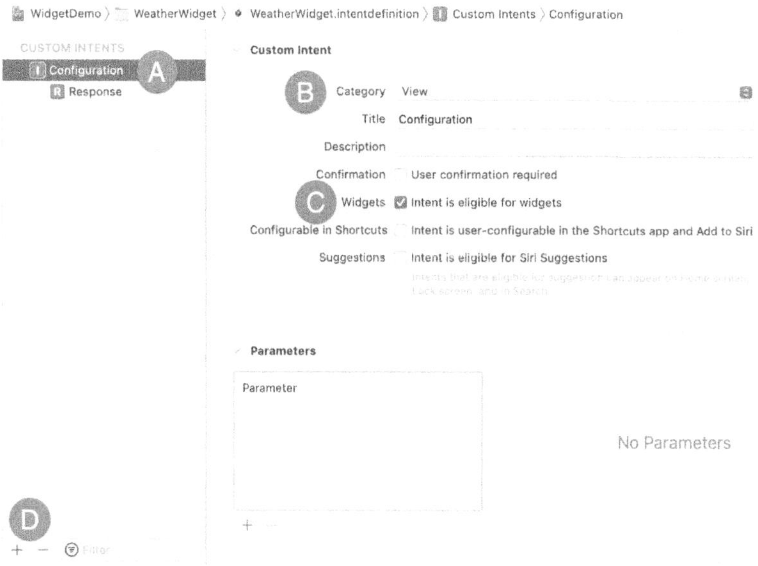

Figure 60-2

Begin by making sure that the Configuration intent (marked A in Figure 60-2 above) is selected. This is the intent that was created by Xcode and will be referenced as ConfigurationIntent in the *WeatherWidget.swift* file. Additional intents may be added to the definition by clicking on the '+' button (D) and selecting *New Intent* from the menu.

The Category menu (B) must be set to *View* to allow the intent to display a dialog to the user containing the widget configuration options. Also ensure that the *Intent is eligible for widgets* option (B) is enabled.

Before we add a parameter to the intent, an enumeration needs to be added to the definition file to contain the available city names. Add this now by clicking on the '+' button (D) and selecting the *New Enum* option from the menu.

After the enumeration has been added, change both the enumeration name and Display Name to *Locations* as highlighted in Figure 60-3 below:

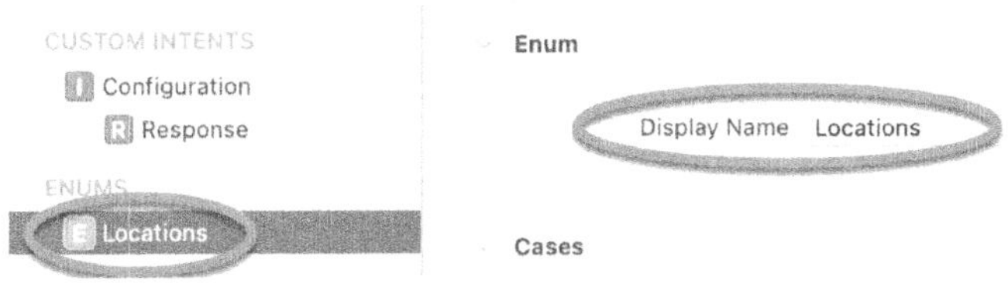

Figure 60-3

With the Locations entry selected, refer to the main editor panel and click on the '+' button beneath the Cases section to add a new value. Change the new case entry name to *londonUK* and, in the settings area, change the display name to *London* so that the settings resemble Figure 60-4:

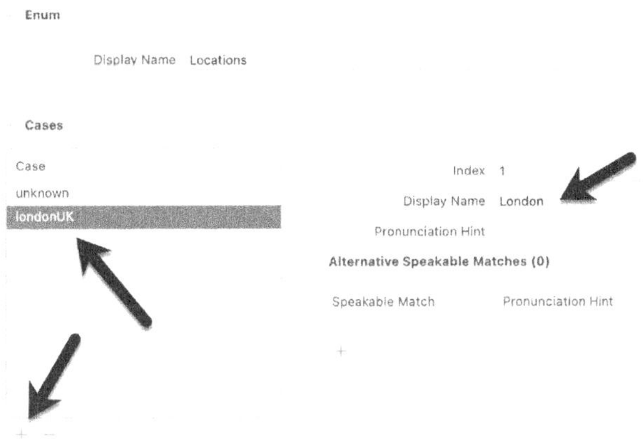

Figure 60-4

Repeat the above steps to add an additional cased named *miamiFL* with the display name set to *Miami*.

In the left-hand panel, select the Configuration option located under the Custom Intents heading. In the custom intent panel, locate the Parameters section and click on the '+' button highlighted in Figure 60-5 to add a new parameter:

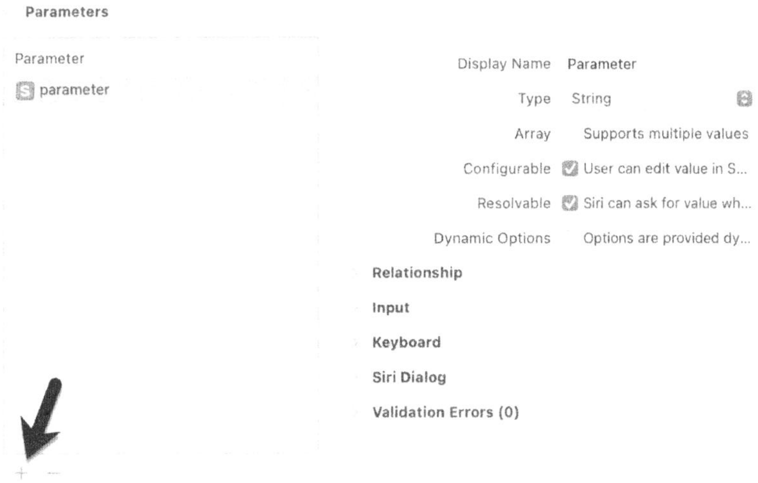

Figure 60-5

Name the parameter *locations* and change the Display Name setting to *Locations*. From the Type menu select *Locations* listed under *Enums* as shown in Figure 60-6 (note that this is not the same as the Location entry listed under System Types):

Figure 60-6

Once completed, the parameter settings should match those shown in Figure 60-7 below:

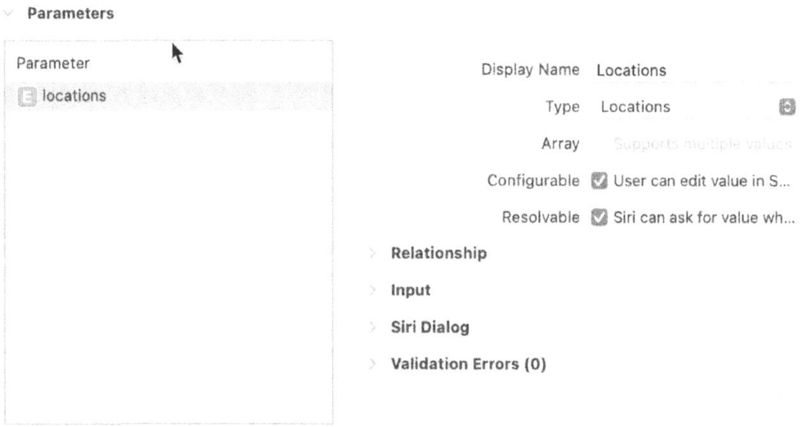

Figure 60-7

60.3 Modifying the Widget

With the intent configured, all that remains is to adapt the widget so that it responds to location configuration changes made by the user. When WidgetKit requests a timeline from the provider it will pass to the *getTimeline()* method a ConfigurationIntent object containing the current configuration settings from the intent. To return the timeline for the currently selected city, the *getTimeline()* method needs to be modified to extract the location from the intent and use it to return the matching timeline.

Edit the *WeatherWidget.swift* file, locate the *getTimeline()* method within the provider declaration and modify it so that it reads as follows:

```
func getTimeline(for configuration: ConfigurationIntent, in context: Context,
              completion: @escaping (Timeline<Entry>) -> ()) {
```

```
    var chosenLocation: LocationData

    if configuration.locations == .londonUK {
        chosenLocation = .london
    } else {
        chosenLocation = .miami
    }

    var entries: [WeatherEntry] = []
    var currentDate = Date()
    let halfMinute: TimeInterval = 30

    for var entry in chosenLocation.timeline {
        entry.date = currentDate
        currentDate += halfMinute
        entries.append(entry)
    }
    let timeline = Timeline(entries: entries, policy: .never)
    completion(timeline)
}
```

In the above code, if the intent object passed to the method has London set as the location, then the *london* entry within the LocationData instance is used to provide the timeline for WidgetKit. If any of the above changes result in syntax errors within the editor try rebuilding the project to trigger the generation of the files associated with the intent definition file.

60.4 Testing Widget Configuration

Run the widget extension on a device (widget testing on a simulator can be problematic) and wait for it to load. Once it is running, perform a long press on the widget to display the menu shown in Figure 60-8 below:

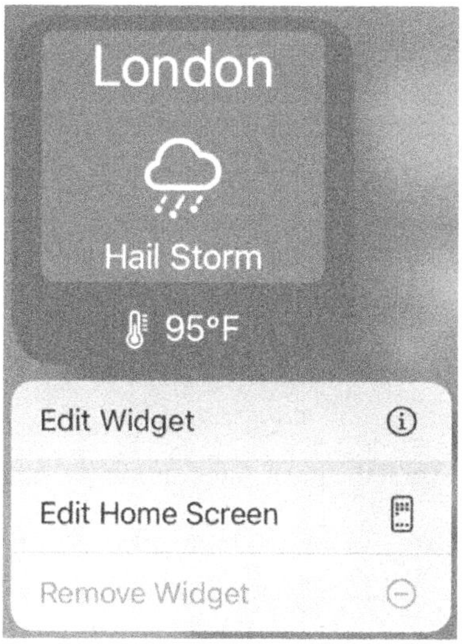

Figure 60-8

Select the *Edit Widget* menu option to display the configuration intent dialog as shown in Figure 60-9:

Figure 60-9

Select the current location (or the Choose button if no city is displayed) to display the list of locations, then select Miami before tapping on any screen area outside of the dialog. On returning to the home screen, the widget should now display entries from the Miami timeline.

60.5 Customizing the Configuration Intent UI

The final task in this tutorial is to change the accent colors of the intent UI to match those used by the widget. Since we already have the widget background color declared in the widget extension's *Assets* file from the steps in an earlier chapter, this can be used for the background of the intent UI.

The color settings for the intent UI are located in the build settings screen for the widget extension. To find these settings, select the WidgetDemo entry located at the top of the project navigator panel (marked A in Figure 60-10 below), followed by the WeatherWidgetExtension entry (B) in the Targets list:

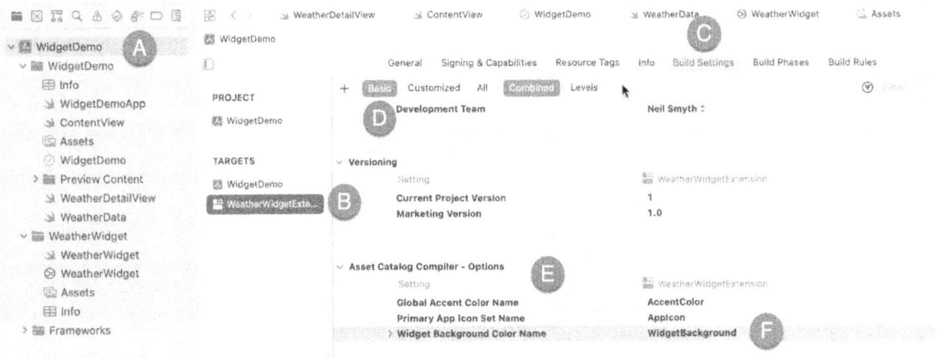

Figure 60-10

In the toolbar, select *Build Settings* (C), then the Basic filter option (D) before scrolling down to the *Asset Catalog Compiler – Options* section (E).

Click on the WidgetBackground value (F) and change it to *weatherBackgroundColor*. If required, the foreground color used within the intent UI is defined by the Global Accent Color Name value. Note that these values must be named colors declared within the *Assets* file.

Test the widget to verify that the intent UI now uses the widget background color:

Figure 60-11

60.6 Summary

When a widget is constructed using the intent configuration type (as opposed to static configuration), configuration options can be made available to the user by setting up intents and parameters within the SiriKit intent definition file. Each time the provider *getTimeline()* method is called, WidgetKit passes it a copy of the configuration intent object, the parameters of which can be inspected and used to tailor the resulting timeline to match the user's preferences.

Chapter 61

61. Integrating UIViews with SwiftUI

Before the introduction of SwiftUI, all iOS apps were developed using UIKit together with a collection of UIKit-based supporting frameworks. Although SwiftUI is provided with a wide selection of components with which to build an app, there are instances where there is no SwiftUI equivalent to options provided by the other frameworks.

Given the number of apps that were developed before the introduction of SwiftUI, it is also important to be able to integrate existing non-SwiftUI functionality with SwiftUI development projects and vice versa. Fortunately, SwiftUI includes several options to perform this type of integration.

61.1 SwiftUI and UIKit Integration

Before looking in detail at integrating SwiftUI and UIKit it is worth taking some time to explore whether a new app project should be started as a UIKit or SwiftUI project and whether an existing app should be migrated entirely to SwiftUI. When making this decision, it is important to remember that apps containing SwiftUI code can only be used on devices running iOS 13 or later.

If you are starting a new project, then the best approach may be to build it as a SwiftUI project (support for older iOS versions notwithstanding) and then integrate it with UIKit when required functionality is not provided directly by SwiftUI. Although Apple continues to enhance and support the UIKit way of developing apps, it is clear that Apple sees SwiftUI as the future of app development. SwiftUI also makes it easier to develop and deploy apps for iOS, macOS, tvOS, iPadOS, and watchOS without making major code changes.

If, on the other hand, you have existing projects that pre-date the introduction of SwiftUI then it probably makes sense to leave the existing code unchanged, build any future additions to the project using SwiftUI, and integrate those additions into your existing code base.

SwiftUI provides three options for performing integrations of these types. The first, and the topic of this chapter, is to integrate individual UIKit-based components (UIViews) into SwiftUI View declarations.

For those unfamiliar with UIKit, a screen displayed within an app is typically implemented using a view controller (implemented as an instance of UIViewController or a subclass thereof). The subject of integrating view controllers into SwiftUI will be covered in the chapter entitled *"Integrating UIViewControllers with SwiftUI"*.

Finally, SwiftUI views may also be integrated into existing UIKit-based code, a topic which will be covered in the chapter entitled *"Integrating SwiftUI with UIKit"*.

61.2 Integrating UIViews into SwiftUI

The individual components that make up the user interface of a UIKit-based application are derived from the UIView class. Buttons, labels, text views, maps, sliders, and drawings (to name a few) are all ultimately subclasses of the UIKit UIView class.

To facilitate the integration of a UIView-based component into a SwiftUI view declaration, SwiftUI provides the UIViewRepresentable protocol. To integrate a UIView component into SwiftUI, that component needs to be wrapped in a structure that implements this protocol.

At a minimum the wrapper structure must implement the following methods to comply with the UIViewRepresentable protocol:

- **makeUIView()** – This method is responsible for creating an instance of the UIView-based component, performing any necessary initialization, and returning it.
- **updateView()** – Called each time a change occurs within the containing SwiftUI view that requires the UIView to update itself.

The following optional method may also be implemented:

- **dismantleUIView()** – Provides an opportunity to perform cleanup operations before the view is removed.

As an example, assume that there is a feature of the UILabel class that is not available with the SwiftUI Text view. To wrap a UILabel view using UIViewRepresentable so that it can be used within SwiftUI, the structure might be implemented as follows:

```
import SwiftUI

struct MyUILabel: UIViewRepresentable {

    var text: String

    func makeUIView(context: UIViewRepresentableContext<MyUILabel>)
                             -> UILabel {
        let myLabel = UILabel()
        myLabel.text = text
        return myLabel
    }

    func updateUIView(_ uiView: UILabel,
                      context: UIViewRepresentableContext<MyUILabel>) {
        // Perform any update tasks if necessary
    }
}

struct MyUILabel_Previews: PreviewProvider {
    static var previews: some View {
        MyUILabel(text: "Hello")
    }
}
```

With the UILabel view wrapped, it can now be referenced within SwiftUI as though it is a built-in SwiftUI component:

```
struct ContentView: View {
    var body: some View {

        VStack {
            MyUILabel(text: "Hello UIKit")
        }
    }
}
```

```
struct ContentView_Previews: PreviewProvider {
    static var previews: some View {
        ContentView()
    }
}
```

Obviously, UILabel is a static component that does not need to handle any user interaction events. For views that need to respond to events, however, the UIViewRepresentable wrapper needs to be extended to implement a *coordinator.*

61.3 Adding a Coordinator

A coordinator takes the form of a class that implements the protocols and handler methods required by the wrapped UIView component to handle events. An instance of this class is then applied to the wrapper via the *makeCoordinator()* method of the UIViewRepresentable protocol.

As an example, consider the UIScrollView class. This class has a feature whereby a refresh control (UIRefreshControl) may be added such that when the user attempts to scroll beyond the top of the view, a spinning progress indicator appears and a method called allowing the view to be updated with the latest content. This is a common feature used by news apps to allow the user to download the latest news headlines. Once the refresh is complete, this method needs to call the *endRefreshing()* method of the UIRefreshControl instance to remove the progress spinner.

Clearly, if the UIScrollView is to be used with SwiftUI, there needs to be a way for the view to be notified that the UIRefreshControl has been triggered and to perform the necessary steps.

The Coordinator class for a wrapped UIScrollView with an associated UIRefreshControl object would be implemented as follows:

```
class Coordinator: NSObject {
    var control: MyScrollView

    init(_ control: MyScrollView) {
        self.control = control
    }

    @objc func handleRefresh(sender: UIRefreshControl) {
        sender.endRefreshing()
    }
}
```

In this case, the initializer for the coordinator is passed the current UIScrollView instance, which it stores locally. The class also implements a function named *handleRefresh()* which calls the *endRefreshing()* method of the scrolled view instance.

An instance of the Coordinator class now needs to be created and assigned to the view via a call to the *makeCoordinator()* method as follows:

```
func makeCoordinator() -> Coordinator {
     Coordinator(self)
}
```

Finally, the *makeUIView()* method needs to be implemented to create the UIScrollView instance, configure it with a UIRefreshControl and add a target to call the *handleRefresh()* method when a value changed event occurs on the UIRefreshControl instance:

```
func makeUIView(context: Context) -> UIScrollView {
    let scrollView = UIScrollView()
    scrollView.refreshControl = UIRefreshControl()

    scrollView.refreshControl?.addTarget(context.coordinator,
            action: #selector(Coordinator.handleRefresh),
                                      for: .valueChanged)

    return scrollView
}
```

61.4 Handling UIKit Delegation and Data Sources

Delegation is a feature of UIKit that allows an object to pass the responsibility for performing one or more tasks onto another object and is another area in which extra steps may be necessary if events are to be handled by a wrapped UIView.

The UIScrolledView, for example, can be assigned a delegate which will be notified when certain events take place such as the user performing a scrolling motion or when the user scrolls to the top of the content. The delegate object will need to conform to the UIScrolledViewDelegate protocol and implement the specific methods that will be called automatically when corresponding events take place in the scrolled view.

Similarly, a data source is an object which provides a UIView-based component with data to be displayed. The UITableView class, for example, can be assigned a data source object to provide the cells to be displayed in the table. This data object must conform with the UITableViewDataSource protocol.

To handle delegate events when integrating UIViews into SwiftUI, the coordinator class needs to be declared as implementing the appropriate delegate protocol and must include the callback methods for any events of interest to the scrolled view instance. The coordinator must then be assigned as the delegate for the UIScrolledView instance. The previous coordinator implementation can be extended to receive notification that the user is currently scrolling as follows:

```
class Coordinator: NSObject, UIScrollViewDelegate {
    var control: MyScrollView

    init(_ control: MyScrollView) {
        self.control = control
    }

    func scrollViewDidScroll(_ scrollView: UIScrollView) {
        // User is currently scrolling
    }

    @objc func handleRefresh(sender: UIRefreshControl) {
        sender.endRefreshing()
    }
}
```

The *makeUIView()* method must also be modified to access the coordinator instance (which is accessible via the *representable context* object passed to the method) and add it as the delegate for the UIScrolledView instance:

```
func makeUIView(context: Context) -> UIScrollView {
    let scrollView = UIScrollView()
    scrollView.delegate = context.coordinator
.
.
```

In addition to providing access to the coordinator, the context also includes an *environment* property that can be used to access both the SwiftUI environment and any @EnvironmentObject properties declared in the SwiftUI view.

Now, while the user is scrolling, the scrollViewDidScroll delegate method will be called repeatedly.

61.5 An Example Project

The remainder of this chapter will work through the creation of a simple project that demonstrates the use of the UIViewRepresentable protocol to integrate a UIScrolledView into a SwiftUI project.

Begin by launching Xcode and creating a new SwiftUI Multiplatform App project named *UIViewDemo*.

61.6 Wrapping the UIScrolledView

The first step in the project is to use the UIViewRepresentable protocol to wrap the UIScrollView so that it can be used with SwiftUI. Right-click on the UIViewDemo folder entry in the project navigator panel, select the *New File...* menu option, and create a new file named *MyScrollView* using the SwiftUI View template.

With the new file loaded into the editor, delete the current content and modify it so it reads as follows:

```
import SwiftUI

struct MyScrollView: UIViewRepresentable {

    var text: String

    func makeUIView(context: UIViewRepresentableContext<MyScrollView>)
             -> UIScrollView {
        let scrollView = UIScrollView()
        scrollView.refreshControl = UIRefreshControl()
        let myLabel = UILabel(frame:
                   CGRect(x: 0, y: 0, width: 300, height: 50))
        myLabel.text = text
        scrollView.addSubview(myLabel)
        return scrollView
    }

    func updateUIView(_ uiView: UIScrollView,
        context: UIViewRepresentableContext<MyScrollView>) {

    }
```

```
}

struct MyScrollView_Previews: PreviewProvider {
    static var previews: some View {
        MyScrollView(text: "Hello World")
    }
}
```

If the above code generates syntax errors, make sure that an iOS device is selected as the run target in the Xcode toolbar instead of macOS. Use the Live Preview to build and test the view so far. Once the Live Preview is active and running, click and drag downwards so that the refresh control appears as shown in Figure 61-1:

Figure 61-1

Release the mouse button to stop the scrolling and note that the refresh indicator remains visible because the event is not being handled. Clearly, it is now time to add a coordinator.

61.7 Implementing the Coordinator

Remaining within the *MyScrollView.swift* file, add the coordinator class declaration so that it reads as follows:

```
struct MyScrollView: UIViewRepresentable {
.
.
    class Coordinator: NSObject, UIScrollViewDelegate {
        var control: MyScrollView

        init(_ control: MyScrollView) {
            self.control = control
        }

        func scrollViewDidScroll(_ scrollView: UIScrollView) {
            print("View is Scrolling")
        }

        @objc func handleRefresh(sender: UIRefreshControl) {
            sender.endRefreshing()
```

```
        }
    }
}
```

Next, modify the *makeUIView()* method to add the coordinator as the delegate and add the *handleRefresh()* method as the target for the refresh control:

```
func makeUIView(context: Context) -> UIScrollView {
    let scrollView = UIScrollView()
    scrollView.delegate = context.coordinator

    scrollView.refreshControl = UIRefreshControl()
    scrollView.refreshControl?.addTarget(context.coordinator, action:
        #selector(Coordinator.handleRefresh),
                                      for: .valueChanged)
.
.
    return scrollView
}
```

Finally, add the *makeCoordinator()* method so that it reads as follows:

```
func makeCoordinator() -> Coordinator {
     Coordinator(self)
}
```

61.8 Using MyScrollView

The final step in this example is to check that MyScrollView can be used from within SwiftUI. To achieve this, load the *ContentView.swift* file into the editor and modify it so that it reads as follows:

```
.
.
struct ContentView: View {
    var body: some View {
        MyScrollView(text: "UIView in SwiftUI")
    }
}
.
.
```

Use Live Preview to test that the view works as expected.

61.9 Summary

SwiftUI includes several options for integrating with UIKit-based views and code. This chapter has focused on integrating UIKit views into SwiftUI. This integration is achieved by wrapping the UIView instance in a structure that conforms to the UIViewRepresentable protocol and implementing the *makeUIView()* and *updateView()* methods to initialize and manage the view while it is embedded in a SwiftUI layout. For UIKit objects that require a delegate or data source, a Coordinator class needs to be added to the wrapper and assigned to the view via a call to the *makeCoordinator()* method.

Chapter 62

62. Integrating UIViewControllers with SwiftUI

The previous chapter outlined how to integrate UIView-based components into SwiftUI using the UIViewRepresentable protocol. This chapter will focus on the second option for combining SwiftUI and UIKit within an iOS project in the form of UIViewController integration.

62.1 UIViewControllers and SwiftUI

The UIView integration outlined in the previous chapter is useful for integrating either individual or small groups of UIKit-based components with SwiftUI. Existing iOS apps are likely to consist of multiple ViewControllers, each representing an entire screen layout and functionality (also referred to as *scenes*). SwiftUI allows entire view controller instances to be integrated via the UIViewControllerRepresentable protocol. This protocol is similar to the UIViewRepresentable protocol and works in much the same way with the exception that the method names are different.

The remainder of this chapter will work through an example that demonstrates the use of the UIViewControllerRepresentable protocol to integrate a UIViewController into SwiftUI.

62.2 Creating the ViewControllerDemo project

As an example, this project will demonstrate the integration of the UIImagePickerController into a SwiftUI project. This is a class that is used to allow the user to browse and select images from the device photo library and for which there is currently no equivalent within SwiftUI.

Just like custom-built view controllers in an iOS app UIImagePickerController is a subclass of UIViewController so can be used with UIViewControllerRepresentable to integrate into SwiftUI.

Begin by launching Xcode and creating a new Multiplatform App project named *ViewControllerDemo*.

62.3 Wrapping the UIImagePickerController

With the project created, it is time to create a new SwiftUI View file to contain the wrapper that will make the UIPickerController available to SwiftUI. Create this file by right-clicking on the ViewControllerDemo folder item in the project navigator panel, selecting the *New File...* menu option, and creating a new file named MyImagePicker using the SwiftUI View file template.

Once the file has been created, delete the current content and modify the file so that it reads as follows:

```
import SwiftUI

struct MyImagePicker: UIViewControllerRepresentable {

    func makeUIViewController(context:
            UIViewControllerRepresentableContext<MyImagePicker>) ->
                    UIImagePickerController {
        let picker = UIImagePickerController()
```

```
        return picker
    }

    func updateUIViewController(_ uiViewController:
            UIImagePickerController, context:
              UIViewControllerRepresentableContext<MyImagePicker>) {

    }
}

struct MyImagePicker_Previews: PreviewProvider {
    static var previews: some View {
        MyImagePicker()
    }
}
```

If Xcode reports that UIViewControllerRepresentable is undefined, make sure that you have selected an iOS device or simulator as the run target in the toolbar.

Click on the Live Preview button in the canvas to test that the image picker appears as shown in Figure 62-1 below:

Figure 62-1

62.4 Designing the Content View

When the project is complete, the content view will display an Image view and a button contained in a VStack. This VStack will be embedded in a ZStack along with an instance of the MyImagePicker view. When the button is clicked, the MyImagePicker view will be made visible over the top of the VStack from which an image may be selected. Once the image has been selected, the image picker will be hidden from view, and the selected image displayed on the Image view.

To make this work, two state property variables will be used, one for the image to be displayed and the other a Boolean value to control whether or not the image picker view is currently visible. Bindings for these two variables will be declared in the MyPickerView structure so that changes within the view controller are reflected within the main content view. With these requirements in mind, load the *ContentView.swift* file into the editor and modify it as follows:

```
struct ContentView: View {

    @State var imagePickerVisible: Bool = false
    @State var selectedImage: Image? = Image(systemName: "photo")

    var body: some View {
        ZStack {
            VStack {

                selectedImage?
                    .resizable()
                    .aspectRatio(contentMode: .fit)

                Button(action: {
                    withAnimation {
                        self.imagePickerVisible.toggle()
                    }
                }) {
                    Text("Select an Image")
                }

            }.padding()

            if (imagePickerVisible) {
                MyImagePicker()
            }
        }
    }
}
.
.
```

Once the changes have been made, the preview for the view should resemble Figure 62-2:

Figure 62-2

Test the view using Live Preview and make sure that clicking on the "Select an Image" button causes the MyPickerView to appear. Note that selecting an image or clicking on the Cancel button does not dismiss the picker. To implement this behavior, some changes are needed within the MyImagePicker declaration.

62.5 Completing MyImagePicker

A few remaining tasks now need to be completed within the *MyImagePicker.swift* file. First, bindings to the two ContentView state properties need to be declared:

```
struct MyImagePicker: UIViewControllerRepresentable {

    @Binding var imagePickerVisible: Bool
    @Binding var selectedImage: Image?
.
.
```

Next, a coordinator needs to be implemented to act as the delegate for the UIImagePickerView instance. This will require that the coordinator class conform to both the UINavigationControllerDelegate and UIImagePickerControllerDelegate protocols. The coordinator will need to receive a notification when an image is picked, or the user taps the cancel button so the imagePickerControllerDidCancel and didFinishPickingMediaWithInfo delegate methods will both need to be implemented.

In the case of the imagePickerControllerDidCancel method, the imagePickerVisible state property will need to be set to false. This will result in a state change within the content view causing the image picker to be removed from view.

The didFinishPickingMediaWithInfo method, on the other hand, will be passed the selected image which it will need to assign to the currentImage property before also setting the imagePickerVisible property to false.

The coordinator will also need local copies of the state property bindings. Bringing these requirements together results in a coordinator which reads as follows:

```
class Coordinator: NSObject, UINavigationControllerDelegate,
                    UIImagePickerControllerDelegate {

    @Binding var imagePickerVisible: Bool
    @Binding var selectedImage: Image?

    init(imagePickerVisible: Binding<Bool>,
                    selectedImage: Binding<Image?>) {
        _imagePickerVisible = imagePickerVisible
        _selectedImage = selectedImage
    }

    func imagePickerController(_ picker: UIImagePickerController,
                             didFinishPickingMediaWithInfo
                info: [UIImagePickerController.InfoKey : Any]) {
        let uiImage =
            info[UIImagePickerController.InfoKey.originalImage] as!
                                                                  UIImage
        selectedImage = Image(uiImage: uiImage)
        imagePickerVisible = false
    }

    func imagePickerControllerDidCancel(_
                        picker: UIImagePickerController) {
        imagePickerVisible = false
    }
}
```

Remaining in the *MyPickerView.swift* file, add the *makeCoordinator()* method within the scope of the MyImagePicker struct, remembering to pass through the two state property bindings:

```
func makeCoordinator() -> Coordinator {
    return Coordinator(imagePickerVisible: $imagePickerVisible,
                            selectedImage: $selectedImage)
}
```

Finally, modify the *makeUIVewController()* method to assign the coordinator as the delegate and comment out the preview structure to remove the remaining syntax errors:

```
func makeUIViewController(context:
        UIViewControllerRepresentableContext<MyImagePicker>) ->
                 UIImagePickerController {
    let picker = UIImagePickerController()
    picker.delegate = context.coordinator
    return picker
}
.
.
/*
struct MyImagePicker_Previews: PreviewProvider {
    static var previews: some View {
        MyImagePicker()
    }
}
*/
```

62.6 Completing the Content View

The final task before testing the app is to modify the Content View so that the two state properties are passed through to the MyImagePicker instance. Edit the *ContentView.swift* file and make the following modifications:

```
struct ContentView: View {

    @State var imagePickerVisible: Bool = false
    @State var selectedImage: Image? = Image(systemName: "photo")

    var body: some View {
.
.
        if (imagePickerVisible) {
                MyImagePicker(imagePickerVisible:
                        $imagePickerVisible,
                           selectedImage: $selectedImage)
        }
```

62.7 Testing the App

With the *ContentView.swift* file still loaded into the editor, enable Live Preview mode and click on the "Select an Image" button. When the picker view appears, navigate to and select an image. When the image has been selected, the picker view should disappear to reveal the selected image displayed on the Image view:

Figure 62-3

Click the image selection button once again, this time testing that the Cancel button dismisses the image picker without changing the selected image.

62.8 Summary

In addition to allowing for the integration of individual UIView-based objects into SwiftUI projects, it is also possible to integrate entire UIKit view controllers representing entire screen layouts and functionality. View controller integration is similar to working with UIViews, involving wrapping the view controller in a structure conforming to the UIViewControllerRepresentable protocol and implementing the associated methods. As with UIView integration, delegates and data sources for the view controller are handled using a Coordinator instance.

Chapter 63

63. Integrating SwiftUI with UIKit

Apps developed before the introduction of SwiftUI will have been developed using UIKit and other UIKit-based frameworks included with the iOS SDK. Given the benefits of using SwiftUI for future development, it will be a common requirement to integrate the new SwiftUI app functionality with the existing project code base. Fortunately, this integration can be achieved with relative ease using the UIHostingController.

63.1 An Overview of the Hosting Controller

The hosting controller (in the form of the UIHostingController class) is a subclass of UIViewController, the sole purpose of which is to enclose a SwiftUI view so that it can be integrated into an existing UIKit-based project.

Using a hosting view controller, a SwiftUI view can be treated either as an entire scene (occupying the full screen) or as an individual component within an existing UIKit scene layout by embedding a hosting controller in a *container view*. A container view essentially allows a view controller to be configured as the child of another view controller.

SwiftUI views can be integrated into a UIKit project either from within the code or using an Interface Builder storyboard. The following code excerpt embeds a SwiftUI content view in a hosting view controller and then presents it to the user:

```
let swiftUIController =
                  UIHostingController(rootView: SwiftUIView())
present(swiftUIController, animated: true, completion: nil)
```

The following example, on the other hand, embeds a hosted SwiftUI view directly into the layout of an existing UIViewController:

```
let swiftUIController =
            UIHostingController(rootView: SwiftUIView())

addChild(swiftUIController)
view.addSubview(swiftUIController.view)

swiftUIController.didMove(toParent: self)
```

In the rest of this chapter, an example project will be created that demonstrates the use of UIHostingController instances to integrate SwiftUI views into an existing UIKit-based project both programmatically and using storyboards.

63.2 A UIHostingController Example Project

Unlike previous chapters, the project created in this chapter will create a UIKit Storyboard-based project instead of a SwiftUI Multiplatform app. Launch Xcode and select the iOS tab followed by the App template as shown in Figure 63-1 below:

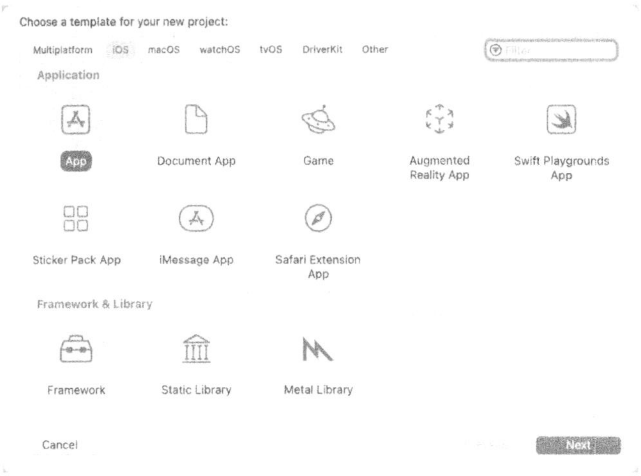

Figure 63-1

Click the Next button and, on the options screen, name the project *HostingControllerDemo* and change the Interface menu from *SwiftUI* to *Storyboard*. Click the Next button once again and proceed with the project creation process.

63.3 Adding the SwiftUI Content View

In the course of building this project, a SwiftUI content view will be integrated into a UIKit storyboard scene using the UIHostingController in three different ways. In preparation for this integration process, a SwiftUI View file needs to be added to the project. Add this file now by selecting the *File -> New -> File...* menu option and choosing the SwiftUI View template option from the resulting dialog. Proceed through the screens, keeping the default SwiftUIView file name.

With the *SwiftUIView.swift* file loaded into the editor, modify the declaration so that it reads as follows:

```
import SwiftUI

struct SwiftUIView: View {

    var text: String

    var body: some View {
        VStack {
            Text(text)
            HStack {
                Image(systemName: "smiley")
                Text("This is a SwiftUI View")
            }
        }
        .font(.largeTitle)
    }
}

struct SwiftUIView_Previews: PreviewProvider {
```

```
    static var previews: some View {
        SwiftUIView(text: "Sample Text")
    }
}
```

With the SwiftUI view added, the next step is to integrate it so that it can be launched as a separate view controller from within the storyboard.

63.4 Preparing the Storyboard

Within Xcode, select the *Main* file from the Project navigator so that it loads into the Interface Builder tool. As currently configured, the storyboard consists of a single view controller scene as shown in Figure 63-2:

Figure 63-2

So that the user can navigate back to the current scene, the view controller needs to be embedded into a Navigation Controller. Select the current scene by clicking on the View Controller button indicated by the arrow in the figure above so that the scene is highlighted with a blue outline and select the *Editor -> Embed In -> Navigation Controller* menu option. At this point the storyboard canvas should resemble Figure 63-3:

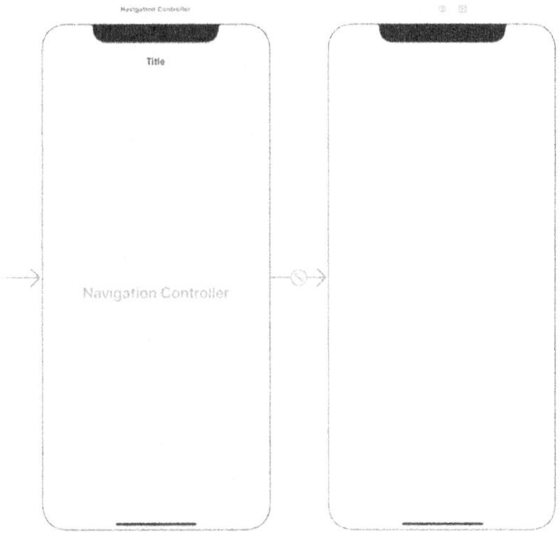

Figure 63-3

The first SwiftUI integration will require a button that, when clicked, will show a new view controller containing the SwiftUI View. Display the Library panel by clicking on the button highlighted in Figure 63-4 and locate and drag a Button view onto the view controller scene canvas:

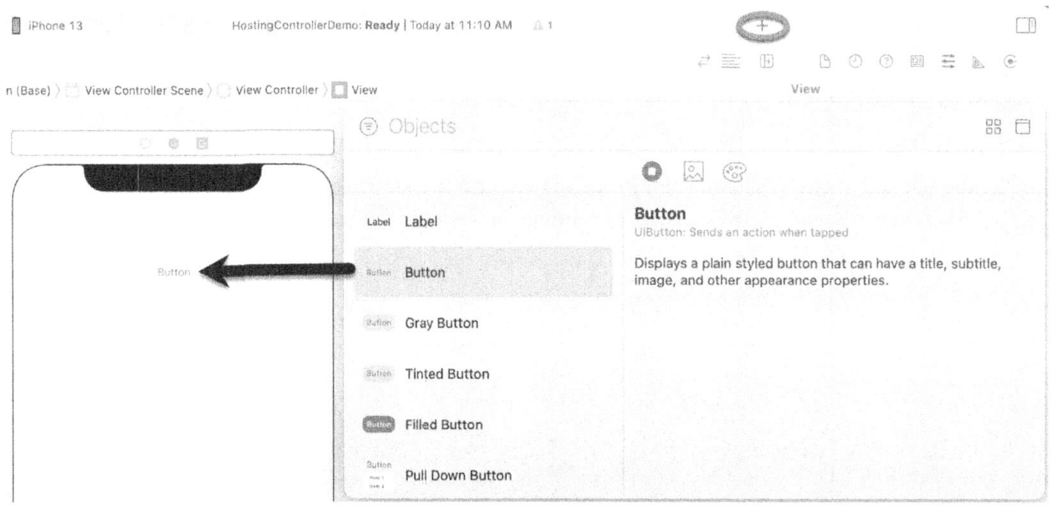

Figure 63-4

Double-click on the button to enter editing mode and change the text so that it reads "Show Second Screen". To maintain the position of the button it will be necessary to add some layout constraints. Use the *Resolve Auto Layout Issues* button indicated in Figure 63-5 to display the menu and select the *Reset to Suggested Constraints* option to add any missing constraints to the button widget:

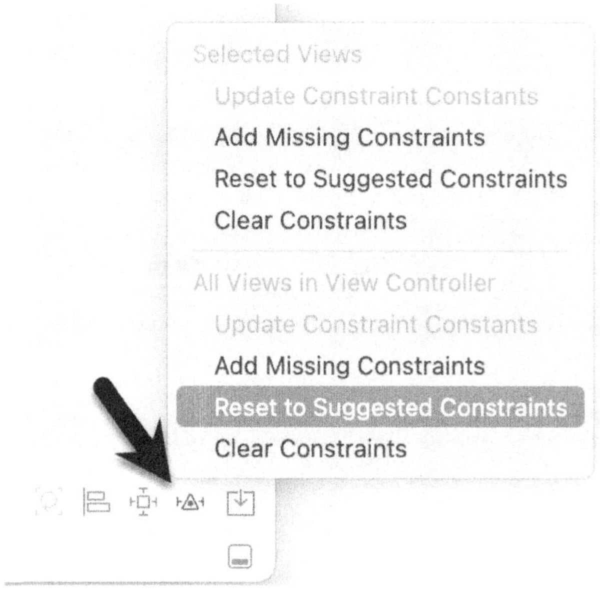

Figure 63-5

63.5 Adding a Hosting Controller

The storyboard is now ready to add a UIHostingController and to implement a segue on the button to display the SwiftUIView layout. Display the Library panel once again, locate the Hosting View Controller, and drag and drop it onto the storyboard canvas so that it resembles Figure 63-6 below:

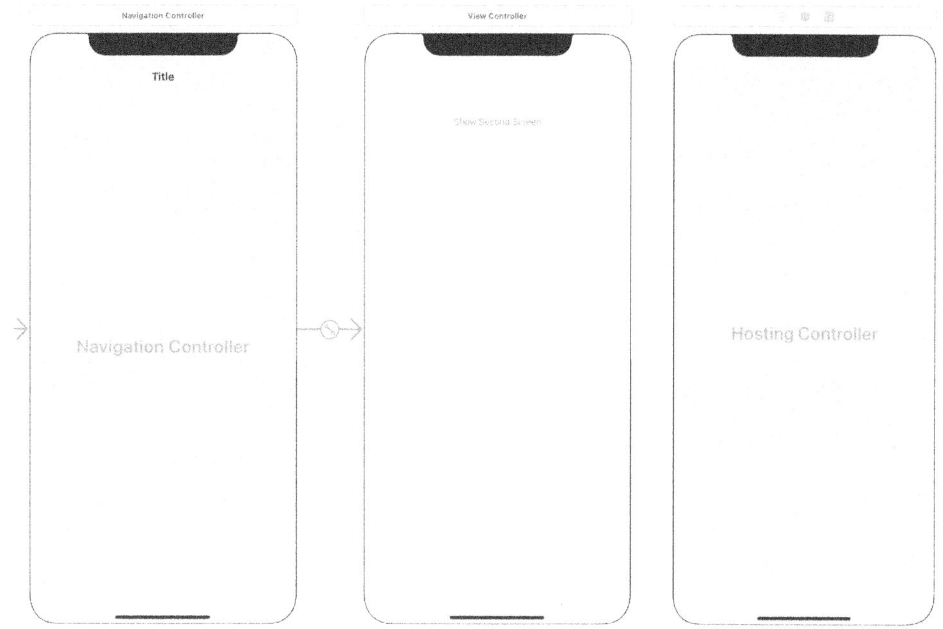

Figure 63-6

Next, add the segue by selecting the "Show Second Screen" button and Ctrl-clicking and dragging to the Hosting Controller:

Figure 63-7

Release the line once it is within the bounds of the hosting controller and select *Show* from the resulting menu.

Compile and run the project on a simulator or connected device and verify that clicking the button navigates to the hosting controller screen and that the Navigation Controller has provided a back button to return to the initial screen. At this point, the hosting view controller appears with a black background indicating that it currently has no content.

63.6 Configuring the Segue Action

The next step is to add an IBSegueAction to the segue that will load the SwiftUI view into the hosting controller when the button is clicked. Within Xcode, select the *Editor -> Assistant* menu option to display the Assistant Editor panel. When the Assistant Editor panel appears, make sure that it is displaying the content of the *ViewController.swift* file. By default, the Assistant Editor will be in *Automatic* mode, whereby it automatically attempts to display the correct source file based on the currently selected item in Interface Builder. If the correct file is not displayed, the toolbar along the top of the editor panel can be used to select the correct file.

If the *ViewController.swift* file is not loaded, begin by clicking on the Automatic entry in the editor toolbar as highlighted in Figure 63-8:

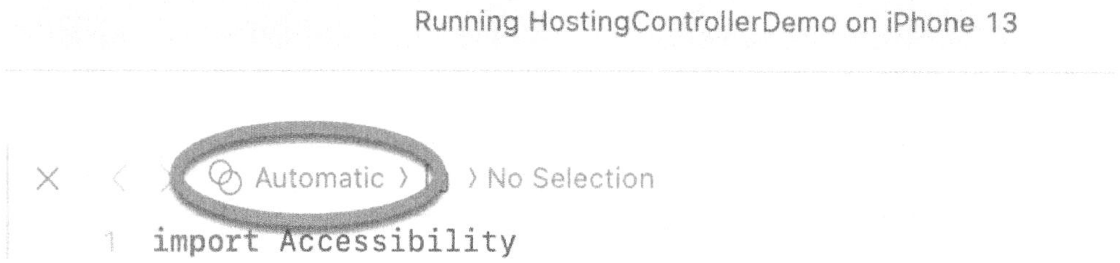

Figure 63-8

From the resulting menu (Figure 63-9), select the *ViewController.swift* file to load it into the editor:

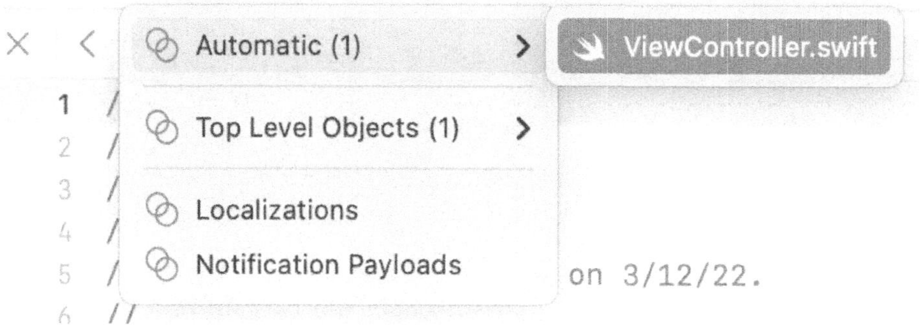

Figure 63-9

Next, Ctrl-click on the segue line between the initial view controller and the hosting controller and drag the resulting line to a position beneath the *viewDidLoad()* method in the Assistant panel as shown in Figure 63-10:

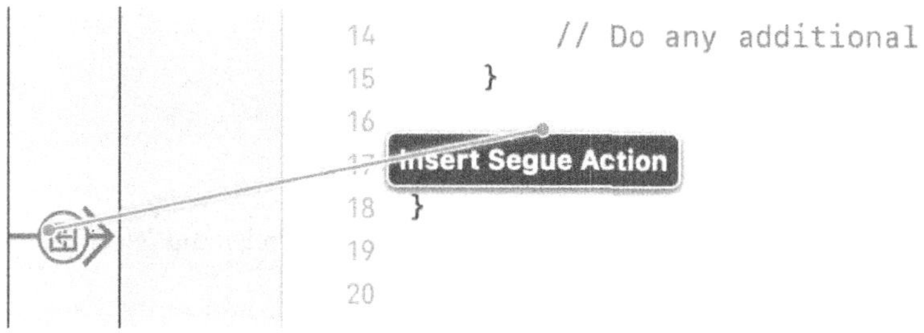

Figure 63-10

Release the line and enter *showSwiftUIView* into the Name field of the connection dialog before clicking the *Connect* button:

Figure 63-11

Within the *ViewController.swift* file Xcode will have added the IBSegueAction method which needs to be modified as follows to embed the SwiftUIView layout into the hosting controller (note that the SwiftUI framework also needs to be imported):

```
import UIKit
import SwiftUI
.
.
@IBSegueAction func showSwiftUIView(_ coder: NSCoder) -> UIViewController? {
    return UIHostingController(coder: coder,
                rootView: SwiftUIView(text: "Integration One"))
}
```

Compile and run the app once again, this time confirming that the second screen appears as shown in Figure 63-12:

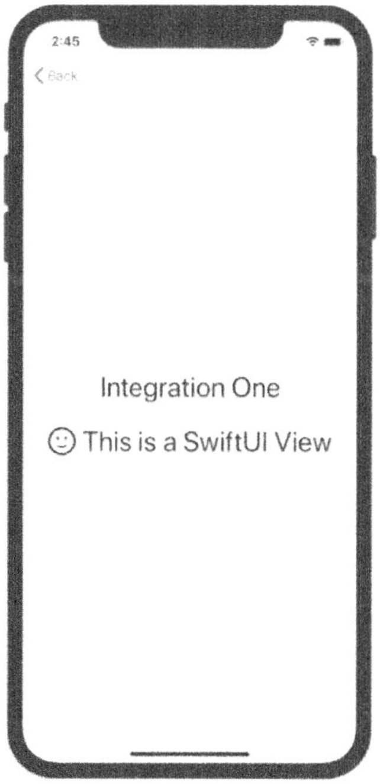

Figure 63-12

63.7 Embedding a Container View

For the second integration, a Container View will be added to an existing view controller scene and used to embed a SwiftUI view alongside UIKit components. Within the *Main* storyboard file, display the Library and drag and drop a Container View onto the scene canvas of the initial view controller, then position and size the view so that it appears as shown in Figure 63-13:

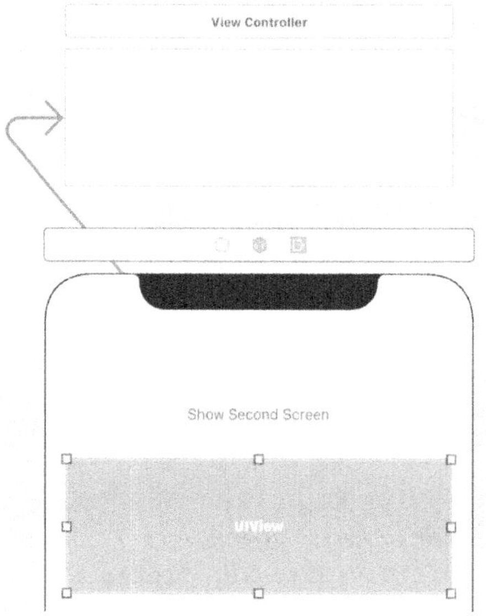

Figure 63-13

Before proceeding, click on the view controller icon in the scene toolbar (as shown in Figure 63-2) before using the *Resolve Auto Layout Issues* button indicated in Figure 63-5 once again and select the *Reset to Suggested Constraints* option to add any missing constraints to the layout.

Note that Xcode has also added an extra View Controller for the Container View (located above the initial view controller in the above figure). This will need to be replaced by a Hosting Controller so select this controller and tap the keyboard delete key to remove it from the storyboard.

Display the Library, locate the Hosting View Controller, and drag and drop it so that it is positioned above the initial view controller in the storyboard canvas. Ctrl-click on the Container View in the view controller scene and drag the resulting line to the new hosting controller before releasing. From the segue menu, select the Embed option:

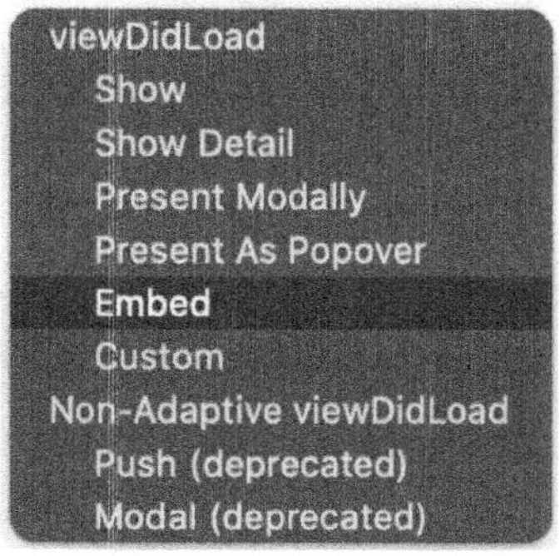

Figure 63-14

Once the Container View has been embedded in the hosting controller, the storyboard should resemble Figure 63-15:

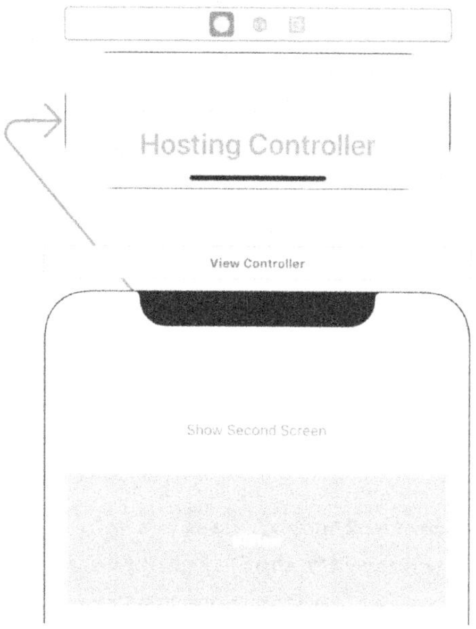

Figure 63-15

All that remains is to add an IBSegueAction to the connection between the Container View and the hosting controller. Display the Assistant Editor once again, Ctrl-click on the arrow pointing towards the left side of the new hosting controller, and drag the line to a position beneath the showSwiftUIView action method. Name the action embedSwiftUIView and click on the Connect button. Once the new method has been added, modify it as follows:

```
@IBSegueAction func embedSwiftUIView(_ coder: NSCoder) ->
                                        UIViewController? {
    return UIHostingController(coder: coder, rootView: SwiftUIView(text:
"Integration Two"))
}
```

When the app is now run, the SwiftUI view will appear in the initial view controller within the Container View:

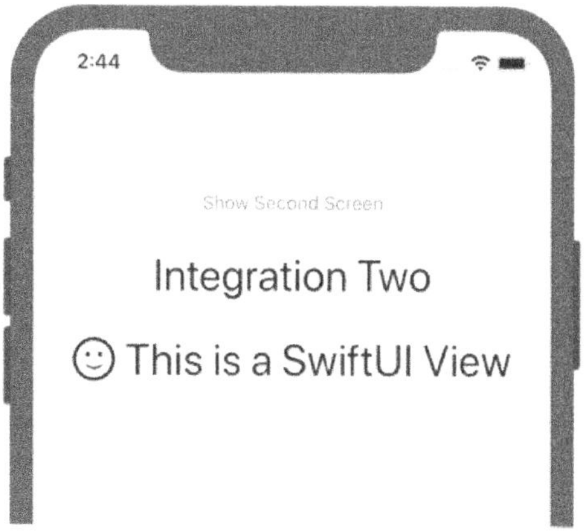

Figure 63-16

63.8 Embedding SwiftUI in Code

In this final integration example, the SwiftUI view will be embedded into the layout for the initial view controller programmatically. Within Xcode, edit the *ViewController.swift* file, locate the *viewDidLoad()* method and modify it as follows:

```
override func viewDidLoad() {
    super.viewDidLoad()

    let swiftUIController = UIHostingController(rootView: SwiftUIView(text:
"Integration Three"))

    addChild(swiftUIController)
    swiftUIController.view.translatesAutoresizingMaskIntoConstraints
                                                            = false

    view.addSubview(swiftUIController.view)

    swiftUIController.view.centerXAnchor.constraint(
              equalTo: view.centerXAnchor).isActive = true
    swiftUIController.view.centerYAnchor.constraint(
              equalTo: view.centerYAnchor).isActive = true

    swiftUIController.didMove(toParent: self)
}
```

The code begins by creating a UIHostingController instance containing the SwiftUIView layout before adding it as a child to the current view controller. The *translates autoresizing* property is set to false so that any constraints we add will not conflict with the automatic constraints usually applied when a view is added to a layout. Next, the UIView child of the UIHostingController is added as a subview of the containing view controller's UIView. Constraints are then set on the hosting view controller to position it in the center of the screen. Finally, an event is triggered to let UIKit know that the hosting controller has been moved to the container view controller.

Run the app one last time and confirm that it appears as shown in Figure 63-17:

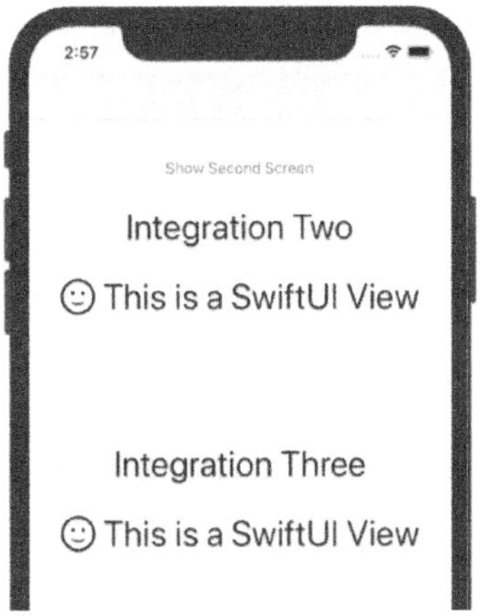

Figure 63-17

63.9 Summary

Any apps developed before the introduction of SwiftUI will have been created using UIKit. While it is certainly possible to continue using UIKit when enhancing and extending an existing app, it probably makes more sense to use SwiftUI when adding new app features (unless your app needs to run on devices that do not support iOS 13 or newer). Recognizing the need to integrate new SwiftUI-based views and functionality with existing UIKit code, Apple created the UIHostingViewController. This controller is designed to wrap SwiftUI views in a UIKit view controller that can be integrated into existing UIKit code. As demonstrated in this chapter, the hosting controller can be used to integrate SwiftUI and UIKit both within storyboards and programmatically within code. Options are available to integrate entire SwiftUI user interfaces in independent view controllers or, through the use of container views, to embed SwiftUI views alongside UIKit views within an existing layout.

Chapter 64

64. Preparing and Submitting an iOS 16 Application to the App Store

After developing an iOS application, the final step is submitting it to Apple's App Store.. Preparing and submitting an application is a multi-step process details of which will be covered in this chapter.

64.1 Verifying the iOS Distribution Certificate

The chapter entitled *"Joining the Apple Developer Program"* covered the steps involved in generating signing certificates. In that chapter, both a development and distribution certificate were generated. Up until this point in the book, applications have been signed using the development certificate so that testing could be performed on physical iOS devices. Before an application can be submitted to the App Store, however, it must be signed using the distribution certificate. The presence of the distribution certificate may be verified from within the Xcode *Preferences* settings.

With Xcode running, select the *Xcode -> Preferences...* menu option and select the *Accounts* category from the toolbar of the resulting window. Assuming that Apple IDs have been configured as outlined in *"Joining the Apple Developer Program"*, a list of one or more Apple IDs will be shown in the accounts panel as illustrated in Figure 64-1:

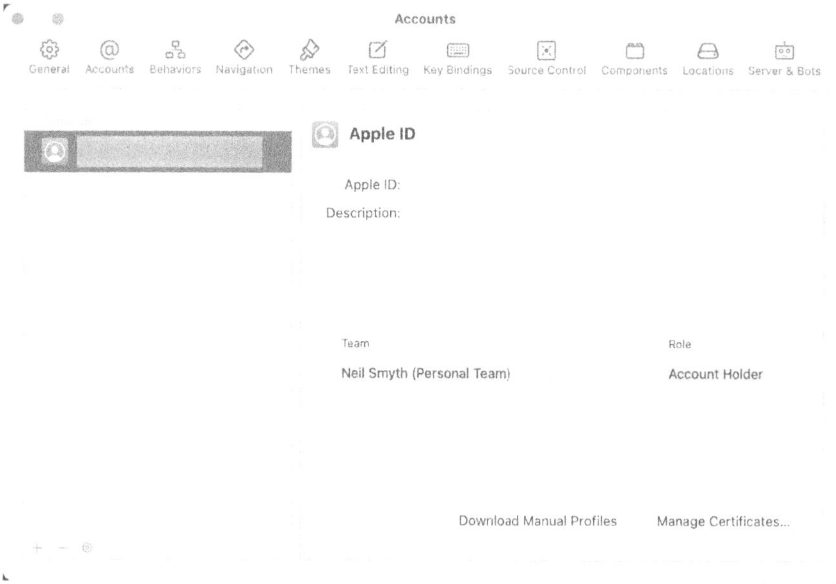

Figure 64-1

Select the Apple ID to be used to sign the application and click on the *Manage Certificates...* button to display the list of signing identities and provisioning profiles associated with that ID:

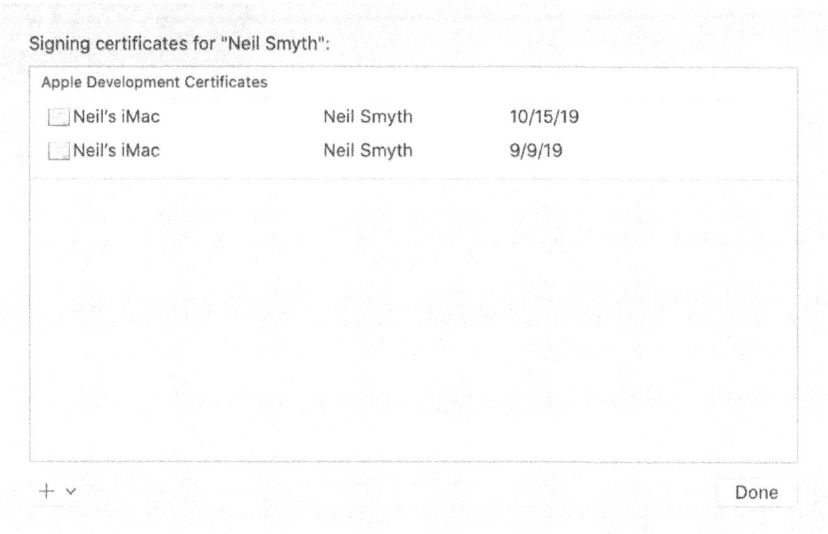

Figure 64-2

If no Apple Distribution certificate is listed, use the menu highlighted in Figure 64-3 to generate one:

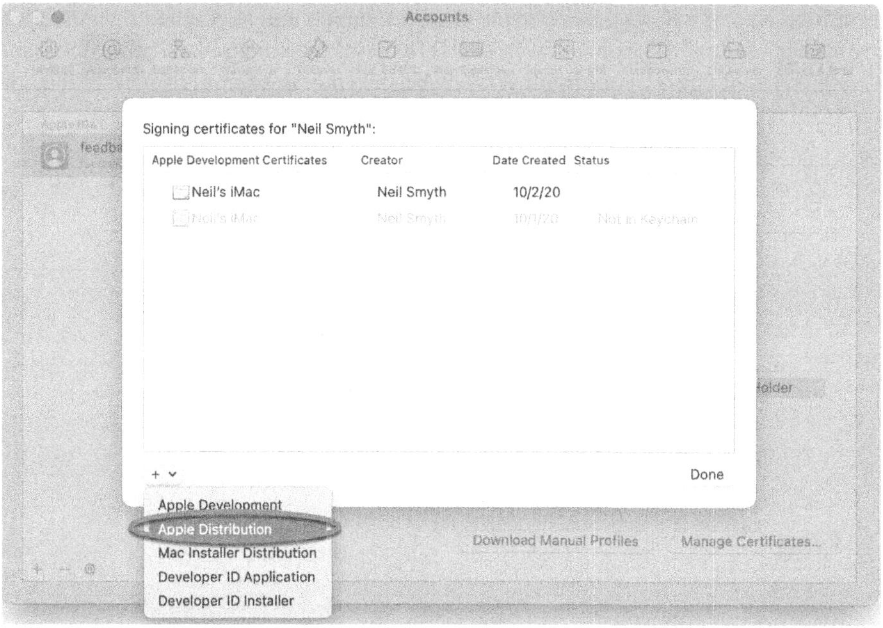

Figure 64-3

Xcode will then contact the developer portal and generate and download a new signing certificate suitable for use when signing applications for submission to the App Store. Once the signing identity has been generated, the certificate will appear in the list as shown in Figure 64-4:

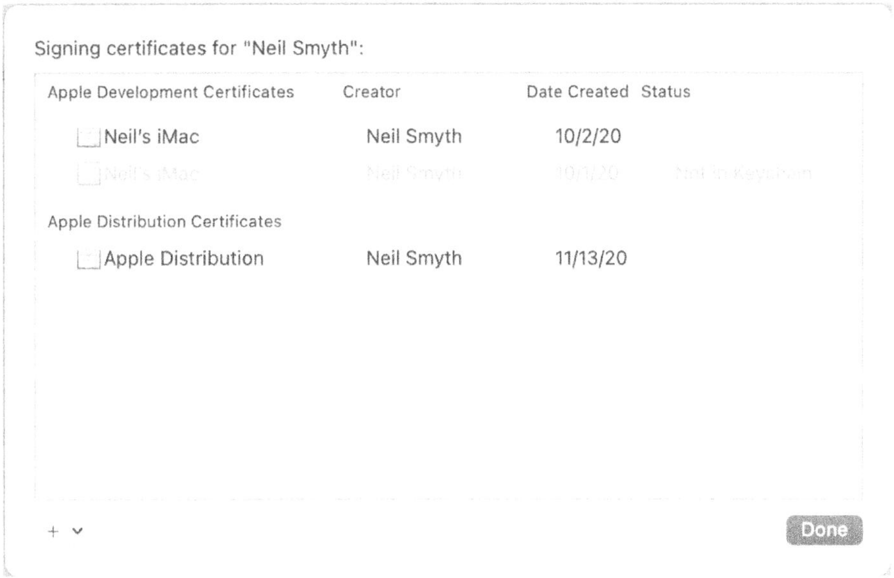

Figure 64-4

64.2 Adding App Icons

Before rebuilding the application for distribution it is important to ensure that app icons have been added to the application. The app icons are used to represent your application on the home screen, settings panel and search results on the device. Each of these categories requires a suitable icon in PNG format and formatted for a number of different dimensions. Alternatively, you can add a single 1024 x 1024 icon to the project and Xcode will adapt it for each requirement.

App icons are added in the *Assets.xcassets* asset catalog within the AppIcon image set. When the AppIcon image set is selected, it will display placeholders for each icon size:

Figure 64-5

To add images, simply drag and drop the missing PNG format image files from a Finder window onto the corresponding placeholders in the asset catalog, or Ctrl-click on the catalog and select *Import* from the menu to import multiple files. To use a single image, change the iOS Size menu in the Attributes inspector panel to *Single Size* as illustrated in Figure 64-6:

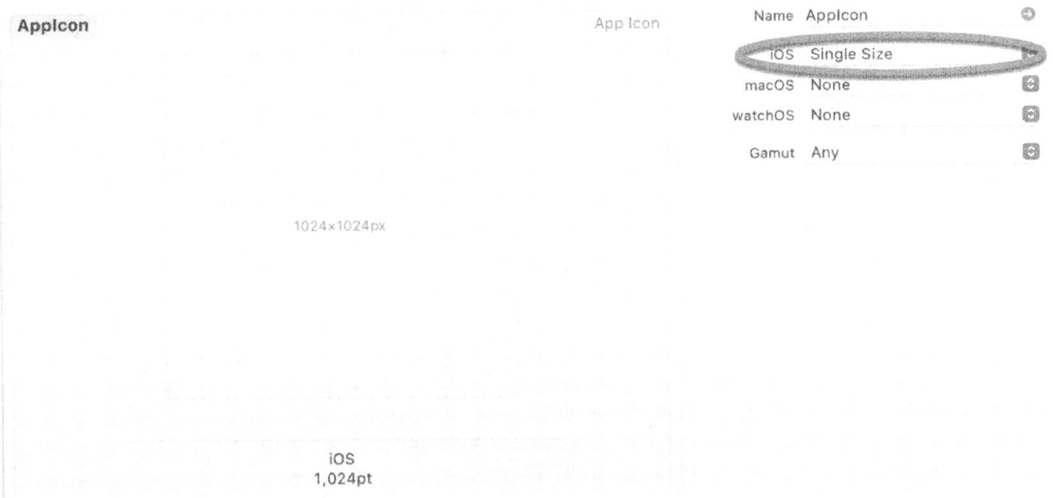

Figure 64-6

64.3 Assign the Project to a Team

As part of the submission process, the project must be associated with a development team to ensure that the correct signing credentials are used. In the project navigator panel, select the project name to display the project settings panel. Click the *Signing & Capabilities* tab and within the Identity section, select a team from the menu as shown in Figure 64-7:

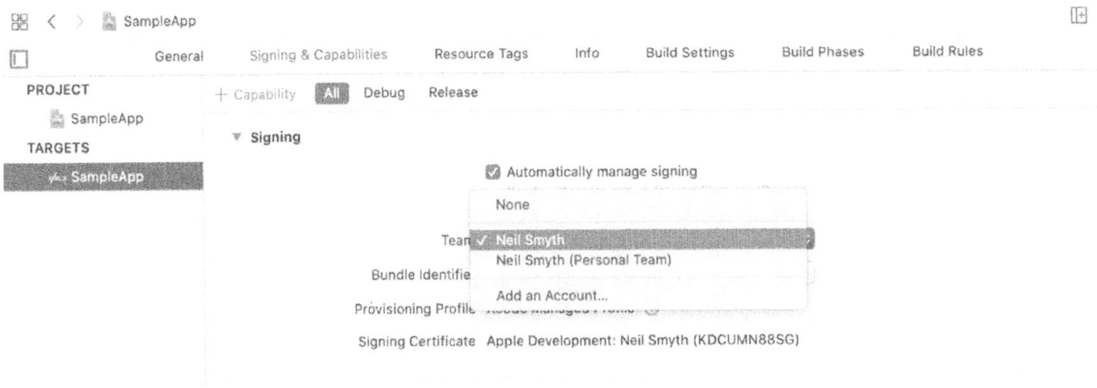

Figure 64-7

64.4 Archiving the Application for Distribution

The application must now be rebuilt using the previously installed distribution profile. To generate the archive, select the Xcode *Product -> Archive* menu option. Note that if the Archive menu is disabled this is most likely because a simulator option is currently selected as the run target in the Xcode toolbar. Changing this menu either to a connected device, or the generic *iOS Device* target option should enable the Archive option in the Product menu.

Xcode will proceed to archive the application ready for submission. Once the process is complete the archive will be displayed in the Archive screen of the Organizer dialog ready for upload and distribution:

Figure 64-8

64.5 Configuring the Application in App Store Connect

Before an application can be submitted to the App Store for review it must first be configured in App Store Connect. Enrollment in the Apple Developer program automatically results in the creation of an App Store Connect account using the same login credentials. App Store Connect is a portal where developers enter tax and payment information, input details about applications and track the status of those applications in terms of sales and revenues.

Access App Store Connect by navigating to *https://appstoreconnect.apple.com* in a web browser and entering your Apple Developer program login and password details.

First time users should click on the *Agreements, Tax, and Banking* option and work through the various tasks to accept Apple's terms and conditions and to input appropriate tax and banking information for the receipt of sales revenue.

Once the administrative tasks are complete, select the *My Apps* option and click on the + button followed by *New App* to enter information about the application. Begin by selecting the *iOS* checkbox and entering a name for the application together with an SKU of your own creation. Also select or enter the bundle ID that matches the application that has been prepared for upload in Xcode:

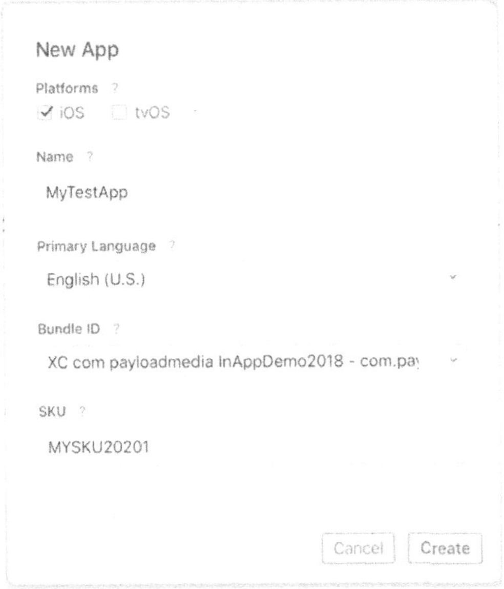

Figure 64-9

Once the application has been added it will appear within the My Apps screen listed as *Prepare for submission*:

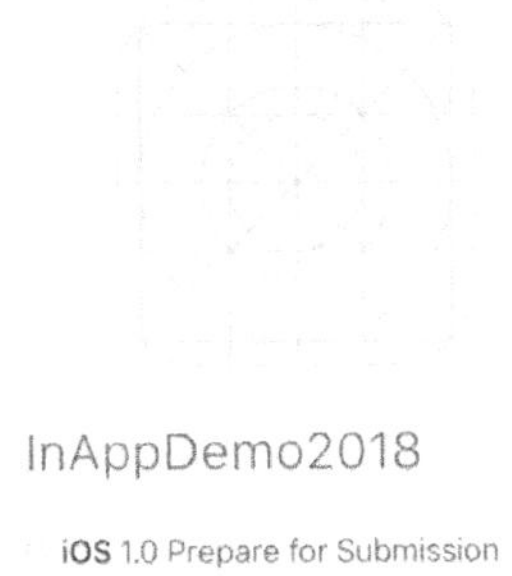

Figure 64-10

64.6 Validating and Submitting the Application

To validate the application, return to the Xcode archives window, make sure the application archive is selected and click on the *Validate App* button. Enter your iOS Developer program login credentials when prompted to do so. If more than one signing identity is configured within Xcode, select the desired identity from the menu.

Xcode will connect to the App Store Connect service, locate the matching app entry added in the previous step and display the summary screen shown in Figure 64-11:

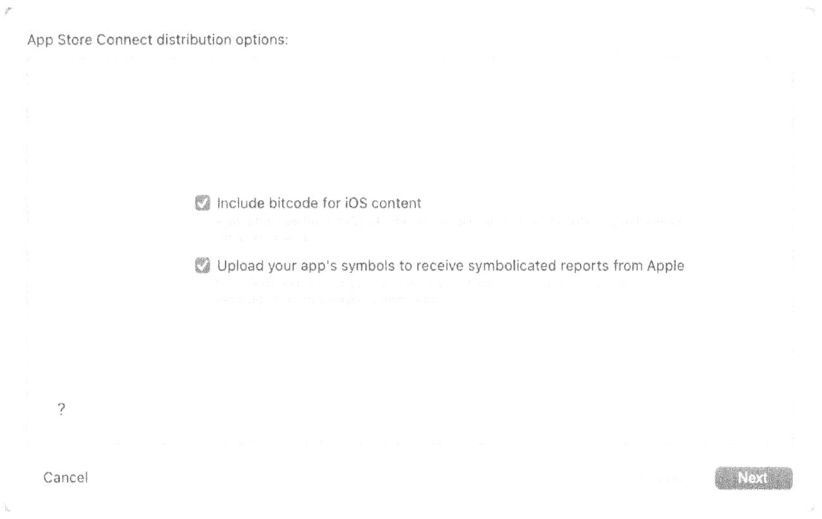

Figure 64-11

This screen includes the following options for selection:

- **Include bitcode for iOS content** – Bitcode is an intermediate binary format introduced with iOS 9. By including the app in bitcode format, it can be compiled by Apple so that it is optimized for the full range of target iOS devices and to take advantage of future hardware and software advances. Selection of this option is recommended.

- **Upload your app's symbols** – If selected, Apple will include symbol information for the app. This information, which includes function and method names, source code line numbers and file paths, will be included in the crash logs provided to you by Apple in the event that your app crashes when in use by a customer. Selection of this option is recommended.

The next screen will provide the option to allow Xcode to automatically manage signing for the app, or to allow you to make manual certificate selections. Unless you are part of a team that uses multiple distribution certificates, automatic signing is usually a good choice:

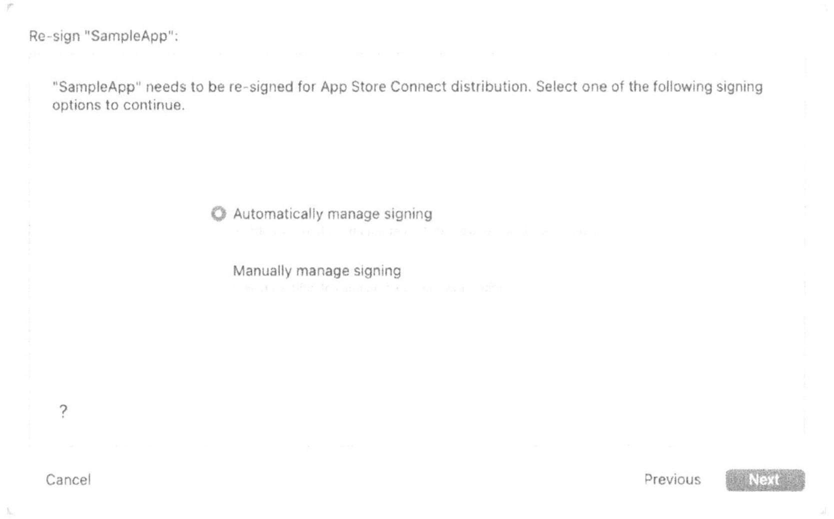

Figure 64-12

The final screen summarizes the certificate, profile and entitlements associated with the app:

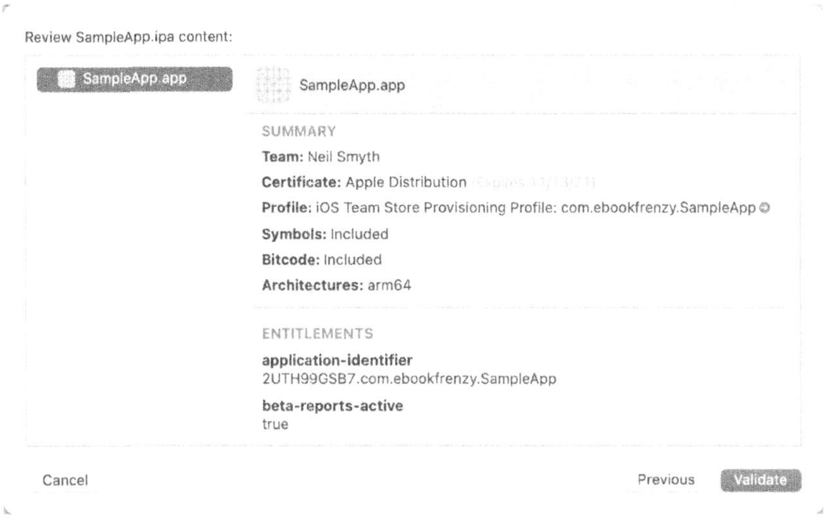

Figure 64-13

Click the *Validate* button to perform the validation and correct any problems that are reported. Once validation has passed, click on the *Done* button to dismiss the panel:

Figure 64-14

The application is now ready to be uploaded for App Store review.

Make sure the application archive is still selected and click on the *Distribute App* button. Work through the screens, selecting the *App Store Connect* and *Upload* options, enter your developer program login credentials when prompted and review the summary information before clicking on the *Upload* button. Wait for the upload process to complete at which point a message should appear indicating that the submission was successful:

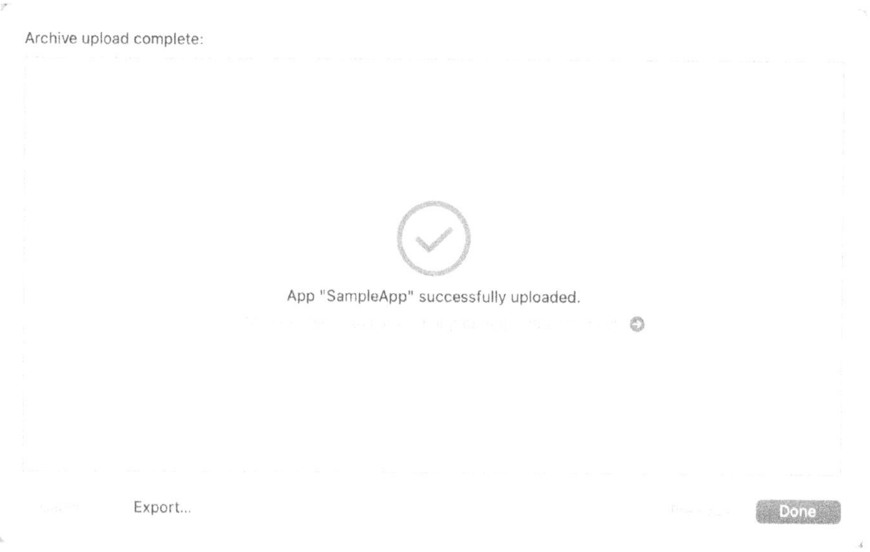

Figure 64-15

64.7 Configuring and Submitting the App for Review

On the My Apps screen of the App Store Connect portal, select the new app entry to display the configuration screen where options are available to set up pre-release test users, designate pricing, enter product descriptions and upload screenshots and preview videos. Once this information has been entered and saved and the app is ready for submission to the App Store, select the *Prepare for Submission* option (marked A in Figure 64-16) followed by the *Submit for Review* button (marked B):

Figure 64-16

Once Apple has completed the review process an email will arrive stating whether the application has been accepted or not. In the event that the application has been rejected, reasons for the rejection will be stated and the application may be resubmitted once these issues have been addressed.

Index

Symbols

A

B

C

M

N

O

P

R

S

X

Y

Z

Made in the USA
Las Vegas, NV
03 November 2022

58684303R00313